ENGLISH EPISCOPAL ACTA
IV

LINCOLN 1186–1206

ENGLISH EPISCOPAL ACTA
IV

LINCOLN 1186–1206

EDITED BY
DAVID M. SMITH

LONDON · *Published for* THE BRITISH ACADEMY
by THE OXFORD UNIVERSITY PRESS
1986

Oxford University Press, Walton Street, Oxford OX2 6DP
London New York Toronto
Delhi Bombay Calcutta Madras Karachi
Kuala Lumpur Singapore Hong Kong Tokyo
Nairobi Dar es Salaam Cape Town
Melbourne Auckland
and associated companies in
Beirut Berlin Ibadan Mexico City Nicosia

Oxford is a trade mark of Oxford University Press

Published in the United States by Oxford University Press, New York

© The British Academy, 1986

All rights reserved. No part of this publication may be reproduced,
stored in a retrieval system, or transmitted, in any form or by any means,
electronic, mechanical, photocopying, recording, or otherwise, without
the prior permission of Oxford University Press

British Library Cataloguing in Publication Data
English episcopal acta
4: Lincoln, 1186–1206
1. Catholic Church — England — Bishops — History — Sources
2. Catholic Church — England — Dioceses — History — Sources
3. England — Church history — Medieval period, 1066–1485 — Sources
I. Smith, David M.   II. British Academy
262'.3   BR750
ISBN 0-19-726050-0

BR
750
.E54
vol.4

Printed in Great Britain by
W. S. Maney and Son Ltd, Leeds

KRAUSS LIBRARY
LUTHERAN SCHOOL OF THEOLOGY AT CHICAGO
1100 EAST 55th STREET
CHICAGO, ILLINOIS — 60615

To P. E. H.

CONTENTS

LIST OF PLATES   viii

PREFACE   ix

MANUSCRIPT SOURCES CITED   xi

PRINTED BOOKS AND ARTICLES CITED,
  WITH ABBREVIATED REFERENCES   xiii

OTHER ABBREVIATIONS   xx

INTRODUCTION   xxi
  The bishops and their staff   xxiii
  The Acta   xxviii
  Editorial method   xlii

PLATES   xlv

THE ACTA
  Hugh of Avalon   nos. 1–215   1
  William of Blois   nos. 216–300   144

APPENDICES
  I. Additional acta and mentions of acta of
     the bishops of Lincoln 1123–1185   189
  II. References to acts of the bishops 1186–1206   204
  III. Itineraries of bishops Hugh and William 1186–1206 208

INDEX OF PERSONS AND PLACES   213

INDEX OF SUBJECTS   244

LIST OF PLATES

(between page xliv *and page* 1 *)*

I. ACTUM OF BISHOP HUGH
    (actum no. 114: scribe **I**)

II. ACTUM OF BISHOP HUGH
     (actum no. 173: scribe **II**)

III. ACTUM OF BISHOP WILLIAM
      (actum no. 268: scribe **III**)

IV. SEAL OF BISHOP HUGH
     (actum no. 173)

PREFACE

The publication of this volume completes the collection of the acta of bishops of Lincoln from 1067 to 1206. In the course of preparing this edition I have incurred many debts of gratitude to scholars, archivists and librarians in this country and abroad. Constant help and encouragement has been received from Professor Christopher Cheney, the Chairman of the Academy's Episcopal Acta Committee, and from Dr Kathleen Major and Professor Christopher Brooke, also members of the Committee. They have all read through the final version of the typescript and I have benefitted much from their valuable comments.

In my examination of manuscripts (often in vain) for Lincoln episcopal acta, I have been greatly assisted in my task by the helpfulness and consideration of custodians of archives in national, local, and ecclesiastical repositories and in libraries. I wish to record my thanks for all their help and I also gratefully acknowledge permission granted by them to publish texts in their possession. Transcripts of Crown-copyright records in the Public Record Office appear by permission of the Controller of HM Stationery Office.

Private owners, like institutions, have been generous in giving me access to their records and have afforded me every facility. I particularly wish to thank His Grace the Duke of Devonshire; His Grace the Duke of Northumberland; His Grace the Duke of Rutland; Lord O'Hagan; Sir Christopher and Lady Chancellor; and the Spalding Gentlemen's Society.

In France, Mlle. Odile Grandmottet of the Institut de Recherche et d'Histoire des Textes, M. Denis Escudier and Dr David Bates have kindly obtained photocopies of documents in municipal and departmental archives.

Over the years many scholars have also helped with information on texts and assistance with editorial problems. I am particularly grateful to Dr Janet Burton; Mr David Farmer; Dr Brian Kemp; Dr Emma Mason; Dr Dorothy Owen; Mr Alan Piper; Mr Martin Snape; and Dr Patrick Zutschi.

Borthwick Institute, York DAVID M. SMITH

MANUSCRIPT SOURCES CITED

Alençon, Archives dép. de l'Orne, H.907: *299*

Aylesbury, Buckinghamshire Record Office, Boarstall cartulary: *43*

Baltimore, Walters Art Gallery, ms. W.15 *135*

Bedford, Bedfordshire Record Office, DD.GY9/2: *29, 228*

Belvoir Castle, Ch.5880: *225*; ms. Add. 105: *20, 225*

Bordeaux, Archives dép. de la Gironde, ms. 769: *171*

Brentford, Syon House, D.i.la: *291*

Caen, Archives dép. du Calvados, H.1251: *6*

Cambridge, University Library, ms. Add. 3021: *196, app. I xviii*

Canterbury, D. and C. Archives, Chartae Antiquae (C.A.) C115/53: *1*; C115/69: *216*; C175: *37*; L135: *38*; L138: *36*; reg. A: *1, 216*

Chatsworth House, Abingdon register: *2, 3*

Colchester, Colchester and Essex Museum, Colchester abbey cartulary: *229, 230*

Dublin, Trinity College Library, ms. E.5.15: *202*

Durham, D. and C., Prior's Kitchen, Cartuarium Vetus: *237*; Cartuarium III: *237*; 1.4. Ebor. 6: *237*

Le Mans, bibl. municipale, ms. 198: *232*

Lichfield, D. and C. Library, Magnum Registrum Album: *90, 251*

Lincoln, Cathedral Library, Sempringham confirmation (no ref.): *173*

Lincoln, Lincolnshire Archives Office, D. and C. records, A/1/5: *91, 92, 93, 94, 99, 100, 102, 104, 106, 107, 252, 253, 254, 255, 256, 257, 260, 261, 262*; A/1/6: *56, 74, 99, 101, 104, 106, 107, 260, 261*; A/1/7: *95*; A/1/8: *110*; A/2/1: *91, 92, 93, 108*; A/2/3: *91, 92, 93*; Dij/20/1/6: *97*; Dij/55/2/8: *102*; Dij/55/3/2: *259*; Dij/63/1/11: *103*; Dij/64/2/1: *4, 28, 41, 117, 141, 174, 175, 176, 177, 178*; Dij/66/3/8: *160*; Dij/69/3/21: *107*; Dij/69/3/22: *101*; Dij/69/3/23: *106*; Dij/69/3/29a: *95*;

Dij/72/3/35: *74*; Dij/73/1/19: *100*; Dij/73/1/30: *81*; Dij/83/3/19(ii): *105*; Dij/83/3/21: *105*; Dij/83/3/21a: *105, 207*; diocesan records, Ep. Reg. I: *30, 113, 218, app. I xii, xiii*; Ep. Reg. II: *290*; Ep. Reg. III: *app. I iii*; misc. roll 6: *102, 252*; Longley ms. 5/29: *app. I iv*

London, British Library, Add. charters, 22002: *192*; 33442: *73*; 33595: *72*; 33596: *72*; 33597: *73*; 46362: *162, 285*; 47573: *139, 140, app. I xxii, xxiii*; 66079: *165, app. I xvii*

– Add. mss. 6118: *app. I viii, xxi*; 8167: *135*; 35296: *180, 181, 182, 183, 184*; 37665: *205, 206*; 37771: *288*; 40008: *25, 26, 27*; 46701: *189, 190*; 47677: *75, 77, 79, 80*

– Cole ms. 43: *182*

– Cotton mss. app. xxi: *191*; Claudius B iii: *300*; Claudius D xi: *116, 117*; Claudius D xii: *48, 49, 50*; Cleopatra A vii: *194, 195*; Cleopatra C vii: *118, 119*; Domitian A x: *161*; Faustina A iii: *210, 212*; Faustina A iv: *168, 169, 170, 239, 287*; Otho B xiv: *286*; Otho D iii: *163*; Tiberius C ix: *205, 206*; Tiberius E v: *133, 134, app. I v*; Vespasian E ii: *157, 158*; Vespasian E xvii: *130, 131, 132*; Vespasian E xviii: *201*; Vespasian E xix: *136*; *137*; Vespasian E xx: *9, 10, 11, 12, 13, 14, 15, 16, 17, 217, 218, 219*; Vitellius E xv: *143, 145, 146, 147, 148, 273*

– Egerton mss. 2827: *54, 55, 238*; 3033: *31*

– Harley charters, 43 H 22: *70*; 43 H 23: *124*; 43 H 25: *244*; 43 H 38b: *123*; 44 F 27: *124*; 84 D 2: *294*; 84 D 3: *298*

– Harley mss. 391: *205, 206*; 742: *181, 289*; 1885: *52, 53*; 2110: *39*; 3640: *208*; 3650: *75, 76, 77, 78, 79, 80*; 3656: *125, 126, 239, 264, 265, 266*; 3688: *120, 121, 122*; 3697: *204*

– Lansdowne mss. 207A: *198*; 402: *214*

– Royal ms. 11 B ix: *130, 131, 132*

London, Charterhouse, De vita et conversacione magistri Ade Cartusiensis: *213A*

London, College of Arms, ms. Arundel 59: *296*

London, Lambeth Palace, Carte Antique et Miscellanee V no. 111: *85*; ms. 415: *32, 33, 36, 37, 38*

London, Public Record Office, C53/57: *71*; C53/150: *85*; C150/1: *66*; D.L. 41/3/25: *286, app. I xvi*; E40/14941: *89*; E40/14946: *app. I xi*; E41/237: *162, 285*; E164/2: *app. I. xiv*; E164/12: *app. I xiv*; E164/19: *202*; E164/20: *67, 68, 211, 242, 243*; E164/28: *157, 158, 159, 284*; E210/7337: *188A*; E315/45/207: *23*; E326/1035: *40*; E326/11398: *40*

Oxford, Bodleian Library, Berkshire Ch. 36: *297*; C.C.C. ms. 160: *274, 275, 276, 277*; DD. All Souls College c.218/17: *84*; DD.Ch.Ch. D.82: *48*; DD.Ch.Ch. O.903: *144*; DD. Queen's College Ch. 286: *166*; ms. Dodsworth 7: *246*; ms. Dodsworth 59: *187, 188*; ms. Fairfax 7: *246*; ms. Fairfax 9: *105, 207*; ms. Gough Lincoln 1: *110*; ms. Laud misc. 625: *88A, 247, 248*; ms. Laud misc. 642: *4, 5, app. I vi*; ms. Lyell 15: *2, 3*; ms. Rawlinson B 408: *67, 211, 242, 243*; Stowell Park, reg. A: *42*; ms. Top. Lincs d 1: *138, 271*; ms. Top. Northants c 5: *133, 134*; ms. Top. Yorks c 72: *51, 235, 236*; ms. Twyne 24: *292*; ms. Willis 5: *121*

Oxford, Christ Church Library, Kitchin's catalogue no. 341: *59, 60, 61, 62, 63, 64, 241*; Notley charter roll: *app. I xv*; Osney cartulary: *142, 144, 146, 147, 272*; St Frideswide's cartulary: *149, 150, 274, 278*

Oxford, Magdalen College, Aynho Ch. 22: *8*; Brackley Ch. 126: *24*; Brackley Ch. A.1: *24*; Brackley Ch. C.64: *24*; Estate records 137/1: *8*; ms. Latin 273: *24*

Paris, Archives Nationales, L.968, no. 224: *172*

Paris, Bibliothèque Nationale, ms. lat. 12880: *127*

Peterborough, D. and C. Library, ms. 1: *152, 154, 155, 156, 279, 280, 281, 282, 283*; ms. 5: *151*

Preston, Lancashire Record Office, DDTO.K/1/10: *268*; DDTO.K/19/5: *app. I ix*

Saint-Brieuc, Archives dép. des Côtes-du-Nord, series H (unlisted): *223*

Southwell, Minster Library, ms. 3: *199*

Spalding, Gentlemen's Society, Crowland cartulary: *44, 45, 46, 47, 233, 234*

Stowell Park *see* Oxford, Bodleian Library

Syon House *see* Brentford

Wells, D. and C. Library, Ch. 39: *221, 222*; Ch. 40: *221*; Liber Albus I: *221, 222*

Westminster Abbey, mun. 2855: *115*; 3057: *114*; 16144: *209*; mun. bk. 10: *114, 115*; mun. bk. 11: *209, 210, 211, 212, app.I, xix, xx*

Winchester, Hampshire Record Office, IM. 54/1: *179*; IM. 54/2: *179*; IM. 54/3: *179*

York, Minster Library, L2/1: *214A, 300*

York University, Borthwick Institute of Historical Research, CP.E.4/2: *26*

PRINTED BOOKS AND ARTICLES CITED,
WITH ABBREVIATED REFERENCES

AASR   *Associated Architectural Societies Reports and Papers.*

Abbreviatio placitorum   W. Illingworth ed., *Placitorum in domo capitulari Westmonasteriensi asservatorum abbreviatio . . .* (Record Commission 1811).

Academia Tertia   F. Peck, *Academia Tertia Anglicana, or the Antiquarian Annals of Stamford* (1727).

Anciens Evêchés   J. Geslin de Bourgogne and A. de Barthélemy, *Anciens Evêchés de Bretagne*, 6 vols. (Paris 1855–79).

Ann. mon.   H. R. Luard ed., *Annales monastici*, 5 vols. (Rolls ser., 1864–9).

Baker, *History of Northants.*   G. Baker, *The history and antiquities of the county of Northampton*, 2 vols. (1822–41).

Beds. Hist. Rec. Soc.   Bedfordshire Historical Record Society publications.

BIHR   *Bulletin of the Institute of Historical Research.*

BJRL   *Bulletin of the John Rylands Library.*

BM Seals   W. de G. Birch, *Catalogue of Seals in the department of manuscripts in the British Museum*, 6 vols. (1887–1900).

Boarstall Cartulary, The   H. E. Salter ed. (Oxford Historical Society 88, 1930).

The Book of John de Schalby   J. H. Srawley ed., *The Book of John de Schalby, canon of Lincoln 1299–1333, concerning the bishops of Lincoln and their acts.* (Lincoln Minster pamph. 2, 1949).

Bracton's Note Book   F. W. Maitland ed., *Bracton's Note Book: a collection of cases decided in the King's Courts during the reign of Henry the Third, annotated by a lawyer of that time, seemingly by Henry of Bratton*, 3 vols. (1887).

Bradenstoke Cartulary   V. C. M. London ed., *The cartulary of Bradenstoke priory* (Wiltshire Record Society 35, 1979).

Brett, M.   *The English Church under Henry I* (Oxford 1975).

Bridlington Chartulary   W. T. Lancaster ed., *Abstracts of the charters and other documents contained in the chartulary of the priory of Bridlington* (Leeds 1912).

Bulloch, J.   *Adam of Dryburgh* (Church Historical Society 1958).

Bushmead Cartulary   G. H. Fowler and J. Godber eds., *The cartulary of Bushmead Priory* (Bedfordshire Historical Record Society 22, 1945).

Cal. Ch. R.   *Calendar of Charter Rolls preserved in the Public Record Office*, 6 vols. (1903–27).

Callus, D. ed.   *Robert Grosseteste: scholar and bishop* (Oxford 1955, repd. 1969).

Canterbury Professions   M. Richter ed. (Canterbury and York Society 67, 1973).

Cartulaire des abbayes de S. Pierre de la Couture et de S. Pierre de Solesmes (Le Mans 1881).

CDF   J. H. Round ed., *Calendar of documents preserved in France, illustrative of the history of Great Britain and Ireland, vol. i, A.D. 918–1216* (1899).

Cheney, C. R. *From Becket to Langton: English Church Government 1170–1213* (Manchester 1956).

Chronica Majora H. R. Luard ed., *Matthaei Parisiensis monachi sancti Albani Chronica Majora*, 7 vols. (Rolls ser., 1872–83).

Chronica Rogeri de Hovedene ed. W. Stubbs, 4 vols. (Rolls ser., 1868–71).

Chronicon Anglicanum Radulphi de Coggeshall ed. J. Stevenson (Rolls ser., 1875).

Church, C. W. *Chapters in the early history of the Church of Wells* (1894).

Churchill, I. J. *Canterbury Administration*, 2 vols. (1933).

Cirencester Cartulary C. D. Ross and M. Devine eds., *The cartulary of Cirencester abbey, Gloucestershire*, 3 vols. (Oxford 1964–77).

Clanchy, M. T. *From memory to written record: England 1066–1307* (1979).

Colchester Cartulary S. A. Moore ed., *Cartularium monasterii sancti Johannis Baptiste de Colecestria*, 2 vols. (Roxburghe Club 1897).

Collectanea Topographica et Genealogica, 8 vols. (1834–43).

Colvin, H. M. *The White Canons in England* (Oxford 1951).

Councils and Synods D. Whitelock, M. Brett and C. N. L. Brooke eds., *Councils and Synods with other documents relating to the English Church I*, 2 vols. (Oxford 1981); F. M. Powicke and C. R. Cheney eds., ibid. *II*, 2 vols. (Oxford 1964).

CRR *Curia regis rolls . . . preserved in the Public Record Office* (1922–).

Danelaw Charters F. M. Stenton ed., *Documents illustrative of the social and economic history of the Danelaw from various collections* (Records of the social and economic history of England and Wales v, British Academy, 1920).

Delisle L. Delisle and E. Berger eds., *Recueil des actes de Henri II concernant les provinces françaises et les affaires de France*, 4 vols. (Paris 1909–27).

Denholm-Young, N., ed. *Cartulary of the Medieval Archives of Christ Church* (Oxford Historical Society xcii, 1931).

Diceto W. Stubbs ed., *Radulf. de Diceto decani Lundoniensis opera historica*, 2 vols. (Rolls ser., 1876).

Dimock, J. F. ed. *The Metrical Life of St Hugh of Lincoln* (1860).

Douie, D. L. *Archbishop Geoffrey Plantagenet and the Chapter of York* (St Anthony's Hall publication 18, York 1960).

Dunkin, J. *Oxfordshire: the history and antiquities of the Hundreds of Bullington and Ploughley*, 2 vols. (1823).

Dunstable Cartulary G. H. Fowler ed., *A Digest of the charters preserved in the cartulary of the priory of Dunstable* (Bedfordshire Historical Record Society 10, 1926).

Early Northants. Charters F. M. Stenton ed., *Facsimiles of early charters from Northamptonshire collections* (Northamptonshire Record Society 4, 1930).

EBC C. R. Cheney, *English Bishops' Chanceries 1100–1250* (Manchester 1950).

Edwards, K. *The English Secular Cathedrals in the middle ages*, 2nd edn. (Manchester 1967).

EEA *English Episcopal Acta*: i *Lincoln 1067–1185*, ed. D. M. Smith (British Academy 1980); ii *Canterbury 1162–1190*, ed. C. R. Cheney and B. E. A. Jones (British Academy

1986); iii *Canterbury 1193–1205*, ed. C. R. Cheney and E. John (British Academy 1986).

EHR   *English Historical Review.*

Emden   A. B. Emden, *A Biographical Register of the University of Oxford to A.D. 1500*, 3 vols. (Oxford 1957–9).

English Baronies   I. J. Sanders, *English Baronies: a study of their origin and descent 1086–1327* (Oxford 1960).

Ep. Cant.   W. Stubbs ed., *Epistolae Cantuarienses* (Chronicles and memorials of the reign of Richard I, vol. 2, Rolls ser. 1865).

EPNS   English Place-Name Society publications.

EYC   *Early Yorkshire Charters* i–iii, ed. W. Farrer (1914–16); iv–xii, and index to i–iii, ed. C. T. Clay (Yorkshire Archaeological Society Record ser., extra ser., 1935–65).

Eynsham Cartulary   H. E. Salter ed., 2 vols. (Oxford Historical Society 49, 51, 1907–8).

Eyton   R. W. Eyton, *Court, household and itinerary of King Henry II* (1878).

Farmer, D. H.   *Saint Hugh of Lincoln* (1985).

Feudal Aids   *Inquisitions and assessments relating to feudal aids . . . A.D. 1284–1431*, 6 vols. (1899–1920).

Final Concords   C. W. Foster ed., *Final Concords of the county of Lincoln from the feet of fines preserved in the Public Record Office, A.D. 1244–1272, with additions from various sources, A.D. 1176–1250*, vol. 2 (Lincoln Record Society 17, 1920).

Foreville, R., ed.   *Un procès de canonisation à l'aube du xiiie siècle (1201–1202): Le Livre de saint Gilbert de Sempringham* (Paris 1943).

Gallia Christiana   D. de Sainte-Marthe ed., 16 vols. (Paris 1715–1865).

Gervase   W. Stubbs ed., *Historical works of Gervase of Canterbury*, 2 vols. (Rolls ser., 1879–80).

Gesta Abbatum   H. T. Riley ed., *Gesta abbatum monasterii S. Albani a Thoma Walsingham (A.D. 793–1401)*, 3 vols. (Rolls ser., 1867–9).

Gesta Henrici II   W. Stubbs ed., *Gesta Regis Henrici secundi Benedicti abbatis*, 2 vols. (Rolls ser., 1867).

Gilbertine Charters   F. M. Stenton ed., *Transcripts of charters relating to Gilbertine houses of Sixle, Ormsby, Catley, Bullington and Alvingham* (Lincoln Record Society 18, 1922).

Gir. Camb.   J. S. Brewer, J. F. Dimock, and G. F. Warner eds., *Giraldi Cambrensis Opera*, 8 vols. (Rolls ser., 1861–91).

Gloucester Cartulary   W. H. Hart ed., *Historia et cartularium monasterii sancti Petri Gloucestriae*, 3 vols. (Rolls ser., 1863–7).

Godstow English Register   A. Clark ed., *The English Register of Godstow nunnery near Oxford*, 3 vols. (Early English Text Society, original ser., 129, 130, 142, 1905–11).

Gorham, G. C.   *The history and antiquities of Eynesbury and St Neot's in Huntingdonshire and of St Neot's in the County of Cornwall* (1824).

Gransden, A.   *Historical Writing in England c.550–c.1307*, i (1974).

Guisborough Cartulary   W. Brown ed., *Cartularium prioratus de Gyseburne Ebor. dioceseos ordinis S. Augustini*, 2 vols. (Surtees Society 86, 89, 1889–94).

Hartley, J. S. and Rogers, A.   *The Religious Foundations of Medieval Stamford* (Nottingham 1974).

xvi   BOOKS AND ARTICLES CITED

Harvey, B.	*Westminster Abbey and its Estates in the Middle Ages* (Oxford 1977).
Hearne, T.	*Liber Niger Scaccarii*, 2 vols. (1774).
Hill, J. W. F.	*Medieval Lincoln* (Cambridge 1948, repd. 1965).
Hill, R. M. T.	'Bishop Sutton and his archives: a study in the keeping of records in the thirteenth century', *Journal of Ecclesiastical History*, 2 (1951), 43–53.
Historians of the Church of York	J. Raine, ed., *The Historians of the Church of York and its Archbishops*, 3 vols. (Rolls ser., 1879–94).
HMC Rutland	Historical Manuscripts Commission, *The Manuscripts of His Grace the Duke of Rutland*, 4 vols. (1888–1905).
HMC Wells	Historical Manuscripts Commission, *Calendar of the Manuscripts of the Dean and Chapter of Wells*, 2 vols. (1907–14).
HMCR	Historical Manuscripts Commission Reports.
HRH	D. Knowles, C. N. L. Brooke, and V. C. M. London eds., *The heads of religious houses: England and Wales 940–1216* (Cambridge 1972).
Hubert Walter	C. R. Cheney, *Hubert Walter* (1967).
Innes, C., ed.	*Liber Sancte Marie de Melros* (Bannatyne Club 1837).
Innocent III and England	C. R. Cheney, *Pope Innocent III and England* (Stuttgart, Päpste und Papsttum 9, 1976).
JL	*Regesta pontificum Romanorum . . . ad annum 1198*, ed. P. Jaffé, 2nd edn. S. Loewenfeld *et al.* 2 vols. (Leipzig 1885–8).
Kennett, W.	*Parochial Antiquities attempted in the history of Ambrosden, Burcester, and other adjacent parts in the counties of Oxford and Bucks.* (Oxford 1695).
LAASR	*Lincolnshire Architectural and Archaeological Society Reports and Papers*.
LCS	H. Bradshaw and C. Wordsworth eds., *The Statutes of Lincoln Cathedral*, 2 vols. in 3 (Cambridge 1892–7).
Le Neve	D. E. Greenway ed., *John Le Neve: Fasti Ecclesiae Anglicanae 1066–1300, iii Lincoln* (1977).
Letters and Papers of Henry VIII	J. S. Brewer, J. Gairdner and R. H. Brodie eds., *Letters and Papers, Foreign and Domestic, Henry VIII*, 21 vols. (1864–1920).
Letters of Pope Innocent III	C. R. and M. G. Cheney eds., *The Letters of Pope Innocent III (1198–1216) concerning England and Wales* (Oxford 1967).
LHA	*Lincolnshire History and Archaeology*.
Lib. Ant.	A. Gibbons ed., *Liber Antiquus de ordinationibus vicariarum tempore Hugonis Wells, Lincolniensis episcopi, 1209–1235* (Lincoln 1888).
Lichfield M.R.A.	H. E. Savage ed., *The great register of Lichfield Cathedral known as Magnum Registrum Album* (William Salt Archaeological Society Collections 1926).
Lincoln Decretals	W. Holtzmann and E. W. Kemp eds., *Papal Decretals relating to the diocese of Lincoln in the twelfth century* (Lincoln Record Society 47, 1954).
Lincolnshire Archives Committee: Archivists' Reports	1948 — in progress.
Lincolnshire Notes and Queries	24 vols. (Horncastle 1888–1936).

Lincs. Assize Rolls *1202–9*	D. M. Stenton ed., *The earliest Lincolnshire assize rolls,* *A.D. 1202–1209* (Lincoln Record Society 22, 1926).
Loomis, R. M. ed.	*Gerald of Wales: The Life of St Hugh of Avalon, bishop of* *Lincoln 1186–1200* (1985).
Luffield Priory Charters	G. R. Elvey ed., 2 vols. (Northamptonshire Record Society 22, 26, 1968–75).
Major, K.	*The D'Oyrys of South Lincolnshire, Norfolk, and Holder-* *ness 1130–1275* (Lincoln, 1984).
Major, K.	*Minster Yard* (Lincoln Minster pamph. 2nd ser., 7, 1974).
Magna Vita	D. L. Douie and D. H. Farmer eds., *Magna Vita Sancti* *Hugonis*, 2 vols. (1961–2 edition reprinted with correc- tions, Oxford Medieval Texts 1985), replacing J. F. Dimock ed., *Magna Vita S. Hugonis Episcopi Lincoln-* *iensis* (Rolls series, 1864).
Missenden Cartulary	J. G. Jenkins ed., *The Cartulary of Missenden abbey*, 3 vols. (Buckinghamshire Archaeological Society, Records Branch 2, 10, 12, 1938–62).
Mon. Angl.	W. Dugdale, *Monasticon Anglicanum*, eds. J. Caley, H. Ellis, and B. Bandinel eds., 6 vols. in 8 (1817–30).
MRH	D. Knowles and R. N. Hadcock eds., *Medieval Religious* *Houses: England and Wales* (2nd edn, 1971).
Newcourt, *Repertorium*	R. Newcourt, *Repertorium ecclesiasticum parochiale* *Londinense*. 2 vols. (1708–10).
Newnham Cartulary	J. Godber ed., *Cartulary of Newnham Priory* (Bedford- shire Historical Record Society 43, 1963–4).
Nicholas, J.	*History and antiquities of the town and county of* *Leicester*, 8 vols. (1795–1815).
Notitiae Ludae	R. S. Bayley (Louth 1834).
Oseney Cartulary	H. E. Salter ed., *Cartulary of Oseney abbey*, 6 vols. (Oxford Historical Society 89–91, 97, 98, 101, 1929–36).
Oxford Formularies	H. E. Salter, W. A. Pantin and H. G. Richardson eds., *Formularies which bear on the history of Oxford c.1204–* *1420*, 2 vols. (Oxford Historical Society, new ser. 4, 5, 1940–2).
Parker, F. ed.	'Chartulary of the "Austin" Priory of Trentham' (William Salt Archaeological Collections xi, 1870).
Patterson, R. B. ed.	*Earldom of Gloucester Charters* (Oxford 1973).
Percy Cartulary, The	M. T. Martin ed. (Surtees society 117, 1911).
Perry, G. G.	*The Life of St Hugh of Avalon* (1879).
Piolin	P. Piolin, *Voyage de Saint Hugues, évêque de Lincoln, à* *travers l'Anjou et le Maine en l'année 1199* (Angers 1889).
PL	J.-P. Migne ed., *Patrologiae latinae cursus completus* (Paris 1844–64).
PUE	W. Holtzmann ed., *Papsturkunden in England*, 3 vols. (Abhandlungen der Gesellschaft der Wissenschaften zu Göttingen, phil.-hist. Klasse, neue Folge, 25 (1930–1), 3 Folge, 14–15 (1935–6), 33 (1952)).
PUFN	J. Ramackers ed., *Papsturkunden in Frankreich*, 2, *Normandie* (Abhandlungen der Gesellschaft der Wissen- schaften zu Göttingen, phil.-hist. Klasse, dritte Folge, 21 (1937)).
Raban, S.	*The estates of Thorney and Crowland* (Cambridge 1977).
Ramsey Cartulary	W. H. Hart and P. A. Lyons eds., *Cartularium monasterii* *de Rameseia*, 3 vols. (Rolls ser. 1884–93).

Records of Merton Priory   A. Heales ed., *The Records of Merton Priory in the county of Surrey* (1898).

Records of the Templars   B. A. Lees ed., *Records of the Templars in England in the Twelfth Century: the Inquest of 1185 with illustrative charters and documents* (Records of the social and economic history of England and Wales ix, British Academy, 1935).

Red Book of the Exchequer, The   H. Hall ed., 3 vols. (Rolls ser., 1896).

Reg. Ant.   C. W. Foster and K. Major eds., *The Registrum Antiquissimum of the cathedral church of Lincoln*, 10 vols. and 2 vols. of facsimiles (Lincoln Record Society 27–9, 32, 34, 41, 42, 46, 51, 62, 67, 68, 1931–73).

Reg. Roff.   J. Thorpe ed., *Registrum Roffense* (1769).

Reg. Sutton   R. M. T. Hill ed., *The Rolls and Register of Bishop Oliver Sutton, 1280–1299*, in progress, 7 vols. so far (Lincoln Record Society 39, 43, 48, 52, 60, 64, 69, 1948–75).

Regesta   H. W. C. Davis, C. Johnson, H. A. Cronne, and R. H. C. Davis eds., *Regesta Regum Anglo-Normannorum 1066–1154*, 4 vols. (Oxford 1913–69).

Regesta Regum Scottorum   G. W. S. Barrow and B. Webster eds., in progress, 3 vols. so far (Edinburgh 1960–82).

RHW   W. P. W. Phillimore and F. N. Davis eds., *Rotuli Hugonis de Welles, episcopi Lincolniensis, A.D. mccix–mccxxxv*, 3 vols. (Canterbury and York Society 1, 3, 4, 1907–9, and Lincoln Record Society 3, 6, 9, 1912–14).

Rot. Chart.   T. D. Hardy ed., *Rotuli Chartarum ... vol. i, pars i, 1199–1216* (Record Commission 1837).

Rot. Cur. Reg.   F. Palgrave ed., *Rotuli Curiae Regis*, 2 vols. (Record Commission 1835).

Rot Grav.   F. N. Davis, C. W. Foster, and A. Hamilton Thompson eds., *Rotuli Ricardi Gravesend, episcopi Lincolniensis, A.D. mcclviii–mcclxxix* (Canterbury and York Society 31 and Lincoln Record Society 20, 1925).

RRG   F. N. Davis ed., *Rotuli Roberti Grosseteste, episcopi Lincolniensis, A.D. mccxxxv–mccliii* (Canterbury and York Society 10, 1913, and Lincoln Record Society 11, 1914).

St Frideswide's Cartulary   S. R. Wigram ed., *The Cartulary of the monastery of St Frideswide at Oxford*, 2 vols. (Oxford Historical Society 28, 31, 1895–6).

Salter, H. E. ed.   *Feet of Fines for Oxfordshire 1195–1291* (Oxfordshire Record Society 12, 1930).

Sayers, J. E.   *Papal Judges Delegate in the Province of Canterbury 1198–1254* (Oxford 1971).

Scammell, G. V.   *Hugh du Puiset, Bishop of Durham* (Cambridge 1956).

Selby Coucher Book   J. T. Fowler ed., *The coucher book of Selby*, 2 vols. (Yorkshire Archaeological Society record ser. 10, 13, 1891–3).

Sheehan, M. M.   *The Will in Medieval England* (Pontifical Institute, Toronto 1963).

Smith, D. M.   *Guide to Bishops' Registers of England and Wales* (Royal Historical Society 1981).

Smith, D. M.   'The rolls of Hugh of Wells, bishop of Lincoln, 1209–35', *BIHR* xlv (1972), 155–95.

Stenton, D. M. ed.	*Rolls of the justices in eyre, being the rolls of pleas and assizes for Lincolnshire 1218–9 and Worcestershire 1221* (Selden Society 53, 1934).
Stoke by Clare Cartulary	C. Harper-Bill and R. Mortimer eds., 3 vols. (Suffolk Records Society, Suffolk Charters iv–vi, 1982–4).
Thame Cartulary, The	H. E. Salter, ed., 2 vols. (Oxfordshire Record Society 25, 26, 1947–8).
Theobald	A. Saltman ed., *Theobald, archbishop of Canterbury* (1956)
Thompson, A. H.	*The Abbey of St Mary of the Meadows, Leicester* (Leicester 1949).
Thompson, A. H.	*The Premonstratensian Abbey of Welbeck* (1938).
Thurston, H.	*The Life of St Hugh of Lincoln* (1898).
TPES	*Transactions of the St Paul's Ecclesiological Society.*
TRHS	*Transactions of the Royal Historical Society*
Tutbury Cartulary	A. Saltman ed., *The cartulary of Tutbury priory* (Staffordshire Record Society, 4th ser., 4, 1962).
VCH	*Victoria County History.*
Wigram, S. R.	*Chronicles of the Abbey of Elstow* (1885).
Woolley, R. M.	*Catalogue of the Manuscripts of Lincoln Cathedral Chapter Library* (Oxford 1927).
Woolley, R. M.	*St Hugh of Lincoln* (1927).
York Minster Fasti	C. T. Clay ed., 2 vols. (Yorkshire Archaeological Society record ser. 123–4, 1958–9).

OTHER ABBREVIATIONS

Add.	Additional
app.	appendix
archbp(s)	archbishop(s)
archdn(s)	archdeacon(s)
Aug.	Augustinian
Ben.	Benedictine
BL	British Library, London
BN	Bibliothèque Nationale, Paris
Bodl.	Bodleian Library, Oxford
bp(s)	bishop(s)
C.A.	Charta Antiqua
C.C.C.	Corpus Christi College
cat.	catalogue
Ch.	Charter
Cist.	Cistercian
Clun.	Cluniac
CUL	Cambridge University Library
D. & C.	Dean and Chapter
dioc.	diocese
d.q.	sur double queue (see Introduction p. oo)
Gilb.	Gilbertine
LAO	Lincolnshire Archives Office, Lincoln
Lib.	Library
m.	membrane
misc.	miscellanea, miscellaneous
ms.	manuscript
Mun.	muniment(s)
opp.	opposite
pd	printed
Prem.	Premonstratensian
PRO	Public Record Office, London
repd	reprinted
s.-ex	late-century
s.-in	early-century
s.-med	mid-century
ser.	series
s.q.	sur simple queue
Trans.	Transactions
(transl.)	in translation, translated

INTRODUCTION

This second and concluding volume of Lincoln episcopal acta covers the episcopates of Hugh of Avalon (1186–1200) and William of Blois (1203–6). From the time of William's successor, Hugh of Wells (1209–35), there exists the earliest known (and possibly the first) systematic enrolment of acts by the episcopal clerks and although there have subsequently been many losses in the series of episcopal rolls and registers and certain categories of acta were not in any case considered for registration, the death of Bishop William of Blois has been taken as a suitable point to conclude this present edition.

This collection is almost as large as the accumulated acta of St Hugh's six episcopal predecessors put together. It numbers 224 acta for Hugh (of which 37 are originals and 45 mere mentions) and 86 for William of Blois (with 10 originals and 21 mentions). Even so as a collection its scope is understandably deficient. As might be expected from the available sources (records from diocesan, capitular and monastic archives predominate), the collection consists for the most part of beneficial grants and confirmations and it is obvious that the resulting collection is both unrepresentative and distorted as an indication of the range of a bishop's administrative activities. If we want to find out about St Hugh's confirmation of children, his consecration of churches and churchyards, his concern for the proper burial rights and ceremonies, his careful examination of the qualifications of prospective ordinands, his celebration of diocesan synods and pastoral visitations, then we must look not to this collection but to the *Magna Vita Sancti Hugonis* and other chronicle sources. Sadly William of Blois had no chronicler to record the discharge of his diocesan duties. Even in respect of routine administrative business there are many gaps. Citations (in the wording of which bishop Hugh, we are told by his biographer Adam of Eynsham, was personally involved),[1] induction mandates, letters of orders, a variety of familiar licences and commissions all fail to find a place in this collection. That all or most of them once existed at this time is highly probable but the restricted nature of the available source material has not encouraged such survivals. As in the earlier collection of Lincoln acta, the grants of privilege and the confirmations of

---

[1] *Magna Vita* ii 48.

churches, lands, pensions, tithes and the like for the cathedral church or religious houses predominate. Considering the main sources of documentary evidence now extant, it is not surprising that records of the appropriation of parish churches to ecclesiastical corporations and the provision of vicarages should also be a significant element in the surviving acta of both bishops. Naturally too, the institution of clergy to benefices in monastic or capitular patronage and any arrangements about pensions, duties and responsibilities are solemnly recorded in the cartularies and registers of these ecclesiastical communities. On the other hand, it is disappointing that Hugh's judicial activities, both as a diocesan and as a papal judge delegate, should be so poorly reflected in the collection. Much more information about his exercise of this judicial authority can be gleaned from the *Magna Vita* than from the few surviving documents and mere mentions noted here. Likewise the evidence for the bishop's activities as a temporal lord and great landowner is scant and of political and personal correspondence there is nothing but an occasional mention abstracted from chronicle sources.[2]

If we compare this collection of 310 acta with the archival evidence for the activities of a bishop of Lincoln exactly one hundred years later we can gain a better idea of the sort of losses that have occurred. Oliver Sutton who was bishop of Lincoln from 1280 to 1299 has left behind, in registered form, an admittedly incomplete record of approximately 4250 administrative acts and the names of approximately 5250 clergy he had ordained.[3] This does not include other material not registered by the episcopal clerks but to be found in capitular and monastic archives or copied into their cartularies. Even accounting for the increase of the diocesan's responsibilities and duties in the course of the thirteenth century it is a salutary indication of the evidential problems facing the historian of the twelfth-century English church, when no substantial episcopal archives have survived and there was no systematic record-keeping by the bishop's staff and reliance has almost exclusively to be placed on the extant archives of recipients of episcopal acta.[4]

---

[2] Readers are referred to the subject index for a fuller indication of the range of business dealt with by both bishops.

[3] These calculations are based on the seven published volumes of *The Rolls and Register of Bishop Oliver Sutton, 1280–1299*, ed. R. M. T. Hill (Lincoln Record Society 39, 43, 48, 52, 60, 64, 69, 1948–75) and the typescript of the eighth and final volume which Professor Hill kindly made available to me. See also Professor Hill's article 'Bishop Sutton and his archives: a study in the keeping of records in the thirteenth century', *Journal of Ecclesiastical History* 2 (1951) 43–53.

[4] For the episcopal *familia* and its activities in the twelfth and early thirteenth centuries see *EBC*; for registration and record-keeping see also M. T. Clanchy, *From memory to written record: England 1066–1307* (1979) 53–5, and my *Guide to Bishops' Registers of England and Wales* (Royal Historical Society 1981) and 'The rolls of Hugh of Wells, bishop of Lincoln, 1209–35', *BIHR* xlv (1972) 155–95.

THE BISHOPS AND THEIR STAFF

The two occupants of the see of Lincoln in this period offer a great contrast: the one a Carthusian monk reluctantly persuaded to be consecrated as bishop and within twenty years of his death to be canonised as a saint of the Universal Church, a figure naturally attractive to contemporary biographers and to modern historians alike;[5] the other a more obscure figure whose period as a teacher in the schools of Paris and service in the household of Hugh du Puiset, bishop of Durham, was followed by ecclesiastical preferment at Lincoln cathedral, firstly as subdean from about 1194 and then precentor from 1197 until his election as bishop in 1203.[6]

The problems the two bishops faced at their elevation were likewise quite different. Hugh came to Lincoln from the Witham charterhouse in succession to a prominent royal official, Walter of Coutances, who had briefly held the see (July 1183–March 1185) before being translated to the archbishopric of Rouen. Apart from Walter's short tenure, the bishopric had virtually been vacant for almost 18 years (for part of that time there was an unconsecrated bishop-elect, Geoffrey Plantagenet) and in the vacancies of the see a great deal of administrative work had devolved upon the eight archdeacons of the diocese.[7] Walter may have

---

[5] The various 'lives' of St Hugh are admirably surveyed by Dr A. Gransden, *Historical Writing in England c.550–c.1307* i (1974) 310–17. The most recent editions are D. L. Douie and D. H. Farmer eds., *Magna Vita Sancti Hugonis* (2 vols., 1961–2 edition repd with corrections, Oxford Medieval Texts 1985); R. M. Loomis's edition and translation, *Gerald of Wales: The Life of St Hugh of Avalon, bishop of Lincoln 1186–1200* (1985), the Latin version also being in *Gir. Camb.* vii 81–147; C. Garton ed., *The Metrical Life of St Hugh of Lincoln*, a translation to be published as a Lincoln Cathedral Library pamphlet in 1986 (the earlier edition edited by J. F. Dimock, 1860). The most recent monograph is D. H. Farmer, *Saint Hugh of Lincoln* (1985).

[6] The account of bp William by John de Schalby (died 1333) includes an incident which took place while the future bishop was teaching in the schools of Paris when he was obliged to resist the amorous advances of a rich Parisian lady (*Gir. Camb.* vii 202–3). Since Canon Srawley considered this passage to have the character of a *chronique scandaleuse* he omitted it from his translation (*The Book of John de Schalby* 10). William occurs as a witness to bp Hugh du Puiset's acta from c.1180 × 1185 (see G. V. Scammell, *Hugh du Puiset, Bishop of Durham* (Cambridge 1956) 70, 235, 255, 257–9, 261–2). From two Salvin deeds deposited in the Durham County Record Office (D/Sa/D.378–9) it would appear that in this period William was rector of the church of St Nicholas, Durham. A nephew, master William de Marum, is also mentioned, and he is likewise found at Lincoln at the close of the century (cf. acta nos. 13–15). He may even be identified with William de Marin' who occurs as a canon of Lincoln 1200 × 10 (*Le Neve* 149). There was also a master William of Blois who attests certain Scottish charters at this period (C. Innes ed., *Liber Sancte Marie de Melros* (Bannatyne Club 1837) 105, 107) but it is uncertain whether he is the future bp.

[7] Before the 1261 composition over vacancy administration between archbp Boniface of Canterbury and the cathedral chapter of Lincoln (Lincoln D. & C. Dij/60/2/8, pd by I. J. Churchill, *Canterbury Administration* (1933) ii 42–7 from Lambeth ms. 1212), it is clear from the extant evidence that at a vacancy the chapter assumed the jurisdiction and the archdns (presumably as agents of the chapter) carried out administrative duties in their respective archdeaconries (e.g. institutions to benefices). Shortly before the Boniface composition the

taken some of his household clerks with him to his Norman diocese. At
any rate, apart from master Wimar, subdean of the cathedral, and the
celebrated theologian John of Cornwall, none of the *magistri* and *clerici*
who feature in Walter's acta are found attesting the charters of his
successor, or are known from other sources to have remained at
Lincoln.[8] Certainly there is no real element of administrative continuity present. In addition, the new bishop's own personal circumstances — a foreigner, with virtually no experience of English diocesan
administration — clearly must have made the formation of a group of
household clerks and administrative assistants a very difficult proposi-
tion. We gain some idea of Hugh's difficulties in an illuminating passage
in the *Magna Vita* when Adam records his request to archbishop
Baldwin of Canterbury for suitable clerks to help him and emphasizes
Hugh's own anxiety to surround himself with capable administrators:

> Ac inprimis quantum studii quantumque impenderit sollicitudinis ut ecclesiam
> sibi commissam uiris adornaret illustribus uideretur commemoratione dignissimum.
> Perpendens quippe altiusque considerans quia absque uirorum proborum adiutorio
> nec populo nec clero quem regebat conuenienter prodesse, nec quibusque iustitiam
> ecclesiastice iurisdictionis expetentibus sufficeret competenter adesse, uiros
> sapientia et scientia preditos et, quod pluris est, in timore Domini probatissimos, suo
> instantius satagebat lateri sociare. Horum siquidem et consiliis fretus et comitatus
> auxiliis, munus suscepti regiminis strenuissime adimplebat. Hiis denique Lincoln-
> iensem ecclesiam cunctis per orbem universum ecclesiis gloriosius copiosiusque
> illustrabat. Hiis enim, cum uacare cepissent, prebendas seu et alia beneficia
> conferebat, hos uariis dignitatibus singulis quoque ecclesiasticis functionibus
> preficiebat; huiusmodi homines, non solum in toto orbe Anglicano, immo et in
> ceteris nationibus scholisque transmarinis omni studio inuestigatos, ecclesie sue
> gremio inserebat.[9]

The two clerks Hugh obtained from the household of archbishop
Baldwin were master Roger of Rolleston, later appointed archdeacon of

---

archdns of the Lincoln diocese claimed to exercise jurisdiction during a vacancy '.. . . habent et
exercent iure et ratione decani et capituli . . . ad quos de iure communi iurisdiccio episcopalis
vacante sede dinoscitur pertinere' (Lincoln D. & C. Dij/60/2/3) and there is certainly considerable
evidence from earlier vacancies to confirm this (e.g. BL ms. Cotton Tib. C ix fo. 41 (archdn of
Huntingdon); *CRR* vi 279 (Bedford), 308 (Lincoln); vii 135 (Bedford); viii 171 (Stow); BL ms.
Royal 11 B ix fo. 36 (Northampton); *RHW* i 239–41, 243–6, 250, 252–3, 256, 264–5, 267–8
(Leicester); iii 186 (Lincoln); *RRG* 158–9 (Northampton); *Eynsham Cartulary* i 3 (Buckingham); BL ms. Add. 47677 fo. 357v (Oxford); BL ms. Cotton Faust. A iii fo. 267 (Northampton);
AASR xxxix (1929) 179–87 (Lincoln, Huntingdon)). In the last-mentioned article Canon Foster
appeared to think that the archdn of Lincoln exercised all manner of episcopal jurisdiction
throughout the diocese. I do not think the documentary evidence supports this view. All the
business dealt with by the archdn of Lincoln concerned parishes within his own archdeaconry. For
a lengthier note on this topic of vacancy administration see appendix I: 'A note on *sede vacante*
administration at Lincoln from the late twelfth century until 1235' in my thesis 'The
administration of Hugh of Wells, bishop of Lincoln 1209–1235' (Nottingham University Ph.D.
1970).

[8] For Walter's *familia* see *EEA* i xlvi; his acta are ibid. nos. 297–323.

[9] *Magna Vita* i 110.

Leicester and then dean of Lincoln cathedral until his death in 1223 and master Robert of Bedford (*in numero clericorum nullus eum zelo iustitie aut ingenii vivacis acumine uidebatur anteire*)[10] who soon became precentor of Lincoln but died young after only a few years in the bishop's service. In that time both clerks acted jointly as the bishop's vicegerents.[11] Other prominent members of his household (if the witness-lists of the episcopal acta are a sufficiently reliable indication) were master Simon of Sywell, the noted canonist, who later joined the household of Hubert Walter, archbishop of Canterbury,[12] the Paris master William de Montibus, who as chancellor of the cathedral greatly enhanced the reputation of the school at Lincoln,[13] and a small group of *magistri* — William of Blois, the future bishop who came to Lincoln after serving bishop Hugh du Puiset of Durham, Geoffrey of Lechlade, Gerard de Rowell, Geoffrey of Deeping, Stephen de Swafeld, Richard of Kent (*uir vita utique et doctrina clarissimus*),[14] Alexander of Bedford, Alexander of Elstow, Hugh of St Edward, Geoffrey of St Edward and possibly Roger of Sumerford. All of these received canonries of the cathedral and some of them further dignities and offices.[15] Richard of Kent became subdean of the cathedral in 1197 and archdeacon of Northampton around 1200; Stephen de Swafeld was successively chancellor and archdeacon of Buckingham; William of Blois became subdean, then precentor of the cathedral. Other clerks, Theobald de Bosell (also appointed to a canonry at Lincoln), Roger Bacon and Eustace de Wilton feature regularly in the acta witness-lists. Hugh of Rolleston, a kinsman of Roger, is described as *clericus episcopi*.[16]

Of the bishop's own kinsmen, master Raymond (*vir multa honestate conspicuus*)[17] and Hamo feature prominently in the acta. Hamo is most probably to be identified with the archdeacon of Leicester and dean of Lincoln cathedral, who was ultimately succeeded in both offices by

[10] *Ibid.* i 112.

[11] BL. ms. Cotton Tib. E v fo. 52v; BL ms. Royal 11 B ix fo. 30.

[12] See *EEA* ii xxvii–viii; C. R. Cheney, *Hubert Walter* (1967) 164–6; S. Kuttner and E. Rathbone 'Anglo-Norman Canonists of the Twelfth Century' *Traditio* vii (1949–51) 279–358, esp. 316–27 *passim*; *EBC* 13.

[13] See H. MacKinnon 'William de Montibus, a medieval teacher' in *Essays in Medieval History presented to Bertie Wilkinson*, eds. T. A. Sandquist and M. R. Powicke (Toronto 1969) 32–45. See also the unpublished thesis by the same author 'The Life and Works of William de Montibus' (Oxford University D.Phil. 1959).

[14] *Magna Vita* ii 185.

[15] See *Le Neve* for the various Lincoln preferments of these clerks.

[16] actum no. 43. He is probably also the Hugh, clerk of the bishop of Lincoln, who occurs in 1198 (N. Denholm-Young ed., *Cartulary of the Medieval Archives of Christ Church* (Oxford Historical Society xcii, 1931) 100).

[17] *Magna Vita* ii 154.

Roger of Rolleston. Master Raymond in turn succeeded Roger as archdeacon of Leicester. Another nephew, William of Avalon, received a canonry from his uncle but does not occur with any great frequency in the episcopal acta. He held this canonry until 1236 and was a donor of books to the cathedral library.[18] Of the clergy at Lincoln when Hugh arrived, master Wimar the subdean has already been mentioned. The only other one who, from the available evidence, seems to have become a member of his *familia* is master Robert de Hardres. At the time of Hugh's consecration he was vice-archdeacon of Lincoln and had been custodian of the vacant bishopric in 1185. He was made a canon shortly afterwards (he first occurs *c*.1187) and by 1192 had been appointed to the archdeaconry of Huntingdon. He regularly attests the bishop's acta until the end of Hugh's episcopate.[19] Of the episcopal chaplains, in addition to his biographer Adam of Eynsham, brief mention is also made of Ralph, William and Walkelin and of course Robert de Capella — *satis erat mansueti lenisque ingenii: preterque ceteros more optimos quibus preditus fuit, quibuslibet afflictis erat compatientissimus, cunctis uero in commune affabilis et benignus*[20] — who survived his episcopal master by only a few days. Reference is also found to two of the bishop's stewards, Pons,[21] and Hugh de Bobi (or Boby).[22] The latter was custodian of the see in the 1200–3 vacancy. No designated chancellor — or head of the household secretariat — is recorded in this period and indeed it is not until the episcopate of Hugh of Wells (1209–35) that a series of episcopal dataries are named.

I have alluded in the first volume of the Lincoln acta to the shortcomings and limitations of witness-lists as an indication of membership of the episcopal *familia*. An initial problem is that often it is not clear in whose service the attesting *clerici* or *capellani* were. For instance, master Ingelram and Luke, who both witness a few of the bishop's acta turn out to have been a chaplain of Roger of Rolleston and a clerk of Robert de Hardres respectively rather than members of Hugh's immediate household.[23] On other occasions only passing reference is made to an individual known from other sources to have been a member of the *familia*. Stephen de Piun, described as *clericus*

---

[18] *Ibid.* i 131n.; R. M. Woolley, *Catalogue of the Manuscripts of Lincoln Cathedral Chapter Library* (Oxford 1927) ix.

[19] See also *Reg. Ant.* vii 206 for his activities as vice-archdn of Lincoln.

[20] *Magna Vita* ii 212.

[21] *Ibid.* ii 203–4.

[22] Acta nos. 179, 212; *Rot. Chart.* 99b. Another temporal official who is found attesting a private charter is Simon de Bukedene, the bishop's bailiff (probably at Newark) (C. J. Holdsworth ed., *Rufford Charters* ii (Thoroton Society record ser. 30, 1974) no. 357).

[23] Ingelram acta nos. 122, 166; Luke acta nos. 123–4.

episcopi, occurs only once in this collection and then as a beneficiary;[24] Ralph *capellanus episcopi* likewise occurs only once.[25] Their isolated appearance in the acta is no real indication of the length or degree of association with the bishop. We are of course fortunate that St Hugh's biographer, the Benedictine monk Adam of Eynsham, described some of the *familiares* with whom the bishop surrounded himself, but it is salutary to record that Adam himself, the bishop's chaplain, never features in a single actum witness-list. Brother Morin, the bishop's almoner for all but the last eighteen months of Hugh's episcopate, occurs only once in a witness-list in this present collection.[26] Other similar examples could be given.

The situation confronting William of Blois on his election was very different from that in 1186. To start with, he was a local man, and most of his erstwhile colleagues in Hugh's *familia* were still in the diocese, often holding archdeaconries or cathedral dignities. There is an appreciable element of continuity, and it is not very surprising that there is little difference in the format and wording of the official documents issued by these two bishops. Roger Bacon, master Hugh of St Edward, master Alexander of Bedford, master Alexander of Elstow (promoted by the bishop to the archdeaconry of Bedford), master Gerard de Rowell, master Geoffrey of Deeping (appointed to the precentorship of the cathedral and possibly also to the archdeaconry of Bedford) are all found on many occasions in his acta. Apart from a kinsman and namesake, who was given the archdeaconry of Buckingham,[27] most of the new names that are found in William's *acta* seem to indicate, by their territorial surnames at least, a local connection — Thomas of Fiskerton, Peter of Kirmond, master Gilbert of Mablethorpe, master William de Stavenby. Other *magistri* who served the bishop and were subsequently rewarded with canonries were Adam of St Edmund and William son of Fulk. Two episcopal clerks are only known by their Christian names — Charles and Waleran, and the bishop's chaplain was one Vacarius, who had been William's chaplain when he was precentor of the cathedral. He was possibly a nephew of the famous civil lawyer, master Vacarius.[28] It is important to note that

---

[24] Acta nos. 76–7.

[25] Actum no. 205.

[26] Actum no. 206.

[27] See *Emden* iii 2153 for his career. He was bp of Worcester 1218–36.

[28] Acta nos. 230, 243, 251, 298–9. For Vacarius as chaplain of William of Blois as precentor see *Reg. Ant.* ix no. 2471. For his possible relationship to the famous lawyer and namesake see R. W. Southern, 'Master Vacarius and the beginning of an English academic tradition' in *Medieval Learning and Literature: essays presented to Richard William Hunt*, eds. J. J. G. Alexander and M. T. Gibson (Oxford 1976) 285.

the careers of some of these *magistri* and clerks spanned three episcopates and it is not uncommon for *familiares* to begin their service under the first Hugh and to continue to serve the second Hugh well into the 1220s.[29] This continuity is obviously an important factor in any study of the ecclesiastical administration of the diocese and of the documents that were produced in the bishop's name.

THE ACTA

St Hugh, we are told by his biographer, Adam of Eynsham, was extremely scrupulous over the use of his seal and the wording of his letters:

> Nec minori quoque observantia veritatis sigilli sui reverentiam tuebatur, nichil umquam non verum in litteris eo signandis contineri permittens. Ubi adeo scrupulosus fuit quod, iuxta tritam scribendi formulam cum citatorias alicui ederet, in eis nullatenus poni sineret 'Meminimus nos te alias citasse', ne forte quod in sua non erat memoria, in ea esse mentiretur sua cartula.[30]

This naturally leads us to ask if the bishop's influence can be seen reflected in the forms and wording of his surviving acta. The answer must be a disappointing no. Understandably enough, it is impossible to gauge from a study of the diplomatic how much personal influence the bishop, as opposed to household clerks, exercised over the actual drafting of the correspondence issued in his name. Adam has perhaps indicated that Hugh was rather more attentive to the form his administrative correspondence took and more closely supervised the activities of his clerks than did many of his episcopal colleagues. But if we look for startling innovation or out-of-the-ordinary phraseology in these documents we shall certainly not find them.

In some ways the period is witnessing a change in the format of administrative documents, as the subsequent study of the diplomatic will attempt to show, but this is a development seen elsewhere at diocesan level and by no means unique to Lincoln. A general impression gained from an examination of the acta of the first Hugh and his successor is that they are becoming more regular and stereotyped. What is particularly striking is that there is considerably less of the

---

[29] Among the familiar names from previous episcopates featuring in the witness-lists of Hugh of Wells's acta are Thomas of Fiskerton, Hugh of St Edward, master William son of Fulk, Adam of St Edmund, Richard of Linwood, Peter of Kirmond and Gilbert of Mablethorpe. Thomas of Fiskerton acted as episcopal datary from 1219 to 1222 and is found in 69 acta of the second Hugh.

[30] *Magna Vita* ii 48.

variation in format found in earlier Lincoln acta and in the case of
original documents, the majority are the product of the episcopal clerks
following accepted forms. Those that by their form or to a lesser extent
from palaeographical evidence may admit of external composition by
the beneficiary or 'casual' scribes are notable rarities. It is perhaps
significant that Professor Cheney has argued that two early thirteenth-
century ecclesiastical formularies are possibly based on a formulary
compiled in St Hugh's household in the last years of his life.[31] Examples
of the *cursus curie romane* are found on occasion in Hugh's acta but not
to any systematic extent.[32] Palaeographically too, as well as in format,
the original acta show a marked similarity, preferring a neat, small
cursive charter-hand, reminiscent of the royal chancery, and in itself
suggestive of a fairly formal clerical 'organisation' within the episcopal
household, even if we cannot yet properly name it the chancery.
Indeed, the handwriting of the acta is often remarkably similar and the
handiwork of individual scribes frequently very difficult to distinguish
from each other. The letter of institution to Melton Mowbray church
(no. 89) is attested by John the clerk *qui hoc scripsit*, but the
handwriting is not found in any other surviving originals and it must
remain an open question whether John was an episcopal scribe or else a
local clerk employed casually or possibly connected with the patron of
the church, Lewes priory. With this single exception, none of the
scribes of the acta or indeed those who drafted the documents can be
named. All that can be said on palaeographical grounds is that when the
same handwriting is found in two or more documents for different
beneficiaries then it is possible to assume that they were written by a
scribe in the episcopal *familia*. Two such identifications have been
positively made for St Hugh (scribe **I** having written nos. 8, 70, 114,
115, 123 and 188A; scribe **II** nos. 23, 105 and 173) and two for William
of Blois (scribe **III** having written nos. 268 and 297; scribe **IV** nos. 244
and 298). To sum up, the acta may not yet have reached the regularity
of form they attained in the thirteenth century and beyond, closely
based on rules and precedents according to the type of business, and
with little scope for flexibility, but they are well on their way to it.

The acta of Hugh of Avalon and William of Blois must obviously be
compared with the diplomatic form of the earlier Lincoln episcopal
charters and also with the products of their immediate successor, Hugh
of Wells (1209–35). The problems faced in the first volume of this

---

[31] *EBC* 124–8.
[32] *Ibid.* 78–9.

Lincoln collection in distinguishing the acta of Robert Bloet (1094–1123) and Robert Chesney (1148–66) are as nothing compared with the difficulties encountered in distinguishing abbreviated copies of acta of St Hugh from those of the second Hugh, and to a lesser extent in deciding if bishop W. is William of Blois or Walter of Coutances (1183 5). Clearly, if originals survive, or at least witness-lists of copies are not truncated or omitted altogether, then the task is usually rendered not too difficult. Besides the internal dating evidence normally provided by the witnesses themselves, the most significant difference between the acta of Hugh I and Hugh II is that the latter's, with a few exceptions (notably, letters missives, mandates, ending with the valediction), are dated by time, place and datary's name. Only a handful of St Hugh's charters bear a date and then only because of the solemnity of the occasion or ceremony, and, unlike Hugh II's, there is no regularity in the way such dates are rendered. However, when a cartulary compiler concludes his copy with 'Hiis testibus etc.', then it is extremely difficult to make a firm distinction between the two on diplomatic grounds alone. Throughout this section on the format of the acta, allusions are made to the diplomatic of Hugh of Wells's acta indicating points of similarity and comparison with his immediate precursors.[33]

TITLES AND ADDRESS

The titles used by Hugh of Avalon and William of Blois followed the practice customary at Lincoln since the time of bishop Alexander (1123–48), namely, the style *dei gratia Lincolniensis episcopus*, which is used for almost all their acta. Once *dei permissione* replaces *dei gratia* in an actum of Hugh (no. 118) and *divina miseratione* is used three times (nos. 134, 169, 170). Likewise under William, only two exceptions to this accepted practice have been found — the use of *dei gratia* (or *miseratione divina*) *Lincolniensis ecclesie minister humilis*, one in a confirmation for the priory of Ware, a cell of St-Évroul (no. 299), the other for St-Évroul itself (no. 286). The form *Lincolniensis ecclesie minister humilis* is used twice by William's successor, Hugh of Wells, as a variant of the standard *dei gratia Lincolniensis episcopus* his clerks also regularly employed.[34] On both occasions it is used by the bishop when specifically addressing a superior, in one case king Henry

---

[33] These allusions to the diplomatic form of Hugh of Wells's acta are based on my study of 400 charters of the bp, edited in my Ph.D. thesis referred to in n. 7 above.

[34] *RHW* ii 204; *LAASR* vi (1956) 111.

III, in the other pope Honorius III. Apart from this, the *dei gratia Lincolniensis episcopus* is used with remarkable regularity at Lincoln from Alexander to Robert Grosseteste (1235–53) and is only superseded in clerical fashion by *permissione divina* or *miseratione divina* during the episcopate of Henry Lexington (1254–8).[35]

It is the same as regards the general address used in beneficial charters of Hugh I and William of Blois (and indeed of Hugh of Wells). *Omnibus Christi fidelibus ad quos presens scriptum pervenerit*, is the norm and the variations on the theme are legion. Sometimes *Omnibus* is replaced by *Universis*, *scriptum* by *carta* or *littere*, and often *Omnibus* (or *Universis*) *sancte matris ecclesie filiis* are substituted for the faithful of Christ. One notably archaic form for the late twelfth century — *omnibus fidelibus sancte dei ecclesie clericis et laycis* (no. 189) — can be shown to have been modelled very closely on a charter of bishop Alexander, issued between 1139 and 1148, and another confirmation of St Hugh using *tam presentibus quam futuris* may, from the evidence of other aspects of the text, borrow phraseology from an earlier document (no. 179). The change of respective positions of general address and episcopal title noted in the time of Walter of Coutances, with the general address preceding the bishop's name and style,[36] is normally observed under Hugh I (139 examples with this sequence and 12 with the reverse order) and becomes the rule under William and Hugh II. No exceptions have been noted in the acta of these two bishops. When a document has a specific address, however, the accepted rule applies that when corresponding with an inferior, the bishop's title precedes the address to the individual, group or corporation, but the position is reversed when the bishop corresponds with someone superior in rank or status, and generally also with episcopal colleagues.

SALUTATION

At first sight the use of the various forms of salutation (fourteen different versions found for St Hugh, six for William) seems to be entirely arbitrary without any distinction being made for categories of business or types of recipient. There is perhaps a noticeable preference for one form in favour of others, which changes from bishop to bishop. From the available evidence, the simple *salutem in domino* is most common under St Hugh, to be supplanted in preference under William

---

[35] Details about the styles employed by Grosseteste and Lexington are taken from *RRG* and additional acta noted in the acta indexes at the Borthwick Institute, York.
[36] *EEA* i, liii–liv.

of Blois by *salutem eternam in domino* (or *eternam in domino salutem*), and then with Hugh II *salutem in domino* once again enjoys the same popularity as under his namesake. It would obviously be a mistake to imagine that rigid rules had been formulated for the employment of different forms of salutation and that convention strictly governed their usage. Yet it does not seem too fanciful at least to discern some developments at this period. The variants of salutation incorporating *benedictionem* (e.g. *salutem et (dei/paternam/fidelem) benedictionem*, *salutem, gratiam et benedictionem*) are used in the acta of St Hugh without distinction for documents with a general address (eight times) or with a specific address (nine times).[37] Under William of Blois this situation changes and the *benedictionem* greeting is exclusively found in acta addressed specifically to inferiors.[38] It is not used with a general address nor is it used in correspondence directed to those superior in rank or status, when much more elaborate forms of greeting were employed. With Hugh of Wells the *benedictionem* greeting is again used only (but not to the total exclusion of other forms) for such correspondence with individuals, groups, or corporations.

THE ARENGA

By the close of the twelfth century, the use of the arenga (harangue, pious preamble) in episcopal documents was fast declining. At Lincoln, however, it does not show such a marked decline as at Canterbury in the same period,[39] perhaps because the Lincoln clerks did not use the inspeximus form of confirmation with any regularity. As it is, 36% of all confirmations and appropriations issued in the names of St Hugh and William of Blois include such a preamble, sometimes as a separate sentence, more often than not as a subordinate clause leading to the *dispositio*. The remaining confirmations restrict themselves to a simple notification before the dispositive clauses. There seems to have been no convention as to usage, and it must be assumed that the arenga's inclusion or omission was governed by the particular preferences of the scribe or the recipient.[40] Of the forty-eight acta of St Hugh which include a preamble, all but four are confirmations of possessions to religious houses or appropriations of churches.[41] Three of the

---

[37] Acta nos. 12, 27, 42, 76, 91–4, 97, 113, 122, 124, 135, 138, 144, 188–9.

[38] Acta no. 217, 253, 256–7, 283.

[39] Cf. *EEA* ii lxii when the use of the preamble in Hubert Walter's time had fallen to under 20% of the total. Professor Cheney notes that 88 inspeximus charters survive for Hubert.

[40] See *ibid*. ii lxiii–iv for a valuable discussion of this point.

[41] Indulgences are another category of business in which the arenga is often found. Unfortunately, no indulgences survive (apart from two mentions) for St Hugh and William.

exceptions relate to Lincoln cathedral and concern pentecostal processions (no. 92) and the residence and jurisdiction of the canons (nos. 93–4). The fourth confirms a settlement of a dispute between the canons of Thornton Curtis and Guisborough (no. 198). Fifteen of William's acta with the arenga are likewise confirmations or grants *in proprios usus*, and the remaining three concern the dean and chapter of Lincoln (nos. 253, 256, 257), the last two being identical with charters of his predecessor.

What is most noticeable about the arengas used in St Hugh's acta is their variation. Although all are confined within the well-laboured themes of the bishop's pastoral responsibilities, charitable benefactions, and the preservation of a written record, the actual form of these preambles is rarely repeated. Of forty-eight examples, forty-four are different. Of the remainder, two with identical preambles are modified versions of the same ordinance (nos. 93–4), a further two are found in confirmations for the same house (Daventry), which could either indicate internal composition or that they were issued at a similar date,[42] and the final three examples are significantly all for Lincolnshire houses of the order of Sempringham (nos. 28, 63, 90). Two have virtually the same witnesses and in fact all three could have been issued together. In stark contrast the preambles found in bishop William's acta are chiefly noteworthy for their monotonous regularity. Eleven acta contain arengas which begin with *ea que viris* (or *locis*) *religiosis pia fidelium largitione rationabiliter collata sunt*, or minor variations, and then conclude with a choice of observations on the theme of the advantages of recording benefactions in writing to prevent losses and difficulties caused by evil-doers or the passage of time.[43] Of the remaining seven acta with preambles, three are verbatim copies of those found in Hugh's acta for the same beneficiaries (nos. 256, 257, 281).

NOTIFICATION

The arenga was generally linked to the narrative or dispositive clauses by such words or constructions as *eapropter* (following the papal pattern), *hinc* (or *inde*) *est quod, quapropter, quocirca, volentes/ attendentes igitur* and so on. The first two examples cited were the most popular at Lincoln in this period as they were earlier in the century.[44] In just under a quarter of the Lincoln examples the arenga was followed by

---

[42] Nos. 48–9. They have only one witness in common, but they are both dated to the same period 1189 × *c*.1194.
[43] Nos. 219, 229, 233, 236, 265, 272–7.
[44] *EEA* i lvi.

c

a notification clause. The episcopal clerks of St Hugh and William preferred two forms of notification, the simple *Noverit universitas vestra*, marginally more popular than *Ad universitatis vestre noticiam volumus pervenire*.[45] Together, they account for 125 of the acta which have a notification. Other forms are found from time to time including *Noveritis* (nos. 9, 90, 184, 238, 255, 266, 287, 298) and *Notum sit universitati vestre* (nos. 39, 152, 158, 172). When addressing papal judges delegate, barons of the exchequer, and royal justices, the form *noverit discretio vestra* is used (nos. 42, 192). Sufficient evidence is just not available to show whether *scire* was normally restricted, as in an earlier period,[46] to charters concerned with enfeoffments, financial matters etc. Whether this reflects that it is declining in use in episcopal acta at the end of the century or merely that the appropriate documentary evidence has not chanced to survive is impossible to answer.[47] *Sciatis quod* occurs only once in Hugh's surviving acta (no. 189) but this is a virtual copy of a similar confirmation by bishop Alexander, issued 1139 × 1148, so that the repeating of the formula cannot be held to represent current practice in the late twelfth century. William's clerks use the form twice, once in a mandate concerning the restitution of revenues to the sacristy of Peterborough abbey (no. 283) and again in announcing the election of a prioress of Stainfield (no. 291).

INJUNCTIO

The injunctive clause is found on only six occasions during St Hugh's episcopate and not at all under bishop William. The six examples are based on the form employed in Angevin royal charters. Five adopt the *volumus et precipimus* form[48] and on the final occasion *volumus et firmiter statuimus* is used (no. 59).[49] Of the six, two are confirmations for Eynsham abbey (nos. 59–60), and the remaining four (confirmations and appropriations) all relate to Gilbertine houses (nos. 28, 41, 141, 178). The *injunctio* usually concludes with a clause saving the

---

[45] Under Hugh of Wells a considerable degree of uniformity was attained in the use of the notification clause. 308 acta contain the standard form *Noverit universitas vestra*. The form *Ad universitatis vestre noticiam volumus pervenire* occurs only five times.

[46] *EEA* i lvi.

[47] Cf. *EEA* ii lxv.

[48] A typical example can be found in the confirmation for Bullington priory: *Volumus etiam et precipimus ut hec omnia prenominata beneficia cum eorum pertinentiis libere et inconcusse sicut eis iuste et canonice collata sunt in perpetuum teneant et possideant* (no. 28).

[49] The one example which does not follow this royal model: *Libertates autem et liberas consuetudines predictis fratribus concessas . . . volumus, statuimus et precipimus inviolabiliter observari*, is to be found in the confirmation for Brackley hospital (no. 24).

episcopal customs and the dignity of the church of Lincoln.[50] This clause, occasionally coupled with other reservation clauses pertinent to the business in hand, is in fact found in most beneficial charters issued by the bishops, but more usually preceding, or else incorporated within,[51] the corroboration-clause. One example of an injunction, used in the episcopal appropriation of churches to Ormesby priory (no. 141) closes with the benediction: *Volumus etiam et precipimus ut hec omnia prenominata beneficia . . . habeant et teneant inperpetuum cum dei benedictione et nostra.*

SANCTIO

As might be expected, the use of a penal clause condemning those who disturbed a grant, possibly coupled with blessings on those who maintained it, is extremely rare by the close of the twelfth century. One of Hugh's acta, surviving as an original, contains a blessings clause without the sanctions. It is a grant *in proprios usus* of the churches of Orston and Edwinstowe to the common fund of Lincoln cathedral (no. 107). This deed of appropriation survives in two forms: once with a list of witnesses following directly on the dispositive clauses (no. 106); the other adding a corroboration clause but omitting the witnesses and concluding with the invocation of the name of Jesus and blessings for those safeguarding the grant. *In nomine igitur domini nostri Ihesu Christi eandem concessionem et assignationem servantibus et ratam habentibus sit pax a deo honor et gloria amodo et in seculorum secula. Amen.* This form of the appropriation was re-issued by William of Blois (no. 260), in virtually a word for word copy.

The only other examples extant for Hugh are confirmations of possessions for St James's abbey, Northampton (no. 133) and for Stixwould priory (no. 189). The former contains both sanctions and blessings: *Si qua igitur ecclesiastica secularisve persona predicte ecclesie bona temere invaserit vel minuerit vel quoquomodo iniuste perturbaverit secundo tertiove commonita, si non satisfecerit, divine subiaceat ultioni. Cunctis autem eidem loco sua iura servantibus sit pax domini nostri Iesu Christi, Amen.* The protocol of this actum and the sanctions and blessings are almost verbatim copies of the relevant sections of a general confirmation, issued between 1174 and 1181 by

---

[50] Usually *salvis episcopalibus consuetudinibus et Lincolniensis ecclesie dignitate* but occasionally variants are found, e.g. *salvis episcopalibus et sinodalibus tantum* (no. 141).

[51] E.g. *Ut ergo hec nostra confirmatio perpetuis perseveret temporibus, eam duximus presenti scripto et sigillo nostro communire, salvis episcopalibus consuetudinibus et Lincolniensis ecclesie dignitate* (no. 84).

Richard of Dover, archbishop of Canterbury. The latter was itself based on a confirmation of archbishop Theobald. Hugh also mentions Theobald's charter, as well as confirmations of two of his predecessors at Lincoln, Alexander (now lost) and Robert Chesney (possibly also lost). In the circumstances the form of this general confirmation suggests close modelling on earlier confirmations and is perhaps an indication of external composition at St James's abbey. The Stixwould confirmation is diplomatically archaic (the first person singular is used) and in fact it can be shown to be very heavily modelled on a similar confirmation by bishop Alexander, issued between 1139 and 1148,[52] including a verbatim copy of the sanctions clause. The only example for bishop William, a general confirmation of possessions for the abbey of St-Évroul (no. 286) is likewise heavily modelled on the confirmation of bishop Chesney of c.1158–9 (see appendix I, no. xvi).

CORROBORATIO

The formula of corroboration, validating the act or business described in the dispositive clauses, and announcing the seal as the form of authentication,[53] affords ample opportunity for great variety. No fewer than one hundred versions of the corroboration clause have been found in the collection of Hugh's acta and thirty-eight in the acta of William of Blois (often, it must be admitted, minor variants on an accepted form). Most of these variations hinge upon the choice of words used for the beginning of the subordinate clause (*Quod ut, ut autem, et ut, ut ergo, ut igitur* being the most frequent), the adjectives used for the strengthening of the act (*firmum, illibatum, inconcussum, inconvulsum, ratum, stabile*), the description of the document (*carta, scriptum, littere, pagina*) as well as the type of act (*assignatio, concessio, confirmatio, donatio, institutio, ordinatio, transactio*), or the verbs employed (*communire, confirmare, corroborare, munire, roborare*) and their tenses. The most popular *corroboratio* used is the simple *Quod ut ratum habeatur et firmum, presenti scripto et sigillo nostro duximus confirmandum* (or *roborandum*).[54] Settlements or compositions may have specific formulae emphasising the bishop's involvement in concluding the dispute e.g. *Et ut ratum sit et stabile imperpetuum quod in presentia*

---

[52] *EEA* i no. 57.

[53] Some confirmations do not mention the seal (nos. 16, 27, 71, 90, 106, 110, 116, 122, 157, 174, 199, 201, 206, 212, 238, 278) in addition to those documents containing injunctive or sanctions clauses.

[54] Nos. 4, 43, 45, 67, 75, 77, 159, 162, 163, 169, 196.

nostra terminatum sit, presentem paginam sigilli nostri appositione duximus muniendam (no. 25). A few corroboration clauses incorporate sentiments to be found frequently expressed in preambles (as reasons for the written record) or in prohibition clauses (as reasons for sanctions or anathema), e.g. *Ne igitur quod intuitu pietatis et favore religionis fecimus succedentibus temporibus possit alicuius malignitate perturbari vel in irritum revocari, hanc concessionem nostram presenti scripto et sigilli nostri appositione duximus roborare* (nos. 48–9) or *Quod ne alicuius astutia vel machinatione possit in irritum revocari, presenti illud scripto et sigilli nostri patrocinio confirmamus* (no. 115).

WITNESSES

Most beneficial acta are attested, the lists of witnesses being introduced by *hiis* (or *his*) *testibus. Teste* is found once (no. 12), as are *huius rei testes sunt* (no. 161) and *huius compositionis et confirmationis sunt testes* (no. 53). Seventy-three acta conclude their witness-lists with *et multis aliis* or *et aliis multis*; eighteen instances of *et aliis* are found, and two of *et pluribus aliis* (nos. 2, 49).

VALEDICTION

The valediction is found on twelve occasions in Hugh's acta (two originals) and on three in William's (one original). Four of Hugh's are jointly issued with fellow judges delegate (nos. 32, 36, 37, 191) and therefore might not properly reflect Lincoln practice. Moreover, since the valediction could so easily be omitted by a cartulary copyist, the extant examples are unlikely to give any real indication of frequency of usage. The simple form *valete* is the most commonly used, but three other versions occur: *bene valete* (nos. 76, 191); *valete in domino* (no. 192) and *valete semper* (no. 37). The majority of acta concluding with the valediction are mandates, legal business, and administrative missives and notifications.[55] However, some beneficial acta are found with it: an exemption from the payment of tolls (no. 113) and three general confirmations for religious houses (nos. 133, 144, 189). Two of these are in fact based on earlier confirmations issued by the bishop's predecessors (nos. 133, 189) and diplomatically follow the practice of an earlier period.[56] The third example, an original for Osney abbey (no.

---

[55] Nos. 32, 36, 37, 42, 191, 192, 217, 237, 283.
[56] See above, pp. xxxv–vi. The Stixwould confirmation (no. 189) ends with the *apprecatio* Amen. The only other acta in this collection with the *apprecatio* are the appropriation of Orston and Edwinstowe churches by Hugh (no. 107) and its re-issue by William (no. 260).

c*

144), is the only actum in the collection to include both witnesses and valediction. Two letters of institution are also found unattested and with the valediction (nos. 76, 184).

THE DATE

It is only with Hugh of Wells (1209–35) that Lincoln episcopal acta are regularly dated.[57] Considering the bishop's former prominence in the chancery of king John, it is not altogether surprising that the dating clauses of his acta were modelled closely on the dating used in royal charters. With very few exceptions the clause was introduced by *dat(um)*,[58] followed by the datary's name, the place-date, the time-date (day and month) according to the Roman calendar and the bishop's pontifical year.[59] Such precise dating was highly exceptional under the first Hugh and is not found at all under William of Blois. Three examples survive for St Hugh, all being dated by the year of incarnation and not by pontifical year. None are originals. On the two occasions when an exact date is provided, and not just the year, the ecclesiastical calendar is used. As might be conjectured, the solemnity of the occasion or the legal rights involved perhaps account for this dating. One of these acta — the settlement of a dispute between the monks of Westminster and the nuns of Godstow (no. 211) — was issued jointly by the bishop and two abbots acting as papal judges delegate, so it cannot be certain whether the episcopal clerks were responsible for its drafting, although it must be pointed out for what it is worth that this document and another recording a clerk's renunciation of his rights in the parish church of Aubourn (no. 20) both begin the dating clause with *Facta est autem hec transactio (inter eos) anno ab incarnatione domini* . . . This similarity may possibly point to the episcopal *familia* for their drafting. In the Aubourn document the practice of referring to a historical event or particular circumstance as part of the date provides useful information for architectural historians of Lincoln cathedral . . . *anno ab incarnatione domini millesimo centesimo nonagesimo tertio die martis*

---

[57] Of the 400 acta of Hugh of Wells I have located, 306 contain a dating clause, a further 39 still retain evidence of having once been dated and the rest are either much-abbreviated cartulary copies or else certain categories of mandates and administrative correspondence which were never dated.

[58] *Actum* is found on seven occasions announcing the date. The range of business (letter of institution, grants of land and tithes, a confirmation, an augmentation etc.) is sufficient to dispel the notion that *actum* was only used for settlements and judgements.

[59] E.g. *Dat' per manum Willelmi de Thornaco archidiaconi de Stowa apud Bannebyr' nono kalendas Septembris pontificatus nostri anno octavo* (PRO E326/3570). On a few occasions the place-date precedes the datary's name. I have only found four instances when the ecclesiastical calendar was preferred to the Roman.

proxima ante annuntiationem dominicam proximam post fundationem novi presbiterii ecclesie nostre. The third dated actum, not obviously connected with the settlement of a dispute or the formal renunciation of claims, is the confirmation for Ramsey abbey of several pensions from churches within the diocese and is dated by place and year of incarnation (no. 157).

THE INSPEXIMUS

In several English dioceses in the last quarter of the twelfth century, as also in the royal chancery, the form of confirmation known as the inspeximus was being evolved. In the time of archbishop Baldwin of Canterbury (1185–90) the inspeximus form accounts for nearly half of the total extant confirmations issued by this archbishop and Professor Cheney has pointed out the development of the inspeximus-confirmation in other dioceses at this period.[60] Perhaps surprisingly, Lincoln is not to be numbered among these, as far as the surviving documents indicate. Only one inspeximus charter (reciting in full the document to be confirmed or approved) exists for St Hugh's episcopate — an inspection of a composition between the priories of St-Fromond and St Michael's, Stamford — and it is not until the first decade of the thirteenth century, that the inspeximus-form is found in any numbers at Lincoln — five such confirmations by William of Blois survive.

St Hugh's clerks, when confirming earlier grants, agreements etc., much preferred to follow the practice of the bishop's predecessors and while alluding to having seen or inspected the document, do not in fact rehearse it *verbatim*. A formula such as *ex inspectione carte dilecti filii nostri Walteri de Evermue ipsiusque confessione cognovimus ipsum concessisse et confirmasse* . . . (no. 71) introduced the matter to be confirmed, or else the terms of the original grant or whatever are recorded and followed by a clause such as *sicut iamdicti Roberti carta quam inspeximus testatur* (no. 31). While continuing with this practice, bishop William's clerks also developed the proper inspeximus form. The statement that the bishop has inspected an earlier document which was to be recited can either follow the notification *Noverit universitas vestra nos inspexisse confirmationem predecessoris nostri Hugonis bone memorie Lincolniensis episcopi in hec verba* (no. 228) or else on occasion the notification can be dispensed with altogether. *Inspeximus cartam . . . sub hac forma* follows directly on the salutation in two instances (nos. 244, 279). The document in question is then

---

[60] *EEA* ii lxvi–viii and *EBC* 90–6.

rehearsed and the *dispositio* concludes with the words of confirmation by the bishop's authority, often the same formula as used in ordinary confirmations, e.g., *Nos itaque dictam abbatis concessionem et donationem ratam et gratam habentes, eam prout rite facta est episcopali auctoritate confirmamus et presenti scripto sigilli nostri appositione roborato communimus* (no. 282). When inspecting a charter of an episcopal predecessor, there was more scope for the insertion of additional phrases such as . . . *vestigiis eiusdem pie recordationis predecessoris nostri Hugonis inherentes* . . . (nos. 241, 244).

THE SEALS

Allusion has already been made to the passage in the *Magna Vita* where Adam of Eynsham records bishop Hugh's concern over the sealing of his acta. It is indeed unfortunate that so few impressions of his episcopal seal survive. Only five good specimens have been located,[61] perhaps the best being the Sempringham confirmation (no. 173),[62] and a further six examples in varying fragmentary states.[63] In design, Hugh's seal is very similar to that of his immediate predecessor, Walter of Coutances.[64] A pointed oval in shape, 75 mm. × 47 mm. with a full length depiction of the bishop, wearing a mitre (horn at the front), and vested in alb and chasuble with a maniple over his left arm. In his left hand the bishop holds his pastoral staff and his right hand is raised in benediction. The legend reads: + HVGO : DEI : GRACIA : LINCOLNIENSIS : EPISCOP'. There is no counterseal on the surviving impressions.

For bishop William's seal we have to rely on one good specimen attached to the composition over Walton chapel (no. 298) and two fragments.[65] Again, though smaller in size (68 mm. × 44 mm.) it resembles Hugh's seal. A pointed oval, with the bishop, full length, vested for mass, and holding a crosier in the left hand and lifting the right hand in benediction. The legend reads : [W]ILL'S DEI GRACIA LI[NC]OLNIENS EPISCOP[ ]. Bishop William used a

---

[61] Acta nos. 24, 115, 123, 144, 173. No. 172, which now lacks a seal, still retained a fragment of seal in 1899 when J. H. Round calendared the charter (*CDF* no. 855). No. 123 is described in *BM Seals* i no. 1705; no. 124 ibid. no. 1707; no. 160 in *Reg. Ant.* ii 337.

[62] Plate IV.

[63] Acta nos. 70, 73, 84, 114, 124, 160, 209.

[64] *EEA* i lxi and plate IIb.

[65] Acta nos. 244, 294. The seal is described in *BM Seals* i nos. 1708 (no. 298), 1710 (no. 294), 1711 (no. 244) and *Reg. Ant.* ii 337-8.

counterseal: a pointed oval (44 mm. × 29 mm.), depicting the Virgin
Mary enthroned, raising her right hand in benediction and holding the
infant Jesus on her knee with her left hand. The legend reads: + AVE
MARIA GRA PLENA DNS TECV. The only predecessor of bishop
William who is known to have used a counterseal on his acta is bishop
Robert Chesney but his was a gem depicting a gryllus.[66] William's
counterseal is the first-known one at Lincoln using a Christian subject
and indeed the Virgin and Child theme was used by all subsequent
bishops of Lincoln in the thirteenth century for their counterseals.[67]
Examples survive of seal impressions in green, red, brown and
brownish-white (varnished natural) wax and like the acta of their
predecessors, there appears to be no significance in the colour used,
certainly not as far as content is concerned. Similarly, with methods of
sealing, no hard and fast rules can be discerned. The bulk of the acta of
both bishops are sealed *sur double queue*. The two distinct methods
described by Professor Cheney are also found here.[68] One involved a
single horizontal cut through the two thicknesses of parchment in the
fold, and then a parchment tag was drawn through the slit to carry the
seal. The other method involved two parallel cuts being made in the
double thickness of the fold and third being made on the crease itself.
The tag was passed through the two thicknesses at the upper slit, its
tails turned inwards at the second slit and emerging together at the slit
on the crease to carry the seal. The first method is described in the text
as 'd.q.1', the second as 'd.q.2'. The choice of one or other of these
methods clearly did not depend on the type of document being drawn
up. It would seem largely to have depended on the personal preferences
of the clerks. Two examples of the use of cords have been found during
Hugh's episcopate (green and white, and green and red, nos. 144, 160)
and the seal for a confirmation for the abbey of Savigny is appended by a
leather thong (no. 172). Three acta of bishop Hugh — all judicial
mandates in connection with the Lambeth dispute — are sealed *sur
simple queue*, but since they were issued in the names of Hugh and his
two colleagues as papal judges delegate, they cannot be used as an
indication of administrative practice at Lincoln. A single example of
sealing *sur simple queue* survives on an actum of bishop William — a
notification of the renunciation of the claims of a presentee to a church

---

[66] *EEA* i lx.
[67] See *Reg. Ant.* ii 338–40 (Wells to Gravesend); W. Greenwell and C. H. Hunter Blair,
Catalogue of Seals in the Treasury of the Dean and Chapter of Durham (Newcastle 1911–21) i
482–3, nos. 3194–5 (Sutton).
[68] *EEA* ii xlvii.

and the presentation of another (no. 237). By the time of Hugh of Wells (1209–35) most documents sealed *sur simple queue* fall within the categories of mandates or missives and unwitnessed letters of institution (attested ones were sealed *sur double queue*). Certainly no beneficial acta are found with such sealing.

Just as in the case of the St James, Northampton confirmation of bishop Chesney (1148–66), printed in the first volume,[69] this collection also produces an interesting example of an attempt to remedy the later loss of a seal. The general confirmation of possessions for Greenfield priory (no. 70), in all other respects an authentic document of St Hugh, has had skilfully appended to it at a later date by a 'new' parchment tag (presumably once on the original mid-thirteenth century charter), the episcopal seal of bishop Richard Gravesend (1258–79).

EDITORIAL METHOD

The editorial method devised for the publication of this series of episcopal acta has been described in detail in the introduction to the first volume (pp. lxi–lxiv). It is only necessary here to rehearse the salient points.

Within the diocesan framework, the acta are arranged chronologically by episcopate; within each pontificate the arrangement is, primarily, alphabetical by beneficiary or recipient, or in the case of judicial documents by person or institution concerned in the proceedings. An asterisk precedes the number given to the actum whenever the text of the document has not survived, a cross whenever a charter is deemed to be a forgery.

The texts of all original acta have been given in full, even if they have been printed elsewhere — similarly all unpublished copies and transcripts, where no original documents survive. Copies which have been printed in satisfactory and easily accessible editions have been calendared, the witness-lists being retained in their original form. A brief English caption and the date precede the actum. Where a copy has already been published, a full calendar of the essential contents is provided, although not every detail contained in the text is recorded. Sigla are used to denote the manuscript sources, A being reserved for original documents and B, C, D, etc. being used for copies. Where A is lacking, B provides the basis for the printed text and in most instances is

---

[69] *Ibid.* i no. 198.

the earliest in date, the later copies following in roughly chronological order. References to post-medieval transcripts — for example, among the compilations of antiquaries — are not included if their presumed exemplars are extant. With originals, medieval endorsements are given together with medial measurements (in millimetres) and brief notes on the seals and sealing methods. Fuller descriptions of the episcopal seals of St Hugh and William of Blois appear in the introduction, pp. xl–xli. Modern endorsements are not noted. With cartulary copies, an indication of the date of the manuscript is provided and a note is made of any former foliation or pagination. The description of the manuscript sources is followed by any references to their previous publication. Textual and historical notes, where appropriate, follow the actum.

In matters of orthography, the spelling of the originals has been retained, except that 'i' has been treated as the equivalent of 'i' and 'j' and 'u' is used as a vowel, 'v' as a consonant. These rules also apply to copies and in the latter case classical practice is followed in using 't' where 'c' is found in some manuscripts, e.g. *donatio*. In originals, the Christian name of the bishop issuing the charter is extended, where appropriate, in parentheses, but all other abbreviated Christian names which can be clearly identified are extended in both originals and copies without parentheses. Names indicated by initials only are not extended. In originals and copies, abridged place-names are extended in adjectival form; if doubt exists, the suspended form is retained. Modern usage has been adopted in respect of capital letters. Editorial corrections are inserted in the text with the manuscript reading indicated in the notes. Conjectural readings or readings supplied from another manuscript are placed in square brackets. Missing sections are indicated by three dots and insertions and interlineations are noted in the printed text by the use of the marks ' '. The punctuation of originals has been retained but has been modernized in the case of copies. Ampersands and tironian symbols have not been reproduced.

Manuscripts are collated but only significant variant readings and necessary editorial corrections are normally recorded. Variations in the spelling of personal and place-names are shown, although where the original exists, the variant spellings of copies are seldom included. Rubrics and marginalia in cartularies and registers have not been noted unless they contain additional information on the contents of the charters or reveal archival arrangements.

The dating of the acta has presented the expected crop of problems. Sometimes the narrowest limits which can be assigned to a document are the dates of the bishop's pontificate. Two dates in square brackets linked by a cross reveal that the document was issued within the limits of those dates. A question mark by the date indicates a possible closer dating, evidence for which is given in the accompanying notes. Modern practice, in starting the year on 1 January, has been used throughout. Certain notable works of reference and chronology have considerably assisted the attempts at dating, not least the Le Neve revision for the Lincoln diocese.[70] This, and *Medieval Religious Houses: England and Wales*,[71] the *Handbook of British Chronology*,[72] and *The Heads of Religious Houses: England and Wales 940–1216*[73] have permitted some welcome economy in the length of the appended notes on dating. Whenever a date is stated to be determined by the dates of a king, bishop, nobleman, or royal official, the tenure of a particular abbot or prior, or of a dignitary or canon of the cathedral church, without further reference, it can be assumed that the information is to be located in one of those works.

[70] D. E. Greenway ed., *John Le Neve: Fasti Ecclesiae Anglicanae 1066–1300, iii Lincoln* (1977).
[71] Eds. D. Knowles and R. N. Hadcock (2nd edn. 1971).
[72] Eds. F. M. Powicke and E. B. Fryde (2nd edn., Royal Historical Society 1961).
[73] Eds. D. Knowles, C. N. L. Brooke, and V. C. M. London (Cambridge 1972).

No. 114 (Scribe I), much reduced   *Dean and Chapter of Westminster*

PLATE I

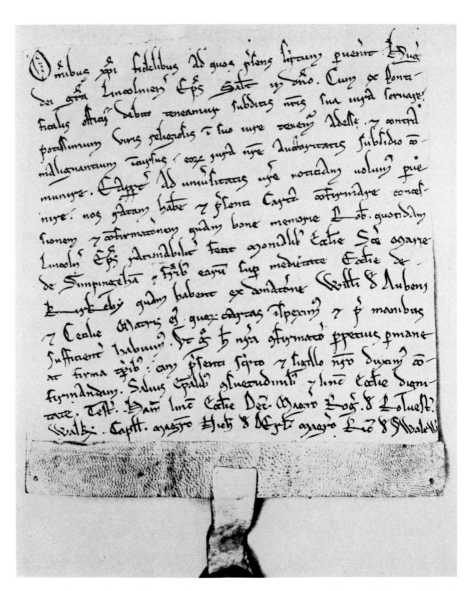

No. 173 (Scribe II), much reduced

Dean and Chapter of Lincoln

PLATE II

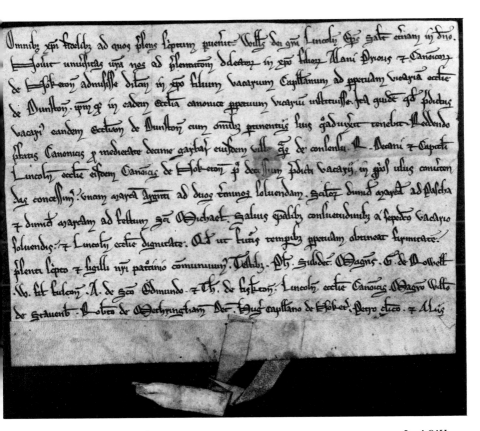

No. 268 (Scribe III), reduced

Lord O'Hagan

PLATE III

Seal of Bishop Hugh (actum no. 173), much enlarged

Dean and Chapter of Lincoln

PLATE IV

HUGH OF AVALON

1. Profession of obedience

Profession of canonical obedience and subjection made to Baldwin, archbishop of Canterbury, and the church of Canterbury.

[21 September 1186]

A = Canterbury D. & C. C.A. C115/53 (facsimile in *TPES* vii (1911–15), opp. 161 and D. H. Farmer, *Saint Hugh of Lincoln* (1985) plate 5). Not endorsed or sealed; approx. 151 × 101 mm.

B = Canterbury D. & C. register A (The Prior's register) fo. 224v. s.xiv med.

Pd (calendar) from A in *Canterbury Professions* no. 124; (in full) in H. Thurston, *The Life of St Hugh of Lincoln* (1898) app. B, p. 604.

Ego Hugo ecclesie Lincolniensis . electus . et a te reverende pater .B. sancte Cantuariensis . ecclesie archiepiscope et totius Anglie primas . consecrandus antistes ? tibi et sancte Cantuariensi . ecclesie . et successoribus tuis canonice substituendis debitam et canonicam obedientiam et subiectionem me per omnia exhibiturum profiteor et promitto . et propria manu subscribendo confirmo. +

The cross appears to be in a different hand from the text, and is presumably autograph. Hugh was consecrated in the chapel of St Katharine at Westminster (*Diceto* ii 42). The wording of William of Blois's profession is different (see no. 216).

2. Abingdon abbey

Confirmation for the monks of Abingdon of a pension of forty-eight shillings and fourpence from the church of Tadmarton for the use of sick brethren of the house.

[c.1192 × ? March 1195]

B = Bodl. ms. Lyell 15 (Abingdon cartulary) fo. 52r–v, particula III (de decretis, confirmationibus, ordinationibus vicariarum et aliis factis episcopalibus et capitul(aribus)), no. iii. s. xiv med. C = Chatsworth House Lib., Abingdon register fo. 32r–v (40r–v). s. xiv med.

Omnibus Christi fidelibus ad quos presens scriptum pervenerit, Hugo dei gratia Lincolniensis episcopus salutem in domino. Ne ea que viri religiosi beneficia iuste possident ecclesiastica per temporum vetustates oblivione sepeliri vel aliquorum malignantium pravitate valeant in irritum revocari, solers[a] antiquorum cavit prudentia huiuscemodi literarum perpetuare memoria. Eapropter ad universitatis vestre notitiam volumus pervenire, nos dilectis filiis nostris monachis de

Abbend'[b] auctoritate episcopali confirmasse pensionem[c] quadraginta et viii[d] solidorum et iiii[e] denariorum quam de ecclesia de Thademerton'[f] percipere consueverunt et adhuc percipiunt ad usus [fo. 52v] infirmorum fratrum eiusdem domus sicut eandem pensionem canonice possident perpetuo possidendam; salvis episcopalibus consuetudinibus et Lincolniensis ecclesie dignitate. Quod ut ratum et inconcussum omni tempore permaneat,[g] presenti scripto sigilli nostri appositione corroborato[h] confirmamus. Hiis testibus: Hamone Lincolniensis ecclesie decano,[i] magistro Ricardo de Swaleclyve, magistro R. archidiacono de Leycestr', Roberto de Capella, Hugone de sancto Edwardo, Galfrido de Depyng', Rogero Bac' et pluribus aliis.

[a] sollers C.   [b] Abendon' C.   [c] pessionem C.   [d] octo C.   [e] quatuor C.
[f] Tademertone C.   [g] permanent B.   [h] coroborato C.   [i] B ends here with etc.

The dates are those of Roger of Rolleston as archdn of Leicester (see no. 11 below). This pension was included in the papal confirmation for Abingdon of 7 March 1201 (*Letters of Pope Innocent III* no. 296 and app.).

3. Abingdon abbey

Confirmation for the abbot and monks of Abingdon of pensions from churches and tithes in the archdeaconry of Oxford.

[1197 × 16 November 1200]

B = Bodl. ms. Lyell 15 (Abingdon cartulary) fo. 52v, particula III (de decretis, confirmationibus, ordinationibus vicariarum et aliis factis episcopalibus et capitul(aribus)), no. iiii. s. xiv med. C = Chatsworth House Lib., Abingdon register fo. 32v (40v). s. xiv med.

Omnibus Christi fidelibus ad quos presens scriptum pervenerit, Hugo dei gratia Lincolniensis episcopus eternam in domino salutem. Ad pastoris spectat solicitudinem[a] ea que viris religiosis divine caritatis intuitu noscuntur rationabiliter esse collata beneficia rata habere et firma. Hinc est quod considerata religiosorum virorum abbatis et monachorum[b] Abbend'[c] religiosa conversatione, attendentes etiam hospitalitatem et opera caritatis que ipsi noscuntur transeuntibus et egenis inpendere,[d] eisdem abbati et monachis pensiones ecclesiarum et decimas quas ipsi in archidiaconatu Oxon' ab antiquo pacifice possiderunt et adhuc possident dignum duximus confirmare, videlicet, de ecclesia sancti Martini in Oxon' pensionem xxx[e] solidorum; de ecclesia de Niweham[f] pensionem xxx[e] solidorum; et de ecclesia de Leukenore[g] pensionem x[h] solidorum; duas etiam partes omnium decimationum de dominico de Niweham;[i] et duas partes omnium rerum que decimari debent de dominio de Grave, de toto villenagio[j] de Codesdone,[k] scilicet, tam de cottariis[l] quam aliis tenentibus duas

partes garbarum de decima et in Wateleia[m] duas partes garbarum
unius hide[n] Ricardi Gernun; [o–]duas partes garbarum de una hyda
Mathie (sic); et[–o] duas partes garbarum de quadam brechia[p] quam
Petrus tenet; de dominio vero Galfridi de Abbefelde[q] omnes decimas;
et de terra quam Robertus et Adam de Rewin'[r] tenent de coquina
similiter omnes decimas. Hec omnia prefatis abbati et monachis sicut
ea favorabiliter[s] adepti sunt et iuste ac debite possident tenenda
inperpetuum[t] episcopali auctoritate confirmamus; salvis in omnibus
episcopalibus consuetudinibus et Lincolniensis ecclesie dignitate.
Quod ut ratum et stabile perseveret, id presenti scripto et sigilli[u]
munimine roboramus.[v] [o–]Hiis testibus: Ricardo Lincolniensis ecclesie
subdecano, Hugone capellano, magistro Galfrido de Depyng' et
Theobaldo de Bosell', Lincolniensis ecclesie canonicis, Hugone de
Ettoneston', Rogero de Rolehyrst' et Ricardo de Tynghirst', clericis,
et aliis multis.[–o]

[a] sollicitudinem C.   [b] conventus *written first B, then dotted for deletion.*   [c] Abendon' C.
[d] impendere C.   [e] triginta C.   [f] Newenham C.   [g] Leuekenor' C.   [h] decem C.
[i] Nywenham C.   [j] villinagio C.   [k] Codesdon' C.   [l] cotariis C.   [m] Wateleya C.
[n] hyde C.   [o–o] *omitted* B.   [p] brachia C.   [q] Abefeld' C.   [r] Rewyn' C.
[s] rationabiliter C.   [t] imperpetuum C.   [u] nostri *added* C.   [v] roboravimus C.

Richard of Kent became subdean of Lincoln in 1197. These pensions and tithes are
also noted in Innocent III's 1201 confirmation (see above, no. 2).

4. Alvingham priory

Confirmation for the nuns of Alvingham of the churches of St Mary,
[North] Cockerington, St Leonard, [South] Cockerington, St Ethel-
wold, Alvingham, St Margaret, Keddington, and St Helen, [Little]
Cawthorpe.   [*c.*1192 × ? March 1195]

  B = Lincoln D. & C. Dij/64/2/1 (in an inspeximus of Roger, the dean and the
  chapter of Lincoln, *c.*1195 × 1200). C = Bodl. ms. Laud misc. 642 (Alvingham
  cartulary) fo. 168r (witnesses omitted). s. xiii ex.

  Pd from B in *Reg. Ant.* ii no. 338(x).

Testibus: Hamone Lincolniensi decano, magistro Rogero archidiacono Leic', magistro Ricardo.

  The dates are those of Roger of Rolleston as archdn of Leicester (see no. 11 below).
  For the grant of these churches by Hamelin the dean, Hugh de Scoteny, William of
  Freiston and Amfred of Legbourne see *Gilbertine Charters* 103–5, nos. 2–5.

5. Alvingham priory

Confirmation for the nuns of Alvingham of two parts of the church of
Stainton[-le-Vale] in proprios usus, saving the right of Robert de
Hardres in his lifetime.   [21 September 1186 × February 1198]

B = Bodl. ms. Laud misc. 642 (Alvingham cartulary) fo. 4v. s.xiii ex. C = ibid.
fo. 144r (147r). D = ibid. fo. 144r (in an inspeximus of archbp Hubert Walter,
April 1195 × February 1198, pd in *EEA* iii no. 329).

Omnibus Christi fidelibus ad quos presens scriptum pervenerit, Hugo
dei gratia Lincolniensis episcopus salutem in domino. Noverit universitas vestra nos, ad presentationem dilecti filii nostri Lamberti de
Scotenay*ᵃ*, recepisse dilectas filias nostras moniales de Alvingham*ᵇ* ad
duas*ᶜ* partes ecclesie beati Andree de Staynton'*ᵈ* easdemque duas
partes cum omnibus pertinentiis ipsis monialibus in usus proprios
concessisse*ᵉ* perpetuo possidendas, salvo iure dilecti in Christo filii
nostri Roberti de Hard'*ᶠ* in vita sua; salvis etiam*ᵍ* in omnibus
episcopalibus consuetudinibus et Lincolniensis ecclesie dignitate.
Quod ut ratum et inconcussum permaneat, presenti scripto et sigilli
nostri patrocinio confirmavimus. Hiis testibus.

ᵃ Scoteni CD.   *ᵇ* Al. CD.   *ᶜ* suas B.   *ᵈ* Staintona C; Staintun D.   *ᵉ* CD *adds* salva
competenti vicaria; *this phrase has been erased in* B.   *ᶠ* Hardr' C; Harden D.   *ᵍ* *omitted* C.

This is one of the documents produced in a dispute over the church between
Alvingham and Thomas de Scoteny in 1208 (*CRR* v 145; *Abbreviatio placitorum*
99b). Lambert's charter is pd in *Gilbertine Charters* 107, no. 10. Robert de Hardres
was vice-archdn of Lincoln and later archdn of Huntingdon. He died in 1207;
details of the subsequent dispute in 1245 can be found in J. E. Sayers, *Papal Judges
Delegate in the Province of Canterbury 1198–1254* (Oxford 1971), app. B,
pp. 315–16.

6. Abbey of Aunay

*Institution of Geoffrey de sancto Edwardo to the perpetual vicarage of
Great Limber on the presentation of John, the abbot and the convent of
Aunay. Geoffrey shall receive one third of everything belonging to the
church, the monks the rest, and he is also to bear episcopal burdens.*

[21 September 1186 × 16 November 1200]

A = Caen, Archives dép. du Calvados, H.1251 (damaged). No medieval endorsements; approx. 140 × 113 + 20 mm. (most of the turn-up eaten away); seal
missing, parchment tag (d.q.1).

Omnibus Christi fid[elib]us ad quos presens scriptum pervenerit ⁊
Hug(o) dei gratia Lincolniensis episcopus salutem eternam in domino. Ad universitatis vestre noticiam volumus pervenire ⁊ nos ad
presentationem Iohannis abbatis de Alneto et conventus ⁊ dilectum
nostrum Gaufridum de sancto Edwardo ad perpetuam vicariam
ecclesie de Magna Limberga recepisse. et ipsum in eadem ecclesia
vicarium perpetuum instituisse . ita quod idem .G. imperpetuum
percipiet terciam partem . universorum quecumque ad prefatam
ecclesiam de Limberga pertinere dinoscuntur . et totum residuum

cedet in usus monachorum. Debebit autem prefatus .G. onera
episcopalia sustinere. Quod ut ratum habeatur et firmum ⸴ presenti
scripto et sigillo nostro duximus confirmandum . salvis quidem in
omnibus ⸴ episcopalibus consuetudinibus . et Lincolniensis ecclesie
dignitate. Testibus . Rogero . domini regis capellano . Drogone de
Frivill' . Gaufredo de Lichelad' . Petro domine regine capellano .
Hugone de sancto Edwardo . Willelmo de Bosco . Waltero . Pagano.

Geoffrey de sancto Edwardo occurs as a canon of Lincoln in the early years of bp
Hugh's episcopate but not later, and this actum may date from a similar time.
Abbot John I of Aunay occurs in 1190 and 1200–1 (*Gallia Christiana* xi 443; *CDF*
no. 842); his predecessor, Christian, is mentioned in 1176 (*Gallia Christiana* xi
443). The occurrence of an abbot Vivian in 1186 (*CDF* no. 534) is clearly an error
(cf. *HRH* 123 under Robert Trianel, St Andrew's, Northampton). Henry II
confirms to Aunay the church of Limber, given to them by Richard de Humet and
Agnes his wife (*CDF* no. 525) and a later charter of Bertram de Verdun gives
further details of the circumstances of the gift (ibid. no. 531). Richard de Humet,
the constable, became a monk at Aunay at the end of his life (*Delisle*, introd.
429–31; *Eyton* 233); for Bertram de Verdun see *Delisle*, introd. 359–60. The
presence of the king's and queen's chaplains suggest that Hugh was with the court
at the time this document was drawn up.

*7. Peter of Avalon

*Grant to the bishop's brother, Peter of Avalon, of two knights' fees in
Histon, formerly held by Geoffrey de Bosco.*

[21 September 1186 × 16 November 1200]

Mention of charter in confirmation of king John, 26 November 1200.

Pd, *Rot. Chart.* 80b.

Bp Hugh's brother, Peter, is mentioned twice in the *Magna Vita* ii (164, 171) when
the bp visited his native region towards the end of his life. The Cambridgeshire fees
of the bp are not mentioned in the Book of Fees. In 1284–6 Philip de Coleville held
two fees of the bp in Histon (*Feudal Aids* i 138, cf. 148, 167, 187), and the Coleville
family certainly were in possession before 1241 (J. W. Clark ed., *Liber memo-
randum de Bernewelle* (Cambridge 1907) 242).

8. Aynho hospital

*Confirmation for the hospital of St James, Aynho, of a hide of land in
Aynho given by Roger son of Richard, and Robert his son, and a
messuage in Aynho given by the aforesaid Robert.*

[c.1192 × ? March 1195]

A = Oxford, Magdalen College, Aynho Ch. 22 (damaged by rodents. Letters in
square brackets supplied from B). Endorsed: Facta est collatio per I. Cyrencestr'
(s. xiii); approx. 181 × 102 + 15 mm.; seal missing, slits for seal tag (d.q.2).
Scribe I.

B = Oxford, Magdalen College, Estate Records 137/1 (charter roll of Aynho hospital) m.3 face (witnesses omitted). s. xiii.

Omnibus Christi fidelibus ad quos presens scriptum pervenerit .⁒ Hugo dei gratia Lincolniensis episcopus salutem in vero salutari. Noverit universitas vestra nos ratam et gratam habere donationem f[acta]m a Rogero filio Ricardi et a Roberto filio eiusdem Rogeri . hospitali sancti Iacobi in Ainho super una hida terre in Ainho .⁒ v[idelicet] una dimidia hida que fuit Turberni et dimidia hida que fuit Sweini .⁒ in liberam . et puram . et perpetuam elemosinam . et quietam ab [omn]i seculari servitio quod ad dominium ipsius ville pertinet. Preterea gratam et ratam habemus donationem factam a prefato Roberto filio Rogeri eidem hospitali super quodam mesagio in supradicta villa de Ainho . videlicet quod fuit Willelmi filii Toke . in liberam . puram . et perp[etu]am elemosinam . ei concessam . ad hospitandum pauperes qui ibi hospicium pro amore dei petierint. Hec omnia predicta sicut supradicto hospitali [rationa]biliter collata sunt cum omnibus pertinentiis suis velud in cartis predictorum donatorum continetur .⁒ ei autoritate qua fungimur presenti scrip[to et] sigilli nostri patrocinio confirmamus. Hiis testibus . Haimone decano Lincolniensis ecclesie . Roberto Huntedon' . et magistro Rogero Leircestren' archidiaconis . magistro Ricardo de Swalewecliva . Ingelramo capellano . Roberto de Capella . Hugone de sancto Edwardo . Willelmo cl[erico d]ecani . Hugone de Rolveston' . Eustachio de Wilton' . et aliis multis .⁒

The dates are those of Roger of Rolleston as archdn of Leicester (see no. 11 below). Aynho hospital was founded during the reign of Henry II, probably by Roger son of Richard.

9. **Bardney abbey**

Confirmation for the abbot and convent of Bardney of an annual pension of twenty shillings from the church of St Peter, Kirkby [Laythorpe], to be paid by the nuns of Sempringham.

[21 September 1186 × 16 November 1200]

B = BL ms. Cotton Vesp. E xx (Bardney cartulary) fos. 230v–231r (225v–226r). s. xiii ex.

Omnibus Christi fidelibus etc. H. dei gratia Lincolniensis episcopus eternam in domino salutem. Noveritis nos concessisse et presenti scripto confirmasse dilectis in Christo filiis abbati et conventui de Bard' annuam pensionem viginti solidorum in ecclesia beati Petri de

Kirkebi a conventu monialium de Sempingh' solvendorum ad hos terminos, scilicet, x solidos ad festum sancti Oswaldi et x solidos ad Purificationem [fo. 231r] beate Marie. Et ut hec nostre confirmationis pagina inperpetuum firma permaneat, eam sigilli nostri appositione corroboravimus. Test(ibus) etc.

The grant of the nuns of Sempringham is on fo. 230v of B.

10. Bardney abbey

Institution of Geoffrey of Steeping, the bishop's clerk, to the perpetual vicarage of Edlington, on the presentation of the abbot and monks of Bardney. Geoffrey shall receive all offerings, except sheaves and all tithes of the abbot's demesne in the village, paying to the monks a pension of three silver marks a year.

[15 September 1189 × September 1193]

B = BL ms. Cotton Vesp. E xx (Bardney cartulary) fo. 32v (28v). s. xiii ex.

Omnibus Christi fidelibus ad quos presens scriptum pervenerit, Hugo dei gratia Lincolniensis episcopus salutem in domino. Ad universitatis vestre notitiam volumus pervenire nos ad presentationem abbatis et monachorum de Bard' recepisse dilectum filium et clericum nostrum Galfridum de Steping' ad perpetuam vicariam ecclesie de Edlington', ipsumque vicarium perpetuum instituisse, ita videlicet quod idem Galfridus omnes obventiones percipiet, preter garbas et preter omnes decimas de dominio abbatis in eadem villa, annuatim solvendo predictis monachis nomine pensionis tres marcas argenti ad duos terminos, videlicet, ad festum beati Martini xx solidos et totidem ad Pentecost'; salvis consuetudinibus episcopalibus et Lincolniensis ecclesie dignitate. Quod ut firmum perseveret, presentis scripti serie et sigilli nostri munimine confirmavimus. Hiis testibus: Haimone decano Lincolniensis ecclesie, Roberto archidiacono Huntund', magistro Rogero de Rolveston', magistro Ricardo de Swalewecliva, Roberto de Capella, Simone decano de Hehham, Hugone de sancto Edwardo, Eustacio de Wiltun' et aliis multis.

Hamo became dean of Lincoln some time after 15 September 1189; Roger of Rolleston is not named as archdn of Leicester in this document. He first occurs as archdn c.1192 × Sept. 1193 (no. 11 below). See also *Le Neve* app. 38. Geoffrey of Steeping is more usually known as Geoffrey of Deeping, later precentor of Lincoln (c.1205/6 × 1225) and perhaps also archdn of Bedford. The identification is confirmed by the agreement between Geoffrey the precentor of Lincoln and vicar of Edlington, and abbot Matthew and the convent of Bardney on the one part, and Robert of Barkwith, lord of Poolham on the other, over the chapel of Poolham (cartulary fo. 102r–v). Matthew was abbot c.1218 × 1223.

11. Bardney abbey

*Confirmation for the monks of Bardney of the church of Edlesborough,
having inspected the charters of Gilbert de Gant I, Hugh de Beauchamp I and Hugh de Beauchamp his nephew, and Robert [Chesney],
the bishop's predecessor [EEA i no. 75]. On the presentation of the
abbot and convent of Bardney, the bishop has admitted Simon de
Beauchamp, clerk, to the church. Simon shall hold the church during
his lifetime paying to the monastery an annual pension of two aurei.*

[1192 × September 1193, ?1192]

B = BL. ms. Cotton Vesp. E xx (Bardney cartulary) fo. 37r–v (33r–v). s. xiii ex.

Omnibus Christi fidelibus Hugo dei gratia Lincolniensis episcopus
salutem in domino. Noverit universitas vestra nos ex inspectione
cartarum Gileberti de Gant primi et Hugonis de Bello Campo primi et
Hugonis de Bello Campo nepotis sui ex carta etiam bone memorie
Roberti Lincolniensis episcopi predecessoris nostri indubitanter accepisse ecclesiam de Edelberg' cum pertinentiis suis deo et sancto^a
Oswaldo de Bard' et monachis ibidem deo servientibus in puram et
perpetuam elemosinam fuisse collatam. Idem etiam ex confessione
predicti Hugonis iunioris in presentia nostra facta plene cognovimus.
Nos igitur eandem donationem et concessionem a predecessore nostro
et predictis patronis factam ratam et firmam habentes, eam auctoritate
pontificali confirmavimus. Ad presentationem etiam abbatis et conventus de Bard' Simonem de Bello Campo clericum ad prefatam
ecclesiam de Edelberg' recepimus, ita videlicet quod idem Simon
eandem ecclesiam cum pertinentiis suis toto tempore suo possideat
annuatim predicto monasterio nomine pensionis solvendo duos
aureos. Et ut hec omnia firma et illibata permaneant, presentis scripti
serie et sigilli nostri appositione, ea duximus corroboranda: salvis
episcopalibus consuetudinibus et Lincolniensis ecclesie dignitate. Hiis
testibus: Hamone Lincolniensis ecclesie decano, Roberto archidiacono de Hunted', magistro [fo. 37v] Rogero de Rolvest,' magistro
Ricardo de Swaleclive, Galfrido de Lichelade, Sampsone de Newerc,
Roberto de Capella, Galfrido de Depighe, Eustacio de Wilton',
Willelmo de Linc' decano, Ricardo de Bard', Galfrido clerico abbatis.

^a *first letter altered from 'k' B.*

This confirmation most probably dates from the time, referred to in the document,
when the younger Hugh de Beauchamp was in the company of the bp. Hugh's
charter confirming this church and attested by bp Hugh is dated 1192 (cartulary
fos. 233v–234r). It is preceded in the cartulary (fo. 233v) by the charter of Hugh de
Beauchamp I. A charter of Gilbert de Gant granting this church to the abbey is on
fos. 72v–73r of the cartulary, cf. also *Mon. Angl.* i 628–9, no. ii. Roger of Rolleston,

who attests here without a title, became archdn of Leicester before September 1193 (see no. 188A); if, as seems likely, the bp's confirmation dates from 1192, then this actum and the Beauchamp document provide a closer date for his appointment to the archdeaconry than otherwise known. Within a short time Roger succeeded Hamo as dean of Lincoln; the latter last occurs ? March 1195.

12. Bardney abbey

Admission of Walter de Neville to a mediety of the church of Cranwell, on the presentation of the abbot and convent of Bardney, to whom he shall pay an annual pension of sixteen shillings. On the presentation of Walter with the consent of the abbot and convent, William of Stainby is admitted to the vicarage of the mediety. He shall hold the mediety, paying sixteen shillings a year to Walter. In this manner the dispute between the abbey and William of Stainby over this mediety is settled.

[15 September 1189 × ? March 1195]

B = BL ms. Cotton Vesp. E xx (Bardney cartulary) fo. 36r (32r). s. xiii ex.
C = ibid. fos. 231v–232r (226v–227r).

Universis sancte matris *a*-ecclesie filiis ad quos presentes littere pervenerint-*a* Hugo dei gratia Lincolniensis episcopus salutem et benedictionem. Noverit universitas vestra nos ad presentationem abbatis et conventus de Bard' Walterum de Novilla ad medietatem ecclesie de Cranewell' ad ipsos pertinentem, sub annua pensione xvi solidorum ecclesie de Bard' solvendorum, recepisse. Nos etiam ad presentationem memorati Walteri de consensu et voluntate eiusdem abbatis et conventus de Bard' Willelmum de Stighenbi*b* ad eiusdem*c* portionis vicariam admisisse, ita quidem quod Willelmus de Stighenbi*d* prefatam medietatem ecclesie de Cranewell'*e* cum pertinentiis suis possidebit, solvendo annuatim eidem Waltero xvi solidos, salvis episcopalibus consuetudinibus et Lincolniensis ecclesie dignitate. Et ita controversia inter abbatem et conventum de Bard' et Willelmum de Stigh' super prescripta medietate ecclesie de Cran'*f* mota coram nobis conquievit. Quod ut ratum permaneat et firmum, presentis scripti munimine confirmamus et sigilli nostri appositione corroboramus. Teste:decano et capitulo Lincolnie*g*.

a–a omitted C and etc added.   *b Stegendebi C.*   *c eius C.*   *d Stegh' C.*
e C reads medietatem de Cranewell' ecclesie.   *f Cranewell' C.*   *g C reads T(este): Hamone decano Lincolniensi et capitulo.*

Hamo became dean of Lincoln after 15 September 1189 and last occurs ? March 1195. The rubric of this charter reads: 'De medietate ecclesie de Cranewell'. Hanc tenent moniales de Sempringham. Unde plura scripta habentur et reddunt xvi solidos'. A William of Stainby was a canon of York at this period (*York Minster Fasti* ii 16) but whether he is to be identified with the vicar of Cranwell is uncertain.

13. Bardney abbey

Confirmation for the abbot and monks of Bardney of the church of [Great] Hale, given to them by Gilbert de Gant and confirmed by his successors. At the presentation of the abbot and monks, he has admitted Gilbert de Lacy, clerk, to the church. Gilbert shall hold the church for as long as he lives, paying an annual pension of one hundred shillings to the monks.   [*c*.1194 × ? March 1195]

B = BL ms. Cotton Vesp. E xx (Bardney cartulary) fo. 33r (29r). s. xiii ex.

Omnibus Christi fidelibus ad quos presens scriptum pervenerit, Hugo dei gratia Lincolniensis episcopus eternam in domino salutem. Noverit universitas vestra nos auctoritate episcopali confirmasse deo et sancto Oswaldo et abbati et monachis de Bard' ibidem deo servientibus ecclesiam de Hale cum omnibus ad eam pertinentibus quam ex donatione bone memorie Gileberti de Gant et confirmatione sucessorum suorum iuste adepti sunt. Ad eorum etiam presentationem recepimus dilectum filium nostrum Gilebertum de Laci clericum ad eandem ecclesiam, ita quidam quod eam cum omnibus pertinentiis suis de predictis monachis tota vita sua teneat, reddendo eis annuatim nomine pensionis centum solidos; salvis episcopalibus consuetudinibus a predicto Gileberto solvendis et Lincolniensis ecclesie dignitate. Quod ut ratum et firmum permaneat, sigilli nostri appositione roboravimus. Hiis testibus: Hamone decano Lincolniensi, Willelmo subdecano, Stephano archidiacono de Bukingham, Willelmo cancellario, magistro Galfrido de Depinge, Roberto de Ardr' archidiacono de Hunted', Laurentio archidiacono de Bedeford' Alexandro archidiacono de Westreing', Petro archidiacono, magistro Gerardo de Rowell', Radulfo avunculo eius, Willelmo filio Ulf, Ricardo de Bard' decano, magistro Willelmo de Marum, Radulfo persona de Fordingt', Galfrido clerico abbatis, Gileberto de Halton', Radulfo capellano de Hale, Roberto clerico de Partheney.

William the subdean, William the chancellor and archdn Stephen of Buckingham all first occur on 22 March 1194; Hamo last occurs as dean *c*.March 1195. The charter of Gilbert de Gant, addressed to bp Robert (II) of Lincoln, confirming the churches of Great Hale and Heckington to the abbey is on fo. 70v of the cartulary. On fo. 72 is a charter of William de Stuteville, as custodian of Gilbert son of Robert de Gant, the heir of earl Gilbert de Gant, presenting the monks of Bardney to the two churches (*EYC* ix no. 34); it is attested by master William the subdean of Lincoln and master Stephen, archdn of Buckingham, and may possibly date from about the time of the bp's confirmation.

14. Bardney abbey

Confirmation for the abbot and monks of Bardney of the church of Heckington, the gift of Gilbert de Gant, and admission, on their presentation, of master Roger of Rolleston, archdeacon of Leicester. He shall hold the church for life, paying to the monks an annual pension of one silver mark and reserving to them a pension of five marks payable after Roger's death. He shall also pay episcopal customs.

[*c*.1194 × ? March 1195]

B = BL ms. Cotton Vesp. E xx (Bardney cartulary) fo. 34r–v (30r–v). s. xiii ex.

Omnibus Christi fidelibus ad quos presens scriptum pervenerit, Hugo dei gratia Lincolniensis episcopus eternam in domino salutem. Noverit universitas vestra nos auctoritate episcopali confirmasse deo et beato Oswaldo et abbati et monachis apud Bard' deo servientibus ecclesiam de Hekington' cum omnibus ad eam pertinentibus quam ex donatione bone memorie Gileberti de Gant et confirmatione successorum suorum iuste adepti sunt. Ad eorum etiam presentationem recepimus dilectum filium nostrum magistrum Rogerum de Rolvestun' archidiaconum Leicest' ad eandem ecclesiam, ita quidem quod eam cum omnibus pertinentiis suis de predictis monachis tota vita sua teneat, reddendo eis annuatim nomine pensionis unam marcam argenti, salva eis pensione quinque marcarum post decessum eiusdem Rogeri solvendarum. Quod ut firmum et ratum permaneat, sigilli nostri appositione roboravimus; salvis episcopalibus consuetudinibus a predicto Rogero solvendis et Lincolniensis ecclesie dignitate. Hiis testibus: Haimone Lincolniensis ecclesie decano, magistro W. subdecano, W. cancellario [fo. 34v], magistro Ricardo de Swaleclive, magistro Alexandro de Alnest', Reimundo, Galfrido de Depinge, Lincolniensis ecclesie canonicis, Hugone de Rolvest', Radulfo de Rowell', Radulfo de Fordingt', Ricardo de Bard' decano, Galfrido clerico abbatis, magistro Willelmo de Mar', Roberto clerico de Partheney et multis aliis.

William of Blois and William de Montibus first occur as subdean and chancellor respectively on 22 March 1194. Hamo last occurs as dean ? March 1195 and was succeeded by Roger of Rolleston (see *Le Neve* app. 41). See no. 13 above for details of the grant of the church by Gilbert de Gant. For the Gant family see the unpublished thesis by Mrs Mary R. Abbott, 'The Gant family in England 1066–1191' (Cambridge Ph.D. 1973).

15. Bardney abbey

Similar document to the above, except that master Roger is to pay an annual pension to the abbey of five silver marks.

[*c.* 1194 × ? March 1195]

B = BL ms. Cotton Vesp. E xx (Bardney cartulary) fos. 34v–35r (30v–31r). s. xiii ex.

Omnibus Christi fidelibus ad quos presens scriptum pervenerit, Hugo dei gratia Lincolniensis episcopus eternam in domino salutem. Noverit universitas vestra nos auctoritate episcopali confirmasse deo et sancto Oswaldo et abbati et monachis apud Bard' deo servientibus ecclesiam de Hekington' cum omnibus ad eam pertinentibus quam ex donatione bone memorie Gileberti de Gant et confirmatione successorum suorum iuste adepti sunt. Ad eorum etiam presentationem recepimus dilectum filium nostrum magistrum Rogerum de Rolvestun' archidiaconum Leicest' ad eandem ecclesiam, ita quidem quod eam cum omnibus pertinentiis suis de predictis monachis tota vita sua teneat, reddendo eis annuatim nomine pensionis quinque*a* marcas argenti, salvis episcopalibus consuetudinibus a predicto Rogero solvendis et Lincolniensis ecclesie dignitate. Quod ut ratum et firmum permaneat, sigilli nostri appositione roboravimus. Hiis testibus: Hamone decano Lincolniensi, Willelmo subdecano, Willelmo cancellario, Stephano archidiacono de Bukingham, magistro Galfrido de Depinge, Roberto de Hardr' archidiacono de Hunted', Laurentio archidiacono de Bedeford', Alexandro archidiacono de Westreing, Petro archidiacono, magistro Gerardo de Rowell', Radulfo avunculo eius, Willelmo filio Ulf, Ricardo de Bard' decano, magistro Willelmo de Marum, Radulfo persona de Fordington' [fo. 35r], G. clerico abbatis, Gileberto de Halt', Radulfo capellano de Hale, Roberto clerico de Parten'.

a quique B.

For the date, see above. Stephen also became archdn of Buckingham *c.*1194. The witness list is very like that in actum no. 13.

16. Bardney abbey

General confirmation of possessions for the abbot and convent of St Oswald, Bardney. The possessions are enumerated in detail: Bardney and Osgodby with appurtenances; in (Great) Steeping four carucates of land and two bovates and the church of Firsby; in Skendleby the church of St Peter with its land and tithes and in the south of the village the chapel of St James with the orchard (virgultum) *next to it, two mills and the land and service of Tholi and Gunnes; in Partney the church of St Nicholas and the chapel of St Mary and the tithe of the village mill; in Bratoft all the demesne tithe of Simon son of William; in Croft twenty sesters of salt, the gift of Philip of Kyme; ten acres of meadow in Firsby, the gift of Geoffrey of Bratoft; twelve acres of meadow beyond 'Scalflet' (? Saltfleet), the gift of Herbert son of Alard; by the gift of Ralph son of Gilbert, made for the soul of his brother Hugh, the land which he held in Firsby and in Ingoldmells and 'Derfletescroft' and the church of (Great) Steeping; in Wainfleet one bovate with the salterns appurtaining; in Halton (Holgate) five and a half bovates of land, a mill and the ninth part of another mill, the gift of William de Roumare; in Hagworthingham six bovates of land and the church, the gift of Walter de Gant, and a knight's fee there, the gift of Gilbert de Gant; in Lusby two bovates of land, the church, a messuage* (mansio), *and a mill, and one bovate in Winceby and Tounecroft (meadow) beside the Lyme (stream); the mill of 'Bradewad', the gift of earl Rannulf of Chester and one silver mark from the rent of Bracebridge mill; the mill of 'Strattona' (? Great Sturton); Edlington with all appurtenances; by the gift of earl Gilbert [of Lincoln] a third part of Baumber and the village mill; the church of Sotby with its lands and tithes; the church of St Hilary at Spridlington, with its tithes; four carucates of land in Burton; in Scampton (the church) with its lands and tithes; in Edlington the church with all appurtenances; Butteyate with all appurtenances, the gift of Robert Marmiun; in Barton(-on-Humber) the church of St Peter with the chapel of All Saints and its lands and tithes, the tithe of the village mills and by the gift of the earl Gilbert [of Lincoln] a bovate of land for the soul of Seer de Arcels and in the south of the village all the demesne tithe; in Folkingham the church with its lands and tithes; the church of Irnham with its lands and tithes, the gift of Robert de Gant; in Aswardby two-thirds of the demesne; in Willoughby (by Skendleby) two-thirds of the demesne tithes; in (Market) Stainton all the demesne tithe; in Southrey all the land which was Ivo son of Schaidman's with his assart and the assarts of William son of Hacon and William Bigot, with the land of Gippolf in the same village; in Sutton(-le-Marsh) half a carucate of land with pastures and meadows adjoining and a meadow in Huttoft; in Strubby two and a half bovates; in Woodthorpe one bovate of land and Thuatt with the land appurtaining and the mill of Withern; Hartsholme with lands and rents; the church of Boultham with appurtenances; in Bracebridge one bovate of land, the gift of William son of Walter*

D

Winterhard; and the churches of Edlesborough, (Great) Hale, and
Heckington.   [c.1194×? March 1195]

B = BL ms. Cotton Vesp. E xx (Bardney cartulary) fos. 62r–63r (58r–59r). s. xiii
ex.

Pd from B in *Mon. Angl.* i 632, no. ix; *PL* cliii cols. 1118–20, no. iii.

Hiis testibus: Hamonc decano Lincolniensi, Willelmo subdecano,
magistro Stephano etc.

William the subdean first occurs on 22 March 1194 and Hamo last occurs as dean
c.March 1195.

The early possessions of Bardney abbey are described by Professor Hamilton
Thompson in *AASR* xxxii (1913) 35–96. The 1147 confirmation of pope Eugenius
III (*PUE* i no. 40) notes that the mill of 'Strattona' was on the river Bain, and it is
thus probably to be identified with the village of Great Sturton. In Hugh's
confirmation the entry relating to Scampton reads: 'in Schamtona cum terris et
decimis suis'; it seems most probable that the word 'ecclesiam' was omitted by the
copyist. Certainly other confirmations of the period corroborate this conclusion.

17. Bardney abbey

Confirmation of the settlement of a dispute in the bishop's presence
between the abbot and monks of Bardney and Gerard of Howell about
the church of Howell and a mediety of the church of Claypole. The right
of presentation of incumbents to these churches shall belong to Gerard,
and the abbot and convent shall receive an annual pension of twenty
shillings from these churches, ten shillings from each, and nothing
more. Gerard and his heirs cannot confer these churches on any other
religious house.   [c.March 1195 × 1197]

B = BL ms. Cotton Vesp. E xx (Bardney cartulary) fo. 35r–v (31r–v). s. xiii ex.

Omnibus ad quos presens scriptum pervenerit, H. dei gratia Lincolniensis episcopus eternam in domino salutem. Noverit universitas
vestra controversiam que vertebatur inter abbatem et monachos de
Bard' et Gerardum de Huwell' super ecclesia de Huwell' et medietate
ecclesie de Claipol' in presentia nostra sub hac forma transactionis
conquievisse, scilicet, quod electio et presentatio personarum que
instituende sunt in ecclesia de Huwell' et medietate ecclesie de Claipol'
ad predictum Gerardum inperpetuum pertinebunt. Abbas vero et
conventus de predicta ecclesia de Huwell' et medietate ecclesie [fo.
35v] de Claipol xx^ti solidos annuatim nomine pensionis inperpetuum
percipient et nichil amplius, scilicet, x solidos de ecclesia de Huwell' et
x solidos de medietate ecclesie de Claipol, ita videlicet quod si altera
vel utraque earum vacaverit, idem Gerardus vel heredes eius personam idoneam vel personas idoneas eligent et presente abbate de Bard'
diocesano episcopo vel eius officiali presentabunt, prestito tamen

sacramento corporali monasterio de Bard' tam coram domino episcopo vel eius officiali quam in capitulo de Bard' ab eodem clerico vel eisdem clericis instituendis super predictis pensionibus in festo sancti Oswaldi fideliter predictis monachis persolvendis. Nec licebit eidem Gerardo vel heredibus suis predictam ecclesiam de Huwell' vel medietatem ecclesie de Claipol alii loco religioso conferre quam monasterio de Bard' si forte illas alicui loco religioso conferre voluerit. Hanc igitur pacem et concordiam in presentia nostra factam ratam et firmam habentes, episcopali auctoritate confirmamus et sigilli nostri appositione roboramus. Testibus: magistro Rogero decano Lincolniensis ecclesie, magistro Willelmo subdecano, magistro Willelmo cancellario, Remundo archidiacono Leggecest', magistro Galfrido de Deping', Alexandro de Alnest', magistro Gerardo de Rowell', Willelmo de Linc' filio Fulconis.

> Roger of Rolleston became dean of Lincoln c.March 1195; William of Blois was succeeded as subdean by Richard of Kent in 1197. The actual settlement of this dispute between Gerard of Howell and abbot Robert and the convent of Bardney is on fo. 224r–v of the cartulary.

*18. Beauchief abbey

Appropriation to Beauchief abbey of the church of Wymeswold, given to them by Robert son of Randolph (or Rannulph).
[21 September 1186 × 16 November 1200]

Mention of confirmation in the Leicester archdeaconry 'matricula' of bp Hugh II.
Pd, *RHW* i 255.

> The 'matricula' records that Beauchief claimed to have held the church for thirty-five years and the abbey was asked to produce St Hugh's charter; for the date of the composition of the 'matricula', see D. M. Smith, 'The rolls of Hugh of Wells, bishop of Lincoln, 1209–35', *BIHR* xlv (1972) 155–95, at 176–84. The church of Wymeswold formed part of the original endowment given by Beauchief's founder, Robert son of Rannulph (H. M. Colvin, *The White Canons in England* (Oxford 1951) 105, app. 1, no. 7).

*19. Beaulieu priory

Appropriation to the prior and monks of Beaulieu of the church of Milton Ernest, saving the life interest of master John of Bedford, the parson.
[21 September 1186 × 16 November 1200]

Mention of charter produced in a dispute between Robert de Middelton and the priors of Beaulieu and Canons Ashby over the advowson of the church, 1214.
Pd, *CRR* vii 135–6; *Abbreviatio placitorum* 89a.

Cecily, mother of Robert de Albini, the founder of Beaulieu, gave the monks the church of Milton Ernest (*CCR* vii 135; *VCH Bedford* i 352, iii 148). Robert de Middelton (Milton) was clearly successful on this occasion and he is found presenting a clerk *c*.1214–15 (*RHW* i 4). Beaulieu must have regained possession at a later date for the church was appropriated to them in 1275 by bp Richard Gravesend and a vicarage ordained (*Rot. Grav.* 202–3, 210).

20. Belvoir priory

Notification that Alexander the clerk of Aubourn has renounced, in the bishop's presence, all the right he claimed in the church of Aubourn and has sworn never again to disturb the prior and convent of Belvoir on the matter.   22 March 1194

B = Belvoir Castle, ms. Add. 105 (Belvoir cartulary) fo. 26v. s. xv in.

Pd (calendar) from B in *HMC Rutland* iv 113–14.

Universis sancte matris ecclesie filiis H. dei gratia Lincolniensis ecclesie episcopus salutem in domino. Universitati vestre notum esse desideramus Alexandrum clericum de Aburn' in presentia nostra constitutum sponte et sine aliqua coactione renuntiasse toti iuri quod se dicebat habere in ecclesia de Aburn' et omnibus pertinentiis eius. Idem etiam Alexander coram nobis iuravit quod nunquam priorem de Beauver vel conventum eiusdem loci inquietabit super ecclesiastico beneficio vel pecunia vel alia re quacumque de qua ante tempus renuntiationis huius aliqua mota fuit controversia inter ipsum et prenominatum priorem et conventum. Facta est autem hec transactio anno ab incarnatione domini millesimo centesimo nonagesimo tertio, die martis proxima ante annuntiationem dominicam proximam post fundationem novi presbiterii ecclesie nostre. Hiis testibus: Haymone decano, magistro Willelmo cancellario, magistro Willelmo subdecano cum ceteris aliis.

The church was given to Belvoir by Ralph d'Aubigny (*HMC Rutland* iv 115). For an earlier confirmation by bp Walter see *EEA* i no. 299.

*21. Bermondsey priory

Institution of Hugh Peverel to the church of Hardwick, on the presentation of the prior and monks of Bermondsey and Henry de Novo Mercato, the patrons, paying an annual pension of half a mark and saving the pension of Richard the vicar.

[21 September 1186 × 16 November 1200]

Mention of charter produced in a dispute between James de Novo Mercato and the prior of Bermondsey over the advowson of the church, 1206.

Pd, *CRR* iv 72.

For details of the grant of Hardwick church to Bermondsey see *EEA* i no. 5.

*22. Bermondsey priory

Institution of Richard the priest to the perpetual vicarage of Hardwick, on the presentation of Hugh Peverel, the parson of the church, with the consent of the prior and convent of Bermondsey and Henry de Novo Mercato, the patrons. Richard is to hold the vicarage for life, possessing the tithes of corn, all small tithes and all the altar offerings, and paying to Hugh a pension of thirty shillings.

[21 September 1186 × 16 November 1200]

Mention of charter produced in a dispute between James de Novo Mercato and the prior of Bermondsey over the advowson of the church, 1206.

Pd, *CRR* iv 73.

*22A. Bermondsey priory

Institution of James de Novo Mercato to the church of Hardwick, on the presentation of William de Novo Mercato, his brother.

[21 September 1186 × 16 November 1200]

Mention of charter produced in a dispute between James de Novo Mercato and the prior of Bermondsey over the advowson of the church, 1206.

Pd, *CRR* iv 73.

23. Bicester priory

Confirmation for the house and canons of Bicester of the gifts of Gilbert Basset, the founder, and of Matilda de Chesney.

[21 September 1186 × 16 November 1200]

A = PRO E315/45/207 (guarded and mounted in a volume, and badly stained, two-thirds of the charter covered with gallic acid solution to 'bring up' the writing). No endorsement; approx. 154 × 85 mm. (originally 154 × 70 + 15 but turn-up now flattened), slit for seal tag; seal missing. Ultra-violet light has greatly assisted the reading of this actum but some parts are quite illegible. Conjectural readings are in square brackets. Scribe **II**.

Omnibus Christi fidelibus ad quos presens scriptum pervenerit ⸴ Hug(o) dei gratia Lincolniensis episcopus salutem in domino. Votis et desideriis dilecti filii nostri Gill(eberti) Basset grato concurrentes affectu ⸴ quod mens sua sincera et karitas ordinata divina preveniente gratia circa domum religionis de Bernecestr' fundandam in summo angulari lapide Christo Jesu preter quod nemo potest aliud funda-mentum ponere . tam devote inchoavit ⸴ ratum et gratum habemus in donis et sanctum ipsius propositum approbamus. Iustis ergo et tam piis votis [ipsius] G. annuentes, et fundationem idem religiose domus de Berencestr' modicum congratul[*section of 60 mm. illegible*] dilat[ari] que cupientes eidem domui [et] canonicis regularibus ibidem deo servientibus ipsam ecclesiam [de Berencestr'] ex dono

prefati Gill(eberti) cum om[nibus pertinentiis] suis sicut carta ipsius
G. testatur . episcopali auctoritate confirmamus . similiter unam
carrucatam terre in villa de Bernecestr' et pratum et pasturam [quod]
sufficit ad carrucatam sustentandam . similiter in villa de Wicumb' de
burgagio duos solidos . preterea ex dono Matillid(is) de Caisneto
quinque summas frumenti in manerio suo de Heiford'. Ut ergo hec
nostra confirmatio in posterum rata et illibata permaneat ⁊ eam
presenti pagina duximus exarare . et sigilli nostri patrocinio roborare.

> Bicester priory was founded by Gilbert Basset 1182×1185. Four charters of
> Gilbert to the priory are BL Add. Ch. 10593, 10595, 10616, 10617 (see also *Mon.
> Ang.* vi 432 and 434, no. i; W. Kennett, *Parochial Antiquities* (Oxford 1695) 135–7,
> 151, 162). Matilda de Chesney's charter to Bicester was inspected by Robert de
> Insula, lord of Heyford Warren in the early 14th century (*HMC Rutland* iv 57; see
> also Kennett, *Parochial Antiquities* 158). The grant was made with the consent of
> her son and heir, Warin FitzGerald. Matilda was dead by Michaelmas 1198
> (*Eynsham Cartulary* i 423) but it is unclear from the wording of this episcopal
> confirmation whether she was alive or dead when it was issued.

24. Brackley hospital

*General confirmation of possessions for the hospital of St John the
Evangelist, Brackley.*   [1189 × 22 March 1194]

> A1 = Oxford, Magdalen College, Brackley Ch. 126. Endorsed: Confirmacio
> Hugonis Lync' episcopi (s. xiv); Nota quod omnia sacramenta et sacramentalia
> possunt ministrari in 'capella' hospitalis sanctorum Iacobi et Iohannis
> omnibus hiis qui manent infra precinctum dicti hospitalis. Et quod eorum
> decime nullo modo pertinent ad vicarium de Bracley (s. xv); Nota in hac charta
> pro una virgata terre in Halsow cum quietancia pannagii ibidem (ss. xvi–xvii);
> approx. 326×180 + 17 mm.; good specimen of seal, green wax, on parchment
> tag (d.q.1), no counterseal.
> A2 = ibid. Brackley Ch. C.64 (slight rodent damage; abbreviated, by comparison
> with A1). Endorsed: Concessio de variis (s. xvi); approx. 280×191 + 20 mm.;
> seal missing, parchment tag for seal (d.q.2).
>
> B = ibid. Brackley Ch. A.1 (inspeximus of A2 by archbp Hubert Walter of
> Canterbury, 1193×1195 *or* 1198×1200). C = ibid. ms. Latin 273 (Brackley
> cartulary) fos. 6v–7v (copied from A1). s.xiii ex.
>
> Pd from B in *EEA* iii no. 345; from C in *Mon. Angl.* vii 751–2, no. vii; *PL* cliii
> cols. 1115–18, no. i.

Universis Christi fidelibus ad quos presens scriptum pervenerit ⁊ .H.
dei gratia Lincolniensis episcopus salutem in domino. Quoniam ea
que ad sustentationem pauperum Christi divino intuitu collata sunt
benefitia ne malignantium possint retractari perversitate ⁊ episcopalis
auctoritatis suffragio tenemur communire ⁊ ad universitatis vestre
noticiam volumus pervenire . nos rata habere et presenti scripto
confirmare deo et ecclesie sancti Iohannis ewangeliste hospitalis de
Braccheleia . et fratribus ibidem deo servientibus . benefitia omnia
que eis a Christi fidelibus fuerint divino instinctu collata . et eorum

usibus deputata. De quibus ut ad omnium noticiam possint pervenire
.ʹ propriis vocabulis precipua*ᵃ* censuimus annotare. Inspectis igitur
cartis quas habent predicti fratres ex dono bone memorie comitis de
Legrecestr' Roberti senioris . et filii eius comitis*ᵇ* de Legrecestr' .
Roberti scilicet iunioris .ʹ in primis ratam habemus et confirmamus
fundationem ecclesie sancti Iohannis apostoli et ewangeliste hospitalis
de Bracchel' . et eandem ecclesiam cum eodem hospitali sicut in cartis
predictorum*ᵃ* patronorum quas vidimus exprimitur .ʹ liberam et
quietam ab omni subiectione esse statuimus . Salomoni vero predicti
hospitalis magistro . et successoribus suis . et fratribus*ᶜ* in ipso
hospitali commorantibus *ᵈ*-ad sacerdotii gradum provectis-*ᵈ* .ʹ concedimus ut ad honorem dei . et pro salute fundatorum et omnium
fidelium divina in ipsa capella celebrent misteria . ita tamen quod
parochiali ecclesia aliquo casu vacante*ᵉ* .ʹ liceat predictis fratribus .
exclusis excommunicatis et interdictis .ʹ submissa voce divina offitia
celebrare . venerabili patre et domino bone memorie .A. iiiᵒ . summo
pontifice .ʹ super hiis auctoritatem prestante . sicut in privilegio
eiusdem patris eis collato .ʹ inspeximus. Sepulturam quoque pauperum et hospitum . qui in ipso hospitali decesserint .ʹ vel eorum qui
in extrema voluntate in territorio hospitalis sepeliendos se devoverint .ʹ
sine vicinarum ecclesiarum iniuria .ʹ liberam esse sanccimus. *ᵈ*-Liber-
tates etiam quas .R. bone memorie abbas sancte Marie de Prato de
Legrecestr' . et eiusdem loci conventus eis contulerunt . sicut in
eorum scripto vidimus digestas .ʹ felici perpetuitate gaudere . et nostra
solidari confirmatione censemus . videlicet ut Salomon predicti
hospitalis iconomus et successores sui habeant ecclesiam intra septa
curtis predicti hospitalis liberam et quietam ab omni subiectione in
qua perpetuo divinum celebretur offitium . et sepulturam pauperum .
et familie sue . et servientium suorum . et peregrinorum . et integram
facultatem regendi . et plenariam dispositionem omnium que ad
predictum hospitale pertinent. Confessiones etiam pauperum et
infirmorum intra septa sua decubantium ex abbatis et conventus
concessu fratribus eiusdem hospitalis qui ad sacerdotii gradum pro-
moti fuerint .ʹ attribuimus . ita ut eisdem infirmis viaticum exhibeant .
familie etiam sue et servientium suorum in Quadragesima confessiones recipiant . et eis die sancto Pasche cum omni solempnitate
eucharistiam prebeant. Preterea decimas omnium que intra curtem
hospitalis aluntur . et intra septa curtis de ortis suis annuatim
innovantur .ʹ ad sustentationem eiusdem hospitalis . et pauperum et
infirmorum consolationem integre habeant et inperpetuum possideant.-*ᵈ* Ex donatione vero comitis de Legrecestr' Roberti senioris .ʹ
confirmamus predictis fratribus unam acram terre in Bracchele . ad

domum et ad edifitia paranda ; in quibus pauperes pro amore dei recipiantur et hospitentur . in qua acra ; ecclesia sancti Iohannis edificata est. Ex donatione autem filii eius comitis de Legrescestr'*f* Roberti scilicet*g* iunioris ; duas acras et dimidiam de Creis iuxta curtem hospitalis . et totam terram de Creis subtus curtem illorum de Grava domini comitis . sicut septis suis includitur. Ex dono eiusdem comitis ; duas virgatas terre . unam scilicet que est de terra de Alsavia*h* cum quietantia pannagii que pertinet ad Halsow . et cum mesuagio quod ad predictam virgatam pertinet ; quod est in Bracchele ad caput fontis de Goldewelle*i* . et unam aliam virgatam que pertinet ad Bracchele*j* . cum mesuagio suo . quod est subtus iuxta rivulum eiusdem fontis . quam virgatam ; Swetman pater magistri Salomonis tenuit. Ex donatione*k* Gileberti de Monte ; xx. et .iii. acras terre in dominico suo mensuratas per perticam in Stochingha*l* . in parte versus Bracchele . et pratum scilicet Kingesham . prout carta ipsius Gileberti exinde facta manifestat. Ex dono*m* Helie*n* de Hinton' ; pratum quod dicitur Herlesham . et aliud pratum quod dicitur Ferham. Ex donatione Alizie*o* de Rumeli ; iiii*or* . acras terre in capite culture de Werveldich . in ea parte ; que extenditur versus Halsow. Ex dono Thome Sorel ; et Symonis filii eius ; iiii*or* . acras in Syresham*p* . Totam quoque terram quam habent in Estwic'*q* ; sicut carte donatorum*r* manifestant. Libertates autem*s* et liberas consuetudines predictis fratribus concessas sicut in cartis patronorum continentur expresse ; volumus . statuimus . et precipimus inviolabiliter observari. Ut ergo prescripte donationes et libertates memoratis fratribus sicut carte donatorum testantur preconcesse . prout rationabiliter eis sunt facte . perpetue stabilitatis optineant firmamentum ; nostre confirmationis eisdem duximus prestare subsidium . et ad noticiam posterorum ; super hiis presenti scripto et sigilli nostri appositione episcopalis auctoritatis adhibere testimonium.*t* Hiis . testibus . R. abbate de Nuttele . magistro Stephano Lincolniensis ecclesie cancellario . magistro Winemero . magistro Giraddo de Rouell' . magistro Ricardo de Sualeuecl' . et multis aliis

---

a *word omitted* A2.   *b* A2 *inserts* scilicet *here*.   *c* capellanis A2.   *d–d* *section omitted* A2.   *e* A2 *inserts* ex episcopi sententia *here*.   *f* Legrecest' A2.   *g* A2 *inserts* scilicet *after* comitis *above*.   *h* Alsow A2.   *i* Goldevell' A2.   *j* Bracchel' A2.
k A2 *inserts* vero *here*.   *l* Stochinga A2.   *m* A2 *inserts* quoque *here*.   *n* Helye A2.
o Alicie A2.   *p* Siresham A2.   *q* Estvic A2.   *r* dominorum A2.   *s* quoque A2.
t A2 *ends here*.

Stephen of Swafeld became chancellor in 1189/90; he had been succeeded in that dignity by 22 March 1194 at the latest. Master Winemer attests without a title even though he was subdean of Lincoln to *c*.1192 and thereafter archdn of Northampton. For the foundation and early history of the hospital see Baker, *History of Northants* i 579–82 and *VCH Northants* ii 151–3.

25. Bridlington priory

*Notification that there was a dispute between abbot Richard and the
canons of Grimsby and prior H(ugh) and the canons of Bridlington
over the sentence pronounced by the abbot of Rievaulx, the prior of
Nostell, and the precentor of York, papal judges delegate, against the
abbot about the tithes of fish of the fishermen of the parish of Filey,
which the abbot and canons were said to have received unjustly in the
port of Grimsby. The execution of this sentence was committed to the
bishop by the pope. At last, the parties being called into the bishop's
presence at Louth, the dispute was settled. The abbot and canons of
Grimsby publicly acknowledged that they had no right to take the
tithes and quitclaimed them to Bridlington. The prior was persuaded
by the judges to remit his claim to tithes already received by Grimsby
and the bishop decreed that the abbot and canons should not
henceforth try to exact the tithes.*   [15 September 1189 × ? 1192]

B = BL ms. Add. 40008 (Bridlington cartulary) fo. 62v (59v, xvii v). s. xiv in.

Pd (calendar) from B in *Bridlington Chartulary* 79.

Omnibus Christi fidelibus Hugo dei gratia Lincolniensis episcopus
salutem. Noverit universitas vestra quod cum contentio fuisset inter
Ricardum abbatem de Grimesby et canonicos eiusdem loci et H.
priorem et canonicos de Brid' super sententia data ab abbate de
Rievall' et priore de Nostela et precentore Eboracensi iudicibus ab
apostolica sede delegatis contra predictum abbatem super decimationibus piscium piscatorum parochie de Fiuele, quas ipse abbas et
canonici iniuste dicebantur accepisse a predictis piscatoribus in portu
de Grimesby et nobis eiusdem sentencie executio a summo pontifice
fuisset commissa. Tandem convocatis partibus in presentia nostra
apud Ludam ipsa controversia inter predictas domos talem finem
sortita est, scilicet, quod predictus abbas de Grimesby et canonici
eiusdem loci puplice recognoverunt coram nobis et multis viris
discretis nobis assidentibus se nichil omnino iuris habere in predictis
decimationibus capiendis et ideo quietas illas domui de Brid'
inperpetuum clamaverunt, renuntiando manifeste omni iuri quo
dicebant se iamdictas decimas percepisse, sed et de perceptis
misericordiam prioris de Brid' humiliter imploraverunt; cumque hoc
priori grave videretur instantia bonorum virorum inductus est quod
consilium nostrum et W. abbatis de Waltham super hoc sequeretur.
Nos vero communicato*a* consilio, attendentes paupertatem domus de
Grimesby, persuasimus iamdicto priori ut sepe nominatas decimas
perceptas canonicis de Grimesby remitteret et ipse eas libenter
remisit, et ego H. Lincolniensis episcopus auctoritate qua fungebar

decrevi ne abbas et canonici decetero decimas a memoratis piscatoribus parochie[b] de Fiuel' exigere attemptarent. Et ut ratum sit et stabile
inperpetuum quod in presentia nostra terminatum est, presentem
paginam sigilli nostri appositione duximus muniendam. Hiis testibus.

[a] communcato B.   [b] parachie B.

The acknowledgement of this settlement by abbot Richard and the convent of
Grimsby is ibid. 79, and is attested by Hamo, dean of Lincoln, master Roger of
Rolleston, and master William of Blois (the last two witnessing without titles).
Hamo became dean of Lincoln between 15 September 1189 and 24 March 1190;
Roger of Rolleston became archdn of Leicester c.1192×September 1193 (see
above, no. 11); and William of Blois was certainly subdean of Lincoln by 22 March
1194 and most probably succeeded in 1192 when his predecessor Winemer was
appointed archdn of Northampton. The earlier judgment of E(rnald), abbot of
Rievaulx, A(nsketil), prior of Nostell, and H(amo), precentor of York is ibid. 79.
    Note that the bp uses the first person singular for his decree, but the first person
plural for the corroboration.

26. Bridlington priory

*Confirmation for the prior and canons of Bridlington, at their instance
and at the instance of master R(obert) de Hardres, archdeacon of
Huntingdon, of the church of Goxhill, which the canons obtained by the
gift of Robert son of Ernis, the patron, and which was confirmed to
them by bishop R(obert Chesney) of Lincoln. After the death of Robert
de Hardres, the perpetual farmer of the church, the priory shall possess
the church* in proprios usus, *saving a portion of the proceeds to the
value of six marks a year for the priest serving there.*

[September 1189×6 June 1199]

B = BL ms. Add. 40008 (Bridlington cartulary) fo. 333r (330r, lxxxx r). s. xiv in.
C = Borthwick Institute, York, CP.E.4/2 (roll of transcripts of charters
    produced in a dispute over Goxhill church between the priory and bp John
    Dalderby of Lincoln, 1308).
Pd (calendar) from B in *Bridlington Chartulary* 442.

Universis Christi fidelibus ad quos presens scriptum pervenerit, H.
dei gratia[a] Lincolniensis episcopus salutem in domino. Noverit
universitas vestra nos divine pietatis intuitu et[b] ad instantiam
dilectorum nostrorum filiorum[c] . . prioris[d] et canonicorum de Brid'[e]
et magistri R. de Hardra[f] archidiaconi Huntendonie ecclesiam de
Gousl'[g] cum omnibus fructibus suis et omnibus ad eam pertinentibus,
quam ex donatione Roberti filii Ernisii eiusdem ecclesie veri patroni et
confirmatione bone memorie R. quondam Lincolniensis episcopi
[*EEA* i no. 88] idem canonici rationabiliter adepti sunt[h], eisdem
canonicis et eorum successoribus in eadem domo de Bridel'[e] imperpetuum domino ministrantibus concessisse et episcopali auctoritate

confirmasse, ita quidem quod post decessum dilecti filii nostri R. de Hardra[f] ipsius ecclesie firmarii perpetui liceat eis fructus eiusdem ecclesie in usus proprios libere convertere et perpetuo possidere, salva tamen aliqua portione[i] de proventibus ipsius ecclesie ad valentiam sex marcarum annuatim ei qui in eadem ecclesia debeat[j] ministrare; salva etiam Lincolniensis ecclesie dignitate. Ut autem hoc factum nostrum firmum[k] sit et inconcussum, presentis scripti testimonio et sigilli nostri appositione[l] id duximus roborandum. Hiis testibus: Roberto de Hardria archidiacono Hunted'[m] et magistro Laurentio archidiacono Bedeford', Ricardo de Hardrie[n], Hugone de Bony[o], Willelmo et Elya[p], canonicis Bridel'[q].

[a] i inserted here B, but dotted for deletion.   [b] omitted C.   [c] filiorum nostrorum C.
[d] prio [sic] B.   [e] Bridlington' C.   [f] Hardria C.   [g] Gousla C.   [h] sunt adepti C.
[i] portione aliqua C.   [j] debiat C.   [k] ratum C.   [l] apositione C.   [m] Huntend' C.
[n] Hardre C.   [o] Boby C.   [p] Helia C.   [q] Bridlingtonie C.

Robert de Hardres was not archdn of Huntingdon in September 1189; his earliest occurrences can be dated c.1189 × 1193 and 4 April 1192. Laurence had been succeeded as archdn of Bedford by 6 June 1199. Robert son of Ernis's grant is in *Bridlington Chartulary* 347, 440.

27. Bridlington priory

Confirmation for the brethren in the church of Bridlington of the churches of Edenham and Witham[-on-the-Hill], and a mediety of the church of South Ferriby, given to them by Walter de Gant.

[c.1194 × 6 June 1199]

B = BL ms. Add. 40008 (Bridlington cartulary) fo. 324v (320v, lxxxvi v). s. xiv in.
Pd (calendar) from B in *Bridlington Chartulary* 429.

Hugo dei gratia Lincolniensis episcopus universis sancte ecclesie filiis sibi successuris imperpetuum, salutem et dei benedictionem. Quoniam divine dispositionis vel iubente vel permittente consilio in ecclesiastici regiminis specula constituti pastoralis cure suscepimus officium, proculdubio exigitur a nobis ecclesiarum virorum religiosorum utilitatibus pro virium quantitate indesinenter providendo consulere. Eapropter fratrum in ecclesia que Bridelingt' sita est sub institutione beati Augustini regulariter conversantium et religione provocati et necessitate compulsi ecclesias de Edenham et de Witham cum capellis suis et dimidiam ecclesiam de Suthferiby, quas in parochia nostra habent ex donatione Walteri de Gaunt firmiter et integre concedimus presentisque cartule nostre pagina confirmamus, ab eisdem fratribus bene et in pace, libere et quiete imperpetuum possidendas, eo videlicet iure eoque tenore quo sua omnia apostolice auctoritatis privilegio communita sunt et corroborata. Hiis testibus:

Roberto de Hardrea archidiacono Huntingd', magistro Laurentio
archidiacono Bedeford', magistro Stephano de Swafeld' archidiacono
de Bukingham, magistro Willelmo cancellario, Hugone de Hoby.

> Stephen of Swafeld became archdn of Buckingham c.1194, being succeeded as
> chancellor by William de Montibus, also a witness; Laurence had been succeeded
> as archdn of Bedford by 6 June 1199 at least. For a similar confirmation of bp
> Robert Chesney see *EEA* i no. 87. These three churches formed part of Walter de
> Gant's original endowment of the priory (*Bridlington Chartulary* 12).

28. Bullington priory

Confirmation for the convent of St Mary, Bullington, of the churches of
St James, Bullington, St Peter, Burgh[-le-Marsh], St Mary, Burgh[-le-
Marsh], St Mary, Winthorpe, a mediety of the church of All Saints,
Friskney, the third part of the church of St Andrew, Fulletby, the
church of St Aubin, Spridlington, the church of All Saints, Ingham, and
a mediety of the church of St Michael, Hackthorn.

[September 1189 × 1192]

> B = Lincoln D. & C. Dij/64/2/1 (in an inspeximus of Roger, the dean and the
> chapter of Lincoln, c.1195 × 1200).
> Pd from B in *Reg. Ant.* ii no. 338 (vi).

Hiis testibus: magistro Hamone summo decano, Winemero subdecano, Roberto de Hard', Sampsone, canonic(o).

> For the date of this charter see *Le Neve* app. 36; cf. no. 178. These churches (along
> with others not named here) were confirmed by bp-elect Geoffrey, 1175 × 1181
> *EEA* i no. 286).

29. Bushmead priory

Confirmation for William the chaplain of Colmworth, and those with
him wearing the religious habit, of the grant made by Hugh de
Beauchamp [Bello Campo] of the land of Bushmead (the boundaries of
which are recited), of common pasture throughout the founder's
demesne, and of priority of grinding at the mill.

[1197 × 31 December 1198]

> B = Bedfordshire Record Office, DD.GY9/2 (Bushmead cartulary) fo. 3r–v. s. xiv
> med.
> Pd from B in *Bushmead Cartulary* no. 8.

Hiis testibus: Ricardo Lincolniensis ecclesie subdecano, magistris
Ricardo de Swalewecliva, Girardo de Rowell', Waltero de Ping',
Hugone capellano, Lincolniensis ecclesie canonicis, Eustachio de
Wilton', clerico, et aliis multis.

Hugh de Beauchamp's charter is ibid. no. 17. Richard of Kent became subdean of Lincoln in 1197 and this episcopal charter was issued before Innocent III's bull of 31 December 1198 (ibid. no. 1; *Letters of Pope Innocent III* no. 76). Bp Hugh's charter was inspected by archbp Hubert Walter (*EEA* iii no. 363) and by bps William (see below, no. 228) and Hugh II (*Bushmead Cartulary* no. 13).

*30. Caldwell priory

Grant of the church of Oakley with the chapel of Clapham in proprios usus *to the prior and convent of Caldwell, saving a suitable vicarage.*

[21 September 1186 × 16 November 1200]

Mention of charter in LAO, Ep. Reg. I (register of bp Sutton) fo. 309v, in the charter of bp Sutton authorising a later appropriation, 18 August 1296.

Sane exhibita nobis ex parte vestra quadam cartula beati Hugonis predecessoris nostri una cum quibusdam aliis documentis comperimus ipsam parochialem ecclesiam de Akele cum capella de Clopham et omnibus pertinentiis suis in usus vestros proprios, salva competenti vicaria in eadem, intuitu paupertatis vestre relevande vobis concessisse perpetuo possidendam, cuius concessionis seu appropriationis fructus et proventus dicte ecclesie percipiendo et pacifice possidendo per plures annos optinuistis effectum.

Bp Sutton's charter also mentions the division of the church by bp Hugh II.

31. Canons Ashby priory

Confirmation for the canons of [Canons] Ashby, having inspected the charter of the donor, of the church of Culworth, given to them by Robert son of William of Culworth.

[21 September 1186 × 16 November 1200]

B = BL ms. Egerton 3033 (Canons Ashby cartulary) fo. 62v (61v, p. 113). s. xiii ex.

Hugo dei gratia Lincolniensis episcopus omnibus Christi fidelibus ad quos presens scriptum pervenerit eternam in domino salutem. Noverit universitas vestra nos donationem quam fecit dilectus filius noster Robertus filius Willelmi de Colewrthe dilectis filiis nostris in Christo canonicis de Esseby et ecclesie eiusdem loci super ecclesia[a] de Colewrda, sicut iamdicti Roberti carta quam inspeximus testatur, ratam habere et presenti scripto atque sigilli nostri patrocinio confirmare; salvis consuetudinibus episcopalibus et Lincolniensis ecclesie dingnitate et hiis testibus.

[a] ecclesiam B.

The charter of Robert son of William of Culworth granting the church to Canons Ashby is on fo. 62r of B, and on the same folio prior Alexander (occurs c.1181 × 1205) confirms the church to Thomas son of William of Culworth.

32.   Canterbury, Christ Church

Mandate by bishop Hugh, bishop Eustace of Ely and abbot Samson of St Edmund's, papal judges delegate, to master Ralph of St Martin, ordering him to restore to the monks of Canterbury the church of Eastry with all the revenues received during his time, or to show cause before the judges, in person or by proxy, at Westminster in the chapel of St Katherine on the day after the Sunday on which Jubilate is sung [10 May].   [early 1199]

> B = Lambeth Palace ms. 415 (Christ Church letter collection) fo. 124r. s. xiii in. Pd from B in *Ep. Cant.* 472 no. dv.

> The mandate recites the bull of pope Innocent III of 20/21 November 1198 ordering the delegates to enforce the papal judgment restoring the disputed churches and revenues to the monks (ibid. 468–9 no. di; *Letters of Pope Innocent III* no. 59). For details of the dispute over the patronage of this church and the three others noted in subsequent mandates (nos. 33–35), see *Innocent III and England* 218; *Hubert Walter* 149, and also below, no. 36n. Master Ralph of St Martin was a clerk of archbishop Hubert Walter. The proposed hearing on 10 May 1199 did not happen, and the judges, acting as arbitrators, ruled on all the questions in dispute on 29 October 1200. They awarded to Ralph possession of the church for his lifetime and to the archbp the advowson of the church, with a pension to the almonry of Christ Church. They ruled in the same manner, with certain modifications, regarding Eynsford, Monkton, and Meopham (see below, nos. 33–35) (*EEA* iii no. 383, cf. nos. 381–2).

*33.   Canterbury, Christ Church

Similar mandate by the judges delegate to J(ohn of Canterbury), former archbishop of Lyon in respect of the church of Eynsford.

[early 1199]

> Mentioned only in a note following no. 32 in Lambeth Palace ms. 415, fo. 124r: 'In eadem forma scripserunt exsecutores ecclesiarum eleemosynarie I. quondam Lugdunensi archiepiscopo pro ecclesia de Aignesford et Symoni archidiacono de Welles pro ecclesia de Muneketune et Virgilio persone de Mapeham.' (*Ep. Cant.* 472).

*34.   Canterbury, Christ Church

Similar mandate by the judges delegate to S(imon de Camera) archdeacon of Wells in respect of the church of Monkton.   [early 1199]

> Mentioned only in a note following no. 32 as above.

*35.   Canterbury, Christ Church

Similar mandate by the judges delegate to Virgil in respect of the church of Meopham.   [early 1199]

> Mentioned only in a note following no. 32 as above.

36. Canterbury, Christ Church

Mandate of bishop Hugh, bishop Eustace of Ely and abbot Samson of St Edmund's to the prior and convent of Christ Church, Canterbury, reciting pope Innocent III's bull of 19 May 1199 about the dispute between the archbishop and monks of Canterbury over the chapel of Lambeth. The recipients of the papal mandate are to work for an amicable composition and failing this they are to proceed to a definitive sentence if the parties agree; if not, they are to report fully to the pope and fix a day for the parties to receive the pope's sentence. The delegates are also instructed to go together to inquire into the state of the church of Canterbury, both within and without, and report to the pope. In accordance with these instructions the delegates summon the convent to the chapel of St Katherine at Westminster on the day after Michaelmas [30 September] to make peace with the archbishop. In case of failure on this occasion the monks are to make answer to the archbishop on the Friday after Michaelmas [1 October].

[summer 1199]

A = Canterbury D. & C. C.A. L138. Endorsed: Littere arbitrum ad conventum citat' certis die et loco et ad tractand' de amicabili concordia . secundum mandatum apostolicum super capella de lamheya (s. xiii); L230; various modern endorsements; approx. 240 × 220 + 22 (step) mm.; seals missing, sealing s.q., tongue and tie torn away.

B = Lambeth Palace ms. 415 (Christ Church letter collection) fol. 130v (omitting text of papal mandate). s. xiii in.

Pd from B in *Ep. Cant.* 496 no. dxxxi (the papal mandate is pd ibid. 490–2 no. dxxv; *Letters of Pope Innocent III* no. 115A).

.H. dei gratia Lincolniensis . et .E. eadem gratia Eliensis . episcopi . et .S. abbas sancti Edmundi . dilectis sibi in Christo priori et conventui ecclesie Christi Cantuariensis . salutem. Mandatum domini . pape . suscepimus in hac forma. Innocencius episcopus servus servorum dei . venerabilibus fratribus . Lincolniensi et Eliensi episcopis . et dilecto filio abbati sancti Edmundi salutem et apostolicam benedictionem. Inter venerabilem fratrem nostrum archiepiscopum et predecessores eius ex una parte . ac dilectos filios priores et monachos Cantuarienses ex altera . super quibusdam capellis . quas ipsi archiepiscopi erigere laborarunt in preiudicium partis alterius sicut monachi proponebant . iam dudum grandis et gravis questio pullulavit . pro qua predecessores nostros et nos ipsos sepius oportuit apostolicas litteras destinare. Verum cum in ipso negocio auctoritate litterarum nostrarum usque adeo sit processum . ut capella de Lameh' dirruta sit penitus et consumpta ⫶ prefatus archiepiscopus predecessorum suorum volens laudabile propositum adimplere ⫶ capellam ad honorem gloriosorum

martirum Stephani et Thome in qua canonicos prebendarios insti-
tueret de novo fundare volebat . de nostra licencia speciali ./ quod sibi
per nuncios et procuratores suos de communi iure competere asserebat . contradictione partis alterius non obstante . cuius indempnitati
per sufficientem et idoneam cautionem poterat provideri . sed neque
per demolitionem capelle prefate de Lameh' suum dicebat desiderium
retardandum . cuius opus ea potissimum ratione fuerat condempna-
tum ./ quod post denunciationem novi operis . inhibitionem predecessorum nostrorum . et appellationem ad sedem apostolicam inter-
positam fuerat attemptatum. Ceterum pro monachis fuit propositum
ex adverso . quod cum mandatum nostrum ad ipsum archiepiscopum
et vos directum circa exeniorum . ecclesiarum . et aliorum restitution-
em adhuc non fuerit adimpletum . nec sopitum scandalum ex ea causa
subortum . nec constaret adhuc de preiudicio in posterum auferendo .
eadem contradictionis causa durante ./ non erat prefati archiepiscopi
petitio admittenda. Cum autem hec et similia fuissent utrinque in
nostro auditorio allegata ./ nos volentes utrique partium pastorali
sollicitudine providere ./ de communi fratrum nostrorum consilio
causam eandem sub ea forma vobis duximus committendam ./ ut ante
omnia inter ipsos amicabiliter componere laboretis. Quod si forte
desuper datum non fuerit ./ vos facta prius restitutione plenaria ./
monachis memoratis eorum que ob hanc causam fuera subtracta ./
inquiratis super hiis que premisimus remoto appellationis obstaculo
plenius veritatem . et si de partium voluntate processerit ./ ad
diffinitivam sentenciam procedatis . facientes quod decreveritis per
censuram ecclesiasticam a partibus irrevocabiliter observari. Alioquin
gesta omnia in scriptis fideliter redigentes ./ ad nos ea sub vestrarum
litterarum testimonio transmittatis . diem assignantes partibus competentem . quo recepture sentenciam nostro se conspectui representent .
ad quem siqua earum venire contempserit ./ nos nichilominus in causa
ipsa quantum de iure poterimus procedemus. Ad hec volumus et
mandamus . ut 'ad' locum ipsum pariter accedentes . super statu
Cantuariensis ecclesie tam interiori quam exteriori inquiratis appella-
tione remota plenius veritatem . et quicquid super hiis inveneritis
nobis fideliter intimetis . ut per relationem vestram certiores effecti ./
quod statuendum fuerit statuamus. Nullis litteris obstantibus preter
assensum partium a sede apostolica impetratis. Quod si omnes hiis
exequendis nequiveritis interesse ./ duo vestrum ea nichilominus
exequantur. Dat' Lateran' .xiiii. kalendas Iunii pontificatus nostri
anno secundo. Volentes igitur in execucione mandati apostolici
secundum eius tenorem procedere prout decet ./ vobis eiusdem
mandati auctoritate mandamus . quatinus in crastino festivitatis sancti

Michaelis in capella beate Katerine apud Westm' vestri nobis copiam exhibeatis . ut inter memoratum venerabilem patrem nostrum archiepiscopum vestrum et vos secundum apostolici mandati tenorem ⸴ de pace tractare valeamus. Quod si desuper datum non fuerit . ut vos ad pacis et concordie reducamus unitatem ⸴ die proximo sequenti . scilicet proxima sexta feria post idem festum sancti Michaelis coram nobis ibidem sufficienter instructi compareatis . prefato domino archiepiscopo nostro secundum tenorem mandati apostolici responsuri et iuri parituri. Valete

> For the detailed background to this quarrel between archbishop Hubert Walter and the monks of Canterbury over the former's attempt to establish a collegiate church at Lambeth (a project begun by his predecessor, archbp Baldwin), see *Ep. Cant.* xcii–cix; *Hubert Walter* 137–57; *Innocent III and England* 209–18. Ironically, the *Magna Vita* tells of bp Hugh's warning to archbp Baldwin when the Lambeth project was first mooted (i 122). In the course of acting as a delegate, Hugh became gravely ill and the dean of Lincoln, Roger of Rolleston, acted in his stead. An award of arbitration settling the dispute over the projected collegiate church, the patronage of the four churches (above, nos. 32–35) and other questions was sealed at Westminster on 6 November 1200 and received papal ratification on 31 May following (*Ep. Cant.* 512–14 no. dxlviii; *EEA* iii nos. 382–3; *Letters of Pope Innocent III* no. 322).
>
> In *HMCR* b (1876) 439 the description of this document is followed by a reference to C.A. L175 'another notice in all respects similar to the last'. The present C.A. L175 bears no relation to the document described in the report, and it must be an error for C.A. C175 (no. 37 below).

37. Canterbury, Christ Church

Notification by the judges delegate to the convent of Christ Church that they intend to visit Canterbury on the octave of St Martin [18 November] in order to try to make peace between the convent and the archbishop, who proposes to be present then. If agreement should be prevented, the delegates will inquire into the state of the church of Canterbury, both within and without, in accordance with the papal mandate (recited in no. 36 above). The date set for the convent to appear at Westminster in connection with this same business, namely the Saturday after the feast of St Katherine [27 November], is nevertheless to be observed. [c.October × early November 1199]

A = Canterbury D. & C. C.A. C175. Endorsed: de lamhethe; littere arbitrum ad conventum (s. xiii); A124; modern endorsement; approx. 160 × 33 + 31 (step) mm.; seal missing, sealing s.q., tongue and tie torn away.

B = Lambeth Palace ms. 415 (Christ Church letter collection) fo. 130v. s. xiii in.

Pd from B in *Ep. Cant.* 496–7 no. dxxxii.

. H . dei gratia Lincolniensis et E. eiusdem permissione Eliensis . episcopi . et . S . eadem gratia abbas sancti Edmundi . karissimis sibi

E

in Christo . priori et monachis beate Trinitatis Cant' salutem in vero
salutari. Super causa que vertitur inter venerabilem patrem nostrum .
H . Cantuariensem archiepiscopum ex una parte . et vos ex altera que
nobis est apostolica auctoritate commissa . cum eodem archiepiscopo
nos noveritis ad pacem inter vos reformandam diligentem habuisse
tractatum . ita quod communi deliberatione providimus quod in
octabis beati Martini ad monasterium vestrum accedemus . et ibidem
inter eumdem archiepiscopum qui presens esse tunc in eodem loco
proposuit . et vos . domino concedente firmam pacem si fieri poterit
faciemus. Et si concordia inter vos aliqua fuerit occasione impedita .
iuxta mandatum apostolicum de interiori . et exteriori statu monasterii
vestri diligenter inquiremus. Nihilominus autem volumus diem quem
inter vos super eodem negotio proxima die sabbati post festum
beate Katerine apud Wesmonasterium constituimus observari. Valete
semper.

38. Canterbüry, Christ Church

*Mandate by the judges delegate to the prior and convent of Christ
Church, Canterbury, noting that the monks had not appeared when
summoned on 27 November, either in person or by proxy (see above),
and fixing the day after the Conversion of St Paul [26 January] in the
chapel of St Katherine at Westminster as the peremptory day for the
hearing of the case between them and archbishop Hubert.*

[27 November 1199 × early January 1200]

A = Canterbury D. & C. C.A. L135. Endorsed: litere arbitrum ad conventum de
lamhethe (s. xiii); de lamhethe (s. xiii); L350; modern endorsements; approx.
192 × 100 + 33 (step) mm.; seals missing, sealing s.q., tongue and tie torn away.

B = Lambeth Palace ms. 415 (Christ Church letter collection) fo. 130v. s. xiii in.

PD from B in *Ep. Cant.* 497 no. dxxxiii.

H. Lincolniensis . et E. Elyensis dei gratia episcopi et S. abbas sancti
Eadmundi . dilectis sibi in Christo priori et conventui ecclesie Christi
Cantuariensis . salutem in domino. Quia die quem venerabili patri
nostro . H. Cantuariensi archiepiscopo et vobis . pro causa quam idem
archiepiscopus auctoritate litterarum domini pape adversus vos insti-
tuit constitueramus scilicet sabbato primo post festum sancte Katerine
nec per vos nec per sufficientem procuratorem coram nobis in loco
conparuistis constituto ꝰ vobis auctoritate qua fungimur alium diem
scilicet crastinum Conversionis sancti Pauli constituimus . mandantes
et iniungentes . quatinus eodem die in cappella beate Katerine apud
Westm' per vos vel per sufficientem procuratorem coram nobis

compareatis . dicto domino archiepiscopo secundum formam mandati apostolici alias vobis editi super iure reedificandi cappellam canonicorum prebendariorum responsuri et iuri parituri   Et quia iam tertio vocati estis pro eadem causa a nobis *: predictum diem vobis constituimus peremptorium . mandantes ut sufficienter instructi veniatis . alioquin nos secundum quod ratio exigerit nichilominus in causa procedemus.

39. Castle Acre priory

Confirmation for the church and monks of St Mary, Castle Acre, having inspected the charters of bishop Robert [Chesney] and Walter [of Coutances] [EEA i nos. 91–6, 300] and the advocati, *of the churches of Fleet and [Long] Sutton with the chapel of Lutton* in proprios usus.

[*c*.1192 × 22 March 1194]

B = BL ms. Harl. 2110 (Castle Acre cartulary) fo. 122v (116v). s. xiii med.

Omnibus Christi fidelibus ad quos presens scriptum pervenerit, Hugo dei gratia Lincolniensis episcopus salutem in Christo. Notum sit universitati vestre nos, inspectis cartis predecessorum nostrorum Roberti et Walteri quondam episcoporum Lincolniensium cartis etiam advocatorum ecclesiarum de Flet et de Sutton', quas nobis exhibuerunt dilecti nobis in Christo prior et monachi de Acra, concessisse et presenti carta confirmasse ecclesie sancte Marie de Acra et monachis ibidem deo famulantibus ecclesias de Flet et de Suttun' cum capella de Lutton' et aliis omnibus pertinentiis in proprios usus eorundem monachorum imperpetuum possidendas, sicut eis a donatoribus rationabiliter collate sunt et carte predecessorum nostrorum prefatorum testantur. Quod ut ratum et inconcussum permaneat, presenti scripto et sigilli nostri testimonio confirmamus; salvis in ipsis ecclesiis competentibus vicariis eis qui in propriis personis in ipsis ministrabunt; salvis etiam episcopalibus consuetudinibus et Lincolniensis ecclesie dignitate. Hiis testibus: Roberto Huntedon' et magistro Rogero Leicestr' archidiaconis, magistro*ᵃ* W. de Monte, magistro Ricardo de Swalewecliva, Galfrido de Lecchelad', Roberto de Capella, Hugone de sancto Edwardo, Eustachio de Wilton' et multis aliis.

ᵃ magister B.

Roger of Rolleston became archdn of Leicester *c*.1192 × September 1193 (see no. 11); William de Monte (or Montibus), who attests here without a title, first occurs as chancellor of Lincoln on 22 March 1194.

40. Catesby priory

Confirmation for the church and nuns of St Mary, Catesby, of the church of Catesby with its chapel of Hellidon, and the church of Ashby [Magna]. [15·September 1189 × 22 March 1194]

A1 = PRO, E326/11398. Endorsed: Confirmatio episcopi Hugonis Linc'. (s. xiv); approx. 168 × 116 + 14 mm.; seal missing, parchment tag for seal (d.q.2).

A2 = PRO, E326/1035 (a small section stained). Endorsed: Episcopus Lincoln' de confirmatione donationum patronorum (s. xiv); approx. 141 × 114 + 12 mm.; seal missing, parchment tag for seal (d.q.2).

Pd from A2 in J. H. Round ed., *Ancient Charters, royal and private prior to A.D. 1200, part 1* (Pipe Roll Society 10, 1888) no. 61, pp. 100–1.

Omnibus Christi fidelibus ad quos presens scriptum pervenerit . Hug(o) dei gratia Lincolniensis episcopus salutem in Christo. Ut ea que locis religiosis a fidelibus pia devotione collata sunt . firmiter et inconcusse ab eis valeant possideri ·/ moris est ea scriptis autenticis ·/ ipsis confirmare. Inde est quod nos indempnitati ecclesie sancte Marie de Chastebi et monialium ibidem deo ministrantium paterna volentes sollicitudine providere ·/ ecclesiam*a* de Cattesbi *b*-cum capella sua de Eliden'*-b* . et ecclesiam*b* de Aissebi Roberti filii Philippi . eis sicut rationabiliter collate sunt confirmamus presenti scripto . et sigilli nostri patrocinio communimus ·/ libere et quiete cum omnibus pertinentiis earum perpetuo possidendas . salvis episcopalibus consuetudinibus . et Lincolniensis ecclesie dignitate. Hiis testibus . Hamone decano Lincolniensis ecclesie . Paulo abbate Leic' . magistro Willelmo de Monte . magistro Rogero de Rolveston' . magistro Ricardo de Swalewecliv'*c* . Galfrido de Lecchelad' . magistro Girardo de Rowell'*d* . Hugone de sancto Edwardo . Eustachio de Wilton' . et aliis multis.

a ecclesias A2   *b* *omitted* A2   *c* Swalewecl' A2.   *d* Rowll' A2.

Hamo became dean of Lincoln between 15 September 1189 and 24 March 1190; Roger of Rolleston became archdn of Leicester *c*.1192 × September 1193 (see no. 11); William de Monte (or Montibus), attesting here without a title, first occurs as chancellor of Lincoln on 22 March 1194.

See *Ancient Charters* p. 101 for a note on Robert son of Philip.

*40A. Pope Celestine III

Letter to pope Celestine III informing him that earl William de Roumare (of Lincoln) has secretly confessed to the bishop that after he had married his first wife, Alice, she had alleged that they were related by ties of consanguinity and petitioned for a decree of nullity from Richard, late archbishop of Canterbury. The earl did not believe there

*was such a relationship but nevertheless did not oppose the petition
and it was granted. After the decree of separation both remarried. The
earl now has a scruple of conscience about the situation and the bishop
asks the pope's advice.*   [14 April × late September 1191]

> Mention of letter in reply of pope Celestine advising the bp to enjoin a suitable
> penance but stating that the earl ought not to leave his second wife, pd, *Lincoln
> Decretals* 56–7, no. xxiii. For the date see *Revue d'histoire ecclésiastique* 50
> (1955) 431–2, no. 44.

*40B.   Pope Celestine III

*Letter to pope Celestine III about the case of one John who had a
lawful wife, Alice, but had committed the crime of adultery with a
woman called Maxilla. While he abjured Maxilla in court, he afterwards set aside his oath and during the lifetime of Alice had dared to
contract a form of marriage with Maxilla and lived with her in
adultery. After Alice died, John still lived with Maxilla for ten years
and she bore him ten sons. John has publicly confessed his adultery
before the bishop. The bishop asks the pope's advice as to whether John
and Maxilla ought to be separated.*

[4 July × *ante* 25 December 1192]

> Mention of letter in the reply of pope Celestine dealing with this matrimonial case,
> pd, *Lincoln Decretals* 60–1, no. xxv. For the date see *Revue d'histoire ecclésias-
> tique* 50 (1955) 440 no. 72.

41.   Chicksands priory

*Appropriation to the house of Chicksands of the churches of Chicksands,
Stotfold, with the chapel of Astwick, Haynes, Cople, Keysoe and
Linslade.*   [*c*.1194 × ? March 1195]

> B = Lincoln D. & C. Dij/64/2/1 (in an *inspeximus* of Roger, the dean and the
> chapter of Lincoln, *c*.1195 × 1200).
> Pd from B in *Reg. Ant.* ii no. 338 (xii).

Hiis testibus: Hamone Lincolniensis ecclesie decano, magistro Rogero
de [. . . pre]centore, Willelmo cancellario, magistro Ricardo de Sualeclif, magistro Gerardo de Rouwell', Galfrido de Lechelade, Hugone
de sancto Edwardo, Eustachio de Wiltun'.

> William de Montibus became chancellor *c*.1194 and Hamo last occurs as dean
> *c*.March 1195 (see no. 11). William de Beauchamp confirmed all these churches to
> Chicksands, which had been granted to the priory by his father, Simon ('Early
> Charters of the Priory of Chicksands' in Beds. Hist. Rec. Soc. i (1913) 104–6,
> no. ii). They were likewise confirmed by king Henry II, 1163 × 1179 (ibid. 118–25,
> no. xvi).

42. Cirencester abbey

Notification to the abbot of Stoneleigh, the dean of Warwick and master Absolom that the bishop has learned in his synod at Northampton from his deans and the maior et sanior pars *of the synod that Philip son of Richard of Oxendon has renounced any right he said he had in the church of Oxendon.*   [1194]

> B = Bodl. (on loan), Stowell Park ms., register A (Cirencester cartulary) fo. 175r–v (no witnesses). s. xiii med.
>
> Pd from B in *Cirencester Cartulary* ii no. 703.

> The judges delegate, abbot William of Stoneleigh, J., dean of Warwick and master Absolom of Aldermaston, were acting on a mandate of pope Celestine III, dated 16 February 1194 (ibid. no. 700; also *PUE* iii no. 468, where Oxendon is wrongly identified).

43. Coventry priory

Institution of the bishop's clerk, Hugh of Rolleston, to the church of Checkendon, vacant by the resignation of master Roger of Rolleston and on the presentation of the prior and convent of Coventry; saving the perpetual vicarage of William de Pentir appointed in the time of master Roger.   [c.1187 × 24 March 1190]

> B = Buckinghamshire Record Office, Boarstall cartulary, Checkendon fo. 2r. s. xv med.
>
> Pd from B in *Boarstall Cartulary* no. 5.

Testibus: Iocelino tesaurario Lincolniensis ecclesie, Haimone archidiacono Legr', magistro Alexandro archidiacono Westriding', magistro Rogero de Rolveston', Walkelino capellano, Roberto de Mora, Gaufrido de Lichelad'.

> Hamo occurs as archdn of Leicester after *c.*1187 (*Le Neve* apps. 33, 35); he had become dean of Lincoln by 24 March 1190. For the institution of Roger of Rolleston and William de Pentir, see *EEA* i no. 301.

44. Crowland abbey

Grant to the abbot and monks of St Guthlac, Crowland, permitting them to convert the church of Whaplode in usus suos, *after the deaths of Geoffrey, Fulk and Hugh, who now possess the church, paying to the monks one hundred shillings a year. The monks shall present a perpetual vicar to the bishop. The vicar shall receive all the offerings of the church, except sheaves. He shall pay the monks two and a half marks a year and shall be responsible for all episcopal customs.*
[? 21 September 1186 × April 1192]

> B = Spalding Gentlemen's Society, Crowland cartulary, fo. 79v, no. xx. s. xiv med.

Omnibus Christi fidelibus ad quos presens scriptum pervenerit, Hugo dei gratia Lincolniensis episcopus salutem in domino. Ad universitatis vestre notitiam volumus pervenire nos divino intuitu et consideratione religionis monasterii sancti Guthlaci de Croiland' concessisse abbati et monachis ibidem deo servientibus ut ecclesiam de Quappelad' cum omnibus pertinentiis suis post decessum Gaufridi et Fulconis et Hugonis qui nunc ecclesiam illam, reddendo inde ipsis monachis annuatim centum solidos perpetualiter, possident, supradicti monachi cum abbate suo tanquam persone in usus suos convertant, eo tamen salvo quod vicarium perpetuum episcopo presentabunt, qui omnes obventiones ecclesie preter garbas percipiet; reddendo inde monachis annuatim duas marcas et dimidiam. Ipse autem vicarius perpetuus episcopo respondebit de omnibus episcopalibus consuetudinibus[a]. Quod ut ratum habeatur et firmum, presenti scripto et sigilli nostri patrocinio duximus confirmandum, salvis in omnibus episcopalibus consuetudinibus et Lincolniensis ecclesie dignitate. Testibus etc.

[a] *word omitted* B.

The church of Whaplode was given to Crowland, along with Gedney church, by Emecina successively the wife of Geoffrey d'Oyry and Walter de Cantelu (cartulary fos. 76r, 106r, pd by K. Major, *The D'Oyrys of South Lincolnshire, Norfolk, and Holderness 1130–1275* (priv. pd Lincoln 1984) app. i no. 14), and was confirmed by various members of the d'Oyry family (ibid. nos. 3, 6, 7). The churches were confirmed by bp Robert Chesney (*EEA* i no. 102) and by archbps Theobald and Richard of Canterbury (K. Major *op. cit.* nos. 5, 8, 9; *EEA* ii nos. 118–19) and by popes Lucius III and Urban III (*PUE* iii nos. 364, 386).

Hugh the chaplain and Fulk and Geoffrey had been admitted to the church by Robert de Hardres, canon of Lincoln and vice-archdn (cartulary fos. 76v–78r, no. ix–no 77 in foliation sequence) and a second charter of vice-archdn Robert (fo. 78r, no. x) institutes Geoffrey and Fulk (described as brothers, the sons of Waleran d'Oyry) to the perpetual vicarage of the church. Robert was vice-archdn from c.1183 until he became archdn of Huntingdon (by April 1192 at the latest) and these charters may have been issued *sede vacante* after Walter of Coutances's translation from Lincoln to Rouen (for vice-archdn Robert see *Reg. Ant.* vii 206 & n.). Alternatively, the second of Robert's charters could indicate that Hugh the chaplain had died or resigned (since he is not mentioned) and that it was issued at a later date (before 4 April 1192). If this is the case then bp Hugh's charter must date before 1192, since it mentions the three incumbents.

This actum was possibly the charter of bp Hugh exhibited in the case between Fulk son of Fulk d'Oyry and abbot Henry of Crowland over Whaplode church in the king's court in Trinity term 1230 (*CRR* xiv no. 169).

The grant was apparently not effective and the church was again appropriated to Crowland by bp Richard Gravesend on 11 December 1266 (cartulary fo. 80r, no. xxii): the abbey was inducted into corporal possession of the church following a mandate of the bp's vicegerent dated 1 July 1267 (ibid. fo. 80v, no. xxv). A vicarage was ordained by bp Gravesend in January 1269 (ibid. fos. 80v–81v, no. xxvi; *Rot. Grav.* 33–4). For the whole question of the churches of Whaplode and Gedney and the disputes between Crowland and the d'Oyry family see K. Major, *op. cit.* 9–15 and app. i, nos. 2–15).

45. Crowland abbey

Confirmation for the monks of Crowland of the church of Gedney, for the repair of the monastery. The monks as parsons shall receive two parts of all garb tithes. The third part of the garbs and all the altar offerings shall remain to the perpetual vicar of the church, who will be instituted by the bishop on the monks' presentation. The vicar shall be responsible for all episcopal customs. The monks shall also continue to receive the tithes of two parts of the whole demesne, which they used to receive before this confirmation.

[? 21 September 1187 × 20 September 1188]

B = Spalding Gentlemen's Society, Crowland cartulary fos. 106v–107r. s. xiv med.

Pd from B in K. Major, *The D'Oyrys of South Lincolnshire, Norfolk, and Holderness 1130–1275* (priv. pd Lincoln 1984) app. i no. 11.

Omnibus Christi fidelibus ad quos presens scriptum pervenerit, Hugo dei gratia Lincolniensis episcopus salutem in domino. Ne ea que viris religiosis beneficia conferuntur ecclesiastica per temporum vetustatem oblivione sepeliri vel aliquorum malignantium pravitate valeant in irritum revocari, solers antiquorum prudentia huiuscemodi viva et inextinguibili literarum perpetuare memoria. Quod ergo intuitu religiose domus de Croiland' ad eiusdem domus emendationem super ecclesia de Gedeneye fecimus, universitati vestre notum fieri volumus, videlicet, quod nos eandem ecclesiam deo et monachis ibidem deo servientibus cum omnibus pertinentiis suis inperpetuum confirmavimus, ita quidem quod monachi illi sicut persone percipient duas partes omnium garbarum. Tertia vero pars omnium garbarum et omnes obventiones altaris cum omnibus aliis ad ecclesiam pertinentibus remanebunt vicario perpetuo qui per nos ad eorum presentationem in eadem vicaria erit institutus, et ipse respondebit super omnibus consuetudinibus episcopalibus. Preterea prefati monachi sicut ante hanc nostram confirmationem [fo. 107r] percipere consueverunt percipient perpetuo omnem decimationem duarum partium de toto dominio; salvis episcopalibus consuetudinibus et Lincolniensis ecclesie dignitate. Quod ut ratum habeatur et firmum, presenti scripto et sigillo nostro duximus confirmandum. Testibus et cetera.

For the gift of the church see no. 44n. above.

This actum probably relates to the settlement between Crowland and Fulk de Oyri over the right of presentation (K. Major *op. cit.* no. 12) which can be dated to bp Hugh's second pontifical year (Fuit autem hec carta facta secundo anno postquam adeptus est episcopatum Lincolniensem Hugo quondam Cartusiensis).

46. Crowland abbey

Confirmation by archbishop Hubert Walter of Canterbury and bishop Hugh of a composition made between abbot Henry and the convent of Crowland and Fulk de Oyri concerning the church of Gedney, specifying the tithes due to the abbey and the portion due to the vicar whom, being chosen by Fulk and his heirs, the abbey shall present to the bishop and who shall do fealty to the church of Crowland.

Chapter-house, Lincoln [1194 × April 1195]

B = Spalding Gentlemen's Society, Crowland cartulary fo. 108r, no. vii (in a record by the abbots of Vaudey and Bourne and the prior of Vaudey, acting on a mandate of pope Honorius III, 24 April 1220, at the instance of Fulk de Oyri, to confirm the composition). s. xiv med.

Pd from B in *EEA* iii no. 424.

For the date see *EEA* iii. The composition between abbot Henry (elected after March 1190) and Fulk de Oyri is in the cartulary (fo. 107r–v, no. vi, pd in K. Major *op. cit.* app. i no. 13). For the 1194–5 dispute over the church see ibid. 10–11.

47. Crowland abbey

Similar confirmation of the composition by bishop Hugh alone.

[? c.1194 × April 1195]

B = Spalding Gentlemen's Society, Crowland cartulary, fo. 107v. s. xiv med.

Pd from B in K. Major, *The D'Oyrys of South Lincolnshire, Norfolk, and Holderness 1130–1275* (priv. pd Lincoln 1984) app. i no. 14.

Omnibus sancte matris ecclesie filiis ad quos presens scriptum pervenerit, Hugo dei gratia Lincolniensis episcopus salutem in domino. Noverit universitas vestra controversiam que mota fuit inter abbatem et conventum Croiland' et Fulconem de Oyri super ecclesia de Gedeneya tali fine conquievisse, videlicet, quod abbas et conventus Croiland' in manu sua quartam partem omnium decimarum in garbis illius ecclesie cum duabus partibus omnium decimarum de dominio Fulconis de Oyri, quas antiquitus receperunt, retinuerunt. Ad reliquam vero partem garbarum et vicariam illius ecclesie, quotiens portio illa vacaverit, clericum quem Fulco de Oyri vel heredes eius elegerint episcopo Lincolniensi presentabunt, qui presentatus et admissus fidelitatem facturus est ecclesie Croiland', nec aliquem alium clericum abbas et conventus Croiland' presentare poterunt, nisi quem Fulco de Oyri et heredes eius ad prefatam portionem elegerint. Promiserunt etiam eos contra Fulconem de Oyri vel heredes eius nullo instrumento inposterum usuros per quod hec amicabilis compositio possit infirmari. Et ut hec perpetua gaudeant firmitate, ea et rescripti pagina et sigilli eorum appositione confirmaverunt et hec se observaturum

utraque pars coram nobis firmiter promisit. Hanc autem conventionem coram nobis in capitulo Lincolniensi factam episcopali auctoritate
confirmamus. Et ut ipsa rata et firma permaneat, presenti pagina et
sigilli nostri appositione communimus; salvis episcopalibus consuetudinibus et Lincolniensis*a* ecclesie dignitate. Hiis testibus: W. Litigt'
decano, magistro W. archidiacono Norhampton', magistro R. archidiacono Leycestr', magistro S. archidiacono de Bukingham, magistro
R. archidiacono Huntyndon', magistro W. subdecano, magistro W.
cancellario et multis aliis.

a Lincolin' B.

The attestation of 'W. Litigt' decano' is very puzzling; the dean of Lincoln would
be Hamo (until *c*.March 1195 and thereafter Roger of Rolleston) and I can suggest
no explanation for this scribal confusion. Stephen became archdn of Buckingham
c.1194 and William of Blois became subdean and William de Montibus chancellor
about the same time; the *terminus ad quem* is 1197 when Richard of Kent
succeeded William of Blois as subdean. If master R., archdn of Leicester is Roger
of Rolleston (rather than Raymond) the charter was issued before *c*.March 1195
when Roger became dean. It is clearly in any case about the same date as the
preceding joint-confirmation.

48. Daventry priory

*Grant for the monks of Daventry of the church of Fawsley, which
master William held of them, permitting them to convert it* in usus
suos.   [21 September 1186 × September 1193]

A = Bodl. DD. Ch.Ch. D.82. Endorsed: Confirmacio Hugonis episcopi de
ecclesia de Falueusl' (s. xiii); appropriacio (s. xiii); 5; approx. 180 × 111 + 15
mm.; seal missing, parchment tag for seal (d.q.2).

B = BL ms. Cotton Claud. D xii (Daventry cartulary) fo. 165v (clxi v) (omits last
witness). s. xiv ex.

Universis sancte matris ecclesie filiis ad quos presens scriptum
pervenerit ∴ .H. dei gratia Lincolniensis episcopus . salutem. Pie
benivolentia karitatis quam ex officio pastorali caris et subditis nostris
impendere tenemur . illis est exhibenda propensius ∴ quos religione
preclaros onere paupertatis videmus pregravari. Eapropter attendentes nimiam paupertatem honestamque conversationem dilectorum
filiorum nostrorum monachorum de Davintr' concessimus eis ecclesiam de Falueslei cum omnibus pertinentiis suis quam magister
Willelmus de eis tenuerat . in usus suos in perpetuum vertendam . ita*a*
ut de ipsa bonis que eius deinceps libere ad utilitatem monasterii sui
disponant . salvis tamen episcopalibus consuetudinibus . et Lincolniensis ecclesie dignitate. Ne igitur quod intuitu pietatis et favore
religionis fecimus . succedentibus temporibis possit alicuius maligni-

tate perturbari . vel in irritum revocari .' hanc concessionem nostram presenti scripto . et sigilli nostri appositione duximus roborare. Testibus . magistro .R. de Rolvestun' . Willelmo decano de Bergebi . magistro Rogero de Sumerford' . magistro Sansone de Bergebi . et multis aliis.

ᵃ followed by the letter 't', dotted for expunction A.

Roger of Rolleston attests without any title; he became archdn of Leicester *c.*1192 × September 1193 (see no. 11). The endowments of the vicarage subsequently ordained in the church are given in *RHW* i 205. Fawsley church was given to Daventry by king Henry II (*temp.* Becket as chancellor (fo. 102v of B); this charter is dated to January 1155 by *Eyton* 4).

49. Daventry priory

Grant for the monks of Daventry of the church of Preston [Capes], permitting them to convert it in usus suos.

[21 September 1186 × September 1193]

B = BL ms. Cotton Claud. D xii (Daventry cartulary) fo. 166r (cxlii r). s. xiv ex.

Universis sancte matris ecclesie filiis ad quos presens scriptum pervenerit, Hugo dei gratia Lincolniensis episcopus salutem in domino. Pie benivolentia caritatis quam ex officio pastorali caris et subditis nostris impendere tenemur, illis exhibenda est propensius quos religione preclaros onere paupertatis videmus pregravari. Eapropter attendentes nimiam paupertatem honestamque conversationem dilectorum filiorum nostrorum monachorum de Daventre, concessimus eisᵃ ecclesiam de Preston' cum omnibus pertinentiis suis in usus suos inperpetuum convertendam, ita ut de ipsa bonisque eius deinceps libere ad utilitatem monasterii sui disponant, salvis tamen debitis consuetudinibus Lincolniensis ecclesie. Ne igitur quod intuitu divine pietatis et favore religionis fecimus succedentibus temporibus possit alicuius malignitate perturbari vel in irritum revocari, hanc concessionem nostram presenti scripto et sigilli nostri appositione duximus roborare. Testibus: magistro R. de Rolvestun', Walkelino priore de Landa, magistro Ricardo de Dodeford', Radulfo decano de Bellinga et pluribus aliis.

ᵃ omitted B.

Roger of Rolleston attests without any title; he became archdn of Leicester *c.*1192 × September 1193 (see no. 11). The endowments of the vicarage subsequently ordained in the church are given in *RHW* i 205. The church of Preston was given by Hugh of Leicester, sheriff of Northampton, the founder (fo. 109r of B). Preston was the site of the first foundation *c.*1090, which was moved to Daventry in 1107–8 (*MRH* 99).

50. Daventry priory

Confirmation for Daventry priory of the chapel of Cold Ashby, permitting them to convert it in proprios usus, *saving suitable maintenance for a vicar who shall serve the chapel in person.*

[1197 × 16 November 1200]

B = BL. ms. Cotton Claud. D xii (Daventry cartulary) fo. 165v (clxi v) s. xiv ex.

Omnibus Christi fidelibus ad quos presens carta pervenerit Hugo dei gratia Lincolniensis episcopus salutem in domino. Noverit universitas vestra nos intuitu dei et honeste paupertatis domus de Daventre concessisse et presenti carta confirmasse prefate domui de Daventre capellam de Coldesseby cum omnibus ad eam pertinentibus in proprios usus convertendam, salva conpetenti et honesta sustentatione vicarii qui in eadem capella in propria persona ministrabit, salvis etiam episcopalibus consuetudinibus et Lincolniensis ecclesie dignitate. Quod ut in posterum firmum et stabile perseveret, sigilli nostri appositione duximus illud communire. Hiis testibus: Rogero decano, et Ricardo subdecano Lincolniensis ecclesie, Roberto archidiacono Huntendon', magistro Ricardo de Swalecluva et multis aliis.

Richard of Kent became subdean in 1197. Hugh Poer gave Cold Ashby to Daventry *temp.* bp Robert Chesney (1148–66) (fos. 2r, 109v of B).

*51. Drax priory

Grant to the prior and convent of Drax of an annual pension of forty shillings from the church of Saltby.

[21 September 1186 × 16 November 1200]

Mention of grant in the Leicester archdeaconry institution roll of bp Hugh II.
Pd, *RHW* ii 307.

This grant is also mentioned in a charter of bp Oliver Sutton of Lincoln (1280–99) in the Drax cartulary (Bodl. ms. Top. Yorks. c 72 fo. 6v), and in the Leicester archdeaconry 'matricula' of bp Hugh II (*RHW* i 267).

52. Dunstable priory

Confirmation for the canons of Dunstable of the church of Studham, after having inspected charters of Alexander of Studham, formerly advocatus *of the church, and Nicholas, formerly archdeacon of Bedford.*   [c.1189 × September 1193]

B = BL ms. Harl. 1885 (Dunstable cartulary) fo. 19r–v (18r–v, pp. 49–50). s. xiii in.

Pd (calendar) from B in *Dunstable Cartulary* no. 100.

Omnibus Christi fidelibus ad quos presens scriptum pervenerit, Hugo
dei gratia Lincolniensis episcopus salutem in vero salutari. Noverit
universitas vestra nos, inspectis cartis Alexandri de Stodham quondam advocati ecclesie de Stodham et Nicholai quondam archidiaconi de
Bedeford' quas dilecti filii nostri canonici de Dunst' habent super
ecclesia de Stodham, ratam habemus presentationem que facta est a
prefato Alexandro atque institutionem a supradicto N. archidiacono
prefatis canonicis in eadem ecclesia factam, ipsamque institutionem
auctoritate qua fungimur confirmamus, scripti quoque presentis testimonio et sigilli nostri appositione et patrocinio roboramus; salvis
[fo. 19v] episcopalibus consuetudinibus et Lincolniensis ecclesie
dignitate. Hiis testibus: magistro Stephano Lincolniensis ecclesie
cancellario, Roberto abbate de Nutel', magistro Rogero de Rolveston',
magistro Ricardo de Swaleweclíva, Petro de Avalun', Roberto de
Capella, Hugone de sancto Edwardo, Eustat' de Wilton et aliis multis.

Stephen de Swafeld first occurs as chancellor 1189/90 and became archdn of
Buckingham c.1194; Roger of Rolleston became archdn of Leicester c.1192×
September 1193 (see no. 11). Alexander of Studham's charter is not copied into the
cartulary but there are confirmations of it by his son, Robert, Hugh and Alice le
Breitt(on), and king Henry II (ibid. nos. 96, 97, 101). The charter of archdn
Nicholas of Bedford (last occurs April 1174×summer 1178) is ibid. no. 99. There
is a pedigree of the Studham family ibid. P/9, between 356–7.

53. Dunstable priory

*Confirmation of the settlement of a dispute between the abbot and
monks of Woburn and the prior and canons of Dunstable over a
mediety of Chesham church.*   [15 September 1189×c.March 1195]

B = BL ms. Harl. 1885 (Dunstable cartulary) fo. 24v (23v, p. 60). s. xiii in.

Pd (calendar) from B in *Dunstable Cartulary* no. 168.

Hugo dei gratia Lincolniensis episcopus omnibus fidelibus ad quos
littere iste pervenerint salutem in vero salutari. Universitati vestre
volumus intimari causam que vertebatur inter abbatem et monachos
de Woburne et priorem et canonicos de Dunst' fine pacifico dei gratia
mediante in nostra presentia conquievisse sub hac forma: abbas
videlicet et monachi de Woburne dederunt in perpetuam elemosinam
et garantizabunt et inpersonari fecerunt priorem de Dunst' ad medietatem altaris de Cestresham et omnium beneficiorum que ad eandem
medietatem pertinent, preter omnes garbas decimarum que simul et
integre remanent monachis, exceptis decimis terre, que ad illam
medietatem pertinet, quam canonici tenebunt, et tota terra cum prato
remanet canonicis, preter terram que intra curtem est et grangias et

domos et totum masuagium, que omnia remanent monachis. Et quia
quidam pars curtis de terra ecclesie dicitur esse que firmam reddit,
monachi pro eadem parte xii denarios domino feudi annue solvent et
canonici reddent quod superest de firma. Omnes etiam episcopales
consuetudines per omnia facient canonici. Set si tailagium super
ecclesiam venerit et dimidiam marcam excesserit, monachi duas partes
tailagii totius solvent et canonici tertiam. Set si dimidia marca tantum
fuerit vel minus canonici totum solvent. Prior quoque et canonici
omnia instrumenta que habuerunt de eodem beneficio reddent
monachis, et monachi similiter omnia instrumenta que prius
habuerunt de canonicis eis restituent. Presbiter vero qui ex parte
prioris in memorata ecclesia ministrabit*a* eidem priori sacramentum
prestabit de fidelitate ei exhibenda et de indempnitate monachis
conservanda. Ut autem hec compositionis forma rata permaneat, eam
sigilli nostri appositione roboravimus. Adiectum est etiam huic
compositioni quod abbas et monachi de Woburne pro posse suo
procurabunt apud dominum feudi ut priori et canonicis ab ipso
predicta portio confirmetur. Huius compositionis et confirmationis
sunt testes: H. Lincolniensis decanus, R. abbas de Notle etc.

a ministravit B.

The dates are those of Hamo as dean of Lincoln. Further disputes between Woburn
and Dunstable over Chesham were settled in 1203 (ibid. no. 169) and in 1221 (ibid.
no. 393).

54. Easby abbey

*Institution of the canons of Easby to the church of Saddington, on the
presentation of Richard de Rollos, the patron, and saving the perpetual
vicarage of William de Bubbenhill. William shall hold the vicarage
from the canons, paying to them each Whitsun an annual pension of
one silver mark.*   [21 September 1186 × ? early 1195]

B = BL ms. Egerton 2827 (Easby cartulary) fo. 302v. s. xiii ex.

Omnibus etc. Hugo dei gratia Lyncolniensis episcopus salutem. Ad
universitatis vestre notitiam volumus pervenire nos, ad presentationem Ricardi de Rollos*a* advocati ecclesie de Sadyngton', recepisse
ad eandem ecclesiam dilectos filios nostros canonicos sancte Agathe de
Richem' et eos canonice in ea personas instituisse, salva dilecto filio
nostro Willelmo de Bubbenhill' clerico perpetua in eadem ecclesia
vicaria quam de ipsis canonicis tenebit, solvendo eis annuatim i
marcam argenti ad Pentecosten nomine pensionis, salvis etiam episcopalibus consuetudinibus et Lincolniensis ecclesie dignitate ab eodem

Willelmo clerico in integrum solvendis. Quod ut ratum et inconcussum permaneat, illud presenti scripto et sigilli nostri patrocinio
confirmamus. Hiis testibus.

a Bollos B.

The charter of Richard II de Rollos granting the church to Easby is on the same
folio of the cartulary. Richard is thought to have died in early 1195 (*EYC* v 97).
This pension is mentioned in the Leicester archdeaconry 'matricula' of bp Hugh II
(*RHW* i 265).

55. Easby abbey

*Institution of William de Bubbenhill to the perpetual vicarage of
Saddington, on the presentation of the abbot and convent of Easby.
William is to pay to the canons each Whitsun an annual pension of one
silver mark and he is also to pay episcopal customs.*
[21 September 1186 × ? early 1195]

B = BL ms. Egerton 2827 (Easby cartulary) fo. 303r. s. xiii ex.

Omnibus etc. Hugo dei gratia Lyncolniensis episcopus. Ad universitatis vestre notitiam volumus pervenire nos, ad presentationem
abbatis et conventus sancte Agathe de Rich', recepisse dilectum filium
et clericum nostrum Willelmum de Bubenhill' ad perpetuam vicariam
ecclesie de Sadyngt' eumque in ipsa vicarium perpetuum canonice
instituisse, ita quod idem W. solvet prefatis canonicis sancte Agathe
annuatim nomine pensionis i marcam argenti ad Pentecosten, salvis
episcopalibus consuetudinibus ab eodem Willelmo solvendis et salva
Lincolniensis ecclesie dignitate. Quod ut ratum habeatur et inconcussum, illud presentis scripti serie et sigilli nostri munimine confirmavimus. T(estibus).

The letter of presentation of R(alph) the abbot and the convent of Easby is on fo.
302v of the cartulary, and William of Bubbenhill's charter recognising his obliga-
tion to pay the pension is on fo. 303r.

56. Edinburgh: Holyrood abbey

*Confirmation for the abbot and canons of Holyrood, Edinburgh, after
having inspected the charters of bishop Robert [Chesney] [EEA i no.
111] and king Malcolm of Scotland, of the church of [Great] Paxton.*
[September 1189 × 16 November 1200]

B = Lincoln D. & C. A/1/6 (Registrum) no. 295. s. xiv med.
Pd from B in *Reg. Ant.* iii no. 818.

Hiis testibus: Roberto archidiacono Huntendon', R. archidiacono
Leircestr', magistro Ricardo de Swaleclive, magistro Galfrido de

Deping', Roberto de Capella, Hugone de sancto Edwardo, Rogero Bact' et multis aliis.

> For king Malcolm IV's charter see *Reg. Ant.* iii no. 804; *Reg. regum Scottorum* i no. 197. Robert de Hardres was not archdn of Huntingdon in September 1189; his first known occurrences can be dated *c.*1189 × 1193 and 4 April 1192. If archdn R. of Leicester is to be identified with Roger of Rolleston, then this charter must have been issued before *c.*March 1195; of course archdn R. could quite easily be Roger's successor, Raymond. Probably 'Rogero Bact'' is a scribal error for Roger Bacon who frequently attests bp Hugh's acta.

*57. Elstow abbey

Confirmation for the abbess and nuns of Elstow of the church of Goddington, given to them by Thomas de Camvill, whose charter the bishop has inspected.   [21 September 1186 × 16 November 1200]

> Mention of charter produced in a dispute between Thomas de Camvill and the abbess of Elstow over the advowson of the church, 1221.
>
> Pd, *CRR* x 251.

> A final concord between Thomas and abbess Mabilia was made in April 1222 whereby Thomas quitclaimed all right in the advowson to Elstow and the abbess received him and his heirs into all benefits and prayers of the abbey (*Feet of Fines for Oxfordshire 1195–1291*, ed. H. E. Salter (Oxfordshire Record Society 12, 1930) 66 no. 64).

*58. William de Longchamp, bishop of Ely

Appeal by the bishop, along with other prelates assembled in council, to the pope against the legation of William (de Longchamp), bishop of Ely.
[Westminster, 10 February 1194]

> Mention of letters of appeal sealed by the bps and others in *Chronica Rogeri de Hovedene* iii 237; also pd in *Councils and Synods* I part ii, 1042, where details of the circumstances of this council are given. 'Deinde appellaverunt ad presentiam domini pape contra Willelmum Eliensem episcopum, ne ipse de cetero fungeretur in Anglia legacionis officio; et appellationem suam sigillis suis confirmaverunt, et miserunt illam domino regi, deinde summo pontifici confirmandam.'

59. Eynsham abbey

Notification to archdeacon J(ohn) of Oxford and all the clergy in the Oxford archdeaconry that the bishop has learned by testimony of the chapter of clergy at Wootton that the abbot and monks of Eynsham have long possessed the whole parish of Eynsham and Yarnton in full right and have appropriated all the offerings from the parish to their

own uses. The bishop confirms that all offerings from Eynsham and Yarnton without any diminution shall be appropriated to the monks.
[21 September 1186 × 20 October 1196]

B = Oxford, Ch. Ch. Lib., Kitchin's cat. no. 341 (Eynsham cartulary) fo. 15v, no. xxi (no witnesses). s. xii ex./s. xiii in.

Pd from B in *Eynsham Cartulary* i no. 21.

John of Coutances, archdn of Oxford, was consecrated as bp of Worcester on 20 October 1196. It is worth noting that in this actum Eynsham and Yarnton are spoken of as a single 'parrochia'; in no. 62 below they are described as 'parrochie'.

60. Eynsham abbey

Confirmation for the monastery and monks of Eynsham of all its churches in the diocese of Lincoln, namely: St Ebbe's, Oxford; Stanton [St John], the gift of John de sancto Iohanne; Merton, the gift of king David of Scotland; Souldern, the gift of Jordan de Sai; [South] Newington, the gift of Hugh de Chesney; Barton [Westcott], the gift of Alexander of Barton; a mediety of [Lower] Heyford, the gift of Peter de Mara; Brizenorton, the gift of Walchelin Hareng; Cornwell, the gift of Stephen de Pinsold and Alice his wife; and those churches situated in the demesne villages of the abbey, to wit, the church of Eynsham with its chapels, the church of [South] Stoke and the church of Charlbury.
[15 September 1189 × September 1193]

B = Oxford, Ch. Ch. Lib., Kitchin's cat. no. 341 (Eynsham cartulary) fos. 15v–16r, no. xxii. s. xii ex./s. xiii in.

Pd from B in *Eynsham Cartulary* i no. 22; (abstract) W. Kennett, *Parochial Antiquities* 139.

His testibus: Hamone decano Lincolniensi, Stephano cancellario, Herberto priore de sancto Neoto, magistro Rogero de Rolveston', magistro Simone de Suwella, magistro Ricardo de Swalecliv'.

Stephen became chancellor at some date between 15 September 1189 and 24 March 1190; he had been succeeded in the office by 22 March 1194. Roger of Rolleston is not described as archdn of Leicester in this document; he first occurs *c*.1192 × September 1193 with this title. Archbp Hubert Walter confirmed Hugh's charter 1195 × 1198 (*EEA* iii no. 462), although the archbp's charter names more churches than the bp's confirmation. For a survey of Eynsham's property, including these churches, see *Eynsham Cartulary* i xx–lxxiv.

61. Eynsham abbey

Confirmation for the monks of Eynsham, having inspected the charter of bishop Robert [EEA i no. 115] of the chapel of Cassington, saving the right of master Nicholas of Lewknor, while he lives. The chapel belongs to the church of Eynsham and was founded by Geoffrey de Clinton in

F

*his fee and in the parish of St Mary, Eynsham, with the consent of
bishop Robert and the abbot and monks. Bishop Robert had confirmed
it to be a chapel of Eynsham and the abbot retained the right of burial
of the dead of Cassington at Eynsham.*   [c.1192 × March 1195]

> B = Oxford, Ch. Ch. Lib., Kitchin's cat. no. 341 (Eynsham cartulary) fo. 15v, no.
> xx. s. xii ex/s. xiii in.
>
> Pd from B in *Eynsham Cartulary* i no. 20.

Hiis testibus: magistro Rogero archidiacono Leucestr', magistro
Ricardo de Swalecliv', magistro Ricardo Grim, Roberto de Capella et
Theobaldo, canonicis Lincolniensis ecclesie, magistro Alexandro de
Elnestow', Galfrido de Deping', Eustachio de Wilton' et aliis multis.

> The dates are those of Roger of Rolleston as archdn of Leicester (see no. 11).

62. Eynsham abbey

*Confirmation for abbot Robert and the convent of Eynsham, having
heard the testimony of the clergy and chapter of Wootton, of the chapel
of Cassington with all the offerings for the use of the monks, together
with the parishes of Eynsham and Yarnton with all their offerings,
saving the right of master Nicholas of Lewknor, while he lives. On
master Nicholas's death there shall be a vicarage of five marks a year
in the chapel of Cassington to be assigned by the monks to the priests
who will serve it. The chapels of Eynsham, Cassington and Yarnton
and the churches of [South] Stoke and Charlbury shall be free, as of
old, from all episcopal burdens, and shall only pay eight shillings for
Peter's Pence. The villages of Shifford and Rollright are quit of the
payment of Peter's Pence.* [11 November 1197 × 16 November 1200]

> B = Oxford, Ch.Ch.Lib., Kitchin's cat. no. 341 (Eynsham cartulary) fos.
> 16v–17r, no. xxiii(a). s. xii ex/s. xiii in. C = ibid. fo. 19r–v, no. xl.
>
> Pd from B in *Eynsham Cartulary* i no. 23A; C mentioned ibid. no. 40; (abstract)
> W. Kennett, *Parochial Antiquities* 140.

Hiis[a] testibus: [b-]B. priore de Wittham',[-b] magistro Ricardo Lincolniensis ecclesie subdecano, Reimundo archidiacono Legrecestr',[c]
magistro Gaufrido de Deping', magistro A. de Bedeford', magistro G.
de Rowell', Roberto capellano.

> [a] His C.   [b–b] *omitted* C.   [c] Legrec' C, *and concludes here with* et multis aliis.

> Robert received benediction as abbot of Eynsham on 11 November 1197; Richard
> of Kent also became subdean of Lincoln in this year. For the later endowment of
> the vicarage of Cassington see *Lib. Ant.* 3. See also *Eynsham Cartulary* ii lxii for a
> note on Peter's Pence collected from Eynsham's parishes (including, at a later date,
> Shifford and Rollright). See note to no. 59 above.

63. Eynsham abbey

Confirmation for abbot Robert and the convent of Eynsham of its churches and pensions, namely: the church of Stanton [St John] and an annual pension of one silver mark from it; the church of [Lower] Heyford and a pension of twenty shillings from it; the church of Barton [Westcott] and a pension of half a silver mark from it; the church of Charlbury and a pension of five silver marks from it; the church of Cornwell and a pension of one pound of wax from it; the church of Rollright and a pension of ten shillings from it; the church of [South] Newington and a pension of four shillings from it; the church of Souldern and a pension of two silver marks from it; the church of [South] Stoke and a pension of one pound of pepper from it; the church of Brizenorton and a pension of four shillings from it . . .

[11 November 1197 × 16 November 1200]

B = Oxford, Ch. Ch. Lib., Kitchin's cat. no. 341 (Eynsham cartulary) fo. 16r–v, no. xxiii (incomplete; a space is left in the cartulary for the completion of the text). s. xii ex./s. xiii in.

Pd from B in *Eynsham Cartulary* i no. 23; (abstract) W. Kennett, *Parochial Antiquities* 140.

Robert received benediction as abbot of Eynsham on 11 November 1197.

64. Eynsham abbey

Institution of William de Wares, nepos of abbot Robert of Eynsham, to the perpetual vicarage of Souldern, on the presentation of the abbot and monks of Eynsham, saving to the abbey an annual pension of one hundred shillings to be paid by the vicar.

[11 November 1197 × 16 November 1200]

B = Oxford, Ch. Ch. Lib., Kitchin's cat. no. 341 (Eynsham cartulary) fo. 46v (witnesses omitted). s. xii ex./s. xiii in.

Pd from B in *Eynsham Cartulary* i no. 185.

Robert received benediction as abbot of Eynsham on 11 November 1197. This charter is probably referred to, together with one of bp William, at the time the patronage was disputed between Eynsham and R. de Mortimer (*RHW* i 20). It is just possible that a general confirmation is meant, although in no. 63 above the Souldern pension was only two silver marks.

*65. Freiston priory

Appropriation of the church of Stonesby to the priory of Freiston.

[21 September 1186 × 16 November 1200]

Mention of grant in the Leicester archdeaconry 'matricula' of bp Hugh II.

Pd, *RHW* i 272.

66. Gloucester abbey

Institution of Richard de Budeford to the church of [Chipping] Norton, on the presentation of abbot Thomas and the convent of Gloucester. Richard is to pay to the abbot and monks sixty shillings a year in two instalments, namely, thirty shillings at Michaelmas and thirty shillings at Easter.

[21 September 1186 × 16 November 1200]

B = PRO C150/1 (Gloucester cartulary) fo. 128r, no. 499 (witnesses omitted). s. xiii ex.

Pd from B in *Gloucester Cartulary* ii no. 499.

The letter of presentation is ibid. no. 498.

67. Godstow abbey

General confirmation of possessions for the house and nuns of St Mary and St John the Baptist, Godstow.   [1189 × September 1193]

B = PRO E164/20 (Godstow cartulary) fo. 17v (v v). s. xv in. C = Bodl. ms. Rawlinson B 408 (Godstow cartulary, English version) fo. 16v. s. xv ex.

Pd from C in *Godstow English Register* ii no. 869.

Omnibus Christi fidelibus ad quos presens scriptum pervenerit, Hugo dei gratia Lincolniensis episcopus salutem in domino. Iustis postulantium petitionibus adesse pio favore volentes precipue domibus religiosis nostri patrocinii presidium tenemur impertiri, ne ea que fidelium largitione ad loca sancta et religiosa collata fuerint beneficia aliquorum prava malignitate possint nimium sive perturbari aut per temporum vetustatem oblivione sepeliri. Ad universitatis igitur vestre notitiam volumus devenire nos rata habere et presenti carta confirmare religiose domui sancte Marie et sancti Iohannis Baptiste de Godestowe et famulabus Christi ibidem deo servientibus ad sustentationem earum perpetuis usibus profutura beneficia fidelium Christi largitate concessa, que propriis nominibus duximus explicanda, videlicet: ex dono bone memorie Alexandri Lincolniensis episcopi centum solidos annuos in theloneo mercati Bannesberi percipiendos [*EEA* i no. 35]; ex dono regis H. filii Matildis imperatricis ecclesias de Wicumbe et de Blockesham cum omnibus pertinentiis suis; ex dono Ailwini filii Godegose ecclesiam sancti Egidii cum omnibus pertinentiis suis, que sita est extra Oxinefordiam; ex dono Agnetis filie Pagani filii Iohannis ecclesiam de Dunigtune cum omnibus pertinentiis suis; ex dono Symonis de Wahille medietatem ecclesie de Pateshille cum omnibus pertinentiis suis. Prefata igitur beneficia sicut eisdem monialibus sunt rationabiliter collata in proprios usus plenarie convertenda et propriis earum capellanis deservienda rata habemus et episcopali auctoritate confirmamus. Concedimus etiam predictis ancillis Christi ut sint libere et quiete ab omni exactione et consuetudine atque gravamine, salvo episcopali iure et Lincolniensis ecclesie dignitate. Quod ut ratum habeatur et firmum, presenti scripto et sigillo nostro duximus confirmandum. Hiis testibus: magistro Sthephano cancellario, magistro Rogero de Rolvestone, magistro Symone de Siwelle, magistro Galfrido de Lechelade, canonicis Lincolniensis ecclesie, Thoma, Walerando, Eustachio, Pagano, sacerdotibus de Godestowe, Galtero diacono, Iohanne clerico, Thomas senescallo, Luca ianitore, Henrico de Eatune, Henrico de Eboraco, Willelmo de Baggeherste.

> Stephen de Swafeld became chancellor of Lincoln in 1189/90 and had been succeeded in that dignity by 22 March 1194 at the latest; Roger of Rolleston, who attests here without a title, became archdn of Leicester c. 1192 × September 1193 (see no. 11).

68. Godstow abbey

Confirmation of the grant made by master John of Bridport, parson of the church of St Mary, Oxford, in the bishop's presence, to the nuns of St Mary and St John the Baptist, Godstow, of land and buildings in Oxford beside the church of St Mary, bequeathed to the nuns by master Robert de Bucketorp in his will. The property is to be held of St Mary's church, subject to a pension of two shillings payable on the feast of the nativity of the Virgin Mary [8 September]. [c. 1192 × March 1195]

> B = PRO E164/20 (Godstow cartulary) fo. 118r (cxv r). s. xv in.

Omnibus Christi fidelibus ad quos presens scriptum pervenerit, Hugo dei gratia Lincolniensis episcopus eternam in Christo salutem. Noverit universitas vestra quod magister Iohannes de Bridport persona ecclesie beate Marie in Oxeneford' concessit in presentia nostra et carta sua confirmavit deo et ecclesie sancte Marie et sancti Iohannis Baptiste de Godestowe et monialibus ibidem deo famulantibus terram et edificia in Oxeneford' que fuit iuxta ecclesiam beate Marie que magister Robertus de Bucketorp' in testamento*a* suo legavit predictis monialibus, tenenda inperpetuum de prefata ecclesia beate Marie sub pensione duorum solidorum in nativitate beate Marie solvendorum. Ut autem quod in nostra presentia factum est firmiori muniatur stabilitate, presenti illud scripto et sigilli nostri patrocinio confirmavimus. Hiis testibus: Haimone decano Lincolniensis ecclesie, magistro Roger archidiacono Lercestr', magistro Ricardo de

Swalewecliva, Galfrido de Lecchelad', Roberto de Capella, Hugone de sancto Edwardo, Ingelramo presbitero, Eustachio de Wilton' et aliis multis.

a testestamento B.

The dates are those of Roger of Rolleston as archdn of Leicester (see no. 11).

*69. Grantham prebend

Institution of Adam son of Reginald to the perpetual vicarage of the chapel of Towthorpe, on the presentation of John [of Coutances], dean of Rouen and canon of Salisbury, saving an annual pension of four shillings.   [c.1188 × 20 October 1196]

> Mention of charter produced in a dispute over Towthorpe chapel between Gerard of Howell and William of Ingoldesby, canon of Salisbury, 1228.
>
> Pd, *CRR* xiii no. 929; *Bracton's Note Book* ii no. 357, p. 295.

> Towthorpe chapel belonged to the prebend of Grantham Borealis in Salisbury cathedral (see *EEA* i no. 306). John of Coutances was dean of Rouen from 1188 or earlier (*Delisle* introd. p. 394) until he became bp of Worcester in 1196.

70. Greenfield priory

General confirmation of possessions for the house of Greenfield.
                                        [c.1192 × ? March 1195]

> A = BL Harl. Ch. 43 H 22. Endorsed: Confirmatio Hugonis episcopi (s. xvi); approx. 164 × 278 + 14 mm.; small fragment of seal of bp Richard Gravesend (1258–79) on 'new' parchment tag (d.q.1), repaired, brownish-red wax, no counterseal. Scribe **I**.
>
> Pd from A in *Mon. Angl.* v 580, no. iii.

Omnibus Christi fidelibus ad quos presens scriptum pervenerit ⠂ Hugo dei gratia Lincolniensis episcopus salutem in domino. Ne donationes locis religiosis a fidelibus facte aliqua malignantium machinatione possint*a* in irritum revocari . sollers antiquorum cavit prudentia . eas episcopali autoritate confirmari⠂ Inde est quod nos eorum sequentes vestigia et domui de Grenefeld atque monialibus in ea deo servientibus quantum in nobis est providere volentes . ea que ipsis pie collata sunt . autoritate qua fungimur duximus ipsis confirmare et ea propriis vocabulis annotata scripto autentico imprimere . videlicet ex dono Eudonis de Grenesbi et Radulfi filii eius fundatorum prefati loci ecclesiam de Abi cum omnibus pertinentiis suis . et culturam de Boland' et de Wargarthweit et Cattecroft cum cultura iuxta boscum de Swnewit . et pratum quod pertinet ad Cattecroft . et sedecim acras prati in campis de Abi . et boscum de Aisterlund . et

Tiedolf Barnewde . et decimam molendinorum de Abi . et totum boscum de Croxhag' quod Normannus habuit . ex dono Rocelini de Riggesbi et Iodlani filii eius . quicquid ipsi habuerunt in Wlurikehag' . ex dono Gilberti de Riggesbi et Herberti filii eius . quicquid ipsi habuerunt in Wlurikehag' et Prestehag' . et sartum iuxta Prestehag' . et quatuor acras terre in Heregereshag' cum communi pastura de Riggesbi . ex dono Amfridi de Hag' quinquaginta acras prati cum communi pastura de Hag' . ex dono Alani de Munbi et Eudonis filii eius . quicquid ipsi habuerunt in Wlurikehag' . et ecclesiam de Cumbrewrd' ·/ quantum ad ipsos pertinebat . scilicet tres partes eiusdem ecclesie . et Snouthecrof . et unam bovatam terre que pertinet ad Snothecroft . cum communi pastura de Sutton' . et unum toftum quod fuit Gunebeni . et pasturam ad trescentas oves . in pastura ultra Havedic de Munbi . ex dono Willelmi filii Otuer(i) . triginta tres acras in campis de Abi et Toresbi . ex dono Ivonis de Strubi et Henrici filii eius ·/ quadraginta duas acras terre in Erareker et Croxhag' . ex dono Willelmi de Wdetorp et Alani filii eius . Matteker . et unam bovatam terre in Farford' cum tofto uno . ex dono Willelmi de Well' et Roberti filii eius . sex acras prati in territorio de Wiern' . in loco qui vocatur Herleham . ex dono Herberti de Alebi et Walteri et Willelmi filiorum eius . quicquid^b ipsi habuerunt in Wlurikehag' . et Prestehag' . et quicquid ipsi habuerunt inter Bolandewang' et Derwennehill' . et inter abbatiam et fossatum de Crakethweit per metas dispositas a Crakethweit usque Trentesic cum communi pastura de Abi . ex dono Gunteri de Alebi quicquid ipse habuit in Wlurikehag' . et quicquid habuit inter culturam de Presthag' . et terram Gileberti de Campania . ex dono Picoti de Houton' et Ricardi filii eius . unam salinam in marisco de Neweton' et quinque acras prati in Twafletes ˙ et in Westenges . ex dono Thome Burgefurn' . duas acras terre in territorio de Hag' . et totam terram suam in Northon . que iacet inter viam et culturam suam . ex dono Gileberti Testard ·/ tres percatas terre in territorio de Abi . ex dono Willelmi Burgefurn' ·/ unam acram terre in territorio de Swabi . in cultura que vocatur Breithebuskewang'. Hec omnia sicut eis iuste collata sunt et rationabiliter ·/ presenti scripto et sigilli nostri patrocinio confirmamus . salvis episcopalibus consuetudinibus et Lincolniensis ecclesie dignitate. Hiis testibus . Haimone decano Lincolniensis ecclesie . magistro Rogero de Rolveston' archidiacono Leic' . magistro Ricardo de Swalewecliva . Galfrido de Lechelad' . Roberto de Capella . Eustachio de Wilton' . et aliis multis .

^a possit A.   ^b quidquid A.

The dates are those of Roger of Rolleston as archdn of Leicester (see no. 11). This confirmation was inspected by bp William (no. 244 below).

71. Heynings priory

Confirmation for the nuns of Heynings, having inspected the charter of
Walter de Evermue, of possessions given to them by Walter and his
father and grandfather.   [*c*.1192 × ? March 1195]

> B = PRO C53/57 (charter roll, 52 Henry III) m.3 (in an inspeximus of king Henry
> III, 16 August 1268).
>
> Pd (calendar) from B in *Cal. Ch. R.* ii 107.

Omnibus Christi fidelibus ad quos presens scriptum pervenerit, Hugo
dei gratia Lincolniensis episcopus salutem in domino. Ex inspectione
carte dilecti filii nostri Walteri de Evermue ipsiusque confessione
cognovimus ipsum concessisse et confirmasse dilectis in Christo
filiabus nostris monialibus de Heyninges omnes decimationes seu
concessiones quas .. R. avus eius et I. pater eius post eum eisdem
monialibus in puram et perpetuam elemosinam contulerant tam in
ecclesiis, decimis, terris, pascuis et libertatibus quam in omnibus aliis
rebus eis a predictis donatoribus pie collatis sicut carta ipsius Walteri
manifeste declarat:eandem igitur concessionem et confirmationem
ratam habentes, eam auctoritate episcopali confirmavimus. Hiis testibus: Haymone Lincolniensis ecclesie decano, magistro R. Leirc',
magistro Alexandro de Westreng' archidiaconis, magistro Ricardo de
Swaluecliva, Roberto de Capella, Gaufrido de Dyeping', Hugone de
sancto Edwardo, Durando de Wivelingh', Roberto de Dunstapill' et
aliis multis.

> The charters of Walter de Evermue, his father Jollan, and his grandfather Reyner
> are all inspected ibid. 106. The dates are those of Roger of Rolleston as archdn of
> Leicester; he succeeded Hamo as dean of Lincoln *c*.March 1195 (see no. 11).

72. Hinchingbrooke priory

General confirmation of possessions for the prioress and nuns of St
James outside Huntingdon (Hinchingbrooke).
                              [21 September 1186 × 18 October 1188]

> A = BL Add. Ch. 33595. Endorsed: Confirmationes episcoporum (s. xiv);
> approx. 160 × 170 + 10 mm.; seal missing, single slit for seal tag (d.q.1).
>
> B = BL Add. Ch. 33596 (in an inspeximus of archbp Hubert Walter of Canter-
> bury, April 1195 × February 1197, pd in *EEA* iii no. 494).

Omnibus Christi fidelibus ad quos presens scriptum pervenerit ﹖
Hug(o) dei gratia Lincolniensis episcopus salutem in domino. Ne ea
que locis religiosis conferuntur beneficia ﹖ maligna pravorum machinatione possint retractari . aut per temporum vetustatem oblivione

sepeliri ⸴ sollers antiquorum cavit prudentia ⸴ ad posterorum cogni-
tionem predicto modo collata beneficia ⸴ per scripture subsidium
longeva perpetuare memoria. Nos igitur veterum vestigia pia sequentes ⸴ dilectis nobis in Christo filiabus priorisse sancti Iacobi extra
Huntendonam et monialibus ibidem deo servientibus donationes sibi
rationaliter factas episcopali auctoritate duximus confirmare . et
attestatione presentis scripti communire . quas propriis vocabulis
censuimus subsequenter exprimere . videlicet ex donatione Willelmi
regis Scotie locum in quo sita est . ecclesia sancti Iacobi in quo loco
prefate moniales manent . ex donatione comitis David pratum turris et
duas virgatas terre in Stivecle . ex donatione Simundi de Turre ⸴
totam terram quam habuit in Huntedon' . excepto loco in quo domus
eius site sunt . ex donatione Clementie de Hamertun' ⸴ unam virgatam
terre in eadem villa . ex donatione Iohannis Vis de Lu . unam
virgatam terre in Abinton' . ex donatione Roberti Engaine ⸴ unam
virgatam terre in Weresle . ex donatione Willelmi de Einesford ⸴ ex
unaquaque acra terre dominii sui de Stoctun' ⸴ unam garbam . ex
donatione Roberti procuratoris vinee regis de Hunted' . redditus
trium solidorum. Supradictas itaque donationes super quibus donatorum cartas inspeximus ⸴ sicut rationaliter facte sunt deo et ecclesie
sancti Iacobi et monialibus ibidem deo servientibus ⸴ ratas habemus et
presentis scripti testimonio ac sigilli nostri patrocinio confirmamus.[a]
Testibus magistro Laurentio archidiacono . Bedeford' . magistro
Roberto de Bedeford' . magistro Garino officiali . Bedef' . magistro
Iohanne de Bedef' . Walk(elino) capellano . magistro Willelmo .
Wacelin' . et aliis.

[a] B ends here.

Robert of Bedford attests here without a title; he had become precentor of Lincoln
by 18 October 1188. Master Warin, the official of Bedford, may be identified with
Warin of Hibaldstow (C. R. Cheney, 'Harrold Priory: a twelfth-century dispute' in
Beds. Hist. Rec. Soc. 32 (1952), repd version with additional notes in *Medieval
Texts and Studies* (Oxford 1973) 303).

73. Hinchingbrooke priory

*Confirmation for the prioress and nuns of St James outside Hunting-
don (Hinchingbrooke), having inspected the charter of king John, of his
grant of sixty acres of land and a meadow outside the town of
Huntingdon.*   [10 June 1199 × 16 November 1200]

A = BL Add. Ch. 33442 (rodent damage at right-hand side). No endorsement;
    approx. 154 × 100 + 16 mm.; fragment of seal on parchment tag (repaired)
    (d.q.1), brownish-red wax, no counterseal.

Omnibus Christi fidelibus ad quos presens scriptum pervenerit . Hug(o) dei gratia Lincolniensis episcopus eternam in domino salutem. Ea que divine caritatis intuitu religiosis conventibus domino iugiter impendentibus famulatum ad sustentationem necessariam noscuntur rationabiliter collata esse beneficia ∴ tanto favorabilius et benignius libentiusque tenemur ipsis sicut ea rationabiliter adepti sunt confirmare ∴ quanto eorum obsequium in religiosiori conversatione et honestiori paupertate credimus domino placere. Hinc est quod considerata honesta paupertate et religiosa conversatione dilectarum in Christo filiarum priorisse et monialium sancti Iacobi extra Huntedon' . s[exa]ginta acras terre et unum pratum que sunt ante portam ipsarum extra villam Huntedon' . que venerabi[lis] dominus Iohannes illustris rex Anglie eis in liberam . puram . et perpetuam elemosinam caritative contulit [sicut] in carta ipsius domini regis continetur quam inspeximus ∴ eisdem priorisse et monialibus episcopali munimine et [patroci]nio confirmamus. Quod ut ratum et inconcussum perpetuo permaneat ∴ id presentis scripti testimonio et [sigilli nostri] appositione roboravimus. Hiis testibus . Ricardo subdecano . magistris Galfrido de Deping' . Giraldo de R[owell' .] Theobaldo de Bosell' . et Willelmo de Avalon' ∴ canonicis . Lincolniensis ecclesie . magistris Nicholao de Radingiis [   ]no subdec(ano) . Roberto de Hulmo . Hugone de Pateshull' . Rogero de Bolehirst' en Ricardo de Tinghirst' . clericis

King John's charter, dated at Westminster, 10 June 1199, is BL, Add. Ch. 33597.

74. Horncastle church

Institution of Osbert de Bisshoppesdun, clerk, to the chapelry of Horncastle, that is to say, the church of Horncastle, with all its appurtenances, namely the churches of [West] Ashby, [High] Toynton, Mareham [on the Hill] and [Wood] Enderby, on the presentation of Richard Revell, with the consent of king Richard; saving the rights of the clerks who hold these churches subject to annual pensions payable to Osbert. [1197 × 6 April 1199]

A = Lincoln D. & C. Dij/72/3/35. Endorsed: Si rector ecclesie de Hornecastr' aliquo tempore indigeat litteris istis ∴ tradantur ei ad tempus certum sub bona pena . infra quod ipsas restituat sine contradictione (s. xiii); de ecclesia de Horncast' (ss. xiii–xiv); iij; approx. 153 × 114 + 19 mm.; seal missing, parchment tag for seal (d.q.2). Scribe **I**.

B = ibid. A/1/6 (Registrum) no. 1808. s. xiv med.

Pd from A in *Reg. Ant.* ii no. 575 (facsimile opp.).

Omnibus Christi fidelibus ad quos presens scriptum pervenerit ∴ Hug(o) dei gratia Lincolniensis episcopus salutem in domino. Noverit

universitas vestra . nos ad presentationem Ricardi Revell' de consensu
illustris regis Anglie Ricardi . recepisse dilectum filium nostrum
Osbertum de Bisshoppesdun' clericum ad capellaniam de Hornecastr'
. videlicet ad ecclesiam de Horncastr' cum omnibus ad eam pertinentibus . scilicet ecclesia de Askebi . ecclesia de Tinton' maiori . ecclesia
de Maringes . et ecclesia de Enderbi . salvo iure clericorum qui
quasdam earum nunc tenent sub annuis pensionibus eidem .O.
solvendis . videlicet Willelmi capellani in ecclesia de Askebi . Iohannis
filii Simonis in ecclesia de Tinton' . Reginaldi capellani et Iohannis
clerici in ecclesia de Maringes. Prefatus igitur .O. predictam capellaniam perpetuo possidebit ; salvis episcopalibus consuetudinibus et Lincolniensis ecclesie dignitate. Quod ut ratum permaneat ; presenti
scripto et sigilli nostri patrocinio confirmamus. Hiis testibus . Rogero
decano . Ricardo subdecano . magistro Roberto de Manecestr' .
magistro Ricardo de Swalewecl' . magistro Alexandro de Bedeford' .
magistro Girardo de Rowell' . Andrea et Hugone . canonicis .
Lincolniensis ecclesie . magistro Willelmo filio Fulconis . Hugone de
Rowell' . Eustachio de Wilton' . et aliis multis .,

Richard of Kent became subdean of Lincoln in 1197; king Richard I died on 6
April 1199.

75. Kenilworth priory

*Confirmation for the prior and canons of Kenilworth of the church of
Barton [Seagrave] and of an annual pension of ten marks payable to
them by the incumbent of the church.*

[21 September 1186 × 18 October 1188]

B = BL ms. Harl. 3650 (Kenilworth cartulary) fos. 49v–50r (pp. 98–9). s. xiii
    med. C = BL ms. Add. 47677 (Kenilworth cartulary) fo. 316v (cccv v). s. xvi
    in.

Omnibus Christi fidelibus ad quos presens scriptum pervenerit, Hugo
dei gratia Lincolniensis episcopus salutem in domino. Quoniam ea
que viris religiosis conferuntur beneficia nostra tenemur protectione
defendere et contra malignantium incursus nostre auctoritatis patrocinio communire, ad universitatis vestre notitiam pervenire volu[fo.
50r]mus nos dilectis filiis priori et canonicis de Kenill'ᵃ ecclesiam de
Barton'ᵇ cum omnibus pertinentiis suis sicut eam rationabiliter adepti
sunt episcopali auctoritate confirmareᶜ, ita quod ipsi annuatim ex ea
decem marcas ab illo percipiant quicumque nomine eorum in ecclesia
illa fuerit institutus. Quod ut ratum habeatur et firmum, presenti
scripto et sigillo nostro duximus roborandum, salva in omnibus
Lincolniensis ecclesie dignitate et episcopalibus consuetudinibus.

Testibus: magistro Roberto de Bedeford', magistro Rogero de Rolv', Gaufrido de sancto Edwardo, Gaufrido de Lichelad', magistro Willelmo Wacelin, Hugone de sancto Edwardo.

a Kenell' C.   *b* Berton' C.   *c* C *adds* etc. *and ends here.*

Robert of Bedford, who attests here without a title, had become precentor of Lincoln at least by 18 October 1188. Barton Seagrave church was among the original endowments of the founder, Geoffrey de Clinton (*Mon. Angl.* vi 220–1, no. i).

76. Kenilworth priory

Institution of Stephen, the bishop's clerk, to the church of Barton [Seagrave], on the presentation of R(obert), the prior and the convent of Kenilworth, saving an annual pension of ten marks payable to the priory. [21 September 1186 × 1194]

B = BL ms. Harl. 3650 (Kenilworth cartulary) fo. 50v (p. 100). s. xiii med.

Hugo dei gratia Lincolniensis episcopus karissimis in Christo amicis suis R. priori de Kenill' et eiusdem loci conventui salutem et dei benedictionem. Dilectioni vestre cuius devotionem sic*a* probavimus sic approbamus nimirum et commendamus presencium latorem Stephanum fidelem vestrum et nostrum clericum transmittimus ut eum tanquam clericum vestrum quem in ecclesia de Berton' ad presentationem vestram instituimus, salva pensione annua x marcarum vobis inde debita, benigne recipiatis et ipsum sicut unum e vestris*b* a latere nostro vobis destinatum honorifice tractetis et in suis agendis promoveatis, ita quod preces nostras sibi sentiat profuisse et pro eo vobis teneamur uberiores gratiarum actiones referre. Bene valete.

a sicut B.   *b* 'vris' *written B, without any contraction sign.*

This document must precede in date the second letter of institution of Stephen [de Piun] (below), when the pension payable to Kenilworth was reduced to seven marks. The date of this actum may be the same as the preceding confirmation.

77. Kenilworth priory

Institution of Stephen de Piun, the bishop's clerk, to the church of Barton [Seagrave], on the presentation of the prior and canons of Kenilworth. Stephen shall pay an annual pension of seven marks to Kenilworth. [15 September 1189 × 22 March 1194]

B = BL ms. Harl. 3650 (Kenilworth cartulary) fo. 49v (p. 98). s. xiii med.
C = BL ms. Add. 47677 (Kenilworth cartulary) fos. 316v–317r (cccv v–cccvi r). s. xvi in.

Omnibus*a* Christi fidelibus ad quos presens scriptum pervenerit, Hugo dei gratia Lincolniensis*b* episcopus salutem in domino. Ad

universitatis vestre notitiam volumus pervenire nos, ad presentationem dilectorum in Christo prioris de Kenill'ᶜ et canonicorum dilectum
in Christo filium Stephanum de Piun clericum nostrum ad ecclesiam
de Barton'ᵈ recepisse et ipsum in ea instituisse, salva pensione septem
marcarum quas idem Stephanus de predicta ecclesia de Barton'ᵈ
tenetur annuatim solvere domui de Kenill'ᶜ et salvis episcopalibus
consuetudinibus et Lincolniensis ecclesie dignitateᵉ. Quod ut ratum
habeatur et firmum, presenti scripto et sigillo nostro duximus confirmandum. Testibus: Hamone Lincolniensis ecclesie decano, magistro Stephano Lincolniensis ecclesie cancellario, magistro Nicholao
de Derleig', Walk(elino) capellano, magistro Ricardo de Swaleweclivʼ,
Ingelramo capellano, Gaufrido de Lichelad'.

ᵃ Omnibus . . . pervenerit *abbreviated to* Omnibus etc. C.   ᵇ Lincolnen' C.   ᶜ Kenell' C.
ᵈ Berton' C.   ᵉ C *adds* etc. *and ends here.*

Hamo became dean of Lincoln at some date between 15 September 1189 and 24
March 1190; Stephen de Swafeld's successor as chancellor first occurs on 22 March
1194. This document must follow in date the similar charters where the annual
pension is stated as ten marks. It is probably in the nature of a 'revised' letter of
institution issued to take into account the altered pension.

78. Kenilworth priory

*Institution of Henry, archdeacon of Stafford, to the church of Hughen-
den, on the presentation of the prior and canons of Kenilworth. Henry
shall hold the church for his lifetime, paying to the canons an annual
pension of ten marks.* [*c.*1192 × ? March 1195]

B = BL ms. Harl. 3650 (Kenilworth cartulary) fo. 50r–v (pp. 99–100). s. xiii med.

Omnibus Christi fidelibus ad quos presens scriptum pervenerit, Hugo
dei gratia Lincolniensis episcopus salutem in domino. Noverit universitas vestra nos, ad presentationem prioris et canonicorum de
Kenill', recepisse dilectum filium nostrum Henricum archidiaconum
Stafford' ad ecclesiam de Uchenden' ipsumque in ea canonice instituisse, ita quidem [fo. 50v] quod idem H. ipsam ecclesiam tenebit
cum omnibus pertinentiis suis tota vita sua, solvendo exinde prefatis
canonicis de Kenill' annuatim de prefata scilicet ecclesia decem marcas
nomine pensionis; salvis episcopalibus consuetudinibus et Lincolniensis ecclesie dignitate. Quod ut ratum et inconcussum permaneat,
presenti scripto et sigilli nostri patrocinio confirmavimus. Hiis testibus: Haimone decano Lincolniensis ecclesie, Roberto Huntedon' et
magistro Rogero Leicestr' archidiaconis, magistro Ricardo de Swaleweclivʼ, Roberto de Neovill', Roberto de Capella, Hugone de sancto
Eadwardo, Hugone de Rolveston,' Eustachio de Wilton' et aliis multis.

The dates are those of Roger of Rolleston as archdn of Leicester (see no. 11). The original grant of the church was made by Nicholas of Hughenden. Three charters of the donor, one addressed to bp Alexander of Lincoln (1123–48) and archdn David of Buckingham (*c*.1142×1177) and a later one addressed to bp Robert Chesney (1148–66) are on fo. 296 of BL ms. Add. 47677 (Kenilworth cartulary).

79.   Kenilworth priory

Confirmation of the settlement of a dispute between the abbot and convent of Osney and the prior and convent of Kenilworth about the church of Iffley. The prior and canons of Kenilworth shall pay to Osney an annual pension of one mark from the church.

[1197 × 16 November 1200]

B = BL ms. Harl. 3650 (Kenilworth cartulary) fo. 50r (p. 99). s. xiii med.
C = BL ms. Add. 47677 (Kenilworth cartulary) fo. 353v (cccxlii v). s. xvi in.

Omnibus*a* sancte matris ecclesie filiis ad quos presens scriptum pervenerit, Hugo dei gratia Lincolniensis*b* episcopus salutem in domino. Noverit universitas vestra controversiam que vertebatur inter abbatem et canonicos de Oseneia et priorem atque*c* conventum de Kenill'*d* super ecclesia de Iftel'*e* in presentia nostra hoc fine quievisse, videlicet, quod prefati prior et canonici de Kenill'*d* persolvent predictis abbati et conventui de Osen'*f* unam marcam annuatim nomine pensionis de supradicta ecclesia de Iftel'*e* scilicet*g* dimidiam marcam ad Pascha et dimidiam marcam ad festum sancti Michaelis, ita quidem quod prefati abbas et canonici de Osen'*f* hac pensione contenti nunquam movebunt predictis priori et canonicis de Kenill'*d* questionem super sepedicta*h* ecclesia de Iftel'*e* vel eius presentatione. Et si aliquis eis questionem super eadem ecclesia vel eius pretaxata*i* pensione movere presumpserit, ipsi sibi mutuo auxilium et consilium fidele inpendent*j*. Nos igitur hanc formam pacis coram nobis factam gratam et ratam habentes, eam auctoritate qua fungimur presenti scripto et sigilli nostri patrocinio confirmamus; salvis episcopalibus consuetudinibus et Lincolniensis ecclesie dignitate*k*. Hiis testibus: Rogero decano et Ricardo subdecano Lincolniensis ecclesie, Stephano archidiacono Bukingham', magistris Ricardo de Swalewecliv', Alexandro de Bedeford', Girardo de Rowll', Henrico de Gilevill', canonicis Lincolniensis ecclesie, Hugone de Rolveston', Angod' de Blackolvest', Eustachio de Wilton' et aliis multis.

*a*Omnibus . . . pervenerit *abbreviated to* Omnibus etc. C.   *b* Lyncoln C.   *c* at C.
d Kennell' C.   *e* Yifteley C.   *f* Oseney C.   *g* C *adds* et.   *h* supradicta C.   *i* pretaxta C.
j impendent C.   *k* C *ends here*.

Richard of Kent became subdean of Lincoln in 1197. For a charter of prior Silvester of Kenilworth about the composition, made in the presence of bp Hugh, see *Osney Cartulary* vi no. 1056.

80. Kenilworth priory

Confirmation for the canons of Kenilworth of the church of Hethe, given to them by Bertram de Verdun.　　　　[1197 × 16 November 1200]

> B = BL ms. Harl. 3650 (Kenilworth cartulary) fo. 49v (p. 98). s. xiii med.
> C = BL ms. Add. 47677 (Kenilworth cartulary) fo. 356v (cccxlv v). s. xvi in.

Omnibus*ᵃ* Christi fidelibus ad quos presens scriptum pervenerit, Hugo dei gratia Lincolniensis episcopus salutem in domino. Cum ex pontificalis*ᵇ* officii debito teneamur ecclesie nostre subditis in iure suo adesse, maxime viris religiosis debemus quantum de iure possumus nostram protectionem exhibere*ᶜ* et ea que presidemus auctoritate eis iura sua illibata conservare. Attendentes igitur religiosam conversationem canonicorum ecclesie de Kenill'*ᵈ* consideratione honestatis eiusdem domus, ratam duximus habere concessionem et donationem ecclesie de Hethre*ᵉ* cum omnibus pertinentiis suis quam habent ex dono Bertram de Verdon' eamque sicut rationabiliter sunt adepti, confirmamus*ᶠ* eis et sigilli nostri patrocinio corroboramus; salvis in omnibus episcopalibus consuetudinibus et Lincolniensis ecclesie dignitate. Testibus: Rogero ecclesie Lincolniensis decano, R. eiusdem ecclesie subdecano, Stephano de Bukingham archidiacono, magistris R. de Swalewecliv', Alexandro de Alnestouu', Henrico de Gilevill', Gerardo de Rowell', Lincolniensis ecclesie canonicis, Eustacio, Hugone de Rolveston', Angod' de Blaculuest' et aliis multis.

ᵃ Omnibus . . . pervenerit *abbreviated to* Omnibus etc. C.　　*ᵇ* pontificali C.　　*ᶜ* exibere C.
ᵈ Kenell' C.　　*ᵉ* Hethra C.　　*ᶠ* C *adds* etc. *and ends here.* ˙

> Richard of Kent became subdean of Lincoln in 1197. For Bertram de Verdun see Delisle, *Recueil* introd. 359–60. Two charters of Bertram confirming this church are on fo. 356r–v of C. One is addressed to John of Coutances, archdn of Oxford; John held this office from ?1184 until, at latest, 20 Oct. 1196, when he was consecrated bp of Worcester.

81. Kingsey church

Institution of Simon de Whitefeld, clerk, to the church of Kingsey, on the presentation of Herbert de Bolebec, knight. The bishop has also instituted William the clerk of 'Eia' to the perpetual vicarage of the church on the presentation of Simon, with the consent of Herbert. The endowments of the vicarage are described.　　[1189 × September 1193]

> A = Lincoln D. & C. Dij/73/1/30. Endorsed: Ista non scribitur in registro (s. xiii); sancti Hugonis de vicaria .W. de Eye (s. xiii); approx. 185 × 142 + 18 mm.; seal missing, parchment tag for seal (d.q.2).
> Pd from A in *Reg. Ant.* iii no. 658 (facsimile opp.).

Omnibus Christi fidelibus ad quos presens scriptum pervenerit Hugo dei gratia Lincolniensis episcopus . eternam in domino salutem.

Noverit universitas vestra nos ad presentationem Herberti de Bolebec militis recepisse Simonem de Whitefeld clericum ad ecclesiam de Kingeseia . ipsum que in ea personam canonice instituisse. Ad eiusdem etiam .S. presentationem de consensu prefati .H. advocati . recepimus Willelmum clericum de Eia quod idem .W. habebit omnes decimationes ad ecclesiam illam pertinentes preter garbam . et omnes obventiones altaris . preterea duas marcas quas iam dictus .S. ci annuatim persolvet ad duos terminos . videlicet unam marcam ad festum sancti Michaelis . et unam ad Pascha . Ipse autem .W. sinodalia persolvet. Prefatus itaque .S. in presentia nostra iuravit . se concessionem istam fideliter et absque tergiversatione observaturum .W. etiam in presentia nostra iuravit . quod nunquam eidem .S. movebit super eadem ecclesia questionem . nec amplius inde exiget. Ut autem hec rata et inconcussa permaneant . presenti scripto et sigilli nostri patrocinio confirmavimus . salvis episcopalibus consuetudinibus et Lincolniensis ecclesie dignitate. Hiis testibus . magistro Stephano cancellario Lincolniensis ecclesie . magistro Rogero de Rolveston' . magistro Ricardo de Swalewecliva . Galfrido de Lecchelad' . Rogero Scotto . Roberto de Capella . Hugone de sancto Edwardo . Eustachio de Wilton' . et aliis multis.

Stephen de Swafeld became chancellor of Lincoln in 1189/90; he had been succeeded in that dignity by 22 March 1194 at the latest. Roger of Rolleston, who attests here without a title, became archdn of Leicester c.1192 × September 1193 (see no. 11). Kingsey, although given parochial status in this document, was in fact a chapel of Haddenham church, and a letter of the archdn of Buckingham in the time of bp Hugh II reveals that Simon eventually had to restore possession of the chapelry to the monks of Rochester, the patrons of Haddenham (*Reg. Ant.* iii no. 665). On the status of Kingsey, or Eia, see *Reg. Roff.* 45, 117, 384–7.

*82. Kyme priory

? Confirmation to Kyme priory of a pension of two and a half marks from the church of All Saints, Wainfleet.

[21 September 1186 × 16 November 1200]

Mention of charter in the first institution roll of bp Hugh II.

Pd, *RHW* i 13.

*83. Langley priory

Confirmation of possessions for the nuns of Langley.

[21 September 1186 × April 1195]

Charter inspected (not recited) and confirmed by archbp Hubert Walter of Canterbury, along with the charter of bp Robert II (*EEA* i no. 142), November 1193 × April 1195.

Pd, *EEA* iii no. 504.

84. Launde priory

General confirmation of possessions for the church and canons of St John the Baptist, Launde.

[15 September 1189 × *c*.March 1195]

A = Bodl. DD. All Souls College c.218/17. Endorsed: Carta sancti Hugonis de omnibus ecclesiis nostris (s. xiii); sanctus Hugo Linc' episcopus (s. xv); pressmark; A nu[mer]us 6; approx. 148 × 155 + 22 mm.; fragment of seal on parchment tag (d.q.2), brownish-white wax; no counterseal (xliiij written on tag, iij on turn-up).

Pd from A in J. Nichols, *History of Leicestershire* iii 1, 302.

Omnibus Christi fidelibus ad quos presens scriptum pervenerit ⁒ Hug(o) dei gratia Lincolniensis episcopus salutem in domino. Ne donationes locis religiosis facte alicuius improbitate vel malignitate possint inposterum retractari ⁒ prudens antiquorum cavit sollertia ⁒ scriptis autenticis ad posterorum memoriam easdem donationes exarare . et scripti munimento perpetuum eis robur commendare. Nos igitur veterum vestigia pia sequentes ⁒ beneficia que ecclesie sancti Iohannis Baptiste de Landa et canonicis ibidem deo servientibus a Christi fidelibus collata sunt ⁒ eidem domus duximus nostra auctoritate confirmare . et ad perpetuitatis memoriam propriis vocabulis designare . videlicet villam de Lodinton' ex dono Ricardi Basset ⁒ cum ecclesia et molendinis . et omnibus pertinentiis . Landas ⁒ ubi canonici manent cum molendino et hominibus ibidem demorantibus . similiter et Friseby cum ecclesia sancti Gudlaci et cum molendino et ceteris pertinentiis . in Oudebi ecclesiam sancti Petri*ᵃ* cum suis pertinentiis . ecclesiam sancte Elene de Ketleby cum capellis et pertinentiis suis . ecclesiam sancte Marie de Warle cum capella de Beltun' . ecclesiam sancte Marie de Weled' . cum pertinentiis suis . ecclesiam sancte Marie de Weston' cum capella de Sutton' . ecclesiam sancti Andree de Welleham . ecclesiam sancti Leodegarii . de Æisseby . ecclesiam sancte Marie Magdalene . de Blarwic . et ecclesiam sancti Andree de Erningworde de dono Ricardi filii Roberti . ecclesiam sancti Nicholai de Bugged' de dono Roberti filii Hugonis . ecclesiam sancti Andree de Glaest' . de dono Phillippi de Pant' . et Iordani fratris eius . ecclesiam sancti Petri de Tilt' . cum capellis et omnibus pertinentiis suis . de dono Everardi de Tilton' . ecclesiam sancte Marie de Eisseby cum capellis et pertinentiis aliis . de dono Radulfi . de Folevile. Ut ergo hec nostra confirmatio perpetuis perseveret temporibus ⁒ eam duximus presenti scripto et sigillo nostro communire . salvis episcopalibus consuetudinibus et Lincolniensis . ecclesie dignitate. Testibus Hamone . Lincolniensis . ecclesie decano . magistro Ricardo de

G

Swalewecl' . magistro Gerardo de Roell' . Eustachio de Wilton' . Hugone de sancto Edwardo.

a Paretri (*sic*) A, *the 'p' having a horizontal 'er/ar' stroke.*

The dates are those of Hamo as dean of Lincoln. For a general confirmation of bp Robert Chesney see *EEA* i no. 143. This charter, along with bp Chesney's and a now missing charter of bp Alexander (1123–48), was confirmed by bp Richard Gravesend of Lincoln on 20 November 1266; the latter's confirmation was inspected by bp John Dalderby on 20 January 1314 (LAO, Ep. Reg. III fo. 295).

85. Leeds priory

Admission of the prior and canons of Leeds into the personatus *of a mediety of the church of Hallaton, at the presentation of Daniel de Crevequer, and institution of Benjamin the clerk to the perpetual vicarage of the mediety. Benjamin shall pay an annual pension of half a mark to the canons.*   [15 September 1189 × September 1193]

B = PRO C53/150 (charter roll, 41 Edward III) m. 9 (in an inspeximus of king Edward III, 22 March 1367).

Pd (calendar) from B in *Cal. Ch. R.* v 202.

Hugo dei gratia Lincolniensis episcopus omnibus Christi fidelibus ad quos presens scriptum pervenerit eternam in domino salutem. Noverit universitas vestra nos, ad presentationem dilecti filii nostri Danielis de Crevequer, recepisse dilectos filios nostros priorem et canonicos de Liedes ad personatum medietatis ecclesie de Halhton' et eos canonice in ea instituisse. Ad eorum etiam presentationem de consensu prefati advocati recepimus dilectum filium nostrum Beniamin clericum ad perpetuam vicariam in ea instituimus, ita quod idem B. solvet de eadem medietate prefatis canonicis nomine pensionis dimidiam marcam; salvis episcopalibus consuetudinibus et Lincolniensis ecclesie dignitate. Ut autem hec nostra donatio firmam optineat stabilitatem, eam presenti scripto et sigilli nostri patrocinio confirmavimus. Hiis testibus: Hamone decano Lincolniensis ecclesie, Roberto abbate Nutel', magistro Rogero de Rolveston', Petro fratre nostro, magistro Ricardo de Swalewecl', Roberto de Capella, Hugone de sancto Edwardo, Willelmo, Eustachio de Wilton' et aliis multis.

This charter is presumably to be identified with the one noted in the list of charters of Leeds priory *c.*1210 (Lambeth Palace Lib., Carte Antique et Miscellanee V no. 111); also mentioned in the Leicester archdeaconry 'matricula' of bp Hugh II (*RHW* i 261), although the pension is then given as four shillings. Hamo became dean of Lincoln between 15 September 1189 and 24 March 1190; Roger of Rolleston became archdn of Leicester *c.*1192 × September 1193 (see no. 11).

*86. Legbourne priory

Confirmation for the priory of Legbourne of the church of Saltfleetby St Peter, given to them by Robert son of Gilbert.
[21 September 1186 × 16 November 1200]

Mention of a charter produced in a dispute between Alice la Constable and the prioress of Legbourne over the advowson of Saltfleetby St Peter, 1202.

Pd, *Lincs. Assize Rolls 1202–9* no. 239.

A confirmation of archbp Hubert Walter (1193–1205) is also mentioned (*EEA* iii no. 521A), but it is not clear that bp Hugh's confirmation was issued at the same time.

*87. Leicester abbey

Confirmation for the abbey of Leicester of the church of [Church] Langton, as in the confirmation of his predecessor, bishop Robert [Chesney].
[21 September 1186 × 16 November 1200]

Mention of charter in Bodl. ms. Laud misc. 625 (Leicester abbey rental) fo. 81v (lxxxv v), being charter no. 5 in the Langton section of the second book of the lost abbey cartulary.

Pd, J. Nichols, *History of Leicestershire* i 2, app. xvii, 92.

For mention of Chesney's charter see *EEA* i no. 150. This church soon passed out of the patronage of the abbey and no institutions on their presentation are found in the Lincoln episcopal rolls and registers (A. Hamilton Thompson, *The Abbey of St Mary of the Meadows, Leicester* (Leicester 1949) 157).

*88. Leicester abbey

Confirmation for Leicester abbey of a mediety of the church of Chesham, the gift of Robert de Sifrewast, saving a suitable vicarage.
[21 September 1186 × 16 November 1200]

Mention of charter produced in a dispute between Richard de Sifrewast and the abbot of Leicester over the advowson of the mediety, 1214.

Pd, *CRR* vii 72.

For Bp Robert Chesney's charter see *EEA* i no. 144; it is stated that both episcopal charters were confirmed by archdn Stephen of Buckingham (*c.*1194 × 1202). For details of Sifrewast's gift see A. Hamilton Thompson, *op. cit.* 115.

88A. Leicester abbey

Institution of master T. to the perpetual vicarage of Hathern, on the presentation of Paul, abbot and the convent of St Mary de Pratis, Leicester, saving to the abbey an annual pension of forty shillings and a stone of wax payable by the vicar.
[1188 × 16 November 1200]

B – Bodl. ms. Laud misc. 625 (Leicester abbey rental) fo. 67r (lxir, 62r). s. xvi in.

Omnibus Christi fidelibus ad quos presens scriptum pervenerit, Hugo dei gratia Lincolniensis episcopus salutem. Ad universitatis vestre notitiam volumus pervenire nos, ad presentationem Pauli abbatis et conventus Leyc', dilectum filium nostrum magistrum T. suscepisse et in perpetuam vicariam*a* ecclesie de Hathurn, salva pencione xl solidorum et i petre cere, quas predictus T. prefato conventui tenetur solvere annuatim. Quod ut ratum habeatur et firmum, presenti scripto et sigilli nostri patrocinio duximus confirmandum.

a memoriam B.

Paul became abbot of Leicester in 1188. Hathern appears to have been one of the churches of the soke of Shepshed, given to the abbey by its founder, earl Robert of Leicester (*Mon. Angl.* vi 466, no. xvi; A. Hamilton Thompson, *op. cit.* 144). Professor Hamilton Thompson notes that the church was not in fact appropriated to the abbey and is described as a rectory in the medieval Lincoln episcopal registers (ibid. 144–6).

89. Lewes priory

Institution of master Helias to the mediety of the church of Melton [Mowbray] formerly held by master Robert de Nuers, on the presentation of the prior and monks of Lewes: saving an annual pension of thirteen silver marks payable to the prior and monks.

[21 September 1186 × 16 November 1200]

A = PRO E40/14941. Endorsed: H. Lincol' de Mautune (? s. xiii); x (ss. xiv–xv); approx. 151 × 97 + 13 mm.; seal and tag missing, slit for seal-tag (d.q.1).

Hug(o) dei gratia Lincolniensis episcopus omnibus Christi fidelibus ad quos presens scriptum pervenerit ./ salutem . in domino. Noverit universitas vestra nos ad presentationem prioris et monachorum Leuiarum recepisse magistrum Heliam ad illam medietatem ecclesie de Mealton' que fuit magistri Roberti de Nuers cum omnibus pertinentiis . et ipsum in eadem medietate canonice instituisse . sub annua pensione .xiii. marcarum argenti solvenda predicto priori et monachis Leuiar' . salva in omnibus Lincolniensis . ecclesie dignitate . et episcopalibus consuetudinibus. Ne autem quod a nobis rationabiliter gestum est temporis diuturnitate in posterum evanescat ./ id litterarum nostrarum testimonio et sigilli nostri impressione duximus roborandum. Hiis testibus . magistro Rogero de Rolvest' . magistro Roberto . de Capella . magistro Gaufrido de Lechelad' . magistro Ricardo de Swalewecl' . magistro Rogero de Sumerford' . magistro Gerardo de Hoiland' . Petro decano de Esford' . magistro Ricardo fratre eius . Symeone decano de Stapelford' . Iohanne clerico qui hoc scripsit . et multis aliis.

90. Lichfield cathedral

Confirmation for the church of Lichfield of the church of Thornton [by Horncastle], given by Robert Marmiun, and institution of Peter the clerk to the vicarage, on the presentation of the dean and canons of Lichfield. Peter shall pay an annual pension of twenty shillings to the church of Lichfield. [1192 × ? March 1195]

B = Lichfield D. & C., Magnum Registrum Album fo. 221r–v. s. xiv in.
Pd (calendar) from B in *Lichfield M.R.A.* no. 514.

Omnibus dei fidelibus ad quos presens scriptum pervenerit, Hugo dei gratia Lincolniensis episcopus salutem. Noveritis nos concessisse et presenti carta confirmasse ecclesie Lich' ecclesiam de Thorneton' quam ei contulit Robertus Marmiun et ad presentationem decani et canonicorum ecclesie de Lich' Petrum clericum ad vicariam iamdicte ecclesie de Thorneton' recepisse, ita quidem quod eam cum omnibus pertinentiis suis tenebit, solvendo pensionem xx solidorum ecclesie Lich' annuatim; [fo. 221v] salvis episcopalibus consuetudinibus et Lincolniensis ecclesie dignitate. Hiis testibus: magistro Winem(er) archidiacono Norh', Rodberto de Hardres archidiacono Huntend', magistro Rogero archidiacono Leyc', Rodberto de Capella, Ricardo de Swalecliv', Ricardo Grim, Galfrido de Licchelade, canonicis Lincolniensis ecclesie, Alexandro de Bedef' et multis aliis.

Winemer became archdn of Northampton in 1192, and Roger of Rolleston, archdn of Leicester, succeeded to the deanery of Lincoln *c*.March 1195. Robert Marmiun's grant is ibid. no. 513. For a similar charter of bp William see no. 251.

91. Lincoln cathedral

Mandate to the archdeacons, deans and other officials of the diocese of Lincoln that the dean and chapter of Lincoln have the power of exercising canonical justice against those who detain anything from the Common; and commanding them to execute the sentence of the dean and chapter. They are not to absolve excommunicates or those placed under interdict except on the authority of the bishop or chapter. [21 September 1186 × 16 November 1200]

B = Lincoln D. & C. A/1/5 (Registrum Antiquissimum) no. 911. s. xiii in. C = ibid. A/2/1 (Liber Niger) fos. 13v–14r. s. xiv in. D = ibid. A/2/3 (Martilogium of John de Schalby) fo. 3r–v. s. xiv in. The document is not witnessed.

Pd from B in *Reg. Ant.* i no. 294; from C in *LCS* i 309.

92. Lincoln cathedral

Mandate to all the archdeacons and officials of the diocese of Lincoln to cause the faithful of every household in the diocese to be moved to a more regular observance of the yearly pentecostal processions.

[21 September 1186 × 16 November 1200]

B = Lincoln D. & C. A/1/5 (Registrum Antiquissimum) no. 914. s. xiii in. C = ibid. A/2/1 (Liber Niger) fo. 13r. s. xiv in. D = ibid. A/2/3 (Martilogium of John de Schalby) fos. 2v–3r. s. xiv in. The document is not witnessed.

Pd from B in *Reg. Ant.* i no. 298; from C in *LCS* i 307–8; from D in *Gir. Camb.* vii 200–1; G. G. Perry, *The Life of St Hugh of Avalon* (1879) 352–3, app. C; R. M. Woolley, *St Hugh of Lincoln* (1927) 63–4; and in transl. *The Book of John de Schalby* 9.

For a similar mandate of bp William see no. 256. For pentecostal processions see *Eynsham Cartulary* i app. ii, 424–30; M. Brett, *The English Church under Henry I* (Oxford 1975) 162–4; *Councils and Synods* II part i 3 and n. 2.

93. Lincoln cathedral

Grant to the dean and chapter of Lincoln of licence to compel all canons who do not make residence to appoint suitable vicars to fill their place. The bishop also grants them liberty to exercise canonical justice against those persons who do injury to the Common, saving in all things the right and authority (potestas) of the bishop. Archdeacons, deans and other officials of the bishopric of Lincoln are not permitted to absolve persons excommunicated or placed under interdict by the chapter except they act on an episcopal or capitular mandate, and they are commanded to carry into effect the sentence of the chapter.

[21 September 1186 × 16 November 1200]

B = Lincoln D. & C. A/1/5 (Registrum Antiquissimum) no. 916. s. xiii in. C = ibid. A/2/1 (Liber Niger) fo. 13r–v. s. xiv in. D = ibid. A/2/3 (Martilogium of John de Schalby) fo. 3r. s. xiv in. The document is not witnessed.

Pd from B in *Reg. Ant.* i no. 300; from C in *LCS* i 308–9; from D in *Gir. Camb.* vii 201–2; G. G. Perry, *The Life of St Hugh of Avalon* (1879) 353–4, app. C; R. M. Woolley, *St Hugh of Lincoln* (1927) 61–2; (transl.) in *The Book of John de Schalby* 10.

For a similar mandate of bp William see no. 257.

94. Lincoln cathedral

Similar grant as above, except for the final section relating to archdeacons, rural deans and other diocesan officials.

[21 September 1186 × 16 November 1200]

B = Lincoln D. & C. A/1/5 (Registrum Antiquissimum) no. 917 (no witnesses). s. xiii in.

Pd from B in *Reg. Ant.* i no. 301.

95. Lincoln cathedral

Assignment to the office of the deanery of the church of Lincoln, with the common assent of the chapter, of the prebend which was formerly Roger of Derby's, substituting it for the prebend which was previously assigned to the deanery. [21 September 1186 × 16 November 1200]

> A = Lincoln D. & C. Dij/69/3/29a. Endorsed: H. de prebenda que fuit quondam Rogeri de Derby data in aumentum decanatus subtracta quadam alia prius decanatui annexa . et fuerunt ecclesie de Oskington' et de Edenestow in comitatu Notinghamie porciones prebende dicti Rogeri nunc date que sunt commune capituli Linc' nunc appropriate . (s. xiv); approx. 165 × 143 + 18 mm.; seal missing, one parchment tag (d.q.2), the other torn away.
>
> B = ibid. A/1/7 (Carte decani) no. 18. s. xiv in.
>
> Pd from A in *Reg. Ant.* iii no. 986 (facsimile opp. p. 278).

Omnibus Christi fidelibus ad quos presens scriptum pervenerit ⸎ Hug(o) dei gratia Lincolniensis episcopus ⸎ salutem in domino. Dignum est ut dignitates ecclesiastice que superiorem in ecclesia dei gradum optinent ⸎ sicut amplioris gratiam honoris . et oneris adiuncti nomen sortiuntur ⸎ ita uberioris beneficii fructum et maioris affluentie commodum ceteris impertiendum consequantur. Cum ergo dignitas decanatus precipuum in ecclesia Lincolniensi nobis commissa locum optineat . et ratione ipsius preminentie ⸎ decanum oporteat gravioris expense pre ceteris onus portare ⸎ de communi assensu capituli prebendam que fuit olim Rogerii de Dereby ⸎ decanatus officio imperpetuum deputavimus . subtracta prebenda que prius fuerat decanatui deputata ⸎ cuicumque alii assumendo in canonicum ecclesie nostre conferenda. Ut igitur hec nostra ordinatio tam sollempniter facta perpetue stabilitatis robur et firmamentum optineat ⸎ eam duximus episcopali auctoritate confirmare . et tam sigillo nostro quam capituli nostri corroborare.

> Roger of Derby was dead at least by September 1187 but possibly much earlier. This document may in fact date from about the same time as the charter relating to Orston and Edwinstowe churches (no. 101).

*96. Lincoln cathedral

Confirmation for the dean and chapter of Lincoln of Philip of Kyme's gift of the prebend of Carlton [Kyme], saving to Philip's son Simon the advowson of the prebend. [21 September 1186 × 16 November 1200]

> Mention of charter in a confirmation of king John, 17 January 1208.
>
> Pd, *Rot. Chart.* 174*b*; *Reg. Ant.* i no. 214.

> For a similar reference to a confirmation by bp Walter (1183 × 1185) see *EEA* i no. 312.

97. Lincoln cathedral

Notification to all parsons, perpetual vicars, chaplains, and clerks, that the bishop has established a new general fraternity of the church of Lincoln. [21 September 1186 × 16 November 1200, ? 1192]

> A = Lincoln D. & C. Dij/20/1/6 (damaged by staining and a hole in the document). No ancient endorsement; approx. 177 × 110/127 + 23 mm.; sealing d.q.2, seal missing.
>
> Pd from A in *Reg. Ant.* ii no. 381 (where it is wrongly attributed to bp Hugh II).

Hugo dei gratia Lincolniensis episcopus omnibus personis . vicariis perpetuis capellanis et clericis . . . [*gap of 40 mm.*] . . . constitutis ? salutem gratiam et benedictionem. Gratia vobis et pax a deo patre nostro . . . [*gap of 50 mm.* ?exhi]betis clericis nostris in negocium ecclesie nostre ad vos missis . quos cum nostri . . . [*gap of 58 mm.*]tis. Unde ad amplioris honoris cumulum vobis multiplicandum ampl [*gap of 55 mm.*] . . . quam vobis fecimus in generali fraternitate Lincolniensis ecclesie nova vobis bo [*gap of 70 mm.*] . . . addere . pro eo quod in ecclesie nostre operatione apparet ex elemosinarum vestrarum . . . [*gap of 30 mm.*] . . . quantum diligitis cum propheta decorem domus d[omini] et locum habitationis eius glorie[1] . Hanc . . . [*gap of 10 mm.*] . . . novam vobis superaddimus indulgentiam ? quod cum inter vos advenerint . . . [*gap of 7 mm.*, ? cleri]ci ecclesie nostre operationis nuntii in die predicationis eorum ubi forte aliquam ecclesiam sub interdicto conclusam . . . [*gap of 8 mm.*, ? inven]erint ? liceat eis auctoritate nostra eclesias reserare . campanas pulsare . parrochianos convocare . . . [*gap of 12 mm.*, ? necnon] . . . divina celebrare atque publice penitentes secum in ecclesias introducere. Preterea si qui casu fo[*gap of 17 mm.*, ? rtuito in]venti fuerint vel aquis submersi vel in locis campestribus defuncti quorum nomina scripta fuerunt in libro fraternitatis nostre nisi excommunicati fuerint ex nomine ? liceat predictis nuntiis fraternitatis nostre sic defunctos ad ecclesias deferre et in cimiterio sollempniter sepelire.

[1] Psalm xxv, v. 8.

Ralph Coggeshall refers to the establishment of this general fraternity of the fabric by bp Hugh and says that 1000 marks were collected each year by this means (*Chronicon Anglicanum*, ed. J. Stevenson (Rolls ser., 1875) 111). For the identification of the bp as Hugh I and further details of the fraternity, see C. R. Cheney, 'Church building in the middle ages', *BJRL* 34 (1951–2) 20–36, esp. 34, repd in *Medieval Texts and Studies* (Oxford 1973) 346–63. It is probable that this letter dates from early in the episcopate, in connection with the rebuilding work begun by the bp after the damage caused by the earthquake on Palm Sunday 1185. According to the Irish annals of Multifernan, written in the late thirteenth century, the building work began in 1192 (*Gir. Camb.* vii xln.). For indulgences for the cathedral fabric by Hugh I and William, see nos. 98, 258.

*98. Lincoln cathedral

Indulgence of eighty days for all those who shall contribute alms towards the building of the (cathedral) church of St Mary, Lincoln.
[21 September 1186 × 16 November 1200]

Mentioned only, in list of indulgences to the cathedral fabric, in *Gir. Camb.* vii 217, app. F.

99. Lincoln cathedral

Confirmation of the church of Wellingore to the common of the church of St Mary, Lincoln, saving the right of Alan of Wellingore, clerk, while he lives. This grant is for the maintenance of canons residing in the church of Lincoln.   [21 September 1186 × 16 November 1200]

B = Lincoln D. & C. A/1/5 (Registrum Antiquissimum) no. 937. s. xiii in. C = ibid. A/1/6 (Registrum) no. 349. s. xiv med. The document is not witnessed.

Pd from B in *Reg. Ant.* iii no. 999.

For bp William's confirmation see no. 261.

100. Lincoln cathedral

Confirmation to the common of the church of St Mary, Lincoln, of a mediety of the church of Glentham, granted by Gilbert of Glentham and Alfred his heir, and saving the right of Geoffrey of Glentham, clerk, while he lives.

[21 September 1186 × 16 November 1200]

A = Lincoln D. & C. Dij/73/1/19. Endorsed: A. xxv; Appropriacio ecclesie de Glentham . primo unius medietatis . et subsequenter alterius medietatis (s. xiv); scrutata (s. xiv); approx. 160 × 46 + 13 mm.; seal missing, slit for seal-tag.

B = Lincoln D. & C. A/1/5 (Registrum Antiquissimum) no. 959. s. xiii in.

Pd. from A in *Reg. Ant.* iii no. 1037.

Omnibus Christi fidelibus ad quos presens scriptum pervenerit ⸴ Hug(o) dei gratia Lincolniensis . episcopus eternam in domino salutem. Noverit universitas vestra nos ad petitionem et concessionem Gileberti de Glenham*a* et Aulfredi*b* heredis sui concessisse et presenti carta nostra confirmasse ecclesie sancte Marie Lincoln' . videlicet eiusdem ecclesie commune medietatem ecclesie de Glenham*a* cum suis pertinentiis ad sustentationem canonicorum ibidem residentium . salvo iure Gaufridi . de Glenham*a* clerici quam diu vixerit. Quod ut firmum et ratum permaneat ⸴ presenti scripto et sigilli nostri appositione confirmavimus.

a Glentham B.   *b* Alveredi B.

Gilbert's original grant of land in Glentham and a mediety of the church was dated
*c.*1190 by Canon Foster (*Reg. Ant.* iv no. 1114) but it cannot be dated so precisely
from the internal evidence. The charter was confirmed by Gilbert's son, Alfred,
presumably at the time of the original grant, since the witnesses to both documents
are identical (ibid. no. 1115). For the confirmation by bp William, see no. 262.

101.   Lincoln cathedral

*Notification that if the prebend of master Robert of Bedford, which was
Roger of Derby's, happens to be vacant before either of the churches of
Orston and Edwinstowe is void, then that prebend and its canon are
charged with the payment to the chapter for the common of the church
of Lincoln of the yearly sum by which the pension of the two churches is
short of twenty marks, until the other church falls vacant.*

[21 September 1186×*c.*1194]

A = Lincoln D. & C. Dij/69/3/22. Endorsed: A. xxvij.; Confirmatio .H. episcopi .
de Oskintun . et de Eden' (s. xii ex.–s. xiii in.); approx. 151×78+23 mm.; seal
missing, slit for seal-tag (d.q.2).

B = ibid. A/1/6 (Registrum) no. 199. s. xiv med.

Pd from A in *Reg. Ant.* iii no. 987.

Omnibus Christi fidelibus ad quos presens scriptum pervenerit ⸴
Hug(o) dei gratia Lincolniensis episcopus salutem in domino. Noverit
universitas vestra quod si prebendam magistri Roberti de Bedeford'
que fuit Rogeri de Dereby contigerit vacare . priusquam alterautra
ecclesiarum de Oskinton' et de Edenestowa vacaverit ⸴ ego onero
prebendam illam et futurum eiusdem prebende canonicum ad sol-
vendum capitulo ad communam annuatim Lincolniensis ecclesie
quicquid defuerit quantitati viginti marcarum supra pensiones ecclesiarum de Oskinton' et de Edenestowa ⸴ quousque alteram illarum
ecclesiarum vacare contigerit.

Roger of Derby was dead at the latest by September 1187 but possibly much
earlier. Robert of Bedford had vacated this prebend by *c.*1194 (*Reg. Ant.* iii no.
989; *Le Neve* 112). For the bp's appropriation of the churches of Orston and
Edwinstowe see below, nos. 106–7.

102.   Lincoln cathedral

*Confirmation, having inspected bishop Robert [Chesney's] charter
[EEA i no. 161], of his grant exempting the prebends of the church of
Lincoln from all episcopal rights and demands, so that the archdeacons
shall have no power to demand anything from the prebends or from the
churches which belong to the common of Lincoln, or to implead their
parishioners. The same liberty is granted to the church of Searby which
is assigned to the lights of the church of Lincoln, the church of Leighton
[Bromswold] belonging to the subdeanery of Lincoln, and the church of*

All Saints [in the Bail], Lincoln, belonging to the chancellorship of
Lincoln.   [15 September 1189 × September 1193]

> A = Lincoln D. & C. Dij/55/2/8 (damaged, letters in square brackets supplied
> from other texts). Endorsed: H. de prebendis . et aliis possessionibus (s. xiii);
> Confirmatio Hugonis episcopi Linc' super iurisdiccione in prebendalibus et
> ecclesiis de communa (s. xiii); Tercia exhit' (*sic*) (s. xv); Memorandum pro
> Bachyler contra Ravenser. v idus Octobris anno domini 1346 .G.T. (s. xiv
> med.); approx. 239 × 165 + 31 mm.; seal missing, parchment tag for seal (d.q.2).
>
> B = ibid. A/1/5 (Registrum Antiquissimum) no. 907. s. xiii in . C = ibid. no. 909
> (inspeximus of Hubert Walter, archbp of Canterbury, ? late 1203 × April 1204).
> D = Lincoln diocesan records, misc. roll 6 (inspeximus of Walter de Gray,
> archbp of York (1215–55)), no. 2.
>
> Pd from A in *Reg. Ant.* i no. 289 (with facsimile opp.); from D in *RRG* 515–16;
> (calendar) from C in *EEA* iii no. 533.

Omnibus Christi fidelibus ad quos scriptum pervenerit hoc .' Hugo dei
gratia Lincolniensis . episcopus . salutem in domino. Ex inspectione
autentici instrumenti bone memorie . Roberti quondam Lincolniensis
episcopi . predecessoris nostri cognovimus ipsum remisisse omnibus
prebendis Lincolniensis ecclesie in perpetuum omnia iura episcopalia
et omnes exactiones . et quod omnes canonici Lincolniensis ecclesie
.' in prebendis suis et omnibus possessionibus que ad prebendas
pertinent .' perpetuam habeant libertatem . ita quod nulli liceat
archidiacono vel archidiaconorum officialibus de prebendis vel possessionibus ad communam [pertine]ntibus aliquid exigere . vel parrochianos prebendarum Lincolniensis ecclesie in placitum ponere. Nos
igitur prefatam indulgentiam ab ipso fact[am rat]am [habe]ntes .' eam
presenti scripto et sigillo nostro duximus confirmare . Hoc adicientes
ut ecclesia de Seuerebi . que ad luminaria L[incolniensis ec]clesie est
assignata et ecclesia de Lehton' que est de subdecanatu Lincolniensi .
et ecclesia omnium sanctorum in Linc' . que pertinet ad cancellariam
Lin[colniensis] ecclesie . eadem plene gaudeant libertate. Precipimus
etiam ut in omnibus causis tractandis et decidendis quecumque in
parrochiis prebendarum emerserint .' ipsi canonici o[mnimo]da et
perpetua gaudeant libertate . et libera utantur potestate. Quod ut
ratum habeatur et firmum .' presentis scripti testimonio et sigillo
nostro roboravimus. Hiis testibus . Hamone decano Lincolniensis
ecclesie . Roberto . archidiacono . Huntedon' . magistro Rogero de
Rolveston' . Iohanne sacrista. Galfrid[o de] Lichelad' . magistro
Ricardo de Swalwecl'. Roberto de Capella . magistro Girardo de Rowell'
. Hugone . de sancto Edwardo . E[ustachio] de Wilton' . et aliis . . .

> For a similar grant of bp William of Blois see no. 252. Hamo became dean of
> Lincoln between 15 September 1189 and 24 March 1190; Roger of Rolleston
> became archdn of Leicester *c.*1192 × September 1193 (see no. 11); and Robert de
> Hardres succeeded to the archdeaconry of Huntingdon *c.*1189 × 4 April 1192.

103.   Lincoln cathedral

Confirmation of the grant of bishop Robert [Chesney] to the churches which belong to the precentorship of Lincoln of the same liberty and exemption as he had granted to the prebendal churches of the canons of the church of Lincoln [EEA i no. 162].

[15 September 1189 × September 1193]

A = Lincoln D. & C. Dij/63/1/11 (badly stained). Endorsed: Lyncon (s. xiv); pressmark; approx. 188 × 88 + 15 mm.; seal missing, parchment tag for seal (d.q.2).

Pd from A in *Reg. Ant.* i no. 305.

Omnibus [Christi] fidelibus ad quos presens scriptum pervenerit . Hugo dei gratia Lincolniensis episcopus salutem in domino . Noverit universitas vestra nos ratam [habentes et] gratam libertatem et immunitatem quam bone memorie Robertus predecessor noster quondam Lincolniensis episcopus concessit ecclesiis de cantaria Lincolniensis ecclesie . volumus itaque et precipimus . ut eedem ecclesie ea plene gaudeant libertate qua gaudent ecclesie prebendarum Lincolniensis ecclesie . sicut in scripto nostro quod ecclesiis prebendarum indulsimus ; plene continetur . salvo denario beati Petri . de quo nichil immutamus . Quod ut ratum et inconcussum permaneat . presenti scripto et sigilli nostri patrocinio confirmamus . Testibus . Haimone Lincolniensis ecclesie decano . magistro Stephano cancellario . magistro Rogero de Rolveston' magistro Ricardo de Swalewecliva . Roberto de Capella . Hugone de sancto Edwardo . Eustachio de Wilton' . et aliis multis .

The attestation of Hamo, dean of Lincoln, and Roger of Rolleston, without an archidiaconal title, provide the date for this document (see above).

104.   Lincoln cathedral

Confirmation for the common of the canons of Lincoln, at the request of master Ralph of Swaton, of Ralph's grant of the church of Scredington. The bishop also confirms master Ralph's gift to the common of the two bovates of land in Scredington which Jungwine held, with a toft and croft and all appurtenances.   [c.1192 × 22 March 1194]

B = Lincoln D. & C. A/1/5 (Registrum Antiquissimum) no. 939. s. xiii in. C = ibid. A/1/6 (Registrum) no. 363. s. xiv med.

Pd from B in *Reg. Ant.* iii no. 1002.

Hiis testibus: Haimone decano et Winemero subdecano Lincolniensis ecclesie, Roberto Huntedon' et magistro Rogero Leic' archidiaconis, magistro Simone de Siwell', Ricarde de Swalewecliva, Galfrido de

Lechelad', Reimundo, Hugone de sancto*a* Edwardo, Eustachio de
Wilton' et aliis multis.

a omitted BC.

Roger of Rolleston occurs as archdn of Leicester *c.*1192×*c.*March 1195, and
Winemer had been succeeded as subdean of Lincoln by 22 March 1194 (see no. 11;
Le Neve app. 39). For a later confirmation by bp William see no. 254.

105. Lincoln cathedral

*Ratification of a concord made in the king's court between the chapter
of Lincoln and the chapter of Warter concerning the advowson of the
church of Melton [Ross], whereby it is agreed that the advowson shall
remain to the church of Lincoln, and the whole church* in prebendam*;
and that the canon of the prebend shall pay one hundred shillings a
year to the chapter of Warter.*   [*c.*1192× ? March 1195]

A = Lincoln D. & C. Dij/83/3/21. Endorsed: Confirmatio episcopi Hugonis .
super ecclesia de Maltona (s. xiii); approx. 216×89+24 mm.; seal missing (no
tag, fold partly eaten away). Scribe **II**.

B = ibid. Dij/83/3/19(ii), in an inspeximus by Nicholas [Heigham], the dean and
the chapter of Lincoln, 29 September 1280, from the muniments of Warter
priory. C = ibid. Dij/83/3/21a(i), in an inspeximus by the Official of the Court of
York, 4 February 1285, from the muniments of Warter priory. D = Bodl. ms.
Fairfax 9 (Warter cartulary) fo. 23r (witnesses omitted). s. xiv in.

Pd from A in *Reg. Ant.* ii no. 577 (facsimile opp. p. 263); *EYC* x no. 33.

Omnibus Christi fidelibus ad quos presens scriptum pervenerit Hugo
dei gratia Lincolniensis episcopus salutem in domino. Noverit universitas vestra nos ratam habere et presenti carta confirmasse concordiam
factam in curia domini regis coram iustic(iariis) eius super ecclesia de
Mealton' inter capitulum Lincolniensis ecclesie et ˙capitulum de
Wartre . ita scilicet quod ecclesie Lincolniensi in perpetuum remanebit advocacio predicte ecclesie . et tota ecclesia in prebendam . et
canonicus eiusdem prebende et successores eius solvent capitulo de
Wartre in perpetuum singulis annis . centum solidos apud Mealton' .
de eadem ecclesia ad duos terminos . scilicet ad festum sancti Botulfi .
quinquaginta solidos . et ad festum sancti Martini quinquaginta
solidos. Quod ut ratum et firmum permaneat presenti scripto sigilli
nostri appositione communito ˙⸱ confirmavimus. Hiis testibus . H.
Lincolniensis ecclesie decano . magistro Rogero archidiacono Leirc' .
magistro Ricardo de Swaleclive . Roberto de Capella . Reimundo .
Galfrido de Deping . Hugone de sancto Edtwardo . Roberto de
Dunestapl' . Rogero Bac' . et multis aliis.

The dates are those of Roger of Rolleston as archdn of Leicester (see no. 11).

106.   Lincoln cathedral

Appropriation of the churches of Orston and Edwinstowe to the church of Lincoln to augment the Common for the maintenance of the residentiary canons.   [c.1194×? March 1195]

> A = Lincoln D. & C. Dij/69/3/23 (damaged). Endorsed: Confirmatio .H. episcopi . de Oskintun' . et Edenstowa (s. xii ex.–s. xiii in.); approx. 125×120 mm.; seal missing (bottom of charter torn away, no sign of sealing).
> B = ibid. A/1/5 (Registrum Antiquissimum) no. 928. s. xiii in. C = ibid. A/1/6 (Registrum) no. 204. s. xiv med.
> Pd from A in *Reg. Ant.* iii no. 977.

Omnibus Christi fidelibus ad quos presentes littere pervenerint . Hug(o) dei gratia [Lincolniensis] episcopus s[alutem i]n domino. Noverit universitas vestra nos considerata modicitate et raritate reddituum commune Lincolniensis ecclesie que in usus fratrum concanicorum residentium [in] ecclesia debet cedere . qui iugiter deo et beate virgin[i gloriose] dei genetrici Marie in eadem ecclesia debent deser[vire] ad ampliandam prefatam communam in sustentatio[nem] canonicorum residentium . dedisse deo et beate Mar[ie] et eiusdem loci capitulo ecclesiam de Oskinton' et eccl[esiam de] Edenestowe habendas et perpetuo po[sside]ndas et in pro[prios usus comm]une convertendas. Hiis testibus [ma]gistro Willelmo Blesensi . Lincolniensis ecclesie subdecano . magistro Winemero archidiacono Norhamt' . magistro Stephano archidiacono Bukingh' . [m]agistro Rogero archidiacono Leicestr' . magistro Ricardo de Swalecl' . Gaufrido de Lichel' . Roberto de Capella . Eustachio de Wilton'.

> Stephen became archdn of Buckingham c.1194; Roger of Rolleston became dean of Lincoln c.March 1195. King William II granted to bp Robert Bloet the churches of Orston and Edwinstowe, the latter being part of the manor of Mansfield (*Reg. Ant.* i no. 14; *Regesta* i no. 337) September 1093. The bp's grant was confirmed by archbp Geoffrey Plantagenet of York, in whose diocese the churches lay (*Reg. Ant.* iii no. 978), bp William (see below, no. 260), and later archbps of York (*Reg. Ant.* iii nos. 982, 985). The existence of two original appropriation deeds of bp Hugh (see no. 107) is puzzling, particularly as the document undergoes no essential modification. The confirmation by bp William (no. 260) follows very closely the wording of no. 107.

107.   Lincoln cathedral

Similar appropriation of the churches of Orston and Edwinstowe to the church of Lincoln to augment the Common for the maintenance of the residentiary canons.   [c.1194×? March 1195]

> A = Lincoln D. & C. Dij/69/3/21. Endorsed: Confirmatio .H. episcopi . de Oskintun . et Edenstowa (ss. xii–xiii); A, j,; A. xxviij.; approx. 160×116+20 mm.; seal missing, slit for seal tag (d.q.2).

B = ibid. A/1/5 (Registrum Antiquissimum) no. 929. s. xiii in. C = ibid. A/1/6 (Registrum) no. 203. s. xiv med.

Pd from A in *Reg. Ant.* iii no. 978.

Omnibus Christi fidelibus ad quos presens scriptum pervenerit . Hug(o) dei gratia Lincolniensis . episcopus . salutem in domino . Quanto maiori dilectione et ferventiori karitate ecclesiam Lincolniensem . nostro regimini commissam amplexamur et diligimus ./ tanto ferventius eius utilitati et commoditati intendere cupimus et desideramus . ut ad honorem dei et beate dei genitricis Marie ./ qui in ea iugiter et devote famulantur ./ dignius et devotius atque honestius possint deo servire. Volentes igitur in posterum canonicis ibidem deo servientibus ad commodiorem ipsorum sustentationem providere ./ considerata modicitate et raritate reddituum commune Lincolniensis ecclesie ./ divino intuitu et consideratione beate dei genitricis Marie in augmentum commune canonicorum residentium concessimus et assignavimus ecclesiam de Oskenton' et ecclesiam de Edenestowa habendas et cum omnibus pertinentiis suis integerrime perpetuo possidendas et in proprios usus commune convertendas. Hanc itaque concessionem nostram et assignationem ut rata sit et firma stabilisque in perpetuum ./ presentis scripti munimine et sigilli nostri appositione confirmamus. In nomine igitur domini nostri Ihesu Christi eandem concessionem et assignationem servantibus et ratam habentibus sit pax a deo honor et gloria amodo et in seculorum secula. Amen.

The date is probably about the same as the preceding actum. See also bp William's appropriation (no. 260).

*108.   Lincoln cathedral

Confirmation of an ordinance made in chapter by dean R(oger) and the chapter of Lincoln, the bishop being present, which established a new division of the psalter among the bishop, dean and canons.

[? March 1195 × 16 November 1200]

Mention of the bp's confirmation of the ordinance at the time it was made in his presence in chapter at Lincoln: 'provisum est ab R. decano adiunctis ei discretis viris de capitulo et institutum in capitulo presente domino Hugone Lincolniensi episcopo et confirmante ut psalmi hoc ordine dicantur ab episcopo et decano atque canonicis' (there then follows the list of the psalms to be said by the canons, arranged by dignity and prebend). LAO A/2/1 (Liber niger) fos. 11r–12v. s. xiv in. Pd, *LCS* i 300–7. The ordinance is headed 'Antiqua constitucio pro psalterio et pro missa singulis diebus dicendis'.

Roger of Rolleston became dean of Lincoln *c*. March 1195. Bradshaw (followed by Edwards) ascribes this confirmation to Hugh I, noting that the psalms would have had to be re-assigned because of the re-building of the cathedral choir *temp.* Hugh I (*LCS* i 79–80; K. Edwards, *The English Secular Cathedrals in the middle ages*

(Manchester, 2nd edn, 1967) 107 and n., 112). It is probable that this ascription is correct, although in fact there is nothing which militates against Hugh II being the bp involved, at some date before dean Roger's death on 28 January 1223.

*109. Lincoln, St Katharine's priory

Confirmation of a composition between the bishop and the chapter of Lincoln on the one hand, and R(oger) the master of the order of Sempringham and the canons of the hospital of (St Katharine's outside) Lincoln on the other, whereby the canons were placed in corporal possession of the churches of Marton and Newton[-on-Trent], to hold in proprios usus. *The master of the order and the prior and convent of the hospital have renounced their claim to the church of Norton [Disney], the gift of bishop Robert Chesney and the chapter of Lincoln [EEA i no. 163].*   [21 September 1186 × 16 November 1200]

Mention of lost charter in a confirmation of bp Hugh II, 1214.

Pd, *Lib. Ant.* 72.

110. Lincoln, St Katharine's priory

Confirmation, with the consent of Hamo the dean and the chapter of Lincoln, for the canons of the hospital of (St Katharine's outside) Lincoln of the prebend of Canwick, which bishop Robert [Chesney] granted to them [EEA i no. 163]. The canons of the hospital have promised to maintain a clerk, who shall be a priest or deacon or subdeacon, to serve in the (cathedral) church of Lincoln. R(oger), master of the order of Sempringham has granted the full fraternity of his order to all the canons of Lincoln, so that there may be done for them, whether living or dead, in the hospital or in the other houses of the order, as the canons of the order are accustomed to do for their own members.   [c.1189 × 22 March 1194]

B = Lincoln D. & C. A/1/8 (Liber de ordinationibus cantariarum) no. 126r. s. xiv.
      C = Bodl. ms. Gough Lincoln 1, pp. 352–3. s. xviii.

Pd from B in *Reg. Ant.* ii no. 348.

Hiis testibus: Hamone decano Lincolniensi, Winemero subdecano.

Hamo became dean c.1189/90 and Winemer had been succeeded as subdean by 22 March 1194.

*111. See of Lincoln

Letters commanding the archdeacons and rural deans in the areas where the bishop has property to assemble the priests of the neighbourhood as soon as the king's escheators come into the district and to

excommunicate all those who order the seizure and occupation of his
church's possessions and those who obey them. [? 1198]

> Mention of letters in the *Magna Vita* ii 116, in connection with Richard I's demand
> for the services of twelve canons of Lincoln for secular purposes (ibid. 110–16).
> This demand was probably made shortly after the Oxford Council of December
> 1197 when, according to Adam of Eynsham, Hugh and bp Herbert of Salisbury
> opposed the king's earlier demand for military service.

*112. London, Haliwell priory

Confirmation to the nuns of Haliwell, Shoreditch, London, of an
annual pension of five marks from the church of Welwyn.
[21 September 1186 × 16 November 1200]

> Mention of confirmation in the second institution roll of bp Hugh II, 1218–9.
> Pd, *RHW* i 136.

> For details of the advowson and the pension granted by the Valognes family see
> *VCH Herts* iii 170. For a similar confirmation by bp William see no. 263.

113. Louth Park abbey

Grant to the monks of Louth Park freeing them from pedage and other
customary tolls throughout the episcopal manors.
[21 September 1186 × 16 November 1200]

> B = LAO Ep. Reg. I (register of bp Sutton, among entries for 1296) fo. 148r (no
> witnesses).
> Pd from B in *Reg. Sutton* v 179.

> The rubric states *Concessio sancti Hugonis* ... and the form of the document
> suggests that the identification is correct.

114. Luffield priory

Confirmation for the monks of Luffield of the churches of Dodford,
Thornborough and a mediety of the church of Beachampton, given to
them by Ralph de Kaynes, Hamo son of Meinfelin and Richard son of
Nigel respectively. [21 September 1186 × September 1193]

> A = Westminster Abbey Mun. 3057. Endorsed: Confirmacio sancti Hugonis
> Lincoln' episcopi (s. xiii); Confirmacio ecclesie . de Torneberg et de Dodeford
> (s. xiii); I. de F. (?ss. xiv–xv); viii; approx. 152 × 137 + 15 mm.; fragment of seal
> in seal-bag (nothing visible), on parchment tag (d.q.2). Scribe I.
> B = Westminster Abbey Mun. bk. 10 (Luffield cartulary) fo. 24r. s. xv ex.
> Pd from A in *Luffield Priory Charters* i no. 32; from B in *Mon. Angl.* iv 349, no. viii;
> *PL* cliii col. 1122, no. vi.

Omnibus Christi fidelibus ad quos presens scriptum pervenerit ∴
Hugo dei gratia Lincolniensis episcopus eternam in domino salutem.

H

Ut ea que locis religiosis dei intuitu a fidelibus collata sunt . absque perturbatione possideantur ⸴ priorum sollicite procuravit prudentia . ipsa eis scriptis autenticis confirmando. Quorum nos vestigia sectantes . dilectis filiis nostris in Christo monachis de Luffeld' beneficia que eis fidelium contulit devotio . sicut ipsis et domui eorum rationabiliter collata sunt ⸴ confirmare et in presenti scripto annotare dignum duximus. Ex dono Radulfi de Caignes ecclesiam sancte Marie de Dudeford' . ex dono Hamonis filii Meinphlin' ⸴ ecclesiam de Torneberg' . ex dono Ricardi filii Nigelli ⸴ medietatem ecclesie sancte Marie de Bechhamton'. Hec omnia beneficia cum omnibus ad ea pertinentibus sicut in cartis donatorum atque archidiaconorum a quibus in ipsis iam dicti monachi sunt instituti ⸴ continentur ⸴ eis concedimus in perpetuum possidenda presenti que scripto atque sigilli nostri patrocinio confirmamus . salvis episcopalibus consuetudinibus et Lincolniensis ecclesie dignitate. Hiis testibus . Roberto abbate Nutel' . magistro Rogero de Rolveston' . magistro Ricardo de Swalewecl' . Galfrido de Lecchelad' . Roberto de Capella   Iohanne decano de Preston' . Eustachio de Wilton' . et aliis multis.

Roger of Rolleston attests without a title; he became archdn of Leicester c. 1192 × September 1193 (see no. 11). Ralph de Kaynes's charter confirming Dodford church to the priory (given by Hugh and Richard de Kaynes) is in *Luffield Priory Charters* ii no. 292; Hamo son of Meinfelin's grant of Thornborough is ibid. no. 546; Richard son of Nigel's gift of a mediety of Beachampton is ibid. no. 730.

115. Luffield priory

Confirmation for the church of St Mary, Luffield of the church of Thornborough in proprios usus, after Thomas the priest shall vacate it, saving a suitable vicarage.   [21 September 1186 × September 1193]

A = Westminster Abbey Mun. 2855. Endorsed: Confirmacio sancti Hugonis Lincoln' episcopi (s. xiii); Confirmacio . ecclesie de Torneberge (s. xiii); de sancto Hugone *added* (s. xiii); I. de F. (? ss. xiv–xv); approx. 154 × 119 + 17 mm.; good specimen of seal, brownish-white wax, on parchment tag (d.q.2), no counterseal.

B = Westminster Abbey Mun. bk. 10 (Luffield cartulary) fo. 25r. s. xv ex.

Pd from A in *Luffield Priory Charters* i no. 37, with a section repeated due to an error in typesetting; *English Bishops' Chanceries* 79, where the cursus is indicated.

Omnibus Christi fidelibus ad quos presens scriptum pervenerit ⸴ Hugo dei gratia Lincolniensis episcopus salutem in domino. Ad universitatis vestre noticiam volumus pervenire . nos divine pietatis intuitu concessisse ecclesie beate Marie de Luffeld et monachis ibidem deo famulantibus ⸴ ecclesiam de Thorneberg' . possidendam perpetuo in proprios usus cum omnibus pertinentiis suis . ex quo eam a Thoma presbitero vacare contigerit . salva in eadem ecclesia competenti vicaria . ei qui in ipsa ministrabit assignanda . salvis etiam episcopalibus consuetudinibus et Lincolniensis ecclesie dignitate. Quod ne alicuius astutia vel machinatione possit in irritum revocari ? presenti illud scripto et sigilli nostri patrocinio confirmamus. Hiis testibus . magistro Rogero de Rolveston' . magistro Simone de Siwell' . magistro Ricardo de Swalewecliva . magistro Radulfo de Ford' . magistro Rogero de Sumerford' . Roberto de Capella . Angod' . et Reimundo . clericis . magistro Ricardo de Doddeford' . Eustachio de Wilton' . et aliis multis .,

Roger of Rolleston, described here without a title, became archdn of Leicester c.1192 × September 1193 (see no. 11).

116. Malton priory

Confirmation for the canons of Malton of the church of [King's] Walden, given to them by Walter de Neville and Alban Hayrun.
[21 September 1186 × 16 November 1200]

B = BL ms. Cotton Claud. D xi (Malton cartulary) fo. 226r (222r). s. xiii med. (witnesses omitted). C = ibid. fo. 53r (51r). s. xiii ex.–s. xiv in. (witnesses omitted).
Pd from B in *Mon. Angl.* vi(2) 972, no. xiii.

In the pd version 'Albani' is reproduced as 'Alani'. For a similar confirmation of bp Robert Chesney, 1154 × 1166, see *EEA* i no. 168. The charters of Walter de Neville and Alban Hayrun are on fo. 226r of B.

117. Malton priory

Confirmation for Malton priory of the churches of Ancaster, the gift of William de Vesci, and of Winterton, the gift of John the constable of Chester.
[c.1189 × 22 March 1194]

B = Lincoln D. & C. Dij/64/2/1 (in an inspeximus of Roger the dean and the chapter of Lincoln c.1195 × 1200). C = BL ms. Cotton Claud. D xi (Malton cartulary) fo. 42v (40v) (witnesses omitted). s. xiii med.
Pd from B in *Reg. Ant.* ii no. 338(xi).

Hiis testibus: Hamone decano Lincolniensis ecclesie, magistro Stephano cancellario Lincolniensi, Roberto archidiacono Huntedon', magistro Vacario, magistro Ricardo de Sualeclif, Theobaldo de Bos', Roberto de Capella, Reimundo, Hugone de sancto Edwardo, Eustachio de Wiltun'.

Hamo became dean of Lincoln c.1189/90 and Stephen de Swafeld had been succeeded as chancellor by 22 March 1194. William de Vesci's charter, made with the assent of bp Robert (II) of Lincoln, is on fo. 36v of the cartulary; John the constable of Chester's charter is on fo. 209r, and a confirmation by Roger de Almaria, precentor of Lincoln and archdn (of the Westriding or Stow) is on fo. 42v.

118. Merton priory

Confirmation for the prior and canons of Merton of the church of Kimpton in the archdeaconry of Huntingdon in usus proprios, *saving a perpetual vicarage. The endowments of the vicarage are described.*

[? March 1195 × 16 November 1200]

B = BL ms. Cotton Clcop. C vii (Merton cartulary) fos. 202v–203r (199v–200r, 219v–220r). s. xiii.

Omnibus Christi fidelibus ad quos presens scriptum pervenerit, Hugo dei permissione Lincolniensis episcopus salutem in domino sempiternam. Ea que viris religiosis et eorum domibus caritatis intuitu ad ipsorum fuerint utilitatem atque proventum decet episcopali auctoritate roborari. Hinc est quod ad universitatis vestre notitiam volumus pervenire nos, dei et pietatis intuitu, concessisse dilectis in Christo filiis nostris priori et canonicis de Merton' ecclesiam de Kymmiton' que est in archidiaconatu Huntend' cum omnibus ad eam pertinentibus in usus proprios inperpetuum convertendam*a*, salva perpetua vicaria ei qui in ipsa ministrabit a prefatis canonicis ad eam presentandis, ad quam videlicet vicariam hec sunt assignata: omnes oblationes altaris, omnia legata, tota*b* terra ecclesie, omnes minute decime, insuper etiam omnes decime de Bigesworde, tam de dominico ipsius ville de Bigesworde ubi ecclesia de Kymmiton' habet tertiam garbam quam de terris hominum ipsius ville [fo. 203r] preterquam de terra quam domina Benedicta et tenentes eius tenent de monachis sancti Albani de quibus terris predicta ecclesia habet plenarie omnes decimas. Preterea idem vicarius habebit omnes decimas que ad predictam ecclesiam pertinent · de exartis Hugonis Bardulf apud eandem villam de Bigesworde*c*; domos quoque ad inhabitandum habebit ubi bone memorie Ricardus presbiter habitare solebat et pomerium et ortum cum illa parte curie ex parte australi usque ad altos*d* fraxinos super vetus fossatum; canonici vero aliam partem curie versus aquilonem habebunt ad colligendum et servandum et tractandum bladum suum. Volumus igitur hec omnia debitam stabilitatem optinere tam de ipsis canonicis quam perpetuo vicario profutura ipsaque presenti scripto et sigilli nostri patrocinio confirmamus; salvis episcopalibus consuetudinibus de quibus omnibus vicarius respondebit; salva Lincolniensis ecclesie dignitate. Hiis testibus: Roberto*e* Huntind', Reimundo Leirc' etc.

a convertendandam B.   *b* tat *written here, then crossed out* B.   *c* Bibesworde B.   *d* altas B.
e Radulfo B.

Raymond succeeded Roger of Rolleston as archdn of Leicester; the latter became dean of Lincoln *c*.March 1195.

119. Merton priory

*Confirmation for the canons of Merton of the church of Flore and two
thirds of the garb tithes* in proprios usus, *with detailed provisions for
the portion of the perpetual vicar.*

[21 September 1186 × 16 November 1200]

B = BL ms. Cotton Cleop. C vii (Merton cartulary) fo. 203r–v (200r–v, 220r–v)
(in an inspeximus of archbp Hubert Walter of Canterbury, November 1193 ×
April 1195 *or* February 1198 × November 1200, pd *EEA* iii no. 544, not including
this actum). s. xiii.

Pd (calendar) from B in *Records of Merton Priory* 55.

Omnibus Christi fidelibus ad quos [fo. 203v] presens scriptum pervenerit, Hugo dei gratia Lincolniensis episcopus salutem in domino.
Ad universitatis vestre notitiam volumus pervenire nos divino intuitu
concessisse et*ᵃ* presenti carta confirmasse dilectis in Christo filiis
canonicis de Merton' ecclesiam de Flora cum omnibus pertinentiis
suis, ita quidem ut prefati canonici duas garbas decimarum ecclesie de
Flora in proprios usus inperpetuum possideant. Perpetuus vero
vicarius qui per presentationem eorum in eadem ecclesia ministrabit
tertiam garbam percipiet cum omnibus obventionibus altaris et
habebit totam terram ecclesie excepta principali domo ad ecclesiam
pertinente cum crofta adiacente, que eisdem canonicis remanebit.
Quod ut ratum et inconcussum permaneat, presenti scripto et sigilli
nostri appositione duximus roborare, salva Lincolniensis ecclesie
dignitate et episcopalibus consuetudinibus de quibus vicarius respondebit et predicte ecclesie in obsequio honeste providebit.

ᵃ ad B.

120. Missenden abbey

*Confirmation for the church and canons of St Mary, Missenden,
having inspected the charters of the donors, of the churches of
Missenden, the gift of William of Missenden, founder of the abbey;
Kimble, the gift of Giffard Palefridus; Caversfield, the gift of Roger
Gargat; Shiplake, the gift of Walter Giffard, earl of Buckingham; and
sixty shillings from the church of Taplow, the gift of William de
Turville.*   [21 September 1186 × September 1193]

B = BL ms. Harl. 3688 (Missenden cartulary) fo. 190r (c iiii xviii r), no. iiii. s. xiv
in. C = ibid. fo. 190r–v (in an inspeximus of bp Oliver Sutton, 4 March 1288).
D = ibid. fo. 191r (another copy of the same inspeximus).

Pd from B in *Missenden Cartulary* i no. 22.

Testibus: magistro Roberto precentore Lincolniensis ecclesie, magistro Rogero de Rotholveston', magistro Willelmo Wacelin, Roberto
Bardulf, magistro Gaufrido de sancto Edwardo, Gaufrido notario.

This charter contains one of three known references to Robert of Bedford as precentor of Lincoln; according to Adam of Eynsham, he died young (*Magna Vita* i 113). Roger of Rolleston is not described as archdn of Leicester, to which office he succeeded *c*.1192 × September 1193 (see no. 11). The inspected charters are ibid. i no. 30 (William of Missenden); no. 245 (Taplow and Lee settlement); ii no. 433 (Giffard Palefridus); iii no. 623 (Roger Gargat); no. 667 (earl Walter of Buckingham).

121. Missenden abbey

Confirmation for the church and canons of St Mary, Missenden, having inspected the charters of the donors, of the churches mentioned in the preceding confirmation [no. 120], with the addition of the church of Chalfont [St Peter], the gift of Richard de Turville, and the chapel of Lee, the gift of William de Turville, on payment of an annual pension of six shillings to the mother church of Weston [Turville].

[21 September 1186 × September 1193]

B = BL ms. Harl. 3688 (Missenden cartulary) fo. 190r (c iiii xviii), no. v. s. xiv in.
C = ibid. fo. 189v, no. iii (in an inspeximus of bp John Dalderby, 1 March 1302). D = Bodl. ms. Willis 5 (copies of a lost Missenden cartulary) fos. 32r, 33r (includes only first witness). s. xviii in.

Pd from B (abridged) in *Missenden Cartulary* i no. 23; from C in ibid. no. 21.

Testibus: magistro Rogero de Rothulveston',*a* magistro Willelmo Wacelin,*b* Roberto Bardulf,*c* magistro Gaufrido de sancto Edwardo, Gaufrido notario.

a Rothelveston' C.   *b* Wacelyn C.   *c* Bardolf C.

From the witness-list, this actum is identical with the preceding Missenden confirmation, apart from the omission of Robert of Bedford, precentor of Lincoln, and must date from the same period. The grant of the advowson of Chalfont was charter no. xviii in the missing Chalfont section of the cartulary (ibid. ii app. A, 175); the chapel of Lee features in the Taplow settlement referred to in no. 120.

122. Missenden abbey

Confirmation of the agreement made between the abbot of Doudeauville and the abbot of Missenden over the church of Glatton. The abbot of Doudeauville grants the church to the church of St Mary, Missenden, in perpetuity, subject to an annual pension of six marks payable at Doudeauville within fifteen days after the feast of St John the Baptist.   [*c*. late 1196 × 1197]

B = BL ms. Harl. 3688 (Missenden cartulary) fo. 163v (clxx r). s. xiv in.

Pd from B in *Missenden Cartulary* iii no. 827.

Testibus: Rogero Lincolniensi decano, Roberto archdiacono de Huntindon', Reymundo archidiacono Leycestr', magistro Alexandro de

Halnestowe, Hugone de sancto Edwardo, Rogero Bacun, Ingelramo capellano Lincolniensis decani.

The agreement is ibid. no. 820, and the confirmation of the church to Missenden by abbot Peter of Doudeauville is ibid. no. 821. The latter charter must date after 21 April 1196 since among the witnesses is archdn Alard of London. Alard of Burnham became archdn between 21 April and 30 December 1196. Abbot Peter of Doudeaville is said to have become abbot of St John, Valenciennes in 1197 (*Gallia Christiana* x 1611, cf. ibid. iii 158, 444). Hugh's confirmation must date from about this time. Certainly he attests abbot Peter's charter.

123.   Newhouse abbey

Confirmation for the church and canons of St Martial, Newhouse, in proprios usus *of the churches of St Peter, [East] Halton, St Margaret, Habrough, St Denis, Killingholme, St Botulph, Saxilby, St Michael, Glentworth, Kirmington, and the sixth part of the church of Brocklesby, saving suitable vicarages.*   [*c.*1192×? March 1195]

A = BL Harl. Ch. 43 H 38b. No endorsement; approx. 164×148+17 mm.; excellent specimen of seal, green wax, on parchment tag (d.q.2), no counterseal. Scribe **I**.

Pd from A in *Danelaw Charters* no. 241.

Omnibus Christi fidelibus ad quos presens scriptum pervenerit ·' Hug(o) dei gratia Lincolniensis episcopus salutem in domino. Noverit universitas vestra nos dei intuitu concessisse deo et ecclesie sancti Marcialis de Newehus et canonicis deo ibidem famulantibus . ecclesiam sancti Petri de Hauton' . ecclesiam sancte Margarete de Haburg' . ecclesiam sancti Dionisii de Kilvingeholm' . ecclesiam sancti Botulfi de Saxelbi . ecclesiam sancti Michaelis de Glentewrd' . ecclesiam de Kirninton' . et sextam partem ecclesie de Broclosbi . cum omnibus ad ipsas pertinentibus sicut eis rationabiliter collate sunt ·' in proprios eorundem canonicorum usus inperpetuum possidendas . salvis in ipsis competentibus vicariis . eis qui in ipsis ecclesiis in propriis personis per prefatos canonicos ministrabunt . salvis etiam episcopalibus consuetudinibus et Lincolniensis ecclesie dignitate. Quod ut ratum et inconcussum permaneat ·' presenti scripto et sigilli nostri patrocinio confirmavimus. Hiis testibus . Haimone decano Lincolniensis ecclesie . Roberto Huntedon' et magistro Rogero Leicestr' archidiaconis . Radulfo de Viren' . magistro Ricardo de Swalewecl' . Galfrido de Lecchelad' . Reimundo . Roberto de Capella . Hugone de sancto Edwardo . Luca clerico archidiaconi Hunted' . Eustachio de Wilton' . et aliis multis.

The dates are those of Roger of Rolleston as archdn of Leicester (see no. 11).

124. Newhouse abbey

Confirmation for Newhouse abbey in proprios usus *of the churches of St Peter, [East] Halton, St Denis, Killingholme, St Margaret, Habrough, St Helen, Kirmington, St Michael, Glentworth, St Botulph, Saxilby and a mediety of the church of All Saints, Brocklesby and the third part of the other mediety of the same church.*

[*c*.March 1195 × 1198, ? 1195]

A = BL Harl. Ch. 43 H 23. Endorsed: Confirmacio ecclesiarum per dominum Hugonem episcopum Lincoln' (s. xiv); note of enrolment; approx. 170 × 129 + 20 mm.; fragment of seal, red wax, on parchment tag (d.q.1), no counterseal.

B = BL Harl. Ch. 44 F 27 (in an inspeximus of William [Lexington], the dean and the chapter of Lincoln, 20 June 1263).

Pd from A in *Danelaw Charters* no. 242.

Omnibus . Christi fidelibus ad quos presens scriptum pervenerit . Hug(o) dei gratia Lincolniensis episcopus salutem et dei benedictionem. Noverit universitas vestra nos dei et pietatis intuitu considerata paupertate fratrum de Nehus concessisse et presenti carta confirmasse deo et ecclesie sancti Marcialis de Nehus atque fratribus ibidem deo servientibus ecclesiam sancti Petri de Halt' . ecclesiam sancti Dionisii de Kilwingholm . ecclesiam sancte Margarete de Haburc . ecclesiam sancte Helene de Kinigt' . et medietatem ecclesie omnium sanctorum de Broclausbi . et terciam partem alterius medietatis eiusdem ecclesie . ecclesiam sancti Michaelis de Glenworhe . ecclesiam sancti Botulfi de Saxolebi cum omnibus pertinenciis suis ita videlicet ut eas habeant et convertant in proprios suos usus salvis episcopalibus consuetudinibus et Lincolniensis ecclesie dignitate. Quod ut inposterum ratum et inconwlsum permaneat presenti scripto et sigilli nostri patrocinio roboravimus. Hiis testibus . R. decano Lincolniensis ecclesie . Roberto archidiacono Huntedon' . Radulfo de Viren' . magistro Ricardo de Swaleclive . magistro Gerardo de Rodhewel' . Raimundo . Roberto de Capella . Hugone de sancto Edwardo . Luca clerico archidiaconi Huntedon' . Eustachio de Wilton' . et aliis multis.

Roger of Rolleston became dean *c*.March 1195 and Raymond who succeeded him as archdn of Leicester first occurs *c*.1198, although he probably came into office in 1195 (*Le Neve* app. 42).

125. Newnham priory

Appropriation to the canons of Newnham, at the presentation of Simon de Beauchamp [Bellocampo], advocatus, *of two parts of the church of Southill. The canons shall pay two marks a year to the vicar who shall serve the church.* [1197 × 19 September 1200]

B = BL ms. Harl. 3656 (Newnham cartulary) fo. 55v. s. xv in.

Pd from B in *Newnham Cartulary* no. 89.

Hiis testibus: R. Lincolniensis ecclesie subdecano, magistro Alexandro Bed' et aliis.

For Simon de Beauchamp's charter see ibid. no. 14. The advowson of the church had been disputed in the court of king Richard I. Richard of Kent became subdean in 1197 and had succeeded as archdn of Northampton by 19 September 1200.

126. Newnham priory

Confirmation for the church and canons of St Paul, Newnham, of the church of Hatley, belonging to the prebends of St Paul, Bedford. Master Alan de Tawell, the perpetual vicar of Hatley, and his successors shall pay an annual pension of four marks to the canons of Newnham. [1197 × 19 September 1200]

B = BL ms. Harl. 3656 (Newnham cartulary) fo. 58v. s. xv in.

Pd from B in *Newnham Cartulary* no. 100.

Hiis testibus: Ricardo subdecano Lincolniensis ecclesie, magistris Alexandro de Bed' et Girardo de Rowelle et multis aliis.

For Simon de Beauchamp's confirmation of this church see ibid. no. 5. For the date of the episcopal confirmation see above.

127. Newport Pagnell priory

General confirmation of churches for the priory of St Mary, Newport [Pagnell]. [21 September 1186 × 16 November 1200]

B = BN ms. lat. 12880 (collection of transcripts concerning Marmoutier made by Dom Edmond Martène) fo. 271v, no. 318. s. xvii.

Pd (calendar) from B in *CDF* no. 1232.

Omnibus Christi fidelibus ad quos praesens scriptum pervenerit, Hugo dei gratia Lincolniensis episcopus salutem in domino. Quoniam ea quae locis religiosis conferuntur beneficia dignum est episcopalis auctoritatis robore communiri, ne malignantium pravitate possint inposterum retractari aut per temporis revolutionem oblivione sepeliri, ad universitatis vestrae notitiam volumus pervenire nos rata habere et praesenti carta confirmare deo et ecclesiae beati Mariae de Neuport beneficia ecclesiastica sicut praefatae ecclesiae et monachis ibidem deo servientibus sunt rationabiliter collata, quae pro propriis nominibus duximus annotanda, videlicet: ipsam ecclesiam de Neuport cum pertinentiis suis, ecclesiam de Tiningonam cum pertinentiis suis, ecclesiam de Srinton cum pertinentiis suis, ecclesiam de Chicheeleia cum pertinentiis suis, capellam de Estwerde cum pertinentiis suis, capellam de Linford cum pertinentiis suis, ecclesiam de Wilingis cum pertinentiis suis, capellam de Bradewelle cum pertinentiis suis, medietatem capellae de Parva Crawleia cum pertinentiis suis, quartam partem ecclesiae ˙de Magna Crawleia, medietatem ecclesiae de Brocton' cum pertinentiis suis. Ut ergo hac nostra confirmatio rata sit inperpetuum praesentis scripti firmamentum et sigilli nostri duximus apponere testimonium; salvis episcopalibus consuetudinibus et Lincolniensis ecclesiae dignitate.

'Tiningonam' may possibly be identified with Tyringham, a church confirmed to the priory by Gervase Paynel (*Mon. Angl.* v 203–4, no. ii). For an earlier confirmation of possessions by bp Robert Chesney see *EEA* i no. 183.

*128. Newport Pagnell priory

Appropriation to the priory of Newport Pagnell of the church of Sherington, to take effect when Gervase the clerk shall vacate the church, saving a suitable vicarage.

[21 September 1186 × 16 November 1200]

Mention of charter produced in a dispute between John de Carn' and the prior of Newport over the advowson of the church, 1229.

Pd, *CRR* xiii no. 2228.

For Gervase (de Carun), the rector of this church, see A. C. Chibnall, *Sherington: fiefs and fields of a Buckinghamshire village* (Cambridge 1965) 2, 29–30, 33, 47–50.

*129. Nocton priory

Grant to the church and canons of St Mary, Nocton Park, at the petition of Thomas de Aresci, of the churches of Nocton and Dunston, saving suitable provision for vicars to serve the churches.

[21 September 1186 × 16 November 1200]

Mention of charter produced in a dispute between the prior of Nocton and the abbot of St Mary's, York over the advowsons of the churches, 1204.

Pd, *CRR* iii 111–12; *Abbreviatio placitorum* 94.

130. Northampton, St Andrew's priory

General confirmation ˙of possessions for the monks of St Andrew, Northampton: namely, the churches of All Saints, Northampton; St Giles, (Northampton); St Michael, (Northampton); Holy Sepulchre, (Northampton); St Mary, (Northampton); St Gregory, (Northampton); St Peter, (Northampton), with (the church of) Kingsthorpe and the chapel of Upton; St Edmund, (Northampton); St Bartholomew,

(Northampton); the chapel of St Thomas, (Northampton); Ryhall; Exton; Newton (in Aveland); Moulton; Brafield (on the Green); Preston (Deanery); (Little) Billing; (Little) Houghton; Quinton; Hardingstone; Stuchbury; Sulgrave; two thirds of the demesne tithe of earl David in Yardley (Hastings), (Earls) Barton, (Great) Dodding-ton and Harringworth; the third part of the demesne tithe of earl David in Fotheringhay; the third part of the demesne tithe of (? Cold) Overton; two thirds of the demesne tithe of Stukeley; twenty shillings from the mills of Paxton for the purchase of wine for mass; three pack-loads (summe) *of corn from the barn of earl David in (Earls) Barton for offerings; two thirds of all the demesne tithe in Wollaston; two thirds of the demesne tithe of Walter son of Winemer in Kingsthorpe; and two thirds of the demesne tithe of the same Walter in Wootton; two thirds of the demesne tithe of Achard de Sproxton in Sproxton (? Spratton), 'Wythyn' and Stretton; two thirds of all tithe of the demesne that was Roger son of Aza's in Isham; two thirds of all the demesne tithe of Henry of Cogenhoe in Harrowden; two thirds of all the demesne tithe of William son of Burchard in Flore; two thirds of all the demesne tithe of Henry de Armenters in Stowe (Nine Churches) and in Kislingbury, which they hold to farm of the monks of St-Prix* (Sanctus Preiectus de Vermendes); *two thirds of the demesne tithe of Walter Luvel in Kislingbury; the church of Potton with all appurtenances and in the same village two virgates of land and twenty acres of heath* (brueria); *two thirds of the demesne tithe of Richard of Heyford in Harlestone; two thirds of all the demesne tithe of Andrew of Braybrooke in Braybrooke; the third part of all the demesne tithe of Richard Foxle in Foxley; and two thirds of all the demesne tithe of (Hanging) Houghton, by Lamport, which they have by the gift of Godfrey de Boloigne.*

[21 September 1186 × 4 April 1192]

B = BL ms. Royal 11 B ix (cartulary of St Andrew's, Northampton) fos. 24v–25r. s. xiii ex. C = BL ms. Cotton Vesp. E xvii (cartulary of St Andrew's, Northampton) fos. 289v–290r (272v–273r). s. xv med.

Pd from C in *Mon. Angl.* v 191, no. viii; *PL* cliii cols. 1120–2, no. iv.

Testibus hiis: Roberto abbate*[a]* de Nuttelega, Walkelino abbate de sancto Iacobo, Walkelino priore de Landa, magistro Roberto de Hard', magistro Rogero de Rolveston', magistro Simone de Siwell',*[b]* magistro Willelmo de Monte, magistro Ricardo de Dodeford',*[c]* Henrico filio Petri, magistro Warino de Bedeford,*[d]* Simone decano de Witlingb',*[e]* Rogero decano de Pateshill',*[f]* magistro Samsone*[g]* de Berehebr',*[h]* magistro Robert de Melhun,*[i]* magistro Roberto Grosseteste.

[a] *word omitted* C.   *[b]* Sywell' C.   *[c]* Dodeforde C.   *[d]* Bedforde C.   *[e]* Witlyngbere C.
[f] Pateshyll' C.   *[g]* Sampsone C.   *[h]* Bereheby C.   *[i]* Melehun C.

Neither Robert de Hardres nor Roger of Rolleston witnesses this confirmation with an ecclesiastical title. Robert first occurs as archdn of Huntingdon on 4 April 1192; Roger of Rolleston became archdn of Leicester c.1192×September 1193. Cf. *Le Neve* app. 36, where this document is cited, and see above no. 11. This charter contains the earliest known attestation of Robert Grosseteste later bp of Lincoln, or another of the same name (*Robert Grosseteste: scholar and bishop*, ed. D. Callus (Oxford 1955, repd 1969) 3–4, where this document is dated 1186×1189/90). See also Royal Commission on Historical Monuments, *County of Northampton* v (1985) 57–67 and inventory (21–9), based on work by M. Franklin and D. A. H. Richmond, for St Andrew's priory and its churches.

131. Northampton, St Andrew's priory

Confirmation for the monks of St Andrew, Northampton, of the church of Potton with all appurtenances, as is contained in the charters of the advocati, *king David of Scotland and earl Simon of Northampton.*

[c.1187×24 March 1190]

B = BL ms. Royal 11 B ix (cartulary of St Andrew's, Northampton) fo. 27v. s. xiii ex. C = BL ms. Cotton Vesp. E xvii (cartulary of St Andrew's, Northampton) fo. 291v (274v). s. xv med.

Omnibus Christi fidelibus ad quos presens scriptum pervenerit, Hugo dei gratia Lincolniensis episcopus salutem in domino. Nostrum est iustis petitionibus adquiescere et quicquid possumus auxilii filiis sancte ecclesie impertiri. Unde et fratribus nostris monachis ecclesie sancti Andree de Norh't*a* episcopali auctoritate*b* qua fungimur confirmamus ecclesiam de Pottona cum omnibus pertinentiis suis sicut in cartis advocatorum eiusdem ecclesie, videlicet, David regis Scotie et Simonis comitis de Norh't*c* continetur. Et ut hoc prefatis monachis ratum et illibatum permaneat, presentis scripti et sigilli nostri attestatione communimus, salva in omnibus Lincolniensis ecclesie dignitate. Testibus: Hamone archidiacono Leicestr'*d*, magistro Rogero de Rolv', magistro Radulfo Nigro, magistro Simone de Siwell'*e*, magistro Willelmo de Monte, Henrico filio Petri, Drogone de Trubleville, Gaufrido de Lichel'*f*.

a North' C. *b* auctoritate episcopali C. *c* Northampton' C. *d* Leycestr' C. *e* Sywelle C. *f* Lychel' C.

Hamo became archdn of Leicester c.1187 and succeeded to the deanery of Lincoln between 15 September 1189 and 24 March 1190 (*Le Neve* app. 35). The charter of king David I, when earl of Huntingdon (before 1136), granting to the priory the church of Potton and the chapel of St Swithin there is on fo. 10v of C (a damaged copy is on fo. 11r of B); that of earl Simon III, addressed to bp Robert of Lincoln and archdn Nicholas of Bedford is on fo. 7r of C (and fo. 7v of B).

132. Northampton, St Andrew's priory

Confirmation for the monks of St Andrew, Northampton, of the church of St Peter, Northampton in proprios usus, *saving a suitable vicarage to be constituted when the church shall become vacant. The right of Henry son of Peter in the church is safeguarded for his lifetime.*

[*c.*1192 × ? March 1195]

B = BL ms. Royal 11 B ix (cartulary of St Andrew's, Northampton) fo. 29v. s. xiii ex. C = BL ms. Cotton Vesp. E xvii (cartulary of St Andrew's, Northampton) fo. 293r (276r). s. xv med.

Omnibus Christi fidelibus ad quos presens scriptum pervenerit, Hugo dei gratia Lincolniensis episcopus salutem in domino. Noverit universitas vestra nos, divine pietatis intuitu, consideratis etiam[a] caritatis operibus que divina propitiante munificentia in eadem domo habundantius et frequentius fiunt, concessisse et auctoritate pontificali confirmasse monasterio beati Andree de Northampton'[b] monachisque ibidem deo deservientibus ecclesiam beati Petri de Norh't[c] cum omnibus ad eam pertinentibus in proprios usus eiusdem domus perpetuo possidendam, salvo iure dilecti filii nostri Henrici filii Petri in eadem ecclesia[d] in vita sua, salva etiam conpetenti[e] vicaria in ecclesia eadem cum vacaverit instituenda; salvis etiam episcopalibus consuetudinibus et Lincolniensis ecclesie dignitate. Quod ut ratum et firmum permaneat, presenti scripto sigilli nostri appositione corroborato[f] communimus. Hiis testibus: magistro Rogero archidiacono de Legrec', magistro Ricardo de Sualeclive[g], magistro Alexandro de Bedeford[h], Roberto de Capella, Galfrido de Lichel'[i], Reimundo, Galfrido de Deping[j], Lincolniensis ecclesie canonicis, magistro Alexandro de Norh't[k], Hugone de sancto Edwardo, Roberto de Dunnestapel'[l] et multis aliis.

[a] C *adds* divine *here*. [b] Northampt' C. [c] North' C. [d] villa BC. [e] competenti C. [f] *Followed by* confirmamus C, *then dotted for expunction.* [g] Swaleclyve C. [h] Bedford C. [i] Lychel' C [j] Depyng' C. [k] Northampton' C. [l] Dunstapull' C.

The dates are those of Roger of Rolleston as archdn of Leicester (see, above no. 11). St Peter's church was among those granted by the priory's founder, earl Simon I (*Mon. Angl.* v 190, no. ii).

133. Northampton, St James's abbey

General confirmation of possessions for the abbot and canons of St James, Northampton. [21 September 1186 × 16 November 1200]

B = BL ms. Cotton Tib. E v (cartulary of St James, Northampton) fo. 3r (badly damaged in the Cottonian fire). s. xiv in. (Letters and words in square brackets are either from C or are conjectural). C = ibid. fo. 51r (45r). D = ibid. fo. 92v (86v) (virtually illegible, referred to in Bodl. ms. Top. Northants c 5 (extracts from the cartulary, s. xviii in.) p. 359).

[Hu]go dei gratia Lincolniensis episcopus universis sancte matris ecclesie filiis ad quos littere presentes pervenerint*a* [s]alutem in vero salutari. Quoniam iuste possidentium quies frequenti temeritate calumpniantium [turbatur] consilii prudentioris usus optinuit, ut [ea] que relligiosis*b* domibus canonice et rationabiliter [su]nt collata scriptorum et testium auctoritate firmentur. Eapropter in puplicam volumus devenire notitiam nos concessisse*c* et confirmasse abbati sancti Iacobi de*a* Norh'pt'*d* et canonicis ibidem deo militantibus universa beneficia que a Christi fidelibus ex eorum donatione rationabiliter [sun]t adepti et que in posterum iustis modis poterunt adipisci. Illis vero possessionibus beneficium [con]firmationis indulgemus que in confirmatione Theobaldi Cantuariensis archiepiscopi bone memorie [ei]s indulta propriis vocabulis exprimuntur. Preterea quecumque predecessores nostri episcopi Alexander [videlice]t et Robertus sive in ecclesiis sive in possessionibus pr[. . .]diis vel in molendinis ceterisque benefi[ciis iuste] adquisitis*e* eisdem canonicis confirmaverunt et nos auctoritate nostra et confirmatione corroboramus*f* quod specialiter propriis vocabulis exprimentes: videlicet, [ecclesi]am de [Wi]ckeleia*g*, ecclesiam de Bosegat'*h*, ecclesiam de Duston', ecclesiam de Hortona*i*, ecclesiam de Roda, cum omnibus appenditiis et pertinentiis earum sicut carte donatorum testantur. Concedimus etiam et nos predictis*j* [canonicis] ecclesiam de Watford'*k*, ecclesiam de Throp'*l*, ecclesiam de Catesden'*m*, ecclesiam de [Craneford' cum] omnibus eisdem ecclesiis pertinentibus prout carte testantur donatorum; preterea molendinum de Heiford', molendinum de Uptona*n* cum appenditiis suis. Quascumque etiam possessiones quecumque bona dono principum, largitione fidelium vel aliis rationabilibus modis in futuro poterint*o* adquirere, simili ratione concedimus et confirmamus, salvo iure et dignitate diocesani episcopi. Si qua igitur ecclesiastica secularisve persona predicte ecclesie bona temere invaserit vel minuerit vel quoquomodo iniuste perturbaverit, secundo tertiove commonita, si non satisfecerit, divine subiaceat ultioni. Cunctis autem eidem loco sua iura servantibus sit pax domini nostri Iesu Christi, Amen. Valete.

a *omitted* C.   *b* religiosis C.   *c* et concessisse *repeated* B.   *d* Norh't' C.
e acquisitis C.   *f* corroboravimus C.   *g* Wicleia C.   *h* Bosegayt' C.   *i* Horton' C.
j eisdem C.   *k* Watfordiam C.   *l* Thorop C.   *m* Gatesden' C.   *n* Upton' C.   *o* poterunt   C.

Theobald's charter is on fo. 228v of B (very badly damaged and ascribed to Thomas Becket). It is not pd by Saltman. Bp Alexander of Lincoln's confirmation is otherwise unknown; that of bp Robert (Chesney) may be *EEA* i nos. 198–9 or else a general confirmation likewise lost. For a confirmation of archbp Richard of Canterbury, issued 1174 × 1181, with a protocol and final clauses almost identical in wording, see *EEA* ii no. 176.

134. Northampton, St James's abbey

Confirmation for the abbot and canons of St James outside Northampton of the church of Bozeat in proprios usus, saving a suitable vicarage. [c.March 1195 × 16 November 1200]

B = BL ms. Cotton Tib. E v (cartulary of St James, Northampton) fos. 91v–92r (85v–86r) (badly damaged in the Cottonian fire). s. xiv in. C = Bodl. ms. Top. Northants c 5 (extracts from the cartulary) p. 359 (much abridged). s. xviii in. (Names of witnesses in square brackets are supplied from C; otherwise words and letters are conjectural).

Omnibus Christi fidelibus ad quos presens scriptum pervenerit, Hugo divina miseratione Lincolniensis episcopus salutem in domino. Ad universitatis vestre notitiam volumus pervenire nos considerata paupertate religiose domus sancti Iacobi extra Norh'pt' divino intuitu confirmasse abbati et canonicis prefate domus ecclesiam de Bosegayt' cum omnibus pertinentiis in proprios usus ad sustentationem eorundem canonicorum, salva competenti vic[aria . . . [fo. 92r, *only a small fragment of which survives*] . . . f]irmum, presenti scripto et sigillo nostro duximus confirmandum; [salvis episcopalibus consuetud]inibus et Lincolniensis ecclesie [dign]itate. Testibus: Rogero Lincolniensi [decano, Reimundo archidiacono] Leicestr', magistro Ricardo de Swalecl', Gaufrido de [Deping, magistro Gerardo de Rowell,] magistro Alexandro de Bedeford', Gaufrido de Lich', Hugone de sancto [Edwardo].

Roger of Rolleston became dean of Lincoln c.March 1195.

135. Northampton schools

Mandate to master A. notifying him that I. and W., scholars of Northampton, have claimed that I.(?) of Bedford, the reeve of Northampton, had violated the immunity of their hostel (hospicium) and that they had been assaulted and their goods removed. Master A. is ordered to cite the reeve to appear before the bishop in London at the nativity (? of St John the Baptist) to answer to these charges. [21 September 1186 × 16 November 1200]

B = Baltimore, Walters Art Gallery, ms. W.15 (formulary) fo. 80v. s. xiii in. C = BL ms. Add. 8167 fo. 118r–v (partial later copy of above).

Pd from B in *EHR* lvi (1941) 596, in the article by H. G. Richardson on 'The Schools of Northampton in the Twelfth Century' (595–605); *Oxford Formularies* ii 276, no. 8 (Salter was doubtful whether this document reflected any historical event).

The form 'H. bishop of London' is given in the formulary. This document provides the earliest evidence for the existence of a *studium* at Northampton in the late twelfth century. H. G. Richardson dates the document to *c*.1192. For this formulary see *EBC* 124–8.

136. Nostell priory

Institution of Ulian to the church of Charwelton, on the presentation of the prior of St Oswald, [Nostell].

[21 September 1186 × 2 April 1196]

B = BL ms. Cotton Vesp. E xix (Nostell cartulary) fo. 112v, no. x. s. xiii ex.

Omnibus Christi fidelibus ad quos presens scriptum pervenerit, Hugo dei gratia Lincolniensis episcopus salutem in domino. Ad universitatis vestre notitiam volumus pervenire nos ad presentationem dilecti filii nostri Asch' prioris sancti Osuualdi dilectum clericum nostrum Ulianum ad ecclesiam de Cherweltona recepisse et ipsum in eandem ecclesiam personam instituisse. Quod ut ratum habeatur et firmum, presentis scripti testimonio et sigilli nostri patrocinio duximus confirmandum. Hiis testibus etc.

Prior Ansketil or Anketil of Nostell died on 2 April 1196.

137. Nostell priory

Confirmation, having inspected the charters of the donors and of bishop Robert Chesney [EEA i no. 202], for the canons of St Oswald, Nostell, of the churches of Charwelton, Cheddington, and [King's] Langley.

[? 21 September 1186 × 16 November 1200]

B = BL ms. Cotton Vesp. E xix (Nostell cartulary) fo. 112v, no. xiii. s. xiii ex.

Omnibus Christi fidelibus ad quos presens scriptum pervenerit, Hugo dei gratia Lincolniensis episcopus salutem in vero salutari. Noverit universitas vestra nos ratam habere et gratam concessionem factam a bone memorie Roberto de[a] Chedneto quondam episcopo Lincolniensi deo et canonicis sancti Osuualdi de Nostle, videlicet, de ecclesiis de Cherwelton' in Norhamt'sir et de Chetend' in Buking'hamsir et de Langel' in Hertford'sir cum omnibus pertinentiis earum, sicut carte donatorum et prefati episcopi quas inspeximus testantur. Et nos iamdictas ecclesias, sicut prefatis canonicis rationabiliter collate sunt, auctoritate qua fungimur confirmamus et sigilli nostri appositione roboramus; salvis episcopalibus consuetudinibus et Lincolniensis ecclesie dignitate. Hiis testibus etc.

[a] Chedned' *written first and then dotted for expunction*.

It is virtually impossible to tell whether this document was issued by bp Hugh I or II, although the form of the greeting and its confirmation of bp Chesney's charter may tend to suggest Hugh I. For details of the original grants of Adeliza and Simon Chesney see *EEA* i no. 202.

138. Nun Cotham priory

Confirmation for the priory of St Mary, Nun Cotham of the church of Cuxwold in proprios usus, *saving a suitable vicarage.*

[? 21 September 1186 × 16 November 1200]

B = Bodl. ms. Top. Lincs. d 1 (Nun Cotham cartulary) fo. 14r. s. xiii in.

[O]mnibus Christi fidelibus ad quos presens scriptum pervenerit, Hugo dei gratia Lincolniensis episcopus salutem et benedictionem dei. Noverit universitas vestra nos, dei et pietatis intuitu considerata paupertate monialium de Cotuna, concessisse et presenti carta confirmasse deo et monasterio beate Marie de Cotun atque monialibus ibidem deo famulantibus ecclesiam de Cuchewald cum omnibus pertinentiis suis, ita videlicet ut eam habeant et convertant in proprios usus, salva in ea competenti vicaria assignanda ei qui in propria persona in eadem ecclesia ministrabit; salvis etiam episcopalibus consuetudinibus et Lincolniensis ecclesie*a* dingnitate. Quod ut inposterum ratum et inconcussum permaneat, presenti carta sigilli nostri appositione roboravimus. Hiis testibus.

a ecclesia *written first, with the final letter dotted for expunction and 'e' interlined.*

It is not certain, even from the diplomatic of the document, whether this confirmation should be ascribed to bp Hugh I or Hugh II.

139. Nuneaton priory

General confirmation of possessions for the nuns of Nuneaton.

[21 September 1186 × 18 October 1188]

B = BL Add. Ch. 47573 (inspeximus by the Official of the Consistory Court of Lincoln, 1453), no. 20.

Hugo dei gratia Lincolniensis episcopus universis Christi fidelibus ad quos presentes littere pervenerint eternam in domino salutem. Cum ad officii nostri pertineat solicitudinem circa pacem subditis nostris conservandam*a* operam et diligentiam exhibere, eos et eorum possessiones propensiori benignitatis studio debemus protegere, qui se artioris*b* religionis iugo noscuntur obligasse. Nos igitur dilectas filias nostras moniales de Eton' ordine Fontis Ebraldi professas sub nostra protectione in securo statu et tranquilla pace permanere volentes, possessiones quas fidelium in subsidium religionis pia eis devotio rationabiliter contulit et episcopalis auctoritas canonice confirmavit, auctoritatis nostre patrocinio dignum duximus communire, de quibus quasdam propriis nominibus censuimus exprimendas: ex dono Ricardi Wyntoniensis episcopi et concessione David de Armenteres ecclesiam de Burgeleya; ex dono Gervasii Painelli ecclesiam de Waltham; ex dono Ricardi filii Nigelli ecclesiam de Muresley; ex dono Arnoldi de Bosco ecclesiam de Claybroke. Ut autem donationes et concessiones memoratis monialibus a predictis viris facte firmam et perpetuam habeant stabilitatem, easdem sicut rationabiliter et canonice facte sunt auctoritate qua fungimur confirmamus et sigilli nostri appositione communimus. Hiis testibus: magistro Roberto de Bedeford', Rogero capellano, magistro David, magistro Galfrido de sancto Edwardo et aliis.

^a concervandam B.   ^b artiorum B.

Robert of Bedford had become precentor of Lincoln by 18 October 1188.

140. Nuneaton priory

Institution of the prioress and nuns of Nuneaton to the church of Ratby, on the presentation of Robert, earl of Leicester.

[1197 × 16 November 1200]

B = BL Add. Ch. 47573 (inspeximus by the Official of the Consistory Court of Lincoln, 1453) no. 19.

Omnibus Christi fidelibus ad quos presens scriptum pervenerit, Hugo dei gratia Lincolniensis episcopus salutem in domino. Noverit universitas vestra nos ad presentationem nobilis viri Roberti comitis Leyc' recepisse dilectas in Christo filias nostras priorissam et moniales de Eton' ad ecclesiam de Roteby cum omnibus ad ipsam ecclesiam pertinentibus, ipsasque in eadem ecclesia canonice instituisse; salvis episcopalibus consuetudinibus et Lincolniensis ecclesie dignitate. Ut autem hec nostra institutio firmum robur obtineat, eam presentis scripti serie et sigilli nostri munimine confirmavimus. Hiis testibus: Ricardo Lincolniensis ecclesie subdecano, magistris Ricardo de Swalewecliva, Alexandro de Bedeford', Girardo de Rowell', Roberto de Capella, Hugone, Lincolniensis ecclesie canonicis, Theobaldo de Cantia, Eustachio de Wilton', clericis, et aliis multis.

Richard of Kent became subdean of Lincoln in 1197.

141. Ormsby priory

Appropriation to the prior and convent of Ormsby of the churches of St Helen, [North] Ormsby, St Andrew, Utterby, St Mary, Fotherby, St Saviour, Little Grimsby, All Saints, South Elkington, and a mediety of the church of St Edith, Grimoldby.

[September 1189 × September 1193]

B = Lincoln D. & C. Dij/64/2/1 (in an inspeximus of Roger, the dean and the chapter of Lincoln, *c*.1195×1200).

Pd from B in *Reg. Ant.* ii no. 338 (ix).

Hiis testibus: Haimone [decano], Rogero de Rollest', Rogero de Bohun, Willelmo de Avaluns, Theobaldo de Buzas, Hamelino decano.

For the date of this charter see *Le Neve* app. 37; and also no. 11 above for Roger of Rolleston.

142. Osney abbey

Confirmation for the church of St Mary, Osney, of the chapel of Blackbourton, the gift of Ralph Murdac and Hugh de Burton (Blackbourton), and the church of Steeple Barton, the gift of Roger of St John.
[21 September 1186×16 November 1200]

B = Oxford, Ch. Ch. Lib., Osney cartulary, fo. 52v (section xxi) (witnesses omitted). s. xiii ex.

Pd from B in *Oseney Cartulary* iv no. 124.

For two versions of Ralph Murdac's charter see ibid. nos. 438–438A; Hugh de Burton's charter is ibid. no. 436. Roger of St John's grant (ibid. no. 119) is attested by John of Coutances, archdn of Oxford from ? 1184 until his election to the bishopric of Worcester in 1196. Archdn John's confirmation of the grant is ibid. no. 119B and among the witnesses is archdn Robert of Nottingham, who was elected bp of Worcester in July 1190. The confirmation of bp Hugh may possibly date from around the same period, relatively early in the episcopate.

143. Osney abbey

Grant to the canons of St Mary, Osney, at the petition and grant of William son of Henry and with the assent of Richard the parson of Ibstone, of ten shillings a year from the church of Ibstone to be paid by the parson in two instalments, namely five shillings at Michaelmas and five shillings at Easter; saving to William and his heirs the patronage of the church. Each parson of the church shall swear on oath to pay this sum to the canons.
[*c*.1189×September 1193]

B = BL ms. Cotton Vit. E xv (Osney cartulary, damaged) fo. 51r–v. s. xiii in.

Pd from B in *Oseney Cartulary* iv no. 411.

[. . .], Gaufrido de Lechelad', Roberto de Capella, Hugone de sancto Edwardo, Eustachio de Wilton et aliis multis.

The charter of William son of Henry granting the ten shillings from the church 'in the presence of bp Hugh of Lincoln at Thame' is ibid. no. 410. The grant is witnessed by abbot Robert of Notley, abbot Eustace of Dorchester, master Stephen the chancellor of Lincoln, master Roger of Rolleston and master Richard of Swalcliffe. Stephen de Swafeld became chancellor of Lincoln in 1189/90 and had been succeeded in that dignity by 22 March 1194 at the latest; Roger of Rolleston, who attests here without a title, became archdn of Leicester *c.*1192×September 1193 (see no. 11). If, as seems likely, bp Hugh's charter was issued on the same occasion or shortly afterwards, it can also be dated *c.*1189×September 1193; the damage to the list of witnesses in the episcopal actum prevents positive confirmation.

144. Osney abbey

General confirmation of possessions for the abbot and canons of Osney.
[*c.*1189×September 1193]

A = Bodl. DD. Ch. Ch. O.903. Endorsed: Confirmatio generalis 'sancti' Hugonis Lincoln' episcopi (s. xiii); Cudelinton' . Weston' . Claidon' . Hokenerton' . Cestreton' . Georg' . Magdal' . Stowe . Couel' . Iftele . Watlinton' . Stanes cum capella de Sutkote   Forsthulle . Waterpiri . Hompton' Barton' . cum capella de Saunford et de Ledwelle   Burton' . Optima est (s. xiii); facta est collacio (s. xiv); I. de Clipston' (ss. xiv–xv); iij; lang' (?); de *(illegible)* camera (s. xiv); press mark; Y; 23; 42; 44; approx. 294×192+20 mm.; excellent specimen of seal in seal bag (open at bottom), brown wax, on green/white strings, no counterseal.

B = Oxford, Ch. Ch. Lib., Osney cartulary fo. 20r–v. s. xiii ex.

Pd from B in *Oseney Cartulary* iv no. 32.

Omnibus Christi fidelibus ad quos presens scriptum pervenerit ⁏ Hugo dei gratia Lincolniensis episcopus salutem . et dei benedictionem. Petitiones a rectitudinis tramite non discrepantes ⁏ dignum est exaudire . et auditas ⁏ effectu prosequente complere. Ea propter karissimorum fratrum nostrorum abbatis et canonicorum ecclesie beate Marie de Oseneia iustis postulationibus annuentes ⁏ ipsos et monasterium in quo divino mancipantur obsequio . sub protectione dei et sancte Lincolniensis ecclesie et nostra suscipimus . possessiones etiam et redditus et precipue ecclesias sive capellas cum vicariis et decimis et aliis earum pertinentiis quas in episcopatu Lincolniensi idem fratres rationabiliter sunt adepti ⁏ eis episcopali qua fungimur auctoritate confirmamus . in quibus hec propriis duximus exprimenda vocabulis . de dono Roberti de Oilli predicti monasterii fundatoris ⁏ necnon et Henrici de Oilli primi . et Henrici et Roberti filiorum eius ⁏ ecclesias de Kedelinton' . de Westona . de Claindon' . de Okenarton' . de Cestreton' . item de dono Henrici de´Oilli primi et Henrici et Roberti filiorum eius . necnon et de dono Iohannis de sancto Iohanne . et Bernardi de sancto Walerico et Bernardi filii eius . et principaliter de dono Matillid(is) imperatricis et filii eius regis Henrici secundi ⁏ ecclesiam sancti Georgii que sita est in castello de Oxeneford' . cum ecclesia sancte Marie Magdal' . et ecclesiis de Stowa . de Couleia . de Ivetele . et cum omnibus aliis ecclesie sancti Georgii pertinentiis ⁏ salva compositione facta inter ecclesiam de Oseneia et Robertum de sancto Remigio super ecclesia de Ivetele . quam quia ratam esse volumus .· presenti scripto confirmamus . item de dono Henrici de Oilli primi . et Henrici et Roberti filiorum eius . necnon et de dono Halinadi de Bidun . et Willelmi Paganelli et Sare uxoris eius .· ecclesiam de Watlinton' .· de dono Willelmi de Braci et Gileberti filii eius .· ecclesiam de Stanes cum capella de Suthcote .· de dono Hugonis de Tiwe . capellam de Forstella .· salva compositione facta inter ecclesiam de Oseneia et ecclesiam sancte Frideswithe super eadem capella . de dono Willelmi filii Helie . et Emme uxoris eius . et Willelmi filii eorum .· ecclesiam de Waterperi . de dono Roberti Gaiti .· ecclesiam de Hamton' Gaitorum . de dono Rogeri de sancto Iohanne et Willelmi fratris eius .· ecclesiam de Bertona cum capellis de Sanford' et de Ledwell' . de dono Radulfi Mur[dac]ᵃ et Hugonis de Burton' .· capellam de Burtona. Volumus igitur et firmiter statuimus . ut iam dicta ecclesia et fratres de Oseneia omnia prenominata libere et integre imperpetuum habeant et possideant .· salvis episcopalibus consuetudinibus . et Lincolniensis ecclesie dignitatibus. Et ut hec nostra confirmatio rata et inconvulsa inperpetuum habeatur .· eam presenti pagina et sigilli nostri appositione duximus corroborandam. His testibus . magistro Stephano cancellario Lincolniensi . magistro Rogero de Rolveston' . magistro Symone de Siwell' . magistro Gaufrido de Lechelad' . Walchalino capellano nostro . magistro Ricardo vicearchidiacono . Nigello decano de Oxeneford' . et multis aliis. Valete.

ᵃ *There is a hole in the parchment at this point.*

For the date see no. 143.

145. Osney abbey

Admission of the abbot and canons of Osney into the personatus of the church of Hampton Gay, on the presentation of Robert Gay(t).

[c.1189 × September 1193, ? 1189]

B = BL ms. Cotton Vit. E xv (Osney cartulary) fo. 52r. s. xiii in.

Pd from B in *Oseney Cartulary* vi no. 964.

Testibus: Hamone Lincolniensi decano, magistro Stephano Lincolniensis ecclesie cancellario, magistro Rogero de Rolv', magistro Roberto de Hardr', Roberto de Capella, Gaufrido de Lichel'.

Hamo became dean of Lincoln c.1189/90 and Stephen de Swafeld had been succeeded as chancellor by 22 March 1194. The fact that neither Roger of Rolleston is described as archdn of Leicester nor Robert de Hardres as archdn of Huntingdon may indicate a date c.1189 × 1190. Roger was archdn by September 1193 (see no. 11). Robert le Gay's letter of presentation is ibid. no. 961. The annals of Osney date this event to 1189 (*Ann. mon.* iv 43) and the episcopal admission presumably followed within a very short while.

146.   Osney abbey

Admission of the abbot and canons of Osney into the personatus *of the church of Waterperry, on the presentation of Emma de Pery (Waterperry), and grant of William her son, then present.*

[c.1189 × September 1193, ? 1189]

B = BL ms. Cotton Vit. E xv (Osney cartulary, damaged — letters in square brackets are conjectural) fo. 74r. s. xiii in. C = Oxford, Ch. Ch. Lib., Osney cartulary fos. 119v–120r (section 1). s. xiii ex.

Pd from B in *Oseney Cartulary* iv no. 343.

Testibus:[a] Hamone Lincolniensis ecclesie decano et magistro Sttefano Lincolniensis ecclesie cancellario, magistro Rogero Rolvestun', magistro Robert de Ha[rdres], Walkelino capellano, [Roberto] de Capella, Gaufrido de [Lech]lade . . .

[a] C *ends here.*

The witness-list of this actum is very similar to no. 145, where reasons are given for the dating. The church of Waterperry was given to Osney by William son of Elias and Emma his wife (ibid. no. 334). The editor dates this grant c.1175–8 but the evidence does not suggest such a precise dating. The annals of Osney record that the abbey obtained the church in 1189 (*Ann. mon.* iv 43). Since William son of Elias entered Newburgh priory c.1180 (*Oseney Cartulary* iv 373, cf. no. 334C) his grant must obviously date before this time. Perhaps the annalist's note of 1189 indicates the year in which they were admitted into the *personatus*. For a confirmation of bp William see no. 272.

147.   Osney abbey

Permission to the abbot and canons of Osney that they may build a chapel in front of the gate of their curia *at their own expense, so that divine service may be celebrated there for their household servants and guests and for parishioners living within the confines of the abbey. The bishop furthermore declares the chapel to be free from the payment of synodals and to enjoy all the immunities which the abbey enjoys.*

[c.1189 × September 1193]

A = Lost original, seen by Anthony Wood in Christ Church Treasury, Oxford, and also by Twyne (mentioned in *Oseney Cartulary* ii no. 1040, n. 1; *Eynsham Cartulary* ii 266).
B = BL ms. Cotton Vit. E xv (Osney cartulary) fo. 86v. s. xiii in. C = Oxford, Ch. Ch. Lib., Osney cartulary fo. 31r (section x). s. xiii ex.

Pd from BC in *Oseney Cartulary* ii no. 1040.

Hiis testibus[a]: magistro Stephano cancellario Lincolniensi, magistro Rogero de Rolvest', magistro Simone de Siwelle, magistro Gaufrido de Lechelad', Walkelino capellano nostro, magistro Ricardo de

Eilesberi vicearchidiacono de Oxenef', Nigello decano de Oxen', et multis aliis.

ᵃ C *adds* etc. *and ends here.*

This chapel has been identified as that of St Thomas (ibid. 433). Stephen de Swafeld became chancellor 1189 × 1190 and had ceased to hold that dignity by 22 March 1194; Roger of Rolleston, who attests here without a title, became archdn of Leicester *c*.1192 × September 1193 (see no. 11).

148. Osney abbey

Admission of the abbot and canons of Osney into a mediety of the chapel of Blackbourton in proprios usus, *on the presentation of Ralph Murdac.* [*c*.March 1195 × 16 November 1200]

B = BL ms. Cotton Vit. E xv (Osney cartulary, damaged — letters in square brackets are conjectural) fo. 85r. s. xiii in.

Pd from B in *Oseney Cartulary* iv no. 438B.

Hiis testibus: Rogero dec[ano Lin]colniensi, Reimundo archidiacono Leiecestr', [Ricardo de Swalewe]clive, Roberto de Capella, Ricardo Grim, [ca]nonicis, Ingelrano capellano, [   ] et multis aliis.

Roger of Rolleston became dean of Lincoln some time after March 1195; Raymond succeeded him as archdn of Leicester. For two versions of Ralph Murdac's charter, one surviving in a cartulary copy, the other in original form, see ibid. nos. 438–438A. The word 'decani' probably followed 'Ingelrano capellano' in the witness-list (cf. no. 166).

149. Oxford, St Frideswide's priory

Notification that the bishop has seen the charter of Henry de Noers, whereby he gave the church of Churchill to the canons of St Frideswide, with the assent of Juliana his wife and Jordan his son-in-law. In the same document Henry and Juliana gave their bodies to the church of St Frideswide, and if they wished to change their present life for a better, they were to be received into the house to lead the canonical life. The bishop confirms the grant of the church to the house of St Frideswide. [? 21 September 1186 × 16 November 1200]

B = Oxford, Ch. Ch. Lib., St Frideswide's cartulary p. 231a (witnesses omitted). s. xv med.

Pd from B in *St Frideswide's Cartulary* ii no. 1037 (ascribed to bp Hugh II).

It may be that this is a charter of bp Hugh II rather than Hugh I. However, since the Noers charter was also confirmed by archbp Richard 1174 × 1181 (*EEA* ii no. 180) and received papal confirmation in 1181 (*St Frideswide's Cartulary* ii no. 1033; *PUE* iii no. 339), it is conceivable that Hugh I confirmed the charter. Against this one must set the fact that bp William, when he confirmed the grant (below, no. 276), did not mention a confirmation of his predecessor. The charters of Henry de Noers and others relating to this grant are in the cartulary (ii nos. 1025–31).

150.   Oxford, St Frideswide's priory

Institution of Hugh of Rolleston to the perpetual vicarage of the church of St Michael at the South Gate, Oxford, on the presentation of the prior and convent of St Frideswide, Oxford. Hugh shall possess the church for his lifetime, paying to the canons of St Frideswide's an annual pension of two silver marks. This pension is to be paid in four instalments. The bishop also confirms the canons' gift to the church of the land once held of them by Bernard the cook, lying between the church and the land of Edith the widow. The church shall hold this land from the canons in perpetuity for an annual rent of two shillings.

[*c.*1192 × ? March 1195]

B = Oxford, Ch. Ch. Lib., St Frideswide's cartulary, p. 337a. s. xv med.

Pd from B in *St Frideswide's Cartulary* i no. 203 (where the annual rent is erroneously given as one shilling).

Hiis testibus: Hamone Lincolniensis ecclesie decano, magistro R. archidiacono Leycestr' etc.

The dates are those of Roger of Rolleston as archdn of Leicester (see no. 11). For the bp's clerk, Hugh of Rolleston, see also no. 43 above.

*151.   Peterborough abbey

Confirmation for the abbot and convent of Peterborough of the advowson of the church of Barnack.

[21 September 1186 × 16 November 1200]

Mention only, in abstract on fo. 63r (78r) of Peterborough D. & C. ms. 5 (Pytchley cartulary): Habetur etiam confirmatio Hugonis Lincolniensis episcopi de presentatione abbatis et conventus de Burgo ad ecclesiam de Bernake.

This entry follows on the note of the confirmation of the same church by archbp Hubert Walter (*EEA* iii no. 570); and if the episcopal confirmation was issued at a similar time, then Hugh of Avalon is the bp of Lincoln in question.

152.   Peterborough abbey

Grant, at the petition of Benedict, abbot of Peterborough, to the almonry of the church of Peterborough of the church of Maxey, saving a perpetual vicarage of six marks.

[21 September 1186 × 10 December 1191]

B = Peterborough D. & C. ms. 1 (Swaffham's register) fo. 105v (xc v) (in an inspeximus of archbp Hubert Walter of Canterbury, November 1193 × April 1195 *or* February 1198 × November 1200, pd in *EEA* iii no. 569). s. xiii med.

Universis sancte matris ecclesie filiis ad quos presens scriptum pervenerit, Hugo dei gratia Lincolniensis episcopus salutem in domino. Notum sit universitati vestre nos, ad petitionem dilecti filii nostri Benedicti abbatis de Burgo, concessisse ecclesiam de Makeseia cum omnibus pertinentiis suis elemosinarie ecclesie sancti Petri de Burgo imperpetuum, salva vicaria sex marcarum que perpetuo vicario sacerdoti residentiamque ibi facienti in eadem ecclesia in loco certo assignabitur; salvis etiam episcopalibus consuetudinibus quas idem vicarius persolvet et Lincolniensis ecclesie dignitate. Quod ut ratum et inconcussum permaneat, presenti scripto et sigilli nostri patrocinio confirmamus. Test(ibus): capitulo*a* Lincolniensi, magistro Girardo de Rouuelle, Roberto de Capella, Eustachio de Wiltona et aliis.

a *an additional 'l' after the 'p' is dotted for expunction B.*

Bp Hugh's grant was confirmed by pope Celestine III in a document dated 10 December 1191 (*PUE* ii no. 265); abbot Benedict died on 25 or 29 September 1193.

*153. Peterborough abbey

Ordination. of a perpetual vicarage in the church of Maxey, in the patronage of the abbot and convent of Peterborough. The vicarage consists of all the altar offerings and small tithes, the manse, and the garb tithes of La Haume. The vicar shall bear all customary charges of the church. [? 21 September 1186 × September 1193]

Mention of ordination in the first institution roll of bp Hugh II.
Pd, *RHW* i 90.

It is possible that the ordination referred to here constituted a separate document describing the provisions of the vicarage in more detail than the original grant (above). Certainly the detail is not contained in the preceding actum.

154. Peterborough abbey

Grant to the almonry of Peterborough abbey, on the presentation of William de Roumare, of the church of Normanby, saving a vicarage of three marks. [15 September 1189 × 10 December 1191]

B = Peterborough D. & C. ms. 1 (Swaffham's register) fo. 106v (xci v). s. xiii med.

Omnibus Christi fidelibus ad quos presens scriptum pervenerit, Hugo dei gratia Lincolniensis episcopus salutem in domino. Noverit universitas vestra nos, ad presentationem dilecti filii nostri Willelmi de Rumar'*a*, concessisse elemosinarie sancti Petri de Burgo ecclesiam de Normannesbi cum omnibus pertinentiis suis inperpetuum, salva

vicaria trium marcarum que vicario perpetuo sacerdoti et residentiam
ibi facienti in eadem ecclesia in loco certo assignabitur; salvis etiam
episcopalibus consuetudinibus et Lincolniensis ecclesie dignitate. Qui
autem vicarius fuerit episcopalia persolvet. Ut autem hec concessio
rata et inconcussa permaneat, presenti scripto et sigilli nostri patrocinio confirmavimus. Hiis testibus: Haimundo decano et capitulo[b]
Lincolniensi, Walkelino priore de Land' et aliis.

^a Dumar' B.   ^b capellano B.

The charter of William of Roumare is on fo. 107v of B, and the following charter
(fos. 107v–108r) is a quitclaim of all right in the church made in the presence of bp
Hugh and attested by William de Roumare by prior Nicholas and the convent of
Spalding. Prior Nicholas was deposed c.1191; Hamo became dean of Lincoln
between 15 September 1189 and 24 March 1190. Bp Hugh's confirmation was itself
confirmed by pope Celestine III in a bull of 10 December 1191 (*PUE* ii no. 265).
Bp Hugh's grant was inspected by bp William (no. 279 below).

155. Peterborough abbey

*General confirmation of possessions for the almonry of Peterborough
abbey, and confirmation of a mill for the infirmary.*

[1192 × ? March 1195]

B = Peterborough D. & C. ms. 1 (Swaffham's register) fo. 106r (xci r) (in an
     inspeximus of archbp Hubert Walter of Canterbury, April 1195 × February 1198,
     pd in *EEA* iii no. 573). s. xiii med.

Universis sancte matris ecclesie filiis ad quos presens scriptum pervenerit, Hugo dei gratia Lincolniensis episcopus eternam in domino
salutem. Quotiens a Christi fidelibus in usus pauperum perpetuos
beneficia conferuntur et ad dei gloriam statuuntur permansura propter
ingeniosas malignantium versutias litteris decet acta ligari et ad future
generationis posteritatem autentici scripti beneficio transmitti. Hinc
est quod decimas et terras in puram et perpetuam elemosinam
elemosinarie Burgi collatas auctoritate episcopali decrevimus confirmare et nominatim singulas exprimere has, scilicet: Suttonam cum
omnibus ad eam pertinentibus, unam virgatam terre et dimidiam in
Wermentona de dono Simonis filii Nigelli, de dono Willelmi de
Cloptona 'septies xx' acras terre et totum pratum de Sinesuuald et
unam virgatam terre, et preterea magnam virgatam terre de dono
Roberti Gargate, unam virgatam terre in Wermentona cum toftis et
pertinentiis suis, duas garbas decime totius parochie capelle de
Pastona et duas partes tertie garbe decimarum quatuor militum in
eadem parochia, Yvonis videlicet de Gunetorp, Ascelini de Pastona,
Roberti Peverel et Roberti Grip, duorum etiam frankelanorum
Alfrici, scilicet, de Widerintona et Odonis de Widerintona, decem

solidos quos Galfridus filius Galfridi ecclesie Burgi in villa de Sutorp assignavit, duodecim denarios annuos quos H'a'uuisa Peverel de terra Henrici clerici de Pastona concessit; de mesagio Wigari de Aia duodecim denarios in villa Burgi, in campis de Dodestorp duas acras terre quas Henricus cocus dedit, unam acram in villa de Thorp quam Willelmus filius Godrici ecclesie Burgi legavit, duodecim denarios de terra quam Thurstanus de Torp elemosinarie dedit, duas acras de terra que fuit Gaufridi braciatoris, unam marcatam redditus ex dono Iordani filii Godrici in Lincolnia de terra que est proxima atrio sancte Trinitatis de Wikeford', de terra de Halebode quadraginta solidos. Hec omnia sicut eis concessa sunt rationabiliter auctoritate qua fungimur elemosinarie Burgi confirmamus. Preterea confirmamus domui infirmorum monachorum Burgi molendinum quod dicitur Briggemilne quod Thuroldus de Suttona ecclesie Burgi dedit. Que omnia ut firma et inconvulsa omni tempore permaneant, presentis scripti serie et sigilli nostri appositione confirmamus. Hiis testibus: Haymone[a] decano Lincolniensis ecclesie, magistro Winemero archidiacono Norhamton', magistro Ricardo de Suualeclive et aliis multis.

[a] Haymo B.

Winemer became archdn of Northampton at some date between 1192 and 8 June 1194, and Hamo ceased to be dean of Lincoln c.March 1195. The grants to the almonry as confirmed by bp Hugh and archbp Hubert were also confirmed by king John in a charter dated at Caen 28 December 1199 (*Early Northants Charters* no. xvi; *Rot. Chart.* 32a). This confirmation was inspected by bp William (see no. 280). For the history of the Peterborough almonry see W. T. Mellows, P. I. King and C. N. L. Brooke eds. *The Book of William Morton* (Northamptonshire Record Society 16, 1954), introd.

156. Peterborough abbey

General confirmation of possessions for the monks of Peterborough.
[c.1194 × ? March 1195]

B = Peterborough D. & C. ms. 1 (Swaffham's register) fos. 106v–107r (xci v–xcii r). s. xiii med.

Omnibus Christi fidelibus ad quos presens scriptum pervenerit, Hugo dei gratia Lincolniensis episcopus salutem in domino. Ne ea que religiosorum agregationes iuste possident alicuius malignitate seu temporis diuturnitate minui possint vel in irritum deduci, sollers antiquorum providit et statuit discretio ea scripture commendare et in scriptum redacta confirmare. Quorum nos vestigia sequentes dilectis in Christo filiis nostris monachis sancti Petri de Burch omnes obventiones ecclesiasticas et decimas et pensiones quas habent de ecclesiis in episcopatu nostro constitutis decrevimus confirmare et eas nominatim singulas exprimere, scilicet, de ecclesia de Castre centum solidos, de ecclesia de Keteringe quadraginta solidos, de ecclesia de Wermintona duas marcas, de ecclesia de Undele duas marcas, de ecclesia de Irtlingburch unam marcam, de ecclesia de Staneuige viginti solidos, de ecclesia de Peichirche xv solidos, de ecclesia de Pastona unam marcam, de ecclesia de Cothingham dimidiam marcam, de ecclesia de Estona tres solidos, de ecclesia de Tineuuelle dimidiam marcam, de ecclesia sancti Martini de Stanford decem solidos, de ecclesia de Scotere quadraginta solidos, de ecclesia de Fiskertona quinquedecim solidos; omnes decimas et obventiones totius parochie Burgi, scilicet, ville Burg' et Torp, Dodestorp, Eie, Neuuert, Eafeld, duas garbas de dominio de Gunetorp et de Suttorp, duas garbas de dominio de Pastona, duas garbas de essartis Willelmi de Wdecroft, duas garbas de dominio Ascelini de Wodint', duas garbas de dominio Rogeri de Helpestona, duas garbas de dominio Waleranni de Helpestona de Moppleshauue, duas garbas de dominio Rogeri 'de' Torpel in Torpel et in Makeseie, duas garbas de dominio Rogeri de Meletona, duas garbas de dominio [fo. 107r] de Turnauue, duas garbas de dominio de Witeringe, duas garbas de dominio de Walecote, duas garbas de dominio Galfridi^a de Pillesgate, duas garbas de dominio Galfridi^a in Badintona, duas garbas de dominio Roberti de Badintona, duas garbas de dominio Radulfi de Widerintona, duas garbas Odonis de Widerintona, duas garbas de dominio Roberti de Tot in Pastona, duas garbas de dominio Roberti Peverel, duas garbas de dominio Roberti Grip, duas garbas de terra Radulfi filii Restuualdi, duas garbas de terra Iohannis de Glintona, duas garbas de dominio de Stokes, duas garbas de dominio de Pappele, duas garbas de dominio de Kinestorp', tertiam garbam de dominio Roberti Flamang in Pokebroc, duas garbas de dominio de Wodeford. Hec omnia sicut eis rationabiliter concessa sunt auctoritate qua fungimur confirmamus et scripti presentis serie sigillique nostri appositione confirmamus, salvis episcopalibus consuetudinibus et Lincolniensis ecclesie dignitate^b. His testibus: Hamundo decano Lincolniensis ecclesie, magistro Willelmo cancellario Lincolniensi, magistro Winemero de Norhamtona^c.

^{a} Galfrido *originally written* B, *and the final 'o' dotted for expunction and 'i' interlined.*
^{b} divinitate *originally written* B,. *and 'vi' dotted for expunction and 'g' interlined.*
^{c} archidiacono *has clearly been omitted here.*

William de Montibus became chancellor of Lincoln *c.*1194 and Hamo ceased to be dean *c.*March 1195.

157. Ramsey abbey

Confirmation for abbot R(obert) and the convent of Ramsey of their pensions from churches in the diocese of Lincoln, namely, five marks a

*year from the church of Elton; four marks from the church of Therfield;
twenty shillings from the church of Cranfield; one mark from the church
of Broughton; one stone of wax from the church of St Andrew,
Huntingdon; and, at the instance of master Herbert of Ramsey, twenty
shillings from his churches of Houghton and Witton and twenty
shillings from his church of Barton. These pensions and other revenues
shall be employed in keeping the monastery roofs (sarta tecta) in repair,
in lights and other necessaries. Sick monks shall, at the arrangement of
the abbot, receive some comforts (consolatio) as shall be necessary and
when their illness demands it.*

Buckden, 1189 [25 March 1189 × 24 March 1190]

B = BL ms. Cotton Vesp. E ii (Ramsey cartulary) fo. 40r–v (39r–v, xxxv r–v), no.
cii. s. xiii med. C = PRO E164/28 (Ramsey cartulary) fos. 187v–188r (clxiii
v–clxiv r). s. xiv med.

Pd from B in *Ramsey Cartulary* ii no. cccii.

Hoc autem*ᵃ* actum est apud Buggeden'*ᵇ* anno incarnationis dominice
mᵒ cᵒ lxxxixᵒ.*ᶜ* Testibus: Hamone Lincolniensis ecclesie decano,
magistro Stephano Lincolniensis ecclesie cancellario,*ᵈ* Roberto abbate
de Parco Nuthel', Waltero capellano, magistro Rogero de Rolweston',
magistro Herberto de Rames', magistro Ricardo de Linchel'.

ᵃ word omitted C.   *ᵇ* Bukedene C.   *ᶜ* mᵒcᵒlxxx nono C.   *ᵈ* C *ends here with* etc.

158. Ramsey abbey

*Confirmation for the church and monks of Ramsey of all garb tithes
pertaining to the church of Shillington (except the sheaves belonging to
the chapel of Gravenhurst), to be applied to the use of the cellarer for
ever, for the better entertainment of guests. The chapel of Gravenhurst
with all appurtenances and other annual dues belonging to Shillington
church are assigned to the vicarage of the church, with lands,
meadows, pasture, orchards (virgulta), fisheries, granges, houses,
revenues, and altar dues. If a dispute should ever arise over the chapel
of Gravenhurst and it should be alienated from the church of Shillington, the monks shall recompense the vicar the value of the chapel in
garb tithes belonging to Shillington church. The monks and the vicar
shall be proportionally responsible for the repair of the church, books,
and ornaments. The vicar shall bear all episcopal charges. The right of
Stephen of Ecton, who now possesses the church, is safeguarded for his
lifetime.*   [c.1192 × ? March 1195]

B = BL ms. Cotton Vesp. E ii (Ramsey cartulary) fo. 40r (39r, xxxv r), no. ci. s.
xiii med. C = PRO E164/28 (Ramsey cartulary) fo. 187r (clxiii r). s. xiv med.

Pd from B in *Ramsey Cartulary* ii no. ccxcviii

Hiis testibus: Haimone[a] decano Lincolniensis ecclesie,[b] magistro Rogero archidiacono Leyc', magistro Haimone de Winton' etc.

[a] Hamundo C.   [b] C *ends here with* et aliis.

The dates are those of Roger of Rolleston as archdn of Leicester (see no. 11).

159. Ramsey abbey

Confirmation of the grant made by abbot Robert and the convent of Ramsey to the prior and monks of St Ives of the church of St Margaret, Hemingford, which is of the fee of the monks of Ramsey, saving the perpetual vicarage of master Aristotle and his successors. The vicar shall pay to St Ives a pension of forty shillings a year, half at Easter and half at Michaelmas. Twenty shillings is to be used for hospitality, the other twenty for the sacristy.   [*c.*1194 × 1195]

B = PRO E164/28 (Ramsey cartulary) fo. 187r–v (clxiii r). s. xiv med.

Pd from B in *Ramsey Cartulary* ii no. ccxcix.

Testibus: Willelmo Lincolniensis ecclesie cancellario, magistro Ricardo Swalewecl', magistro Galfrido de Depingis, Reimundo, Gaufrido de Lichel', Petro de Hungr', canonicis.

William de Montibus first occurs as chancellor on 22 March 1194 and Raymond became archdn of Leicester some time after March 1195. For the career of master Aristotle see Sir Charles Clay in *EHR* lxxvi (1961) 303–7.

160. Richard the usher

Grant to Richard the usher of two virgates of land of the bishop's fee outside Banbury. Richard and his heirs shall pay ten shillings a year for all service, except for ploughing once a year and reaping once a year as boonwork.   [15 September 1189 × September 1193]

A = Lincoln D. & C. Dij/66/3/8 (damaged in top right-hand corner). Endorsed: Bannebyr' .x. (ss. xiii–xiv); approx. 169 × 103 + 12 mm.; seal (damaged at edges, repaired), brown wax, on green and red cords, no counterseal.

Pd from A in *Reg. Ant.* iii no. 924.

Hug(o) dei gratia Lincolniensis episcopus omnibus Christi fidelibus ad quos presens scriptum pervenerit eternam in d[omino salutem.] Noverit universitas vestra nos dedisse et concessisse dilecto filio et fideli nostro Ricardo hostiario duas virgatas terre extra Bannebir' de feodo nostro . videlicet virgatam quam Gilebertus Chethun et virgatam quam Radulfus telarius tenuerunt. Quas prefatus Ricardus tenebit libere et quiete . ipse et heredes sui de nobis et successoribus nostris . reddendo singulis annis decem solidos ad quatuor terminos pro omni servicio ·' excepto quod idem Ricardus et qui prefatas virgatas post eum tenebit ·' semel in anno ad precarias nostras arabit . et semel metet. Hanc nostram donationem et concessionem presenti scripto et sigilli nostri patrocinio confirmavimus. Testibus . Hamone Lincoln-iensis ecclesie decano . magistro .R. Rolveston' . magistro Ricardo de Swalewecl' . Galfrido de Lecchelad' . Roberto de Capella . Hugone de sancto Edwardo . clericis . Waltero constabulario . Eustachio de Wilton' et aliis multis.

Hamo became dean between 15 September 1189 and 24 March 1190, and Roger of Rolleston, who attests here without a title, became archdn of Leicester *c.*1192× September 1193 (see no. 11).

161. Rochester priory

Confirmation for the church and monks of St Andrew, Rochester, of the church of Haddenham, with its chapel of Cuddington. The church of Haddenham, together with the manor, was given to Rochester by king William. The bishop confirms that all the offerings from the church shall be used for the lights of the church of Rochester in accordance with bishop Ernulph of Rochester's charter, which he has inspected.

[*c.*1194×16 November 1200]

B = BL ms. Cotton Domit. A x (Rochester cartulary) fo. 107r–v, no. xvii. s. xiii in.
Pd from B in *Reg. Roff.* 385.

Huius rei testes sunt: magister Stephanus archidiaconus de Buchinge-ham, magister Ricardus de Swaleweclive.

Stephen of Swafeld became archdn of Buckingham *c.*1194. For charters relating to Haddenham, Cuddington and Kingsey see *Reg. Ant.* iii nos. 658–69. William II's confirmation (1088) is in *Regesta* i no. 301.

162. Royston priory

Grant of the church of Owersby in proprios usus *to prior H(arpin) and the canons of Royston, on the presentation of Eustace de Merk. The prior and canons shall present a perpetual vicar to the bishop and suitable provision is to be made for him.*

[? 21 September 1186×September 1193, ? 1186×10 October 1188]

B = PRO E41/237 no. 3 (transcript of Royston priory charters). s. xiii ex.
C = ibid. no. 5 (in an inspeximus of bp William of Lincoln, see no. 285 below).
D = BL Add. Ch. 46362 (leaf of Royston cartulary). s. xiv.

Omnibus Christi fidelibus ad quos presens scriptum pervenerit, Hugo dei gratia Lincolniensis episcopus salutem in domino. Ad universitatis

vestre notitiam volumus pervenire nos divino intuitu et consideratione
paupertatis novelle domus canonicorum regularium de Cruce Roys[a]
concessisse H.[b] priori et canonicis ibidem deo servientibus ut
ecclesiam sancti Martini de Ouerisby[c] in qua eos ad presentationem
Eustachii de Merk instituimus in usus suos proprios convertant, eo
tamen[d] salvo quod prior et canonici presentabunt episcopo vicarium
perpetuum ad ecclesiam illam ad portionem competentem secundum
dispositionem[e] episcopi. Quod ut ratum habeatur et firmum presenti
scripto et sigillo[f] nostro duximus confirmandum, salvis quoque in
omnibus episcopalibus consuetudinibus et Lincolniensis ecclesie dignitate. Testibus: magistro Roberto[g] de Bedeford[h], magistro Rogero
de Rulveston', magistro Luca, Rogero capellano, Roberto Bardolf[i].

[a] Rosie D.   [b] Harpino D.   [c] Ouresbi D.   [d] mihi D.   [e] disposisionem D.
[f] sigilli D.   [g] Radulfo D.   [h] Bedeforde D.   [i] Bardeleton' D.

Neither Robert of Bedford nor Roger of Rolleston is described by their dignities.
Robert had become precentor of Lincoln by 18 October 1188; Roger had become
archdn of Leicester c.1192 × September 1193 (see no. 11). If this is not merely an
omission by the copyist, then this actum must have been issued in the early months
of bp Hugh's episcopate. It must be noted that Luke and Robert Bardolf who also
attest this charter occur as canons of Lincoln in the list of c.1187, but are not so
described here. At all events the document must have been issued by c.1194 when
Robert of Bedford died.
    Charters confirming the church to Royston by Eustace de Merk and his nephew,
Ralph de Rouecestre, are PRO E41/237 nos. 1 and 2; Merk's charter is also copied
on the leaf of BL Add. Ch. 46362.

163. St Albans abbey

*Confirmation for the church and monks of St Albans of the church of
Luton, after the bishop's inspection of the charter of king Henry.*

[21 September 1186 × 16 November 1200]

B = BL ms. Cotton Otho D iii (St Albans cartulary) fo. 117r (damaged in the
Cottonian fire; words in square brackets conjectural). s. xiv ex.

Omnibus Christi fidelibus ad quos presens scriptum pervenerit, Hugo
dei gratia Lincolniensis episcopus salutem in domino. Quoniam ea
que locis religiosis conferuntur beneficia ex suscepti pontificatus
officio tenemur protegere et episcopali auctoritate contra malignorum
machina[tionem ? *one or two words here* ? confirmare]. Ad universitatis vestre notitiam volumus vero pervenire nos ratam habere et
presenti carta confirmare deo et ecclesie sancti Albani et monachis
ibidem deo servientibus concessionem quam rex Henricus eis rationabiliter fecit super ecclesia de Luyton' cum omnibus pertinentiis suis
sicut carta domini regis exinde facta quam inspeximus testatur. Quod
ut ratum habeatur et firmum, presenti scripto et sigillo nostro

duximus roborandum; salvis tamen in omnibus episcopalibus consuetudinibus et Lincolniensis ecclesie dignitate.

> The charter of king Henry II respecting the churches of Luton and Houghton is on
> fo. 117r of B. For the earlier history of Luton church see *Gesta Abbatum* i 113–24.
> Richard of Dover, archbp of Canterbury, confirmed the church to St Albans,
> 1174×1177 (*EEA* ii no. 199, which see for further details about the church).

*164.   St Albans abbey

*Institution of William son of Peter to the church of Wingrave, on the
presentation of St Albans abbey.*   [*c*.1191]

> Mention of charter in the possession of the abbot of St Albans in a dispute between
> the abbot and Ralph de Waddon over the advowson of the church, 1201.
>
> Pd, *CRR* i 401.

The abbot stated that William had been parson of the church for ten years.

165.   Priory of St-Fromond

*Institution of master Samson of Stamford to the perpetual vicarage of
St John, Stamford, on the presentation of the prior and convent of St-
Fromond. Samson shall possess the church with all appurtenances,
saving a pension of one mark a year to the convent of St-Fromond.*

[15 September 1189×4 April 1192]

> B = BL Add. Ch. 66079 (roll of charters of priory of St-Fromond, dioc.
> Coutances), m. 1. s. xv.

Omnibus sancte matris ecclesie filiis ad quos presens scriptum*a*
pervenerit, Hugo dei gratia Lincolniensis episcopus salutem in
domino. Ad universitatis vestre notitiam volumus pervenire nos ad
presentationem prioris et conventus sancti Fromundi recepisse dilectum filium nostrum magistrum Samsonem de Stamford' ad ecclesiam
sancti Iohannis in Stamford' et eum perpetuum vicarium in ea
canonice instituisse. Volumus autem et precipimus ut idem Samson
prefatam ecclesiam cum omnibus pertinentiis suis habeat et possideat,
salva pensione unius marce prefato conventui sancti Fromundi annuatim solvenda ad duos terminos: dimidiam, videlicet, marcam ad
festum sancti Michaelis et dimidiam*b* marcam ad terminum Rogationum; salvis episcopalibus consuetudinibus et Lincolniensis ecclesie
dignitate. Hiis testibus: Hamone decano Lincolniensis ecclesie,
magistro Rogero de Rolveston', Roberto de Hardr', magistro Ricardo
de Swaleweclin' (*sic*), magistro Adam de Lincoln', magistro Girardo
de Rowell', Hugone de sancto Edwardo, Eustachio de Wylton' et aliis
multis.

a *word omitted* B.   *b* ad *inserted here* B, *then dotted for expunction.*

K

Hamo became dean of Lincoln some time after 15 September 1189; Roger of Rolleston and Robert de Hardres are not named as archdns in this document. Roger became archdn of Leicester *c*.1192 × September 1193 (see no. 11); Robert became archdn of Huntingdon *c*.1189 × 4 April 1192.

166. Priory of St-Fromond

Judgment by the bishop, R(oger of Rolleston), dean of Lincoln, and R(aymond), archdeacon of Leicester, acting upon a mandate of pope Celestine III, in respect of a dispute between the monks of St-Fromond and master S. of Stamford and master R. of Stapleford over the church of St John, Stamford. Master R. of Stapleford has renounced all rights he claimed in the church of St John and has similarly renounced all claims to the church of All Saints in the Market, Stamford, against the monks of St-Fromond, the nuns of St Michael, Stamford, and master S. of Stamford. [*c*.March 1195 × *c*.February 1198]

A = Bodl. DD. Queen's Coll. Ch. 286. Endorsed: pro ecclesia (ecclesiis *interlined*) sancti Iohannis et omnium sanctorum de Stanford' (ss. xiv–xv); approx. 151 × 142 + 10 mm.; seals missing, two parchment tags (d.q.1).

Universis Christi fidelibus ad quos presens scriptum pervenerit ⸴ H. dei gratia Lincolniensis episcopus et R. Lincolniensis ecclesie decanus . et R. archidiaconus Leic' salutem. Ad communem omnium volumus devenire noticiam . quod cum causa que vertebatur inter monachos sancti Fromundi et magistrum .S. de Stanford' et magistrum .R. de Stapelford' super ecclesia sancti Iohannis de Stanford' . de mandato summi pontificis Celestini pape . tercii . nobis commissa . fuisset audienda et fine canonico terminanda ⸴ predicto magistro .R. et prefato magistro .S. procurante causam propriam et causam iamdictorum monachorum . in presentia nostra constitutis ⸴ idem .R. pure et sponte renuntiavit in perpetuum iuri quod vendicabat in supradicta ecclesia . omni que questioni super ea coram nobis mote . et omnibus instrumentis ab eo super ea habitis. Preterea coram nobis iuramentum prestitit . quod nec prenominatis monachis nec prenominato .S. super ea de cetero questionem movebit. Iuravit etiam idem .R. in presentia nostra quod nec monachis sancti Fromundi nec monialibus sancti Michaelis de Stanford' nec sepedicto S. tam propriam quam illorum causam procuranti ⸴ super ecclesia omnium sanctorum in foro de Stanford de cetero questionem movebit . iuri quod in eadem ecclesia prius vendicabat sponte renuntians. Nos vero habito virorum prudentum consilio auctoritate qua fungebamur per sententiam diffinitivam eidem .R. perpetuum silentium super iamdictis ecclesiis inposuimus . et iamdictum .S. et supradictos monachos et

moniales ab eiusdem .R. impetitione super prefatis ecclesiis absolv-
imus. Ne igitur que in presentia nostra tam sollempniter acta sunt in
dubium tractu temporis possint revocari ? ea huius scripti serie et
sigillorum nostrorum testimonio corroboravimus. Hiis testibus .
magistro .W. Norhanton' . R. Huntend' . S. Bukingham . archidiaconis . magistro .G. de Rowell' . magistro .A. de Alnestow' .
magistro .R. de Malmecestr' . magistro .R. de Sumerford' .
Ing(elramo) . capellano decani . W. clerico de Bannebir' . et multis
aliis.

Roger of Rolleston became dean of Lincoln c.March 1195; pope Celestine III died
on 8 January 1198, and news of his death would not reach England before
February.

*167. Priory of St-Fromond

*Confirmation of an exchange to be made between the prior and canons
of Merton and the prior and monks of St-Fromond. The prior and
canons of Merton are to exchange their church of Caen ('Kaanes') in
Normandy for the tithes of Stamford castle, a pension of two silver
marks from the church of All Saints [in the Market], Stamford, the
Stamford churches of St John, St Paul, St Michael [Cornstall] and St
George, and the churches of Saxby and Bonby in Lindsey.*
                        [21 September 1186 × 17 February 1200]

Mention of charter assenting to the exchange in a confirmation by king John, 17
February 1200. The royal charter also mentions the permission given by pope
Lucius III (1181–5) and the charter of bp H(enry) of Bayeux (1165–1205).
Pd, *Rot. Chart.* 36a; noted in *Records of Merton Priory* 55.

These and other churches in England were confirmed to St-Fromond by pope
Alexander III, 8 March 1179 (*PUFN* no. 191). The exchange with Merton did not
take effect (see J. S. Hartley and A. Rogers, *The Religious Foundations of Medieval
Stamford* (Nottingham 1974), esp. 72). For the identification of 'Kaanes' see the
note to *Reg. Ant.* i no. 284.

168. St Neot's priory

*Confirmation for the prior and monks of St Neot's of the church of St
Mary in the town of St Neot's, the church of St Mary, Everton, and the
church of 'Auco' [? Ayot St Peters], granted to them by Gilbert de
Munfichet and Richard his heir, as an inspection of their charters
indicates.*   [21 September 1186 × 16 November 1200]

B = BL ms. Cotton Faust. A iv (St Neot's cartulary) fo. 37r (36r), no. i (witnesses
omitted). s. xiii med.

Pd from B in *Mon. Angl.* iii 476, no. xxix; abstract in G. C. Gorham, *History . . . of
Eynesbury and St Neot's* (1824), supplement p. x.

I have identified 'Auco' with Ayot St Peters, since the latter formed part of the Gernon estates which were granted to William de Munfichet in the mid-twelfth century (*VCH Essex* i 347). Gilbert de Munfichet died in 1186/7; his son, Richard I, in 1204 (*English Baronies* 83).

169. St Neot's priory

Confirmation for the church and monks of St Neot's of the charter of bishop Robert [Chesney] confirming the church of Tempsford (EEA i no. 243], which he has inspected, and also confirmation of the church of Knotting, in accordance with the agreement between the monks of St Neot's and the prior and brethren of the Hospitallers in England made before B(artholomew), bishop of Exeter [1161–1184].

[21 September 1186 × 16 November 1200]

B = BL ms. Cotton Faust. A iv (St Neot's cartulary) fo. 39v (38v), no. xvii. s. xiii med.

Pd (abstract) in Gorham, *op. cit.* supplement p. xii.

Omnibus Christi fidelibus ad quos presens scriptum pervenerit, Hugo divina miseratione Lincolnienc' episcopus salutem in domino. Ad universitatis vestre notitiam volumus pervenire nos ratam habere et presenti carta confirmasse deo et ecclesie sancti Neoti et monachis ibidem deo servientibus concessionem et confirmationem sicut eis rationabiliter facta est super ecclesia de Tamiseford a bone memorie Roberto predecessore nostro quondam Lincolnienc' episcopo, cuius cartam super hoc inspeximus. Confirmamus etiam prefatis monachis ecclesiam de Cnotting' quam habent ex concessione prioris et fratrum hospitalis Ierusalemitani in Anglia*a* sicut eorum carta testatur et secundum formam transactionis inter ipsos et predictos fratres coram egregie memorie B. olim Exoniensi episcopo factam auctoritate apostolica. Confirmamus quoque eisdem monachis alia omnia beneficia sua eis rationabiliter collata secundum tenorem cartarum suarum. Quod ut ratum habeatur et firmum, presenti scripto et sigillo nostro duximus roborandum, salvis tamen*b* in omnibus episcopalibus consuetudinibus et Lincolniensis ecclesie dignitate.

a Angliam B.   *b* tam B.

170. St Neot's priory

Confirmation for the prior and monks of St Neot's of the churches of Clopton, Hemington, Brampton [Ash], and Barnwell [All Saints].

[21 September 1186 × 16 November 1200]

B = BL ms. Cotton Faust. A iv (St Neot's cartulary) fo. 41v (40v), no. xxxi. s. xiii med.

Pd (abstract) in Gorham, *op. cit.* supplement p. xiii.

Omnibus Christi fidelibus ad quos presens scriptum pervenerit, Hugo divina miseratione Lincolnienc' episcopus salutem in domino. Ut beneficia que viris religiosis intuitu caritatis sunt collata rata et inconcussa inperpetuum permaneant, dignum duximus ea scripto nostro perpetue memorie comendare et sigilli nostri atestatione firmiter roborare. Eapropter dilectis in Christo filiis nostris priori et monachis de sancto Neoto ecclesiam de Cloptona cum omnibus pertinentiis suis et ecclesiam de Hemmingtona cum suis pertinentiis, ecclesiam de Bramthona de feudo Willelmi de Albineyo, et ecclesiam de Bernewella cum 'omnibus' que ad eam pertinent eis rationabiliter concessas sicut ex eorum cartis testatur*a* concedimus*b*, presenti carta nostra confirmamus et sigilli nostri appensione roboramus; salvis tamen in omnibus episcopalibus consuetudinibus*a* et Lincolnienc' ecclesie dignitate.

a Word omitted b.   *b* concepimus B.

Barnwell was given to St Neot's by king Henry I (*Regesta* ii no. 1969; cf. *EEA* i no. 54). In 1219 there was a final concord between St Neot's and Peterborough abbey, whereby Peterborough quitclaimed to St Neot's all right in the advowson of Hemington, and St Neot's quitclaimed to Peterborough all right in the advowson of Clopton (fo. 50r of B, no. xxxviii).

171. Abbey of La Sauve-Majeure

Confirmation for the abbey of La Sauve-Majeure and its cell, the monastery of Burwell, of the church of Burwell, with its chapel of Authorpe, and the church of Walmsgate.

[*c.*1194 × ? March 1195]

B = Bordeaux, Archives de la région Aquitaine et du département de la Gironde, ms. 769 (cartulary of La Sauve-Majeure) tome ii, pp. 297–8. s. xiii.

Omnibus Christi fidelibus ad quos presens scriptum pervenerit, Hugo dei gratia Lincolniensis episcopus salutem. Noverit universitas vestra nos gratas et ratas habere donationes factas*a* deo et ecclesie sancte Marie Silve Maioris atque monasterio de Burwell' monachisque ibidem deo famulantibus tam in ecclesiis quam in aliis possessionibus eis iuste collatis, videlicet, ecclesiam de Bur[p.298]well' cum capella sua de Aggleptort et ecclesiam de Walmesgar' cum omnibus ad easdem ecclesias pertinentibus, sicut in donatorum cartis continetur, ipsas igitur ecclesias prefato monasterio sancte Marie Silve Maioris et monasterio de Burguell' auctoritate qua fungimur confirmamus et sigilli nostri appositione roboramus, salvis episcopalibus consuetudinibus et Lincolniensis ecclesie dignitate. Hiis testibus: Roberto abbate de Bardeney, magistro Willelmo Blesen', subdecano Lincolniensi, magistro Rogero archidiacono Leirc', magistro Waltero Blund', magistro Gyrart de Rowell', magistro Ricardo de Swalewetua, Roberto de Capella, Galfrido de Lectelad', Samson de Rowell', Philippo Apostolorum, Hamelino decano, Hugone de sancto Edwardo, Eustachio de Wilton', magistro Willelmo de Muketon', Roberto capellano de Walmesgare, Herberto clerico de Burwell', et multis aliis.

a followed by a, *dotted for expunction* B.

William of Blois first occurs as subdean of Lincoln on 22 March 1194. Roger of Rolleston, who witnesses here as archdn of Leicester, succeeded Hamo as dean of Lincoln; Hamo last occurs *c*.March 1195.

172. Abbey of Savigny

Confirmation for the abbot and monks of Savigny of the church of [Long] Bennington, provision being made for a perpetual vicarage, the endowments of which are described.

[15 September 1189 × September 1193]

A = Paris, Archives nationales L.968, no. 224 (top edge trimmed). Endorsed: Carta Hugonis . Lincon' episcopi super ecclesia de Beligton' (s. xii ex.–s. xiii); T. ii; approx. 182 × 162 + 43 mm.; seal missing, white leather thong.

B = Cartulary of Savigny (formerly in the Archives dép. de la Manche, St Lô), destroyed in 1944.

Pd (calendar) from A in *CDF* no. 855 (at this time a fragment of the seal was still attached).

Hugo dei gratia Lincolniensis episcopus omnibus Christi fidelibus ad quos presens scriptum pervenerit ⫶ eternam in [domino] salutem. Notum sit universitati vestre nos concessisse et presenti carta confirmasse dilectis filiis nostris in Christo abbati et monachis Savign' ecclesiam de Benigton' . cum omnibus pertinentiis suis perpetuo possidendam .⫶ ita quod ipsi perpetuum vicarium presentabunt . assignatis ei ad sustentationem suam . et portanda onera episcopalia omnibus obventionibus altaris . et medietate terre ecclesie domorum et hominum et pratorum . reddendo inde annuatim prefatis monachis unum aureum ad Pascha. Abbas autem et monachi Savig[n' omnes] decimas bladi illius parrochie . et alteram medietatem terre domorum hominum et pratorum ad usus proprios possidebunt . salvo iure et Lincolniensis ecclesie dignitate. Quod ne in posterum alicuius malignitate possit infirmari ⫶ presentis scripti serie et sigilli nostri munimine confirmavimus. Testibus . Haimone decano Lincolniensi . magistro Rogero de Rolvestun . magistro Rogero de Sumerford' . magistro Symone de Sudwell[e . Iohanne .] et Galfrido de Lichelad' . canonicis Lincolniensibus . magistro Ricardo de Sualecliv' . Hugone de sancto Edwardo . magistro Luca et Eustacio de Wilton'.

Hamo became dean of Lincoln between 15 September 1189 and 24 March 1190; Roger of Rolleston, who attests here without a title, became archdn of Leicester *c*.1192 × September 1193 (see no. 11). The confirmation of this charter by the dean and chapter of Lincoln is *CDF* no. 856.

The leather thong may be a local Savigny production, cf. *EEA* ii no. 311; *Delisle* ii no. ccxxv.

173. Sempringham priory

Confirmation for the nuns and brethren of the church of St Mary, Sempringham, having inspected the charters, of the mediety of the church of Kirkby [Underwood], given to the priory by William d'Aubigny and Cecilia his mother, and confirmed by the bishop's predecessor, Robert [Chesney].

[15 September 1189 × September 1193]

A = Lincoln Cathedral Lib. (charter formerly in the possession of Sir Christopher and Lady Chancellor and previously in the possession of the Earl of Winchelsea and Nottingham). Endorsed: Confirmatio episcopi de Kirkebi (ss. xii ex.–xiii); Confirmacio .H. episcopi Linc' recapitulans confirmationem R. episcopi super advocatione ecclesie de Kyrkeby iuxta Aslakeby (s. xiii); approx. 156 × 140 + 18 mm.; splendid specimen of seal (plate IV), red wax, on parchment tag (d.q.1), no counterseal. Scribe **II**.

Omnibus Christi fidelibus ad quos presens scriptum pervenerit . Hug(o) dei gratia Lincolniensis episcopus salutem in domino. Cum ex pontificalis officii debito teneamur subditis nostris sua iura servare ⁊ potissimum viris religiosis in suo iure tenemur adesse . et contra malignantium incursus ⁊ eorum iura nostre auctoritatis subsidio communire. Eapropter ad universitatis vestre noticiam volumus pervenire . nos ratam habere et presenti carta confirmare concessionem et confirmationem quam bone memorie Rob(ertus) . quondam Lincolniensis episcopus rationabiliter fecit monialibus ecclesie sancte Marie de Simpingeham et fratribus earum super medietate ecclesie de Kirkeby quam habent ex donatione Willelmi de Aubeni et Cecilie matris eius . quorum cartas inspeximus et pre manibus sufficienter habuimus. Ut ergo hec nostra confirmatio perpetuis permaneat firma temporibus ⁊ eam presenti scripto et sigillo nostro duximus confirmandam . salvis episcopalibus consuetudinibus et Lincolniensis ecclesie dignitate. Test(ibus) . Hamone Lincolniensis ecclesie decano . magistro Rogero . de Rolvest' . Walk(elino) . capellano . magistro Nicholao de Derl' . magistro Ricardo de Swalew'

Hamo became dean of Lincoln at some date between 15 September 1189 and 24 March 1190; Roger of Rolleston, who attests here without a title, became archdn of Leicester *c*.1192 × September 1193 (see no. 11). this charter is almost certainly the one referred to in *HMCR* i (1874), ix, 14.

The original charter of William D'Aubigny [Dalbini] granting all his land in Kirkby to the nuns of Sempringham and confirming the gift of William de Raines of the wood of Frethegestahac in Kirkby Underwood is in the possession of Sir Christopher and Lady Chancellor. The original grant of William de Raines (Rennes) is BL Add. Ch. 21137.

174. Sempringham priory

Confirmation for the convent of St Mary, Sempringham, of the churches they possess in the diocese, in accordance with the charters of the donors and the confirmation of bishop Robert [Chesney], namely: the church of St Andrew, Sempringham, with the chapel of Pointon, the gift of Roger son of Jocelin; the church of St Aethelthryth, Stow by Threckingham, with the chapel of Birthorpe, the gift of William Pikenot; the church of St Peter, Kirkby by Sleaford [Kirkby Laythorpe], the gift of countess Alice de Gant and Hugh de Neville; and the church of St Mary, West Torrington, the gift of Agnes daughter of Jocelin and her son, Roger Musteil.

[15 September 1189 × September 1193]

B = Lincoln D. & C. Dij/64/2/1 (in an inspeximus of Roger, the dean and the chapter of Lincoln, c.1195 × 1200).
Pd from B in *Reg. Ant.* ii no. 338 (i).

Hiis testibus: Hamone decano Lincolniensi, Roberto archidiacono Huntend', Stephano cancellario Lincolniensi, magistro Rogero de Rolvestun, magistro Willelmo de Monte, magistro Ricardo de Sualeclif, Roberto de Insula, Galfrido de Lechelad', Eustachio clerico, Gerardo de Rouwell'.

Hamo became dean between 15 September 1189 and 24 March 1190; Roger de Rolleston became archdn of Leicester before September 1193 (see no. 11). For the dating of this charter see *Le Neve* app. 38. See also *EEA* i app. i, no. 23.

175. Sempringham priory

Grant to the convent of Sempringham in proprios usus *of the church of Stow [by Threckingham] and the chapel of Birthorpe, given to them by William Pikenot, the patron.*   [c.1194]

B = Lincoln D. & C. Dij/64/2/1 (in an inspeximus of Roger, the dean and the chapter of Lincoln, c.1195 × 1200).
Pd from B in *Reg. Ant.* ii no. 338 (ii).

Testibus: Hamone Lincolniensis ecclesie decano, magistro Willelmo subdecano, magistro Rogero archidiacono Leic', magistro Winemero archidiacono de Norhamt', magistro Stephano archidiacono de Bukingham, magistro Willelmo Lincolniensis ecclesie cancellario, magistro Ricardo de Sualeclif et magistro Gerardo de Rouwelle, magistro Symone de Siwelle, Radulfo de Virin, Ricardo de Kime, Galfrido de Lechelad', canonicis.

For the date of this charter see *Le Neve* app. 41. This document was most probably the one produced in the dispute between the prior of Sempringham and Walter of Birthorpe over the advowson of the chapel of Birthorpe in 1222 (*CRR* x 320; *Bracton's Note Book* ii no. 211, p. 171).

176. Sempringham priory

Grant to the convent of Sempringham in proprios usus *of the church of Laughton [by Folkingham], given to them by Hubert de Rye and Ralph Child, the patrons. Master Robert de Beaufoe, who had claimed against the convent, resigns any rights in the church into the bishop's hands.* [*c.*1194]

B = Lincoln D. & C. Dij/64/2/1 (in an inspeximus of Roger, the dean and the chapter of Lincoln, *c.*1195 × 1200).
Pd from B in *Reg. Ant.* ii no. 338 (iii).

Testibus: Hamone Lincolniensis ecclesie decano, magistro Willelmo subdecano, magistro Rogero archidiacono Leic', magistro Winemero archidiacono de Norhamt', Robert archidiacono de Hunt', magistro Stephano archidiacono de Bukingh', magistro Willelmo Lincolniensi cancellario, magistro Ricardo de Sualeclif.

For the date of this charter see *Le Neve* app. 41.

177. Sempringham priory

Grant to the convent of Sempringham in proprios usus *of the church of Billingborough, given to them by Roger Burnel, the patron.* [*c.*1194]

B = Lincoln D. & C. Dij/64/2/1 (in an inspeximus of Roger, the dean and the chapter of Lincoln, *c.*1195 × 1200).
Pd from B in *Reg. Ant.* ii no. 338 (iv).

Hiis testibus: magistro Willelmo cancellario Lincolniensi, magistro Ricardo de Sualeclif, Roberto de Capella, magistro Gerardo de Rouwell', magistro Alexandro de Aunest', Galfrido de Deping', canonicis Lincolniensibus.

For the date of this charter see *Le Neve* app. 41.

178. Sixhills priory

Confirmation for the convent of St Mary, Sixhills, of the churches of All Saints, Sixhills, St Helen, Ludford [Magna], St Thomas, [North]

Willingham, All Saints, Tealby, St Thomas, East [Market] Rasen, St Mary, East Wykeham, a mediety of the church of St Edward, West Wykeham, and the churches of St Margaret, Saleby and St Peter, [South] Cadeby.   [15 September 1189 × 1192]

B = Lincoln D. & C. Dij/64/2/1 (in an inspeximus of Roger, the dean and the chapter of Lincoln, c.1195 × 1200).

Pd from B in *Reg. Ant.* ii no. 338 (viii).

Hiis testibus: magistro Hamone summo decano, [Wi]nemero sub-decano, Roberto de Hardr', Sampsone, canonico Lond', magistro Rogero de Rolvest', Roberto Bardulf, magistro Ricardo.

For the date of this charter see *Le Neve* p. 144 and app. 36; cf. no. 28. It is probable that 'canonico Lond'' is a scribal error for 'canonico Linc''.

179. Southwick priory

General confirmation of possessions for the canons of St Mary, Southwick, after having inspected the charters of the donors.
                                [1197 × 16 November 1200]

B = Hampshire Record Office, IM.54/1 (Southwick cartulary I) fo. 29r. s. xiii.
C = bid. IM.54/3 (Southwick cartulary III) fo. 19v. s. xiv ex.

Omnibus sancte matris ecclesie filiis tam presentibus quam futuris ad quos presens scriptum pervenerit, Hugo dei gratia Lincolniensis episcopus eternam in domino salutem. Ea que religiosis domibus divino intuitu pia largitione*ᵃ* fidelium conferuntur perpetua debent stabilitate gaudere et ne inposterum malignantium molestiis agitentur episcopalis confirmationis debent beneficio communiri. Inde est quod ad universitatis vestre volumus notitiam pervenire quod nos inspectis pariter et auditis cartis virorum illustrium Willelmi de Hum' super donatione redditus quatuor marcarum in terris et hominibus apud Keten'*ᵇ*, et Roberti de Novo Burgo de duabus bovatis terre apud Coteshmore*ᶜ*, et Guidonis de Diva de redditu duarum marcarum in terris et hominibus et in parte molendini apud Holewel'*ᵈ* in parochia de Gildeburg', predictas donationes ecclesie sancte Marie de Suwic'*ᵉ* et canonicis eiusdem loci rationabiliter factas ratas habentes, eas eidem ecclesie episcopalis autoritatis*ᶠ* munimine confirmamus. Paci quoque et indempnitati prescriptorum canonicorum religionis gratia providere volentes, distrixius*ᵍ* inhibemus ne quis homines seu possessiones eorum que in Lincolniensi diocesi sunt indebite vexari vel molestare presumat. Ut autem hec donationes firmius et liberius perseverent, sigilli nostri appositione ipsas duximus roborare. His*ʰ* testibus: magistro Ricardo Lincolniensis ecclesie subdecano*ⁱ*, Roberto de Capella*ʲ*,

Hugone presbitero, et magistro Galfrido de Dep', Lincolniensis ecclesie canonicis, Hugone de Bobi senescallo nostro, Rogero Bacun, Eustachio de Wilton' et aliis multis.

a largione B.   *b* Ketena C.   *c* Cotteshmor' C.   *d* Holewell' C.   *e* Suthewyk' C.
f auctoritatis C.   *g* districtius C.   *h* Hiis C.   *i* subdiacono C.   *j* C *adds* et multis aliis *and ends here.*

Richard of Kent became subdean of Lincoln in 1197. The inventory of deeds in Southwick cartulary II (Hampshire Record Office, IM.54/2, fo. 25r) records that bp Hugh's confirmation was kept in *cophinus primus* among the priory's archives. The charter of William de Humet is on fo. 11r (no. xlvi) of B, with related documents, fo. 11r–v, nos. xlvii–l; that of Robert de Novo Burgo on fo. 13r (no. lvi); and that of Guy de Diva on fo. 26r–v. The Humet and Novo Burgo charters were probably issued at a similar time since they have twelve witnesses in common, including archbp John of Dublin and the abbots of Durford and Croxden.

180. Spalding priory

Institution of William the chaplain to the perpetual vicarage of Spalding, on the presentation of the prior and convent of Spalding. The endowments of the vicarage are described.

[? 21 September 1186 × 16 November 1200]

B = BL ms. Add. 35296 (Spalding cartulary) fo. 285r (57r). s. xiv in.

Universis sancte matris ecclesie filiis ad quos presens scriptum pervenerit, H. dei gratia Lincolniensis episcopus salutem in domino. Noverit universitas vestra nos, ad presentationem prioris et conventus de Spalding' patronorum ecclesie de Spalding', dilectum in Christo filium Willelmum capellanum*a* ad perpetuam eiusdem ecclesie de Spald' vicariam admisisse et ipsum in eadem vicarium perpetuum instituisse. Consistit autem*b* eadem vicaria in exhibitione capellani qui debet accipere panem monachalem et servisiam*c* cum generali de coquina et ad palefridum suum necessaria in avena et foragine. Consistit etiam vicaria in decimationibus operariorum et omnium mercatorum ville de Spalding' cum legatis capellano*d* debitis et visitationibus infirmorum cum denariis missalibus et denariis cum pane benedicto oblatis et caseis ad Pentecost' et gallinis ad natale predicte ecclesie de Spald' debitis; salvis in omnibus episcopalibus consuetudinibus et Lincolniensis ecclesie dignitate. Et ut hec institutio nostra perpetuam optineat firmitatem, eam presenti scripto et sigilli nostri duximus appositione confirmandam. T(estibus) etc.

a *The scribe of* B *has inserted an extra minim in this word.*   *b* ante B.
c 'c' *originally written at the beginning and altered to* 's'; *also an extra minim inserted in this word* B.   *d* capelpellano B.

It is not quite certain which bp Hugh issued this document. The vicarage was ordained before the Fourth Lateran Council (*Lib. Ant.* 65); on the other hand bp

Hugh II instituted a William of Alkborough, chaplain, to the vicarage, 20 December 1228 × 19 December 1229 (*RHW* iii 167). This might be the occasion when this letter of institution was issued, merely with a rehearsal of the vicarage endowments.

181. Spalding priory

Confirmation of the release by the abbot and monks of Peterborough to the prior and monks of Spalding of all rights in the church of Alkborough and the chapel of Walcot; and furthermore, confirmation of the grant made by the abbot and monks of Peterborough to Spalding priory of one carucate of land in Alkborough and one bovate of land in Walcot, subject to an annual pension of one silver mark, and also the payment of three shillings and three loaves of hastybere bread (panes de hastivell') *each year.*   [15 September 1189 × c. 1191]

B = BL ms. Add. 35296 (Spalding cartulary) fo. 330v (332v). s. xiv in. C = BL ms. Harl. 742 (Spalding cartulary) fo. 270v (ccxxix v). s. xiv in.

Universis[a] sancte matris ecclesie filiis ad quos presens scriptum pervenerit, Hugo dei gratia Lincolniensis episcopus salutem in domino. Noverit universitas vestra nos ratam habere relaxationem factam primo priori et monachis de Spald' ab abbate et monachis Burgi de universo iure quod ipsi dicebant se habere in ecclesia de Hautebarge et capella de Walecote[b] et in appenditiis suis. Ratam etiam habemus[c] concessionem factam eidem priori et monachis a iamdictis abbate et monachis Burgi de una carucata terre in Hautebarg'[d] et una[e] bovata terre in Walecot'[f] quas prenominati prior et monachi de Spald' tenebunt de prefatis abbate et monachis de Burgo, solvendo inde singulis annis i marcam argenti ad firmam de Walecote[f] ad duos terminos in natale domini et in nativitate sancti Iohannis Baptiste et preterea solvendo inde memoratis abbati[g] et monachis Burgi iii solidos et iii panes de hastivell'[h] singulis annis[i] in passione apostolorum Petri et Pauli apud Burgum. Quod ut ratum habeatis et inconvulsum,[j] presentis pagine in scriptione et sigilli nostri appositione corroboravimus.[k] T(estibus).[l]

[a] Oniversis C.   [b] Walcote C.   [c] et *added here* B.   [d] Hautebarge C.   [e] *altered later to* duabus B.   [f] Walcot' C.   [g] abbatis C.   [h] hast' C.   [i] anns C.   [j] *There is one minim too many in this word in* C.   [k] corroboravinus C.   [l] Dat' C.

The use of 'Dat'' in C might reasonably suggest bp Hugh II rather than Hugh I but other evidence in the cartularies confirms that this actum was issued by Hugh I. On fos. 270v–271r of C there is a ratification by abbot William and the convent of St Nicholas, Angers (the mother-house of Spalding) of this agreement between abbot Benedict and the convent of Peterborough and prior Nicholas and the convent of Spalding. Prior Nicholas was deposed c.1191. His own charter is on fo. 271v of C and is attested by Hamo, dean of Lincoln. Hamo became dean at some date

between 15 September 1189 and 24 March 1190. It is more than likely that bp
Hugh's confirmation dates from a similar time soon after the agreement was made.

182. Spalding priory

*Decision made by the bishop, the abbot of Revesby and master Roger of
Rolleston settling a dispute between the prior and monks of Spalding
and the prior and convent of Trentham over the church of Belchford.
The prior and monks of Spalding shall have the mediety of the church
which was Alexander Malebisse's, quit of all exactions, saving the
dignity of the church of Lincoln; likewise the prior and convent of
Trentham shall possess the other mediety. The bishop has admitted
Peter son of William of Paris into the mediety, formerly Alexander
Malebisse's, on the presentation of the prior and monks of Spalding,
saving to the priory an annual pension of fifteen shillings to be paid by
Peter.*   [21 September 1186 × September 1193]

B = BL ms. Add. 35296 (Spalding cartulary) fos. 386v–387r ($\overset{xx}{v}$ vi v–$\overset{xx}{v}$ vii r,
389v–390r). s. xiv in.

Pd (inaccurately) from a later transcript (BL ms. Cole 43, p. 430) in 'Chartulary of
the "Austin" Priory of Trentham', ed. F. Parker (*Collections for a history of
Staffordshire* xi (William Salt Archaeological Society, 1870) 317).

Omnibus Christi fidelibus ad quos presens scriptum pervenerit, Hugo
dei gratia Lincolniensis episcopus salutem in domino. Noverit universitas vestra controversiam[a] que vertebatur inter priorem et monachos
de Spald' et priorem et conventum de Trentham super ecclesiam de
Beltisford arbitrio nostro et abbatis de Revisbi et magistri Rogeri de
Rovelesto in quos compromiserant post multas et longas altercationes[b]
sub tali forma sopitam fuisse, videlicet, quod prior et monachi Spald'
medietatem ecclesie de Beltisford' que fuit Alexandri Malebissi
quietam et solutam ab omni exactione, salva in omnibus Lincolniensis
ecclesie dignitate, inperpetuum tenebunt. Prior vero et canonici de
Trentham aliam medietatem eadem libertate presidebunt inperpetuum. Sopita itaque inter eos con'tro'versia facta pace firmiter
atque conconditer[c], Petrum filium Willelmi de Paris ad presentationem predictorum prioris[d] et monachorum Spald' in illam [fo. 387r]
medietatem prefate ecclesie que fuit Alexandri Maleb' recepimus et
eum in eadem medietate vicarium perpetuum sine omni contradictione instituimus[e], salva in omnibus domui Spald' xv solidorum
pensionem annuatim a predicto Petro solvendorum.

[a] conversiam B.   [b] alternationes B.   [c] concordiam B.   [d] prior B.   [e] instituius B.

Roger of Rolleston, who is not described here as archdn of Leicester, succeeded to
that office c.1192 × September 1193 (see no. 11). For Alexander Malebisse, who
was a canon of Lincoln, see *Le Neve* 120–1.

183. Spalding priory

Institution of Roger de Gene, clerk, to the church of Addlethorpe, on the presentation of I., prior and the monks of Spalding.

[*c*.1191 × 16 November 1200]

B = BL ms. Add. 35296 (Spalding cartulary) fo. 385r ($\overset{xx}{v}$ v r, 388r). s. xiv in.

Omnibus Christi fidelibus ad quos presens scriptum pervenerit, H. dei gratia Lincolniensis episcopus eternam in domino salutem. Noverit universitas vestra nos, ad presentationem I. prioris et monachorum de Spald', recepisse dilectum filium nostrum Rogerum de Gene clericum ad ecclesiam de Hardelistorp, ipsumque in ea personam canonice instituisse, salvis episcopalibus consuetudinibus et Lincolniensis ecclesie dignitate. Quod ut ratum permaneat, presenti scripto et sigilli nostri patrocinio illud confirmavimus. T(estibus).

> On fo. 385v of B there is recorded the letter of presentation of Roger de Genn' by prior G. and the convent of Spalding, attested by bp Hugh and G. de Rowell, canon of Lincoln. The prior must be Jollanus or Goslenus; his predecessor, Nicholas I, was deposed *c*.1191.

184. Spalding priory

Institution of John of St Edward, clerk, to a mediety of the church of Belchford, on the presentation of the prior and monks of Spalding, saving the due and ancient pension to the priory.

[*c*.1191 × 16 November 1200]

B = BL ms. Add. 35296 (Spalding cartulary) fo. 387v ($\overset{xx}{v}$ vii v, 390v). s. xiv in.

Omnibus Christi fidelibus ad quos presens scriptum pervenerit, Hugo dei gratia Lincolniensis episcopus eternam in domino salutem. Noveritis nos ad presentationem dilectorum in Christo filiorum prioris et monachorum de Spald' patronorum medietatis ecclesie de Beltisford' recepisse dilectum filium Iohannem de sancto Eduuardo clericum ad prefatam medietatem eiusdem ecclesie ipsumque in ea personam canonice instituisse, salva dictis priori et monachis debita et antiqua de eadem medietate pensione; salvis etiam in omnibus episcopalibus consuetudinibus et Lincolniensis ecclesie dignitate. In huius itaque robur et testimonium presenti scripto sigillum nostrum apposuimus. Valete.

> On fo. 387r of B is the letter of presentation of John of St. Edward by prior I. and the convent of Spalding. This must be prior Jollanus or Goslenus, who succeeded Nicholas I (deposed *c*.1191). The previous incumbent of the mediety is named as Peter of Paris (see no. 182 above).

*185. Stainfield priory

Admission of the prioress and nuns of Stainfield into the personatus *of a mediety of the church of Quadring, on the presentation of Ralph de Fenne, the patron, and in the presence of Waleran of Rochford and Albreda his wife, daughter of the aforementioned Ralph. This was done in Lincoln cathedral.*   [21 September 1186 × 16 November 1200]

> Mention of charter produced in a dispute between Waleran of Rochford and
> Albreda his wife, and the prior of Stainfield over the advowson of the mediety,
> 1201.
>
> Pd, *CRR* i 460.

*186. Stainfield priory

Similar charter, confirming Ralph de Fenne's gift of the mediety of the church of Quadring to the nuns of Stainfield.
[21 September 1186 × 16 November 1200]

> Mention of charter produced in a dispute between Waleran of Rochford and
> Albreda his wife, and the prior of Stainfield, 1201.
>
> Pd, *CRR* i 460.

187. Stamford, St Michael's priory

Confirmation for the nuns of St Michael, Stamford, of a third part of the church of Corby, given to them by Matilda de Dive and Hugh her son, in usus proprios.   [*c.*1192 × 6 June 1199]

> B = Bodl. ms. Dodsworth 59 (ex quibusdam antiquis rotulis in pergameno penes
> me Rogerum Dodsworth) pp. 166–7. s. xvii.
>
> Pd from B in *Academia Tertia* lib. viii, 7 & n.b (omitting some witnesses).

Omnibus Christi fidelibus ad quos presens scriptum pervenerit, Hugo dei gratia Lincolniensis episcopus eternam in domino salutem. Noverit universitas vestra nos divine pietatis intuitu consideranda et paupertate domus beati Michaelis de Stanford' auctoritate episcopali concessisse et confirmasse deo et beate Mariae et sancto Michaeli et monialibus ibidem deo servientibus tertiam partem ecclesie de Corbi cum omnibus ad eandem portionem pertinentibus ad eorundem monialium sustentationem in usus proprios perpetuo possidendam, quam 'quidem' partem ex donatione et presentatione domine Matill(dis) de Diva et Hugonis filii et heredis eius rationabiliter adepte sunt; salvis episcopalibus consuetudinibus et Lincolniensis ecclesie dignitate. Ut firmum et illibatum cunctis diebus permaneat, presenti scripto sigilli nostri appositione corroborato communivimus. Hiis testibus: magistro R. [p. 167] archidiacono de Leircest', magistro L. archidiacono de Bedeford', magistro Ricardo de Swaleclive, Roberto de Capella, Galfrido de Lichelad, Galfrido de Deping, canonicis Lincolnensis ecclesie, Rogero Bacc(un), Hugone*a* de Rolveston', Roberto de Dunestaple, Galfrido de Stanford' decano et multis aliis.

a Hugo B.

It is not certain whether archdn R. of Leicester is Roger of Rolleston or his successor, Raymond; Roger became archdn *c.*1192 × September 1193 (see no. 11). Archdn Laurence of Bedford last occurs *c.*1198 and certainly was no longer in office by 6 June 1199.

188.   Stamford, St Michael's priory

Confirmation for the nuns of St Michael, Stamford, of the churches of St Martin, All Saints, St Andrew and St Clement in Stamford, the church of St Firmin, Thurlby, the third part of the church of Corby, and the tithes of the assarts of Matilda de Dive.

[21 September 1186 × 16 November 1200]

B = Bodl. ms. Dodsworth 59, p. 166. s. xvii.
Pd from B in *Academia Tertia* lib. viii, 7–8 & n.c.

Omnibus Christi fidelibus ad quos presens scriptum pervenerit, Hugo dei gratia Lincolniensis episcopus salutem et benedictionem. Licet ex suscepte administrationis officio teneamur ea quae locis religionis offeruntur beneficia nostrae autoritatis 'patrocinio' defendere et contra malignantium incursus episcopali protectione communire. Ad universitatis vestre' volumus notitiam pervenire nos ratas habere et presenti carta confirmare*a* donationes sicut rationabiliter factae sunt deo et ecclesiae sancti Michaelis de Stanford' et monialibus ibidem deo servientibus super ecclesiis sancti Martini et omnium sanctorum et sancti Andree et sancti Clementis in villa Stanford' et sancti Firmini de*b* Turlebi et super tertiam partem ecclesiae de Corbi et de decimis de sartis Matild(is) de Diva, sicut cartae donatorum testantur. Quod ut inperpetuum ratum et firmum permaneat*c*, presenti carta et sigillo nostro duximus confirmandum; salva Lincolniensis ecclesie dingnitate et episcopalibus consuetudinibus.

a confirmasse *originally written* B, *with 'r' interlined.*   *b* de *repeated* B, *the first one crossed through.*   *c* *omitted* B.

For the priory of St Michael and its churches in Stamford see J. S. Hartley and A. Rogers, *The Religious Foundations of Medieval Stamford* (Stamford Survey Group Report 2, 1974); Royal Commission on Historical Monuments, *The Town of Stamford* (1977), 31–2.

188A.   Stamford, St Michael's priory

Inspeximus of a charter of prior Robert and the convent of St-Fromond settling the dispute between his house and the nuns of St Michael,

Stamford, over the church of All Saints, Stamford, by amicable composition. The prior confirms the church to the nuns of St Michael's, saving the ancient pension of two silver marks each year payable to St-Fromond. The nuns shall pay episcopal dues and shall bear all ordinary burdens. The bishop confirms the composition and institutes the nuns into corporal possession of the church of All Saints.

[1192 × September 1193]

A = PRO E210/7337 (damaged and repaired — conjectural reconstructions in square brackets). Endorsed: Confirmacio .H. episcopi . Linc' ; super composicione facta monialibus . de Stanf' . a priore et conventu sancti Fromundi de ecclesia omnium sanctorum in foro. (s. xiii); approx. 196 × 184 + 18 mm. (seal fold flattened); no seal or seal-tag (the section of the turn-up round the slit for the seal-tag torn away). Scribe **I**.

Omnibus Christi fidelibus ad quos presens scriptum pervenerit ; Hugo dei gratia Lincolniensis episcopus salutem in domino. Ad universitatis vestre notitiam volumus pervenire . dilectas filias nostras priorissam et moniales sancti Michaelis in Stamford' nobis exhibuisse scriptum autenticum inter ipsas et priorem atque conventum sancti Fromundi super ecclesia omnium sanctorum in foro de Stamford' ; factum . in hec verba . Universis sancte matris ecclesie filiis ad quos presens scriptum pervenerit . Robertus dictus prior sancti Fromundi et conventus eiusdem loci ; salutem in Christo. Noverit universitas vestra . quod controversia que mota erat inter nos et moniales sancti Michaelis de Stamford' super ecclesia omnium sanctorum in foro eiusdem ville . ita amicabili compositione sopita est. Ex communi etenim consilio concessimus et presenti carta nostra confirmavimus predictis monialibus antedictam ecclesiam cum omnibus ei a[di]acentibus solvendo nobis antiquam pensionem ; scilicet duas marcas argenti . ad terminum rogationum omni anno. E[t] predicte sanctimoniales episcopalia solvent et omnia onera ordinaria agnoscent . salva pensione nostra du[arum mar]carum. Hiis testibus . Willelmo monacho . Andrea monacho . Gaufrido tunc decano . Alstano capellano [   ] capellano . Matheo capellano . Alexandro capellano . Waltero capellano . Reiner(o) diacono . magistro Samson(e) . Gaufrido filio Reiner(i) . et aliis pluribus. Nos itaque hanc pacis formam et compositionem sicut rationabiliter facta est gratam et ratam habentes ; eam episcopali autoritate confirmamus et presentis scripti serie sigilli que nostri appositione robboramus. Sanctimoniales quoque prefatas in iam dicta ecclesia omnium sanctorum canonice instituimus . salvis episcopalibus consuetudinibus et Lincolniensis ecclesie dignitate. Hiis testibus . Haimone decano Lincolniensis ecclesie . Benedicto abbate Burg' . Winem(ero) Norhamton' . Roberto Huntedon' . et Rogero Leircestren' ; archidiaconis .

L

magistro Ricardo de Swaleweclíva . Galfrido de Lecchelad' . et
Roberto de Capella ·' Lincolniensis ecclesie canonicis . Walkelino
priore de Land' . Virgilio . magistro Roberto de Glamford' . magistro
Damiano . Roberto de Neovill' . Eustachio de Wilton' . et aliis multis.

This confirmation can be closely dated by the witnesses, and furnishes a closer date
for the appointments of Winemer and Roger of Rolleston to their respective
archdeaconries than previously known. Benedict of Peterborough died as abbot 25
or 29 September 1193 — one source gives 1194 but 1193 is the generally accepted
year (*HRH* 61). Roger of Rolleston was still not archdeacon in an actum probably
datable to 1192 and certainly 1192×September 1193 (see no. 11 above). The
original composition of prior Robert is pd in T. Madox, *Formulare Anglicanum*
(1702), p. 24, no. xliii. The church was granted to St Michael's by Achard of
Stamford in the reign of Henry II (*Mon. Angl.* iv p. 263, no. xx). The dating of the
St-Fromond dispute, noted in J. S. Hartley and A. Rogers, *The Religious
Foundations of Medieval Stamford* (Stamford Survey Group Report 2, 1974),
p. 18, needs amending in the light of this actum.

189. Stixwould priory

*Confirmation for the nuns of Stixwould of their lands in Bassingthorpe
and Stixwould, given by countess Lucy and confirmed by Rannulf,
earl of Chester, and William de Roumare.*

[21 September 1186 × 16 November 1200]

B = BL ms. Add. 46701 (Stixwould cartulary) fo. 2r (p. 3). s. xiii ex.

H. dei gratia Lincolniensis episcopus omnibus fidelibus sancte dei
ecclesie clericis et laycis salutem et paternam benedictionem. Sciatis
quod ego confirmo et firmiter concedo quod moniales de Styk' teneant
bene et in pace et quiete et honorifice totam terram de Torp et de
Stykeswald liberam et solutam*ᵃ* ab omni seculari servitio et cum
omnibus pertinentiis suis sicut Lucia comitissa eis dedit et concessit in
elemosinam pro salute anime sue et sicut Rannulfus comes Cest' et
Willelmus de Romar' illud postea confirmaverunt et concesserunt per
cartas suas et precor vos sicut filios karissimos sancte ecclesie ut eas
pro salute animarum vestrarum adiuvetis et manuteneatis et de
beneficiis vestris eis impertiamini et sub anatemate pono ne aliquis
violentia vel rapina illud donum eis auferat. Valete.

ᵃ liberas et solutas B.

This confirmation is modelled very closely on the confirmation by Hugh's
predecessor, Alexander, issued 1139×1148 (*EEA* i no. 57), except that the
Honington property mentioned in the latter document is not noted here. The fact
that the form of this confirmation is, diplomatically, archaic for the late twelfth
century does not necessarily mean that the document is spurious, merely that the
scribe closely copied an earlier confirmation with only the most necessary altera-
tions (cf. ibid. liii).

190. Stixwould priory

Confirmation for the nuns of Stixwould of the church of Lavington, and its chapels, in proprios usus.

[21 September 1186 × 16 November 1200]

B = BL ms. Add. 46701 (Stixwould cartulary) fos. 98v–99r (pp. 196–7). s. xiii ex.
C = ibid. fo. 100v (p. 200) (in an inspeximus of archbp Hubert Walter of Canterbury, 1201 × 1205).

Universis etc.[a] Hugo dei gratia Lincolniensis episcopus eternam in domino salutem. Ad pastoris spectat sollicitudinem subditis et maxime religionis nomen professis pacem providere, et que eorum recte deputata sunt usibus summo opere fovere et perpetuo stabilire. Huius igitur rationis intuitu dilectis nobis in Christo filiabus nostris monialibus de Styk', quas conversatio religiosa et paupertas honesta favorabiles et commendabiles reddunt, ecclesiam de Lavingtun' cum capellis suis et omnibus ad eam pertinentibus sicut eam rationabiliter adepte sunt, auctoritate episcopali confirmamus, tenendam et possidendam et fructus eiusdem ecclesie et pertinentium in usus proprios earundem sanctimonialium convertendos et perpetuo possidendos, salvis etiam episcopalibus consuetudinibus et Lincolniensis ecclesie dignita[fo.88r]te. Quod ut ratum et firmum permaneat, presenti scripto sigilli nostri[b] appositione communito confirmavimus. Test(ibus).

[a] Universis sancte matris ecclesie filiis ad quos presens scriptum pervenerit C.   [b] mei *written first B and dotted for expunction.*

Archbp Hubert's inspeximus is pd (except for bp Hugh's charter) in *EEA* iii no. 619.

191. Stoke by Clare priory

Notification by the bishop, Hamo dean of Lincoln and master R(oger) of Rolleston to Godfrey bishop of Winchester that in the case heard by them as papal judges delegate between the prior of Stoke by Clare and Jordan, Robert, and Theoderic, clerks, concerning the church of Woking, the clerks have resigned the church with its chapels into the hands of the judges and the latter have restored it to the prior, saving to the clerks the perpetual vicarages acknowledged by the prior.

[22 October 1189 × September 1193]

B = BL ms. Cotton app. xxi (Stoke by Clare cartulary) fo. 50r (no witnesses). s. xiii med.

Pd from B in *Stoke by Clare Cartulary* i no. 102.

Godfrey de Lucy was consecrated bp of Winchester on 22 October 1189, and Roger of Rolleston, here described without title, became archdn of Leicester *c.*1192 × September 1193 (see no. 11).

192. Sulby abbey

Notification to the barons of the Exchequer and the king's justices of
proceedings in a case about the church of [Great] Harrowden between
the abbot of Sulby and Robert de Muschamps.

[21 September 1186 × 16 November 1200]

B = BL Add. Ch. 22002 (in an inspeximus of bp Oliver Sutton of Lincoln, 3 July
1288).

H. dei gratia Lincolniensis episcopus venerabilibus amicis baronibus
de scaccario et aliis iust(itiariis) domini regis salutem in Christo.
Noverit discretio vestra quod cum Alexander de Cranel' quondam
persona ecclesie de Harwedon' esset de medio sublatus, decanus loci,
qui decanatum illum de novo adeptus est, ecclesiam illam in manum
nostram recepit. Postmodum autem Robertus de Muschamps ad nos
accedens clericum ad prefatam ecclesiam presentavit. Abbas vero de
Suleby, qui tunc presens erat, asserebat se eiusdem ecclesie personam
esse per presentationem Marie de Muschamp' et a Savarico archidiacono Norham' institutum fuisse. Affuit etiam clericus quidam
Helias nomine qui se eiusdem ecclesie de Harwedon' vicarium esse
proponebat, presentatum videlicet a prefato abbate et a prenotato
archidiacono similiter institutum. Nos igitur volentes utrique parti ius
suum conservare diem eis statuimus quo coram nobis comparerent in
sinodo Norham' et ius quod in eadem ecclesia haberent ibidem
ostenderent. Die igitur assignata abbas cartam M. de Muschamp' et
cartam Savarici archidiaconi protulit in medium quibus testimonium
perhibuerunt. Hii qui testes in carta archidiaconi conscripti erant qui
tunc interfuerunt, H. clericus nichilominus cartam archidiaconi S.
de institutione sua exhibuit. Interim autem ne quid precipitanter
ageremus alium partibus diem assignavimus, ad quem diem comparentibus coram clericis abbate et H. clerico, R. de Muschamp' non
comparens Reginaldum Murdac procuratorem suum pro se destinavit.
Abbas igitur et H. clericus cartas suas denuo exhibuerunt et preterea
de ⸱possessione sua testes ydoneos produxerunt. Quibus omnibus
instructi clerici nostri, procuratore quoque R. de Muschamp' nichil in
contrarium probante, abbati et prefato clerico possessiones suas
restituerunt, abbati scilicet personatus et clerico vicarie possessionem
adiudicantes. Valete in domino.

It is not definitely certain from the wording of the document whether Savaric was
still archdn of Northampton. The use of 'quondam' might be expected if the
document was issued after 1192 when he became bp of Bath; on the other hand, if
he was still archdn, it is surprising that he was not called on to verify his part in the
earlier proceedings.

*193. Sulby abbey

Appropriation to the abbey of Sulby of the church of Addington, given to them by Alnath Papillun. [? 21 September 1186 × 20 September 1192]

> Mention of charter produced in a dispute between Richard de Waterville and the abbot of Sulby over the advowson of the church, 1233.
>
> Pd, *CRR* xv no. 831; *Bracton's Note Book* ii no. 820, p. 628.

A charter of archdn Savaric of Northampton admitting the abbey to the church on Alnath's presentation was also produced in the case. Savaric was consecrated as bp of Bath on 20 September 1192. See also no. 293.

194. Tewkesbury abbey

Confirmation for the monks of Tewkesbury, after inspection of the charters of Robert FitzHamon and the earl of Gloucester, of the churches of [Great] Marlow and Hambleden, given to them by these patrons.   [? 21 September 1186 × 16 November 1200]

> B = BL ms. Cotton Cleop. A vii (abstract of Tewkesbury abbey charters) fo. 84r (80r, 82r). s. xiii med.
>
> Pd from B in *Mon. Angl.* ii 75, no. lxxii.

The bp could be either Hugh I or Hugh II. Robert FitzHamon died in 1107 (*Ann. mon.* i 9, 44) and the charter of the earl of Gloucester referred to may be the confirmation of earl William, dated 11 January 1148 (*Earldom of Gloucester Charters*, ed. R. B. Patterson (Oxford 1973) no. 179).

195. Tewkesbury abbey

Institution of Robert Bardulf to the church of Hambleden, on the presentation of the monks of Tewkesbury, saving an annual pension of sixty shillings.   [? 21 September 1186 × 16 November 1200]

> B = BL ms. Cotton Cleop. A vii (abstract of Tewkesbury abbey charters) fo. 84r (80r, 82r). s. xiii med.
>
> Pd from B in *Mon. Angl.* ii 75, no. lxxii.

The bp could be either Hugh I or Hugh II, although there is no record of this institution in the latter's enrolments (*RHW*). A Robert Bardolf or Bardulf was a canon of Lincoln (*Le Neve* 72) and according to the Barlings cartulary was rector of thirty churches (see C. Clay, 'Hugh Bardolf the Justice and his Family' in *LHA* i (1966) 4–28). Whether the rector of Hambleden is to be identified with him is uncertain.

196. Thorney abbey

Institution of Simon de Hillegha to the church of Stanground, on the presentation of the abbot and convent of Thorney, saving to the abbey an annual pension, namely a tenth of the tithes of corn which Simon receives from the parish and the whole tithe of the corn which he, or another in his name, cultivates.

[15 September 1189 × 22 March 1194]

B = CUL ms. Add. 3021 (Thorney cartulary) fos. 410v–411r (pars nona, ix v–x r), no. xii. s. xiv in.

Omnibus Christi fidelibus ad quos presens scriptum pervenerit, Hugo dei gratia Lincolniensis episcopus salutem in domino. Ad universitatis vestre notitiam volumus pervenire nos, ad presentationem abbatis et conventus de Thorn', Simonem de Hillegha clericum ad ecclesiam de Stangrund' recepisse et ipsum in eadem instituisse, salva pensione annua quam debet monasterio de Thorn', scilicet decima decimarum bladi quam de parochia percipit et tota decima bladi quod vel ipse propriis sumptibus vel alius eius nomine excolit; salvis etiam episcopalibus consuetudinibus et Lincolniensis ecclesie dignitate. Quod ut ratum habeatur et firmum, presenti scripto et sigillo nostro duximus confirmandum. Testibus: Hamone Lincolniensis ecclesie decano, magistro Stephano Lincolniensis ecclesie cancellario, Roberto de Hardres archidiacono Huntend' etc.

Hamo the dean and Stephen the chancellor both first occur after 15 September 1189; Stephen had been succeeded as chancellor by 22 March 1194.

*197. Thornton Curtis abbey

Confirmation for the abbey of Thornton [Curtis] of the church of Welton le Marsh, saving the life interest of Herbert the clerk, son of Matthew, the donor of the church. [21 September 1186 × 16 November 1200]

Mention of charter produced in a dispute between Walter de Hamby and the abbot of Thornton [Curtis] over the advowson of the church, 1221.

Pd, *CRR* x 42.

See also no. 295.

198. Thornton Curtis abbey

Confirmation of the composition made between the canons of Thornton and the canons of Guisborough over the church of Kirklevington, the chapel of Yarm, the church of Skelton [in Cleveland], and the church of Kelstern with its appurtenances and six bovates of land. The canons of Thornton renounce their claim to Kirklevington, Yarm and Skelton, and shall hold Kelstern and its land of the canons of Guisborough for an annual pension of one aureus *or two shillings. The right of T. the parson of Kelstern is safeguarded in accordance with the rescript of the judges delegate, the abbot of Meaux and the priors of Bridlington and Warter.* [late May 1191 × 1197]

B = BL ms. Lansdowne 207A (collections of Gervase Holles) fo. 151r–v (pp. 281–2). s. xvii in.

Omnibus etc. Hugo dei gratia Lincolniensis episcopus salutem. Ea que inter viros religiosos solempniter acta sunt ad posterorum memoriam decet scripture testimonio communire et episcopalis auctoritatis subsidio roborare. Ad universitatis igitur vestre notitiam volumus pervenire, nos ratam habere et presenti carta confirmare compositionem rationabiliter factam inter canonicos de Torenton et canonicos de Giseburn super ecclesiam de Levington et capellam de Iarum*a* et ecclesiam de Scelton, quibus canonici de Torenton spontanea voluntate renuntiaverunt, et super ecclesiam de Kelesterne cum pertinentiis suis et cum sex bovatis terre, quam quidem ecclesiam canonici de Torenton debent in perpetuum tenere de canonicis de Giseburn cum predicta terra sub annua [fo. 151v] pensione unius aurei vel duorum solidorum ipsis canonicis de Giseburn annuatim solvendorum; salvo iure quod T. persona ecclesie de Kellesterne in eadem ecclesia dinoscitur habere, sicut rescriptum iudicum delegatorum T. abbatis de Melsa et H. et I. de Bledlington et de Wartria priorum coram quibus compositio illa facta est protestatur etc.

a Sarum B.

The charter of the abbot and convent of Thornton about this composition is to be found in *Guisborough Cartulary* ii no. dclxxii. It indicates that the commission to the judges delegate was issued by pope Celestine III (consecrated 14 April 1191), so it cannot have reached them before late May 1191; one of the judges, abbot Thomas of Meaux, resigned as abbot in 1197.

199. Thurgarton priory

Confirmation of the institution, made during the vacancy of the see, of Richard de Hayden to the vicarage of Timberland, on the presentation of the prior and convent of Thurgarton. The vicarage consists of the third part of the church. [21 September 1186 × 16 November 1200]

B = Southwell Minster ms. 3 (Thurgarton cartulary) fo. 145v, no. 989. s. xiv med.

Omnibus Christi etc. Hugo dei gratia Lincolniensis episcopus salutem in domino. Noverit universitas vestra ratam habere institutionem quam fecit vacante sede Lincolniensi Robertus de Hayden tunc officialis episcopatus eiusdem dilecto filio nostro Ricardo de Hayden ad presentationem prioris et conventus de Thurg' in ecclesie de Timberlund vicaria, ad quam videlicet vicariam pertinet*a* tertia pars totius ecclesie cum omnibus ad partem illam pertinentibus. Idem itaque Ricardus ipsam vicariam cum omnibus pertinentiis suis perpetuo possidebit et omnia onera ipsius ecclesie sustinebit. Nos igitur hanc concessionem et supradicti Ricardi institutionem sicut rationabiliter facta est ratam habemus eamque auctoritate qua fungimur confirmamus, salvis episcopalibus consuetudinibus et Lincolniensis ecclesie dignitate. Hiis testibus etc.

a pertinent B.

Robert de Hayden is probably to be identified with Robert de Hardres who was vice-archdn of Lincoln and later archdn of Huntingdon until his death in 1207. Before the 1261 Boniface composition, the archdns of the diocese exercised jurisdiction during a vacancy, together with the cathedral chapter. It is likely that he instituted Richard de Hayden (or ? Hardres, cf. *Reg. Ant.* ix nos. 2459, 2501, 2503) to Timberland when he was acting in the Lincoln archdeaconry, probably during the vacancy between Walter of Coutances and Hugh I. A charter of Robert de Hardres, canon of Lincoln and vice-archdn, regarding this church is on fo. 105r–v (no. 756) of the cartulary. Timberland was among the churches confirmed to Thurgarton by bp Robert Chesney (*EEA* i no. 273).

*200.   Torksey priory

Confirmation for the priory of Torksey of the churches of St Mary, Torksey, the gift of Philip the priest, of All Saints, Torksey, the gift of Rocelin the priest, and of St Peter, Torksey, the gift of William of Adlingfleet, knight.   [21 September 1186 × 16 November 1200]

Mention of charter in quo warranto proceedings against the prior of Torksey, 1236. Pd, *CRR* xv no. 1965.

201.   Torksey priory

Confirmation for the nuns of St Peter, Torksey, of the place where they live, namely, the part of the churchyard on the north side of the church.
[*c.*1187 × 24 December 1198]

B = BL ms. Cotton Vesp. E xvii (Kirkstead cartulary) fo. 102r (p. 185). s. xiii med.

Hugo dei gratia Lincolniensis episcopus universis sacrosancte ecclesie filiis salutem in vero salutari. Noverint presentes et posteri quod ego, iustis petentium desideriis annuens et piis piorum virorum R. abbatis de Kyrk' et Odonis persone ecclesie sancti Petri de Torkesey petitionibus obtemperans, concessi et hac presenti pagina confirmare curavi incluse sancti Petri de Torkesey et ancillis Christi ibidem deo servientibus locum ipsum in quo resident, videlicet, illam partem cimiterii que est ad aquilonem etc.

The use of the first person singular in this document is most unusual for this late date, and suggests external composition or borrowing from an earlier document.

More details about this community of nuns in the parish church of St Peter at Torksey and under the protection of Kirkstead abbey are provided by the charter of Odo the clerk of Torksey (fo. 102r of B, no. xxii): '. . . confirmasse deo et ecclesie sancte Marie de Kyrk' et monachis eiusdem loci ad opus monialium habitantium ex aquilonari parte ecclesie beati Petri de Thorkesey que sunt in custodia et protectione prefate domus de Kyrk' omnem illam partem cimiterii ex nord parte eiusdem ecclesie beati Petri ubi edificia predictarum monialium sunt constructa cum ipsis edificiis . . .'. This community must surely be identified with the later nunnery of Fosse. Odo's charter is attested by archdn Alexander (of the West Riding or Stow) and master Simon of Sywell, among others. Alexander became archdn c.1187 and Simon had become treasurer of Lichfield (he is not so described here) by 24 December 1198 (*EEA* ii no. 340n).

202. Torre abbey

Institution of the abbot and canons of Torre to the church of Skidbrook, on the presentation of Richard de Parco, saving the possession of Osbert, Walter, William and Richard son of Hernisius, clerks, who now hold the church, for as long as they live.

[21 September 1186 × 16 November 1200]

B = Dublin, Trinity College Lib., ms. E.5.15 (Torre cartulary) fo. 107v, no. cxxxix. s. xiii med. C = PRO E164/19 (Torre cartulary) fos. 49v–50r. s. xv.

Omnibus Christi fidelibus ad quos presens 'scriptum' pervenerit, H. dei gratia Lincolniensis episcopus eternam in domino salutem. Noverit universitas vestra nos, ad presentationem Ricardi de Parco, recepisse dilectos nostros abbatem et canonicos de Thorre[a] ad ecclesiam de Schitebroc[b] ipsosque canonice in ea instituisse, salva in ea possessione clericorum qui eam nunc tenent, videlicet, Osberti, Walteri, Willelmi, [c]-Ricardi filii-[c] Hernisii quamdiu vixerint; salvis episcopalibus consuetudinibus et Lincolniensis[d] ecclesie dignitate. Quod ut ratum et inconcussum permaneat, presenti scripto et[c] sigilli nostri patrocinio communimus.[e] Hiis testibus etc.

[a] Torre C.   [b] Skidebrok C.   [c] *omitted* C.   [d] Lyncolniensis C.   [e] communivimus   C.

The charters of Richard de Parco, his wife Beatrice (daughter of Roland Haket) and his son William are all on fo. 107r of B. For the appropriation of this church by bp Hugh II see *Lib. Ant.* 73 (also on fo. 107v of B; and on fo. 50r of C).

*203. Low Toynton church

Confirmation of the institution by Alexander, archdeacon of the West Riding, then official of the church of Lincoln sede vacante, of Richard the clerk to the church of Low Toynton, on the presentation of Robert of Sausthorpe.

[? late 1186]

Mention of charter produced in a dispute between Robert of Sausthorpe and Osbert, parson of Horncastle over the advowson of the church, 1219.

Pd, *CRR* viii 171.

The charter of archdn Alexander was also produced in this dispute. It is conceivable that he was not yet archdn at the time he instituted Richard, for his predecessor, Richard de Almaria, is thought to have still been in office when Hugh became bp. The vacancy in question is clearly the period between Walter of Coutances and St Hugh. It is likely that Richard's institution was confirmed soon after Hugh's consecration.

204. Walden abbey

Institution of Ralph de Vireneto to the church of Aynho, on the resignation of Ralph de Diceto and on the presentation of the abbot and convent of Walden. He shall pay an annual pension of two shillings to the abbot and monks. At the petition of Ralph de Vireneto, the bishop has confirmed the perpetual vicarage in the church to Turbert son of Turbert, who had been presented by Ralph de Diceto with the consent of William, then prior of Walden, and had been instituted by Robert [Chesney], bishop of Lincoln. Turbert shall possess the church for ever, paying to Ralph de Vireneto two aurei *a year, one at Easter, the other at Michaelmas.* [*c*.1192 × ? March 1195]

B = BL ms. Harl. 3697 (Walden cartulary) fo. 64r (49r), no. i. s. xiv ex.

Pd from B in *Diceto* ii lxviii–lxix, no. ii; Newcourt, *Repertorium* i 34 (abridged).

Hiis testibus: R. archidiacono Leiric', magistro Ricardo Trim,[a] magistro Ricardo de Sualeclive, Alexandro de Bedford, Reumundo, Galfrido de Doping',[b] Lincolniensis ecclesie canonicis, Rogero Bacun, Hugone de Rolveston' et multis aliis.

[a] *recte* Grim.   [b] *recte* Deping'.

The dates are those of Roger of Rolleston as archdn of Leicester; his successor, Raymond, is still described here as a canon. The charter of Ralph de Vireneto, canon of Lincoln, confirming this pension to the monks of Walden is no. ii on the same folio of B. For Ralph de Diceto, dean of St Paul's, London, see D. E. Greenway ed., *John Le Neve: Fasti Ecclesiae Anglicanae 1066–1300, i St Paul's, London* (1968) 5–6, 15–16.

205. Waltham abbey

Institution of abbot Walter and the canons of Waltham into the vacant church of Arlesey, provision being made for a vicarage.
[15 September 1189 × September 1193, ? 1189 × 1192]

A = Lost original, in the possession (1840) of Stacey Grimaldi.

B = BL ms. Harl. 391 (Waltham cartulary) fo. 102r. s. xiii in. C = BL ms. Cotton Tib. C ix (Waltham cartulary) fo. 142r. s. xiii med. D = BL ms. Add. 37665 (Waltham cartulary) fo. 176r–v (in an inspeximus of Richard [de Mepham] the dean and the chapter of Lincoln, 1273). s. xvi in.

Pd from A in *Collectanea Topographica et Genealogica* vi (1840) 202 (at that time the seal was broken away).

Omnibus Christi fidelibus Hugo dei gratia Lincolniensis episcopus salutem. Noverit universitas vestra nos instituisse Walterum abbatem de Waltham*a* et canonicos eiusdem loci in vacantem*b* ecclesiam de Alricheseia et ipse abbas in presentia nostra inperpetuum*c* vicarie eiusdem ecclesie concessit omnes decimationes et obventiones que dantur in ipsa parrochia*d* preter garbas, quas ex integro sibi retinuit, ita quod vicarius episcopo et officialibus suis omnibus respondebit in omnibus que ad ipsos pertinent, et etiam ipsam ecclesiam adversus eos adquietabit*e*; salvis episcopalibus consuetudinibus et Lincolniensis ecclesie dignitate. His testibus: Haimone*f* decano Lincolniensi*g*, Ricardo*h* abbate de Grimesbi*i*, H. priore*j* de Brellingt', Laurentio archidiacono de Bedef'*k*, magistro R. de Rolvest', magistro W. de Bleis*l*, Radulfo et Willemo capellanis nostris, Ricardo de Sualeclive*m*, Galfrido de Lechelad', H. de sancto Edwardo, R. de Bradel'*n*.

a Walth' C.   *b* vocantem D.   *c* imperpetuum C.   *d* parochia C.   *e* acquietabit D.
f Haymone D.   *g* C *adds* etc. *and ends here*..   *h* dicto *(sic)* D.   *i* Grymmesby D.   *j* pryore D.
k Bed' D.   *l* Bleys D.   *m* Sualeweifme *(sic)* D.   *n* Bradell' D.

Hamo became dean of Lincoln at some date between 15 September 1189 and 24 March 1190; William of Blois was subdean by 22 March 1194 at the latest and it is possible he succeeded in 1192 when Winemer became archdn of Northampton. Roger of Rolleston, who attests here without title, became archdn of Leicester *c.*1192 × September 1193 (see no. 11).

206.   Waltham abbey

Confirmation for the abbot and canons of Waltham of the church of Wrangle, given to them by Simon le Bret, whose charter the bishop has inspected, saving the right of Alan the parson during his lifetime. After Alan's death, the abbey shall have the church in proprios usus, *saving a suitable vicarage.*   [1197 × ? May 1199]

B = BL ms. Harl. 391 (Waltham cartulary) fo. 106v. s. xiii in. C = BL ms. Cotton Tib. C ix (Waltham cartulary) fo. 143r. s. xiii med. D = BL ms. Add. 37665 (Waltham cartulary) fos. 174–175r. s. xvi in. E = ibid. fos. 175v–176r (in an inspeximus of Richard [de Mepham], the dean and the chapter of Lincoln, 18 September 1273).

Omnibus Christi fidelibus ad quos presens scriptum pervenerit, Hugo dei gratia Lincolniensis*a* episcopus salutem in domino. Noverit universitas vestra nos, ad presentationem et petitionem dilecti in Christo filii*b* Symonis*c* le Bret*d*, advocati ecclesie de Wrengl'*e* concessisse ecclesiam de Wrengl'*f* cum omnibus pertinentiis suis abbati et canonicis regularibus de Waltham'*g* quam predictus S.*h* le Bret*i* eis dedit et concessit, sicut carta eiusdem S.*j* testatur quam inspeximus et eandem ecclesiam eis episcopali auctoritate confirmasse, salvo iure Alani persone eiusdem ecclesie quamdiu vixerit, ita quidem*k* quod in

proprios usus eorum cedat post decessum[l] predicti Alani, salva
competenti vicaria et salvis episcopalibus consuetudinibus et salva in
omnibus Lincolniensis ecclesie dignitate. Hiis testibus[m]: Reimundo[n]
archidiacono Leic'[o], magistro Ricardo de Cant' subdecano Lincolniensi[a], magistro Ricardo de Swalewecl'[p], magistro Alexandro de
Bedeford'[q], Roberto de Capella, Theobaldo[r] de Busello[s], Lincolniensis ecclesie canonicis, Hugone de sancto Edwardo[t], Willelmo de
sancta Cruce, fratre Rogero elemosinario, Willelmo de Bernewude[u]
preceptore Templi Lond'[v], fratre Morino elemosinario, Willelmo
clerico de Lond'[v] et aliis.

[a] Lincolnienc' D.   [b] fili C.   [c] Simonis DE.   [d] Brett D.   [e] Wrengle D.
[f] Wrengle CD.   [g] Walth' C; Waltham DE.   [h] Symon C; Simon D.   [i] Brett E.
[j] Symonis C; Simonis DE.   [k] quidem *repeated twice* C.   [l] discessum C.   [m] C *adds* etc.
and ends here.   [n] Reing' D.   [o] Leycestr' E.   [p] Sualeweel' E.   [q] Bedeford E.
[r] Teobaldo E.   [s] Bussello E.   [t] Eadwardo DE.   [u] Bernwd' E.   [v] London' DE.

Simon le Bret's charter is on fo. 106r of B. Richard of Kent became subdean of
Lincoln in 1197. This charter was inspected and confirmed by archbp Hubert
Walter, 1200 × 1203 (*EEA* iii no. 642). The grant was also confirmed by pope
Innocent III, 15 June 1199 (*Letters of Pope Innocent III* no. 137). If, as seems
likely, brother Morin the almoner is the bp's almoner mentioned by Adam of
Eynsham (*Magna Vita* ii 212–13), then the charter can be dated more closely.
Morin, we are told, died eighteen months before the bp.

207. Warter priory

Grant to the canons of Warter in proprios usus *of the mediety of the
church of Ulceby which Geoffrey the king's chaplain held, and which
they possess by the gift of the late Geoffrey Trussebut, saving a suitable
vicarage.*   [*c.*1190 × ? March 1195]

B = Lincoln D. & C. Dij/83/3/21a (in an inspeximus by the Official of the Court of
York, 4 February 1285). C = Bodl. ms. Fairfax 9 (Warter cartulary) fo. 23r
(witnesses omitted). s. xiv in.

Pd from B in *Reg. Ant.* ii no. 578 (iv); *EYC* x no. 40.

Hiis testibus: Hamone Lincolniensis ecclesie decano, magistro
Ricardo de Swaleclive, magistro Gerardo de Rowell', Roberto de
Capella, Reymundo, Galfrido de Deping', magistro Willelmo de
Fryseby, Willelmo filio Fulconis, Roberto de Dunstapl' et multis aliis.

Geoffrey Trussebut had died by Michaelmas 1190 (*EYC* x no. 40n.) and Hamo had
been succeeded as dean of Lincoln by *c.*March 1195. Geoffrey Trussebut's charter
is *EYC* x no. 71, dated 1175 × 1178; it was confirmed by pope Alexander III on 25
April 1178 (ibid. no. 72; *Reg. Ant.* ii no. 578 (v)). Geoffrey, Henry II's chaplain,
was drowned when crossing to Normandy on 27 September 1177 (*Gesta Henrici II*
i 195).

208. Welbeck abbey

Grant to the church and canons of St James, Welbeck, of the churches of Whitton and Cotes[-by-Stow] in proprios usus, saving a suitable vicarage to be assigned to those serving the churches.

[*c.*1189 × 22 March 1194]

B = BL ms. Harl. 3640 (Welbeck cartulary) fo. 125r (p. 228). s. xiv med.
C = ibid. fo. 125v (p. 229) (in an inspeximus by William [Lexington] the dean and the chapter of Lincoln, 2 January 1264).

Omnibus Christi fidelibus ad quos presens scriptum pervenerit, Hugo dei gratia Lincolniensis episcopus salutem in domino. Ad universitatis vestre notitiam volumus pervenire nos dei et pietatis intuitu concessisse deo et ecclesie sancti Iacobi de Well' atque canonicis ibidem deo famulantibus *ᵃ*-ecclesias de Whiten' et de Cotes⁻*ᵃ* in proprios usus eorum inperpetuum possidendas et habendas cum omni integritate; salva in eis perpetuo competenti vicaria eis qui in eisdem*ᵇ* ecclesiis ministrabunt assignanda; salvis etiam episcopalibus consuetudinibus et Lincolniensis ecclesie dignitate. Ne igitur hec nostra concessio alicuius astutia vel malignitate possit in irritum reduci, eam presentis scripti serie et sigilli nostri munimine confirmamus. Hiis testibus: Roberto archidiacono Huntend',*ᶜ* magistro Willelmo de Monte, magistro R. de Walewecliva,*ᵈ* Galfrido de*ᵇ* Lectelad',*ᵉ* Roberto de Capella, Galfrido de Deping', Luca.

ᵃ⁻ᵃ section underlined B.   *ᵇ word omitted* C. *ᶜ* Huntedon' C.   *ᵈ* Shwalucliva C.
ᵉ C *adds* et aliis *and ends here.*

Robert de Hardres became archdn of Huntingdon *c.*1189; William de Monte is not described as chancellor of Lincoln, an office he held at least by 22 March 1194. For details of these two churches and their donors, see A. Hamilton Thompson, *The Premonstratensian Abbey of Welbeck* (1938), 51–4.

209. Westminster abbey

Institution of Edmund the bishop's clerk to the church of Deene, on the presentation of the abbot and convent of Westminster, saving the perpetual vicarage of Simon the clerk during his lifetime.

[21 September 1186 × 18 October 1188]

A = Westminster Abbey Mun. 16144. Endorsed: Sanctus Hugo episcopus Lincoln' admisis *(sic)* Edmundum ad ecclesiam de Dene ad presentationem abbatis Westm' (ss. xv–xvi); approx. 142 × 77 + 20 mm.; fragment of seal, whitish-brown wax, on parchment tag (d.q.1), no counterseal.

B = Westminster Abbey Mun. bk. 11 ('Domesday') fo. 242r (253r). s. xiv in.

Omnibus Christi fidelibus ad quos presens scriptum pervenerit ⸴ Hug(o) dei gratia Lincolniensis episcopus salutem in domino. Ad universitatis vestre noticiam volumus pervenire ; nos ad presentationem abbatis Westmonasterii et conventus dilectum clericum nostrum Eadmundum ad ecclesiam de Dene recepisse . et ipsum in eadem ecclesia personam instituisse . ita quod ipse ecclesiam illam cum omnibus pertinentiis suis libere inperpetuum possideat salva tamen vicaria perpetua Simonis clerici quamdiu vixerit . et salvis in omnibus ; episcopalibus consuetudinibus et Lincolniensis ecclesie dignitate. Quod ut ratum habeatur et firmum ; presenti scripto duximus confirmandum et sigilli nostri patrocinio roborandum. Hiis testibus . magistro Alexandro . magistro Roberto de Bedeford' magistro Rogero de Rulveston' . Roberto Bard' . Rogero capellano . Gaufrido de sancto Edwardo . Roberto de Mora . Roberto de Hardr' . Gaufrido de Lichelad' . magistro Alexandro de Bedeford'

> Robert of Bedford, who attests here without a title, had become precentor of Lincoln by 18 October 1188 at the latest.

210. Westminster abbey

Confirmation for master Nicholas of Westminster of the churches of Thorpe [on the Hill] and Doddington, which he holds by grant of the abbot and monks of Westminster, paying to the abbey an annual pension of two aurei *and saving the perpetual vicarage of master Alexander, archdeacon of the West Riding [Stow] during his lifetime. Alexander shall pay to Nicholas an annual pension of one hundred shillings.*   [*c.*1192 × ? March 1195]

> B = BL ms. Cotton Faust. A iii (Westminster cartulary) fo. 289r–v (297r–v). s. xiii ex.–s. xiv in. C = Westminster Abbey, Mun. bk. 11 ('Domesday') fo. 501v (525v). s. xiv in.

Omnibus Christi fidelibus ad quos presens scriptum pervenerit, Hugo dei gratia Lincolniensis episcopus salutem in domino. Ad pastoris spectat sollicitudinem subditorum et maxime clericorum [fo. 289v] quos vite honestas et morum gravitas commendant paci et securitati providere. Huius igitur rationis consideratione dilecto filio nostro magistro Nicholao de Westm' ecclesias de Thorp[a] et de Dudington'[b] sicut eas ex concessione abbatis et monachorum de Westmonasterio[c] rationabiliter possidere dinoscitur, sub annua pensione duorum aureorum eidem abbati et monachis annuatim[d] nomine pensionis solvenda, episcopali auctoritate confirmamus, salva perpetua vicaria dilecti filii nostri magistri Alexandri archidiaconi de Westrid'[e], qui easdem ecclesias quamdiu vixerit cum omnibus pertinentiis suis, solvendo annuatim[f] predicto magistro N. nomine pensionis C[g] solidos tenebit. Ut autem hec que prenotata sunt robur optineant perpetuum, presenti scripto sigilli nostri appositione corroborato confirmamus; salvis episcopalibus consuetudinibus et Lincolniensis ecclesie dignitate. Hiis testibus:[h] magistro Rogero archidiacono Leyrc', magistro Ricardo de Swaleweclive, Roberto de Capella, magistro Alexandro de Bedeford', Reimundo, Galfrido de Depig', Hugone de sancto Edwardo, Hugone de Rolvest' et multis aliis.

[a] Torp C.   [b] Dudinton' C.   [c] Westm' C.   [d] annuatis B.   [e] Westriding' C.
[f] annutim B.   [g] centum C.   [h] B ends here.

The dates are those of Roger of Rolleston as archdn of Leicester (see no. 11).

211. Westminster abbey

Settlement by the bishop, J(ohn de Cella), abbot of St Albans, and B(enedict), abbot of St Mary, Stratford (Langthorne), judges delegated by pope Celestine III to hear the case between W(illiam Postard), the abbot and the monks of St Peter, Westminster and the nuns of Godstow over the church of Bloxham. The abbot and convent of Westminster have granted the church to the nuns of Godstow and quitclaimed all rights in it, saving an annual pension of five silver marks which they were to receive for providing the altar light.

13 June 1197

B = Westminster Abbey Mun. bk. 11 ('Domesday') fos. 378v–379r (391v–392r). s. xiv in. C = PRO E164/20 (Godstow cartulary) fo. 27r–v (xiiii r–v). s. xv in. D = Bodl. ms. Rawlinson B 408 (Godstow cartulary, English version) fos. 25v–26r. s. xv ex.

Pd from B in J. E. Sayers, *Papal Judges Delegate in the Province of Canterbury 1198–1254* (Oxford 1971), app. B no. 5, pp. 354–5; from D in *Godstow English Register* i no. 309.

Facta est autem hec transactio inter eos anno ab incarnatione domini m° c° xc° vii° die tertia post festum sancti Barnabe apostoli, mediante ex parte domini Huberti Cantuariensis archiepiscopi et apostolice sedis legati viro [fo. 379r] venerabili Hugone abbate Abbendonie[a] et huic compositioni opem et operam adhibente. Hiis testibus: domino Hugone abbate Abendonie[b], Nicholao et Ricardo monachis et capellanis eius, Waleranno capellano, Iohanne de Kensinton'[c] et Henrico de Kensinton' fratre eius, Marino clerico domine regine, Godefrido de la Dene, Willelmo de Haggehurste[d], Roberto de Clere, magistro Ernulfo Postard[e], magistro Simone[f] de Bareswrde[g], Theodbaldo senescallo Westm', Radulfo de[h] Septem Fontibus et Henrico fratre eius et multis aliis.

[a] Abendonie C.   [b] et *added* C.   [c] Cunsinton' C.   [d] Hauggehurst C.   [e] Hernulfo Posthard C.   [f] Simon C.   [g] Bareswrd' C.   [h] *word omitted* C.

For details of the case see Sayers *op. cit.* 265–6.

212. Westminster abbey

Confirmation for the abbot and convent of Westminster of the churches of Oakham and Hambleton, given to them by king William I, and a pension of thirty marks a year from these churches towards the entertainment of guests.   [1197×c.1198]

> B = BL ms. Cotton Faust. A iii (Westminster cartulaiy) fos. 267v–268r (275v–276r), cap. lxx. s. xiii ex. C = Westminster Abbey Mun. bk. 11 ('Domesday') fo. 594r (621r). s. xiv in.

Omnibus Christi fidelibus ad quos presens scriptum pervenerit, Hugo dei gratia Lincolniensis episcopus salutem in domino. Noverit universitas vestra nos divine pietatis intuitu concessisse et presenti scripto sigillique nostri patrocinio confirmasse dilectis in Christo filiis abbati et monachis sancti Petri*a* Westm' ecclesias de Okham*b* et de Hameldon'*c*, quas ex donatione illustris regis Willelmi primi adepti sunt cum omnibus ad eas pertinentibus sicut eas rationabiliter adepti sunt, ita quidem quod iamdicti monachi percipient de supradictis ecclesiis annuatim nomine pensionis xxx*d* marcas, ad hospitum*e* susceptionem deputatas, ab eo qui prefatas ecclesias de eisdem monachis tenebit. Recipient autem has*f* xxx*d* marcas ad quatuor anni terminos, videlicet, C*g* solidos [fo. 268r] ad Natale, C*g* solidos ad Pascha, C*g* solidos ad Nativitatem sancti*h* Iohannis Baptiste et*i* C*g* solidos ad festum sancti Michaelis; salvis episcopalibus consuetudinibus et Lincolniensis ecclesie dignitate. Hiis testibus:*j* Rogero decano et Ricardo subdecano Lincolniensis ecclesie, Roberto archidiacono Hontindon', magistro Ricardo de Swalewed', magistro Alexandro de Bedeford', magistro Gerardo de Rowell', Hugone et Andrea capellanis, Lincolniensis ecclesie canonicis, Ricardo de Hardr', Hugone de Rolveston', Eustachio de Wilton', Hugone de Bobi tunc senescallo episcopi, Teobaldo de Feringes, Andrea de Scaccario, Roberto Mauduyt, Rogero Enganet et multis aliis.

> *a* de *added* C.   *b* Ocham C.   *c* Hameledune C.   *d* triginta C.   *e* hospitium *originally written* B *and* hospitum *written in the margin.*   *f* hiis C.   *g* centum C.   *h* beati C.   *i* omitted C.   *j* B ends here.

> Richard of Kent became subdean of Lincoln in 1197; for the dating of this charter see *Le Neve* app. 44. For the churches of Oakham and Hambleton see *Reg. Ant.* ii no. 374 and Professor Hamilton Thompson's note; ibid. iii nos. 1008–17; B. Harvey, *Westminster Abbey and its Estates in the Middle Ages* (Oxford 1977), 49–50, 389–90, 404.

*213. William son of Adam

Letters signifying to the royal justices that William son of Adam was of legitimate birth.   [Easter × Michaelmas 1199]

Mention of letters in a case between William son of Adam and Eustace of Watford over a plea of land before the itinerant justices at Northampton, Easter 10 Richard I–Michaelmas 1 John [1199].

Pd, *Rot. Cur. Reg.* i 406, 413; ii 42.

In one of these entries a William son of Hervey is mentioned, but this is most probably an error for William son of Adam.

*213A. Witham charterhouse

Letters of recommendation to the prior and convent of Witham in favour of Adam of Dryburgh who wished to become a Carthusian.

[1188]

Mention of letters in *De vita et conversacione magistri Ade Cartusiensis* (London, Charterhouse ms.), pd by E. M. Thompson in *Bulletin of the John Rylands Library* xvi (1932) 500, and by A. Wilmart in *Analecta Praemonstratensia* ix (1933) 221.

It is thought that Adam first came to Witham charterhouse in 1188 (J. Bullock, *Adam of Dryburgh* (Church Historical Society 1958) 29, 138).

214. Archbishop Geoffrey of York

Notification by bishop Richard [FitzNeal] of London, bishop Hugh of Lincoln, and abbot B(enedict) of Peterborough, delegated by pope Celestine III to hear the case between G(eoffrey Plantagenet), archbishop of York and H(ugh du Puiset), bishop of Durham. The parties being present before the judges at Northampton on the feast of St Calixtus [14 October], the case was adjourned until the octaves of St John to enable peace to be made. If there is not a peaceful settlement within this time, the papal letters directed to the judges are to be as effective as if there had been no adjournment.   [c.14 October 1192]

B = BL ms. Lansdowne 402 (cartulary of the see of York) fo. 67v (60v), no. 203. s. xiv in.

Ricardus Lond(oniensis) et H.[a] Lincolniensis dei gratia episcopi et B. eadem gratia de Burgo abbas[b] omnibus ad quos presens scriptum pervenerit salutem in domino. Noverit universitas vestra quod causa inter venerabiles fratres nostros G. Eboracensem archiepiscopum et H. Dunelmensem episcopum nobis a summo pontifice Celestino tertio commissa, partibus in nostra presentia apud Norhampton' in festo beati Calixti constitutis, mediante gratia divina nobis etiam partes interponentibus de consensu ipsorum usque ad octavas sancti Iohannis proximo venturas cepit dilationem; ut interim honore invicem prevenientes, ad plenioris pacis consummationem[c] per dei gratiam facilius inducantur, rebus omnibus inter eos in eodem statu quo fuerunt die prefato interim permanentibus. Si vero quod[d] deus avertat

M

infra prefatum terminum ad plenum pax inter eos refirmata[e] non
fuerit, littere ad nos a domino papa[f] transmisse[g] eundem vigorem sunt
habiture, quem haberent si dilatio prefata 'non' intercessisset et
per tantum temporis, salvis utrique parti omnibus excepcionibus suis.
Citatione etiam, si qua fieri debebit, facienda sub eodem spatio
temporis et eadem forma et ad eundem diem quo facta fuit primo,
scilicet ad diem beati Kalixti.

[a] *followed by* dei *dotted for expunction* B.   [b] *word omitted* B.   [c] confirmationem *originally written* B, *with* 'fir' *crossed out and* 'sum' *interlined.*   [d] vero quod: vos B.   [e] confirm-
ata *originally written* B, *with* 'con' *dotted for expunction and* 're' *interlined.*   [f] papae B, *with
second* 'a' *dotted for expunction.*   [g] transmissae B, *with second* 'a' *dotted for expunction.*

For details of the background of this case arising from the failure of bp Puiset to
profess obedience to the new archbp, see G. V. Scammell, *Hugh du Puiset, Bishop
of Durham* (Cambridge 1956) 176–81. The wording of this document is followed
very closely in the relevant extract in *Chronica Rogeri de Hovedene* (iii 172), where
the adjournment date is given more precisely as 'ad octavas nativitatis beati
Iohannis baptiste' (1 July).

214A.   Archbishop Geoffrey of York

*Notification by bishop Hugh, archdeacon W(inemer) of Northampton
and prior H(ugh) of Pontefract, delegated by pope Celestine III to
investigate charges made against archbishop Geoffrey of York in his
dispute with the canons of York (the papal mandate dated at St
Peter's, Rome, 8 June 1194, is recited in full). They report that the
archbishop was cited to appear before them many times but he did not
do so. Finally his clerks have appeared and excused their master's
absence by stating that the archbishop had appealed to the apostolic
see and had gone to Rome in person. In accordance with the papal
mandate the judges delegate have admitted witnesses and have
condemned the archbishop to make restitution in the matter of various
sums (listed in detail).*   [January 1195]

B = York Minster Muniment Room, L2/1 (Magnum Registrum Album) part iii,
    fo. 14v. (no witnesses). s. xiv med.

Pd from B in *Historians of the Church of York* iii 99–104, no. lxxvi.

The judges delegate arrived in York to investigate the charges on 15 January 1195
(*Chronica Rogeri de Hovedene* iii 278). Pope Celestine's bull commissioning the
three judges is also pd ibid. 279–81; in *Historians of the Church of York* the year of
the bull is erroneously rendered as 1195, not 1194. For further details of archbp
Geoffrey's dispute see D. L. Douie, *Archbishop Geoffrey Plantagenet and the
Chapter of York* (St Anthony's Hall publications 18, York 1960).

*214B.   Archbishop Geoffrey of York

*Similar notification from the judges delegate, addressed specifically to
pope Celestine, reporting their actions and informing him that they*

have assigned dates for the two parties to appear in Rome, allowing the archbishop four and a half months and his opponents until 1 June.

[January 1195]

Mention of letters sent under their seals to Rome in *Chronica Rogeri de Hovedene* iii 282.

*214C. Archbishop Geoffrey of York

Publication by the same judges delegate of the papal suspension of archbishop Geoffrey of York. The archbishop's spiritual jurisdiction is to be temporarily exercised by the dean of York. [*c*.January 1196]

Bp Hugh had previously refused to suspend the archbp and the canons of York had consequently appealed to pope Celestine (*Chronica Rogeri de Hovedene* iii 306). The papal bulls informing Simon de Apulia, dean of York and the clergy of the province of York that the archbp has been suspended are dated 23 December 1195 (ibid. 309–11). Celestine's letter to the three judges delegate of the same date orders them to publish the suspension in all the churches of the diocese and province (ibid. 312–16). Subsequent events show that the suspension was duly published.

*215. Testament of bishop Hugh

The author of the *Magna Vita* states (ii 186–7) that in his last illness, (after making his confession on 21 September 1200), the bp was advised to make his will and records his comments on the custom of churchmen making wills: 'Tedet me sane huius consuetudinis iam passim in ecclesiam traducte. Nam quo ad animum meum, nichil omnimodis aut possedi umquam uel possideo quod censerem meum et non potius ecclesie quam regebam proprium.' However, in order to prevent the royal exchequer laying hands on his goods, he summoned the dean, Roger of Rolleston, and two archdns and commissioned them to supervise the distribution to the poor of whatever goods he possessed. He then asked for his stole, and excommunicated anyone who tried to carry off anything belonging to him or to prevent his executors having complete freedom to carry out his instructions. On 6 October following king John confirmed the testament of the bp in a document dated at Freemantle: 'Sciatis quod nos ratum et gratum habemus testamentum venerabilis patris nostri domini Lincolniensis episcopi sicut illud rationabiliter et secundum deum condidit de feodis suis.' (*Rot. Chart.* 98a). This document may have been occasioned by the king's visit to the dying bp when he confirmed (?verbally) his testament (*Chron. Rogeri de Hovedene* iv 141). However, chronological problems arise later in the *Magna Vita* when it is recorded that at a council held at Westminster the bp renewed the anathema he had already laid on those who tried to misappropriate any bequests made in his testament. This was extended into a general sentence of excommunication against those who abused bequests in legal testaments (ii 205; cited in *Councils and Synods* I part ii, 1053–5). The editors of *Councils and Synods* have discussed the circumstances and possible dates of the council and have concluded that it probably took place in May 1199. This would suggest that the bp made an earlier testament and the death-bed version described above was in some way a modification of the earlier version. It certainly was not unusual for bps to change their testamentary dispositions, cf. the two extant testaments of bp Hugh II (*HMC Wells* i 431–2; *Reg. Ant.* ii no. 372). For a brief comment on Hugh I's testament see M. M. Sheehan, *The Will in Medieval England* (Toronto 1963), 245–6.

WILLIAM OF BLOIS

216. Profession

Profession of canonical subjection made to the church of Canterbury and archbishop Hubert. [24 August 1203]

> A = Canterbury D. & C. C.A. C115/69. Endorsed: Hec professio facta est in ecclesia Christi Cant' anno gracie mcciii ix kalendas Septembris et quia tunc egrotabat Hubertus archiepiscopus Cant' sacravit Willelmus episcopus Lundoniensis, astantibus et cooperantibus G. episcopo Roffensi, H. Sarisberiensi, H. Exoniensi, S. Bathoniensi, Gaufrido Cestrensi, Egidio Herefordensi. Alii episcopi tam Anglie quam Wallie literas excusatorias archiepiscopo miserunt preter G. Wintoniensem, qui recessit indignans eo quod episcopi consecratio eidem non concederetur; approx. 222 × 90 mm.; not sealed.
>
> B = Canterbury D. & C. register A (the Prior's register) fo. 224v. s. xiv med.
>
> Pd from A in *Canterbury Professions* no. 143.

Ego Willelmus ecclesie Lincolniensis electus ꞏ sancte Cantuariensi ecclesie et reverendo patri Huberto eiusdem ecclesie archiepiscopo . et tocius Anglie primati suisque successoribus canonice substituendis ꞏ canonicam subiectionem et obedientiam me per omnia exhibiturum promitto . et per manum propriam signo crucis confirmo ; +

> The cross appears to be in a different hand from the text, presumably autograph. For the circumstances of this consecration see *EEA* iii no. 532.

217. Bardney abbey

Notification to all the archdeacons, officials and deans of the diocese that he has taken the abbey of Bardney and its possessions into his protection. [24 August 1203 × 10 May 1206]

> B = BL ms. Cotton Vesp. E xx (Bardney cartulary) fos. 37v–38r (33v–34r). s. xiii ex.

W. dei gratia Lincolniensis episcopus dilectis in Christo filiis archidiaconis, officialibus et decanis universis per episcopatum Lincolniensem constitutis salutem et benedictionem. Noverit universitas vestra nos domum de Bard', quam propter dilectorum filiorum monachorum ibidem deo iugiter famulantium religionem et honestatem speciali [fo. 38r] devotione tenemur amplecti, possessiones etiam ad eam pertinentes in protectione nostra recepisse. Mandamus ergo vobis firmiter iniungentes quatinus auditis eorum querimoniis si quos inveneritis contumeliose eis iniurias inferre, possessiones eorum contra iustitiam

inquietare, averia eorum capere vel detinere, beneficiaque rationabiliter eis collata occupare vel aliqua violentia perturbare, ipsis super
hiis celerem et districtam exhibeatis iustitiam, ita ne ipsos pro defectu
iustitie ad nos oporteat laborare. Valete.

The rubric identifies bp W. as William, but it is equally possible that the charter
was issued by bp Walter (1183–5).

*218. Bardney abbey

Ordination of the vicarage of [Great] Hale.

[24 August 1203 × 10 May 1206]

Mention of lost ordination being exhibited before bp. Oliver Sutton, 1280.
'Consistit autem dicta vicaria in toto alteragio secundum ordinationem Willelmi
episcopi coram domino episcopo exhibitam, videlicet in omnibus oblationibus et
minutis decimis cum tofto quod fuit Godewini Grikke et cum terra pertinente ad
ecclesiam, excepto tofto quod fuit Radulfi Pilat iuxta ecclesiam ex parte
aquilonari et excepto loco in marisco de Hal qui dicitur parcus, et vicarius de
episcopalibus consuetudinibus respondebit.'

Pd, *Reg. Sutton* i 7.

There is another ordination of the vicarage of Great Hale by bp Thomas Bek of
Lincoln, dated 22 November 1346 (BL ms. Cotton Vesp. E xx fo. 284r–v).

219. Bardney abbey

*Appropriation to the monks of Bardney of two garbs of the tithes
belonging to the church of Edlesborough, saving the rest for the vicar
who shall serve the church. The vicar shall also pay all episcopal
charges.* [25 September 1205 × 10 May 1206]

B = BL ms. Cotton Vesp. E xx (Bardney cartulary) fo. 37v (33v). s. xiii ex.

Universis Christi fidelibus ad quos presens scriptum pervenerit,
Willelmus dei gratia Lincolniensis episcopus salutem eternam in
domino. Ea que viris religiosis pia fidelium largitione rationabiliter
collata sunt inperpetuum inconcussa permaneant autentici scripti
decet munimine roborari et episcopalis auctoritatis subsidio stabiliri.
Eapropter dilectorum in Christo filiorum monachorum de Bard'
religionem et honestatem attendentes, duas garbas totius decime ad
ecclesiam de Edelberg' pertinentis in proprios usus inperpetuum
convertendas confirmamus et presenti scripto cum sigilli nostri patrocinio communimus, salvo toto residuo ad opus vicarii qui in dicta
ecclesia eorum nomine perpetuo ministrabit; salvis in omnibus episcopalibus consuetudinibus a vicario persolvendis et Lincolniensis
ecclesie dignitate. Testibus: W. archidiacono Bukingham, magistro
W. filio Fulconis, T. de Fiskerton', canonicis Lincolniensibus,

magistro W. de Stavenebi, R. de Bolehurst', P. de Cheueremund', Waleranno, Karolo, clericis et multis aliis.

Master William son of Fulk became a canon of Lincoln 25 September 1205 × 10 May 1206. The church of Edlesborough formed part of the abbey's original endowment by Gilbert de Gant (*AASR* xxxii (1913) 38, 42).

*220.   Barlings abbey

Confirmation for Barlings abbey of the church of Snelland, given to them by Helto of Snelland the patron, whose charter the bishop has inspected, and grant of an annual pension of half a mark from the church.   [24 August 1203 × 10 May 1206]

Mention of charter produced in a dispute between Robert of Snelland and the abbot of Barlings over the advowson of the church, 1219.

Pd, D. M. Stenton ed., *Rolls of the justices in eyre, being the rolls of pleas and assizes for Lincolnshire 1218–9 and Worcestershire 1221* (Selden Society 53, 1934) no. 234.

No copy of the charter survives in the Barlings cartulary.

221.   Jocelin of Wells, bishop of Bath and Glastonbury

Letters testimonial of W(illiam) bishop of London, G(ilbert) bishop of Rochester, H(enry) bishop of Exeter, H(erbert) bishop of Salisbury, E(ustace) bishop of Ely, G(eoffrey) bishop of Coventry, M(auger) bishop of Worcester, J(ohn) bishop of Norwich, W(illiam) bishop of Lincoln, S(imon) bishop of Chichester and P(eter) bishop of Winchester to pope I(nnocent III) informing him of the canonical election of master Jocelin, canon of Wells, as bishop of Bath upon the death of bishop Savaric, and of the assent of king John. The bishops petition the pope, in the vacancy of the see of Canterbury, to confirm the election.
                    [February × May 1206]

B = Wells D. & C. Ch. 39 (in an inspeximus of William Brewer, bp of Exeter, April 1242). C = ibid. Ch. 40 (in an inspeximus of Jocelin, bp of Bath, William Brewer, bp of Exeter, and William Raleigh, bp of Norwich, July 1242). D = ibid. Liber Albus I, fo. 56r, no. ccxi, s. xiii med. The document is not witnessed.

Pd from B in *Archaeologia* lii (1890) 106; C. M. Church, *Chapters in the early history of the Church of Wells* (1894) app. S, 404–5; calendared in *HMC Wells* i 64 (from D); ibid. ii 554–4 (from BC).

Jocelin, the brother of Hugh of Wells, was elected in February 1206 and consecrated the following 28 May. For a discussion of the circumstances see J. Armitage Robinson, *Somerset Historical Essays* (1921), 145–7.

222.   Jocelin of Wells, bishop of Bath and Glastonbury

Similar letters on the same subject addressed to J(ohn) cardinal deacon of Sta Maria in Via Lata and apostolic legate.

[February × May 1206]

B = Wells D. & C. Ch. 39 (in an inspeximus of William Brewer, bp of Exeter, April 1242). C = ibid. Liber Albus I, fo. 56r–v, no. ccxii. s. xiii med.

Pd from B in *Archaeologia* lii (1890) 106–7; C. M. Church, *Chapters in the early history of the Church of Wells* (1894) app. S, 405–6; calendared in *HMC Wells* i 64 (from C); ibid. ii 554 (from B).

223.   Abbey of Beauport

Confirmation for the canons of St Mary, Beauport, of the grant by Alan son of the count (Henry) of the churches of Waltham, Barnoldby(-le-Beck), Beelsby, Hatcliffe, Ravendale, Brigsley, Hawerby, Aswardby, and Beesby, and of ten pounds a year from the manor of Ravendale. The bishop has inspected Alan's charter and the confirmatory charters of king John and archbishop Hubert of Canterbury.

[25 September 1205 × 10 May 1206]

B = Saint-Brieuc, archives du département des Côtes-du-Nord, vidimus of official of the bp of Tréguier, 7 August 1415, series H (unlisted) (stained and damaged).

Pd from B (with some errors) in J. Geslin de Bourgogne and A. de Barthélemy, *Anciens Évêchés de Bretagne* (6 vols., Paris 1855–79) iv *Diocèse de Saint-Brieuc* 58, no. xvii.

Omnibus Christi fidelibus ad quos presens scriptum pervenerint, Guillelmus dei gratia Lincolenensis episcopus salutem eternam in domino. Noverit universitas vestra nos, ex inspectione cartarum Alani filii comitis et excellentissimi domini Iohannis dei gratia illustris regis Anglorum et Huberti bone memorie quondam Cantuariensis[a] archiepiscopi pendisse quod dictus Alanus dilectis in Christo filiis canonicis sancte Marie de Bello Portu omnes ecclesias ad presentationem suam sitas in archidiaconatu Lincolenensi, scilicet, in socha de Waltham pertinentes, caritative contulit: videlicet, ecclesiam de Waltham, de Bernelobi, de Belesbi, de Haudclive, de [Rav]endal,[b] de Brigehesl, de Hawaudebi, de Abwaldebi et de Besebi cum earum pertinentiis; necnon ad vestituram dictorum canonicorum decem libras sterlingorum annuatim in manerio suo de Ravendale percipiendas; et quod tam dicti dominus rex quam archiepiscopus ea sibi confirmaverunt. Ut igitur eadem pia donatio prescripti nobilis viri futuris temporibus perpetuam obtineat firmitatem, eam sicut rationabiliter facta est auctoritate nostra confirmamus et presentis scripti[c] et sigilli nostri patrociniis communivimus, salvis in omnibus episcopalibus consuetudinibus et Lincolenensis ecclesie dignitate. Testibus: Galfrido

precentore, Philippo subdecano,[d] magistris Symone de Sywell',
Girardo de Rowell', Gilberto de Malbertorp, Adam de sancto
Edmundo et Thoma de Fiskerton', Linconensis ecclesie canonicis,
magistro Willelmo de Stavenb', Rogero Bacun, Petro de Chevermund',
clericis, et multis aliis.

   [a] Cartuariensis b.   [b] *The missing place-name is Ravendale (cf. EEA iii no. 334).*
[c] presenti scripto B.   [d] subdecentore B.

Details of the churches (including Ravendale) are given in the charters of Alan son
of count Henry and Conan his brother (*Anciens Évêchés* iv 57–8, nos. xv–xvi) and
in the original confirmation of archbp Hubert Walter, dated 28 April 1202, referred
to by bp William (*EEA* iii no. 334). Philip became subdean of Lincoln at the very
close of bp William's episcopate; William de Bramfeld, his predecessor but one, was
murdered on 25 September 1205.

   I am most grateful to M. Denis Escudier of the Institut de Recherche et
d'Histoire des Textes for help in locating this document.

*224. Begbroke church

Institution of Thomas the chaplain to the vicarage of Begbroke.
Thomas shall hold the church as long as he lives, paying to the rectors a
pension of one aureus.   [? 24 August 1203 × 10 May 1206]

   Mention of letter of institution of bp W. shown in the chapter, in an entry on the
   Oxford archdeaconry institution roll of bp Hugh II for the twenty-third
   pontifical year, beginning 20 December 1231.

   Pd, *RHW* ii 38.

   Bp W. could be William of Blois or Walter of Coutances but the fact that Thomas
   was still vicar in 1231–2 would tend to suggest bp William.

225. Belvoir priory

Confirmation of the gift made by William d'Aubigny the third to the
church and monks of St Mary, Belvoir, of the third part of all the tithes
of his demesne of Woolsthorpe with the two parts of the same tithes
which they previously used to receive, and the third part of all the
small tithes of his castle of Belvoir belonging to Woolsthorpe church,
together with the two parts of the same tithes which they previously
received. The bishop has inspected William's charter.
                                [25 September 1205 × 10 May 1206]

   A = Belvoir Castle, Ch. 5880 (not accessible. Typescript catalogue indicates that
      the seal is missing).
   B = Belvoir Castle, ms. Add. 105 (Belvoir cartulary) fo. 98v. s. xv in.
   Pd (calendar) from B in *HMC Rutland* iv 167.

Universis Christi fidelibus ad quos presens scriptum pervenerit,
Willelmus dei gratia Lincolniensis episcopus salutem eternam in

domino. Noverit universitas vestra quod nos ratam et gratam habemus donationem et concessionem quam dilectus filius Willelmus de Albeniac' tertius fecit deo et ecclesie beate Marie de Belver' et monachis ibidem deo servientibus super tertia parte omnium decimarum de dominico suo de Wulstorp cum duabus partibus decimarum dominici sui predicti quas prius percipere solebant, simul cum tertia parte omnium minutarum decimarum castelli sui de Belver predicte ecclesie de Wullestorp pertinentium, simul etiam cum duabus partibus decimarum illarum quas prius percipiebant sicut in carta sua super hoc confecta*a* quam inspeximus continetur, eamque prout rite facta est auctoritate nostra confirmamus et presenti scripto cum sigilli nostri patrocinio communimus; salvis in omnibus episcopalibus consuetudinibus et Lincolniensis ecclesie dignitate. Testibus: W. archidiacono Bukingham, magistris W. Blund', G. de Malbertorp et aliis.*b*

a confectam B.   *b* The calendar notes that the witnesses to the original document continue after Malbertorp as follows: W. filio Fulconis, T. de Fiskerton, canonicis Lincolniensibus, magistro W. de Staveneby, Rogero, Petro, Walerano, clericis.

William son of Fulk became a canon of Lincoln at some date between 25 September 1205 and 10 May 1206 (see no. 259 below).

*226.   Bermondsey priory

Notification that the church of Hardwick was now vacant.

[*c*.January 1206]

Mention of letters produced in a dispute between James de Novo Mercato and the prior of Bermondsey over the advowson of the church, Hilary term 1206.

Pd, *CRR* iv 72.

It is stated later in the case that these letters had been issued in error, since Hugh Peverel was still parson of the church.

*227.   Simon le Bret

Letters patent excommunicating Simon le Bret, iuvenis, *on account of his manifest contumacy.*

[*c*.April × May 1206]

Mention of notification to the royal justices of the issue of letters patent of excommunication in a plea of service, Trinity term, 1206.

Pd, *CRR* iv 182.

228.   Bushmead priory

Inspeximus of bishop Hugh's confirmation [no. 29] for William the chaplain of Colmworth and those with him wearing the religious habit at Bushmead.

[24 August 1203 × 10 May 1206]

B = Bedfordshire Record Office, DD.GY9/2 (Bushmead cartulary) fos. 3v–4r. s. xiv med.

Pd from B in *Bushmead Cartulary* no. 10.

Hiis testibus: magistris Roberto de Hardr' archidiacono Huntend', Henrico de Gilewill', Gilberto de Malbertorp', Thoma de Fiskerton', Lincolniensis ecclesie canonicis, magistris Willelmo filio Fulconis, Adam de sancto Edmundo, Willelmo de Stasnebi, Gilberto de Ywardbi, Petro de Cheuermund' et Karolo, clericis, et multis aliis.

This inspeximus may date from early in the episcopate since William son of Fulk became a canon of Lincoln between 25 September 1205 and 10 May 1206 (see below, no. 259). For a similar confirmation by bp Hugh II see *Bushmead Cartulary* no. 13; *Lib. Ant.* 79–80.

229. Colchester abbey

General confirmation of possessions for the monks of Colchester.

[24 August 1203 × 10 May 1206]

B = Colchester and Essex Museum, Colchester cartulary p. 69 (particula xi, ar(marium) i). s. xiii ex.

Pd from B in *Colchester Cartulary* i 123.

Universis Christi fidelibus ad quos presens scriptum pervenerit, Willelmus dei gratia Lincolniensis episcopus salutem eternam in domino. Ea que viris religiosis pia fidelium largitione rationabiliter collata sunt ne pravorum hominum molestatione turbentur auctentici scripti decet perpetuare munimine et episcopalis auctoritatis subsidio stabilire. Eapropter religionem et honestatem dilectorum nobis in Christo monachorum de Col' attendentes, duas partes decimarum dominii de Estun', duas partes decimarum dominii de Walcra, et totam decimam molendini de Walcra, et duas partes decimarum pannagii de Walcra, duas partes decimarum dominii de Hamerton', duas partes decimarum de blado dominii de Sandeya, dimidiam partem de veteribus decimis dominii de Eatun', totam autem decimam molendinorum et pannagii in parochia de Etun', ipsis sicut eas rationabiliter adepti sunt auctoritate nostra confirmamus et presenti scripto cum sigilli nostri patrocinio communimus; salvis in omnibus episcopalibus consuetudinibus et Lincolniensis ecclesie dignitate. Testibus: R. decano, W. archidiacono Bukinham, magistris A. de Bedeford, G. de Louuell',[a] A. de sancto Eadmundo, T. de Fiskertun', canonicis Lincolniensibus, magistro Willelmo filio Fulconis, W. persona de Cleipol, G. de Iwareb', et multis aliis.

[a] *recte* Rouuell'.

William son of Fulk is not described as a canon of Lincoln; he received the prebend of Decem Librarum at some date between 25 September 1205 and 10 May 1206 (see no. 259). For an earlier confirmation by bp Robert Chesney where most of these possessions are mentioned see *EEA* i no. 99.

230.   Colchester abbey

Admission and institution of the abbot and monks of Colchester into the church of Walkern, at the petition and grant of William de Lanval son of William de Lanval the patron of the church, and confirmation of an annual pension of one mark from the church. Geoffrey de Bocland shall hold the church for as long as he lives, paying the aforesaid annual pension to the abbot and monks.   [24 August 1203 × 10 May 1206]

> B = Colchester and Essex Museum, Colchester cartulary p. 69 (particula xi, ar(marium) i). s. xiii ex.
>
> Pd from B in *Colchester Cartulary* i 124.

Omnibus Christi fidelibus ad quos presens scriptum pervenerit, Willelmus dei gratia Lincolniensis episcopus salutem eternam in domino. Noverit universitas vestra nos, ad petitionem et concessionem dilecti in Christo filii Willelmi de Lanval' filii Willelmi de Lanval' patroni ecclesie de Walcre, admisisse dilectos filios nostros abbatem et monachos de Colecestr' ad eandem ecclesiam de Walcre et ipsos in ea canonice instituisse et eis in eadem ecclesia pensionem unius marce annuatim percipiendam episcopali auctoritate confirmasse, ita quidem quod dilectus filius Galfridus de Bocland' predictam ecclesiam cum omnibus pertinentiis suis tota vita sua de eis tenebit, reddendo eisdem abbati et monachis predictam marcam annuatim nomine pensionis; salvis in omnibus episcopalibus consuetudinibus et Lincolniensis ecclesie dignitate. Quod ut ratum et inconcussum inposterum perseveret, id presenti scripto sigilli nostri munimine roborato communimus. Testibus: magistris Girardo de Rowell', Gileberto de Malbertorp' et Thoma de Fiskerton', Lincolniensis ecclesie canonicis, Vacario capellano, magistro Willelmo filio Fulconis, Petro de Parisiis,[a] Rogero de Rolehust', Henrico de Ramburc', Ricardo de Rowell', Petro de Cheuermund' et Waleranno, clericis, et multis aliis.

[a] Parisius B.

William son of Fulk is not described as a canon of Lincoln (see above). For Geoffrey de Bocland see *Le Neve* 123.

*231.   Henry de Colevill

Grant to Henry de Colevill of one knight's fee in Attington and Moreton, formerly held of the bishop by Odo de Braimuster.
[23 August 1203 × ? February 1205]

Mention of charter in a confirmation by king John, undated but enrolled between
entries dated 7 February and 22 February 1205.

Pd, *Rot. Chart.* 141*b*–142*a*.

Henry de Colevill is listed as holding a knight's fee of the bp of Lincoln in Thame in
the 1210–12 inquest (*Red Book of the Exchequer* ii 515). For the grant of a knight's
fee in Attington and Moreton to Henry by Odo de Braimuster see *The Thame
Cartulary* i no. 72; cf. Henry's confirmation of a gift to Thame abbey by Odo, ibid.
no. 63. Henry witnesses many Lincoln charters in the early years of the thirteenth
century (see *Reg. Ant.* ii nos. 342–3, 379, 616–7; iii nos. 772, 875, 877; v no. 1555;
x no. 2839).

232. Abbey of La Couture

*Notification of the settlement before the bishop of a dispute between the
abbot and monks of La Couture and master Hugh of Gloucester over
the manor and church of [Little] Woolstone and the church of
Toddington, the abbey being represented by Peter des Roches, their
proctor. Master Hugh shall hold the manor and churches as long as he
lives, paying ten silver marks to the abbey each year in mid-Lent at
the New Temple, London, to the master of the Temple or to whomsoever is appointed by the abbey, on condition that Hugh provides one
monk from La Couture, living with him in his house, with food and
clothing.*   [24 August 1203 × 10 May 1206,
                              ? 24 August 1203 × 25 September 1205]

B = Le Mans, Bib. mun. ms. 198 (cartulary of St-Pierre de la Couture) fo. 17v (Di
    v). s. xiii in. C = ibid. fo. 18r (Dii r).
Pd from B in *Cartulaire des abbayes de S. Pierre de la Couture et de S. Pierre de
    Solesmes* (Le Mans 1881) 144; (calendar) in *CDF* no. 1041.

Omnibus Christ fidelibus *ᵃ*-ad quos presens scriptum pervenerit,⁻ᵃ
W. Lincolniensis episcopus *ᵃ*-eternam in domino⁻ᵃ salutem. Noverit
universitas vestra controversiam que fuit inter abbatem et monachos
de Cultura ex una parte et magistrum Hugonem*ᵈ* de Glocestria*ᶜ* ex
altera*ᵈ* super manerio et ecclesia de Wisiton cum suis pertinentiis et
super ecclesia de Todingedona cum suis pertinentiis comparentibus*ᵉ*
coram nobis predictis*ᶠ* abbate et monachis per procuratorem*ᵍ* suum
Petrum*ʰ* de Rupibus et eodem H. in propria persona hoc fine
conquievisse, videlicet, quod idem Hugo*ᵇ* dictum manerium et prefatas ecclesias cum suis pertinentiis tenebit et possidebit nomine
ipsorum toto tempore vite sue libere et quiete, reddendo exinde dictis
abbati et monachis xᵉᵐ*ⁱ* marcas argenti ad mediam quadragesimam
singulis annis solvendas London' apud Novum Templum magistro
Templi vel ei quem ad hoc predicti abbas et monachi destinaverint, eo
adiecto quod prefatus Hugo*ᵇ* unum monachum*ʲ* de monasterio de

Cultura secum in domo commorantem in victu vel in^f vestitu honorifice exibebit.^{k} Remiserunt autem predicti abbas et monachi querelas
omnes predicto Hugoni^b quas contra eum proposuerunt tam super
monacatione^l quam ei obiciebant quam etiam super summam^m
quamdam pecunie ab eodem H. ut dicebant eis debitam; necnon
etiam omnes querelas ex quacumque causa eo tempore sibi contra
predictum Hugonem^b competentes; dictus quoque Hugo vice
versa omnes querelas sibi contra prefatos abbatem et monachos et
Petrum^h de Rupibus eorumdem procuratorem et quoscumque
eorumdem servienes competentes penitus remisit. Hanc pacis formam
inposterum fideliter observandam tam predictus Petrus^h de Rupibus
procurator eorumdem quam predictus H. corporaliter prestito
iuramento promiserunt. Ut ergo hec compositio perpetuam^n obtineat
firmitatem, eam presentis scripti testimonio sigilli nostri patrocinio
roborato communivimus.^{o} Hiis testibus: R. de Rollestan' decano
Lincolniensi, Hermerico archidiacono Dunhelmensi,^{p} Roberto archidiacono Norhanton',^{q} Gaufrido archidiacono, Gaufrido de Moneta et
multis aliis.

$^{a-a}$ omitted B. ^{b} H. B. ^{c} Glowcestria C. ^{d} alia parte C. ^{e} comparantibus B.
^{f} omitted C. ^{g} procuratore C. ^{h} P. B. ^{i} decem C. ^{j} monachum unum C. ^{k} exhibebit C.
^{l} monachitione C. ^{m} summa C. ^{n} perpetue C. ^{o} communinivimus (sic) BC. ^{p} Dunholm' C.
^{q} B ends here with et plures alii (sic).

Archdn Geoffrey may be Geoffrey, archdn of Bedford. For references to a
continuation of this case see *Letters of Pope Innocent III* nos. 980, 1174. If Peter des
Roches, the abbey's proctor, is to be identified with the future bp of Winchester,
then this actum must have been issued before the latter's consecration on 25
September 1205.

233. Crowland abbey

*Confirmation for the monks of Crowland of the church of Langtoft,
saving a perpetual vicarage. The vicar shall receive all the income of
the church, save garb tithes, and shall pay to the monks a pension of
half a mark. He shall also be responsible for episcopal charges.*

[24 August 1203 × 10 May 1206]

B = Spalding Gentlemen's Society, Crowland cartulary fo. 143r, no. i. s. xiv med.

Universis Christi fidelibus ad quos presens scriptum pervenerit,
Willelmus dei gratia Lincolniensis episcopus salutem in domino. Ut ea
que viris religiosis pia fidelium largitione rationabiliter collata sunt
perpetua gaudeant firmitate episcopali auctoritate decet ea firmari et
auctentici scripti patrocinio roborari. Quapropter nos religionem et
honestatem dilectorum in Christo filiorum monachorum de Croiland'
attendentes, ipsis ecclesiam de Langtoft' cum pertinentiis suis sicut

eam rationabiliter adempti sunt, auctoritate nostra confirmamus possidendam sicut eam ante tempus administrationis nostre in episcopatu
Lincolniensi pacifice noscuntur possedisse, salva perpetua vicaria ei
qui in dicta ecclesia eorum nomine perpetuo ministrabit. Qui quidem
omnes obventiones ad dictam ecclesiam pertinentes preter garbas
percipiet, reddendo inde dictis monachis dimidiam marcam nomine
pensionis, salvis etiam episcopalibus consuetudinibus de quibus idem
vicarius respondebit et Lincolniensis ecclesie dignitate. Quod ut
inposterum perpetuam optineat firmitatem, presenti scripto et sigilli
nostri patrocinio communimus. Testibus etc.

> The abbey increased the portion of the vicar after a dispute in 1222 by the addition
> of 2 acres of arable land, one acre of meadow and a toft (see below no. 234n. for the
> dispute; and cf. *RHW* ii 133–4 for a description of the endowment, 20 December
> 1224 × 19 December 1225).

234. Crowland abbey

*Institution of Robert the chaplain to the perpetual vicarage of Langtoft,
on the presentation of the abbot and monks of Crowland. Robert shall
receive all the income of the church, save garb tithes, and shall pay to
the abbey each year a pension of half a mark. He shall also pay all
episcopal charges.* [24 August 1203 × 10 May 1206]

B = Spalding Gentlemen's Society, Crowland cartulary fo. 143r, no. ii. s. xiv med.

Omnibus sancte matris ecclesie filiis ad quos presens scriptum pervenerit, Willelmus dei gratia Lincolniensis episcopus salutem eternam
in domino. Noverit universitas vestra nos ad presentationem dilectorum in Christo filiorum abbatis et monachorum de Croiland'
admisisse dilectum filium Robertum capellanum ad vicariam ecclesie
de Langtoft' ipsumque in ea perpetuum vicarium canonice instituisse,
ita quidem quod idem Robertus omnes obventiones eiusdem ecclesie
preter garbam percipiet, reddendo annuatim dictis abbati et monachis
dimidiam marcam in festo sancti Bartholomei apostoli, salvis in
omnibus episcopalibus consuetudinibus ab eodem Roberto solvendis
et Lincolniensis ecclesie dignitate. Quod ut perpetuam optineat
firmitatem, presenti scripto et sigilli nostri patrocinio roborato confirmamus. Hiis testibus etc.

> Robert the chaplain is probably to be identified with Robert de Maneton, vicar of
> Langtoft, who was involved in a dispute with the abbey of Crowland over the
> payment of archidiaconal procurations in respect of his benefice. The dispute was
> settled by the priors of Ely, Barnwell, and Swavesey, papal judges delegate, in a
> judgment dated the day after St Brice's day [14 or 15 November] 1222 (cartulary
> fo. 143r–v, no. iii). Dispute over the liability for the payment of procurations and
> also over the annual pension of half a mark mentioned in this actum again occurred

in the early fourteenth century, and was finally settled in 1311 by the abbot of Vaudey, delegated by pope Clement V (ibid. fos. 143v–145v, nos. iii–v).

235. Drax priory

Institution of Peter of Kirmond, clerk, to the church of Garthorpe, on the presentation of the prior and canons of Drax; saving to the priory an annual pension of three marks. [24 August 1203 × 10 May 1206]

B = Bodl. ms. Top. Yorks. c 72 (Drax cartulary) fo. 6r (p. 11). s. xiv med.

[U]niversis Christi fidelibus ad quos presens scriptum pervenerit, Willelmus dei gratia Lincolniensis episcopus salutem eternam in domino. Ad universitatis vestre notitiam volumus pervenire nos, ad presentationem dilectorum in Christo filiorum .. prioris et canonicorum de Drax, admisisse dilectum filium Petrum de Cheuermund clericum ad ecclesiam de Garthorp' ipsumque in ea canonice instituisse, salva eisdem .. priori et canonicis exinde annua pensione trium marcarum; salvis etiam in omnibus episcopalibus consuetudinibus et Lincolniensis ecclesie dignitate. Quod ut ratum et inconcussum inposterum perseveret, id presenti scripto et sigilli nostri patrocinio communivimus. Testibus etc.

This pension is mentioned in *RHW* i 267–8.

236. Drax priory

Confirmation for the canons of Drax of the church of Garthorpe and an annual pension of forty shillings from it.
[24 August 1203 × 10 May 1206]

B = Bodl. ms. Top. Yorks. c 72 (Drax cartulary) fo. 6r–v (pp. 11–12). s. xiv med.

[O]mnibus Christi fidelibus ad quos presens scriptum pervenerit, Willelmus dei gratia Lincolniensis episcopus salutem eternam in domino. Ea que viris religiosis pia fidelium largitione rationabiliter collata sunt beneficia episcopali decet auctoritate muniri. Hinc est quod nos, religionem et honestam conversationem dilectorum in Christo canonicorum de Drax attendentes, ipsis ecclesiam de Garthorp' cum omnibus pertinentiis suis quam sicut in eorum instrumentis que inspeximus continetur rationabiliter adepti sunt et in ea pensionem annuam quadraginta solidorum confirmavimus et presenti scrip[fo.6v]to sigilli nostri munimine roborato communivimus, salvis in omnibus episcopalibus consuetudinibus et Lincolniensis ecclesie dignitate. Hiis testibus etc.

Garthorpe formed part of the original endowment of William Paynel, the founder of Drax priory (see note to *EEA* i no. 106).

237. Durham priory

Notification that Bertram, the prior and the convent of Durham have presented to the bishop on the feastday of the Circumcision next after the death of archbishop H(ubert) of Canterbury [1 January 1206] master Henry of Stamford to the church of St Mary, Bynwerk, [Stamford]. Helias son of William son of Acard, previously presented to the church by the prior and convent, has resigned all right in the same church and in the churches of St Mary at the Bridge, Stamford, and Normanton on Soar. [1 January × 10 May 1206]

A = Durham D. & C. 1.4. Ebor.6. Endorsed: Willelmi Lincoln' episcopi de renuntione (*sic*) trium ecclesiarum et presentatione magistri Henrici ad ecclesiam de Binneweyc. (s. xiii); approx. 133 × 64 mm.; seal missing, tongue and tie torn away, sealing s.q.

B = ibid. Cartuarium III part ii fo. 122v. s. xv in.

Omnibus Christi fidelibus ad quos presens scriptum pervenerit . Will(elmu)s dei gratia Lincolniensis episcopus salutem in domino . Noverit universitas vestra Bertramum priorem et conventum Dunolm' ecclesie presentasse nobis die circumcisionis domini proximo post obitum venerabilis .H. Cantuariensis archiepiscopi . magistrum Henricum de Stamford' ad ecclesiam beate Marie de Binnewerc litteris suis patentibus per Iohannem de Radinge monachum . Heliamque filium Willelmi filii Acardi prius ad eandem ecclesiam a predictis priore et conventu nobis presentatum . totum ius quod dicebat se in eadem ecclesia . et in ecclesia beate Marie ad pontem Stanford' . et in ecclesia de Normant' super Sor . in manu nostra penitus resignasse . Hoc igitur literis nostris presentibus sigillo nostro signatis universitati vestre protestamur . Valete .

William son of Acard (or Achard) gave the two Stamford churches of St Mary to Durham cathedral priory in the mid-twelfth century; Normanton on Soar was given by Richard de Estona. All these and other priory possessions in Lincolnshire and Nottinghamshire were administered by the Durham cell of St Leonard's at Stamford (J. S. Hartley and A. Rogers, *The Religious Foundations of Medieval Stamford* (Stamford Survey Group Report 2, 1974); A. Piper, 'St Leonard's Priory, Stamford' in *Stamford Historian* 5 (1980) 5–25; 6 (1982) 1–23).

238. Easby abbey

Confirmation, after inspection, of the charter of bishop Hugh [no. 54], instituting the canons of Easby to the church of Saddington. [24 August 1203 × 10 May 1206]

B = BL ms. Egerton 2827 (Easby cartulary) fo. 302v. s. xiii ex.

Omnibus etc. Willelmus dei gratia Lincolniensis episcopus. Noveritis quod nos ratam et gratam habemus institutionem quam venerabilis

Hugo Lincolniensis episcopus predecessor noster[a] fecit dilectis filiis canonicis sancte Agathe de Rich' ad ecclesiam de Sadyngton' ad presentationem Ricardi de Rollos eiusdem ecclesie patroni, sicut in carta ipsius predecessoris nostri quam inspeximus continetur, scilicet, salva dilecto filio nostro Willelmo de Bubbenhill' clerico perpetua vicaria quam de ipsis canonicis tenebit, solvendo eis annuatim i marcam argenti ad Pentecosten nomine pensionis, salvis etiam episcopalibus consuetudinibus et Lincolniensis ecclesie dignitate. Nos igitur eandem institutionem sicut rationabiliter facta est episcopali auctoritate confirmamus. Hiis testibus.

[a] *altered from* nostri B.

239. Eynesbury church

Confirmation of the settlement of a dispute in his presence between Saher de Quincy and the canons of Newnham and the monks of St Neot's over the church of Eynesbury. Saher and his heirs shall have the right of presentation to a mediety of the garb tithes belonging to the church, all the altar offerings and all the land belonging to the church. The other mediety shall belong to the monks of St Neot's together with a third part of the garb tithes of the demesne of the village and they shall hold it as they held it of old, and in the name of this mediety they shall pay each year in perpetuity to the canons of Newnham one hundred shillings, as is contained in the chirograph drawn up between the aforesaid monks and canons. Every clerk whom Saher shall present to the benefice shall swear that he will do nothing against this composition to the prejudice of the monks and canons, and when necessary he shall proceed against those withholding the tithes of the monks without delay. [c.Whitsun 1204]

B = BL ms. Cotton Faust. A iv (St Neot's cartulary) fo. 43r–v (42r–v), no. xliii (witnesses omitted). s. xiii med. C = BL ms. Harl. 3656 (Newnham cartulary) fo. 56v. s. xv in.

Pd from C in *Newnham Cartulary* no. 93.

Testibus: Galfrido archidiacono Bed', Alexandro de Haunestou' et aliis.

The composition is pd ibid. no. 92 (another copy is on fo. 89r of the St Neot's cartulary, pd by G. C. Gorham, *The history and antiquities of Eynesbury and St Neot's in Huntingdonshire and of St Neot's in the county of Cornwall* (1824) i 302, no. G). The latter is dated the Monday before Whitsun 1204 [7 June]. An additional witness to the composition is master Henry de Gilevill. Since the bp was present at the time the settlement was made it is probable that he issued his confirmation on or shortly after this occasion.

N

*240. Eynsham abbey

Confirmation for Eynsham abbey of the chapel of Sarsden and a pension of one mark from it.   [24 August 1203 × 10 May 1206]

Mention of confirmation in a list of charters on fo. 1r of the Eynsham cartulary.

Pd, *Eynsham Cartulary* i 2.

241. Eynsham abbey

Inspeximus of bishop Hugh's confirmation for the abbot and convent of Eynsham of its churches and pensions in the diocese [no. 62].
[24 August 1203 × 10 May 1206]

B = Oxford, Ch. Ch. Lib., Kitchin's catalogue 341 (Eynsham cartulary) fo. 19v. s. xiii med. (addition).

Pd from B in *Eynsham Cartulary* i no. 40A.

Hiis testibus: Eustachio abbate de Dorkecestre et aliis.

The witness list of Hugh's charter has been curtailed, only the names of B., prior of Witham and master Richard, subdean of Lincoln, occurring. This charter of William's is the charter referred to ibid. i 1–2, 396–7, but it is not absolutely clear whether it is also the charter mentioned, along with one of St Hugh (no. 64 above), when the patronage of Souldern was disputed between Eynsham and R. de Mortimer *temp.* bp Hugh II (*RHW* i 20).

242. Godstow abbey

Confirmation for the religious house and nuns of St Mary and St John the Baptist, Godstow, of one hundred shillings a year from the toll of Banbury market, given by bishop Alexander [EEA i no. 35], the churches of [High] Wycombe and Bloxham, given by king Henry II, the church of St Giles, [Oxford], given by Alwin son of Godegos, the church of Dinton, given by Agnes daughter of Pain son of John, and a mediety of the church of Pattishall, given by Simon de Wahill (Odell). The churches shall be converted in proprios usus *and be served by their own chaplains. The bishop also grants the nuns freedom from all exaction, custom, and grievance, saving the episcopal right and dignity of the church of Lincoln.*   [24 August 1203 × 10 May 1206]

B = PRO E164/20 (Godstow cartulary) fo. 18r (vi r). s. xv in. C = Bodl. ms. Rawlinson B 408 (Godstow cartulary, English version) fo. 17r–v. s. xv ex.

Pd from C in *Godstow English Register* ii no. 870.

Universis Christi fidelibus ad quos presens scriptum pervenerit, Willelmus dei gratia Lincolniensis episcopus salutem eternam in domino. Iustis postulantium desideriis adesse pio favore volentes precipue domibus relligiosis nostri patrocinii presidium tenemur impertiri, ne ea que fidelium largitione ad loca sancta et relligiosa collata fuerint beneficia aliquorum prava malignitate possint nimium seu turbari aut per temporum vetustatem oblivione sepeliri. Ad universitatis igitur notitiam volumus devenire nos rata habere et presenti carta confirmare relligiose domui sancte Marie et sancti Iohannis Baptiste de Godestow et famulabus Christi ibidem deo servientibus ad earum perpetuis usibus pro futura beneficia fidelium Christi largitate concessa que propriis nominibus duximus explicanda, videlicet, ex dono bone memorie Alexandri Lincolniensis episcopi centum solidos annuos in teloneo mercati de Bannebir' percipiendos; ex dono regis H. filii Matild(is) imperatricis ecclesias de Wicumb' et de Blokesham cum omnibus pertinentiis suis; ex dono Alwini filii Godegos ecclesiam sancti Egidii cum omnibus pertinentiis suis que sita est extra Oxonf' ; ex dono Agnetis filie Pagani filii Iohannis ecclesiam de Dunington' cum omnibus pertinentiis suis; ex dono Simonis de Wahill' medietatem ecclesie de Pateshill' cum omnibus pertinentiis suis. Prefata igitur beneficia sicut eisdem monialibus rationabiliter sunt collata in proprios usus plenarie convertenda et propriis earum capellanis deservienda, rata habemus et episcopali auctoritate confirmamus. Concedimus etiam predictis ancillis Christi ut sint libere et quiete ab omni exactione, consuetudine atque gravamine; salvo episcopali iure et[a] Lincolniensis ecclesie dignitate. Quod ut ratum habeatur et firmum, presenti scripto et sigillo nostro duximus confirmandum. Testibus: R. archidiacono Norhamtun', magistris Alexandro de Elnestow, Gilberto de Malbertorp', Thoma de Fiskert', Lincolniensis ecclesie canonicis, magistris Willelmo filio Fulconis, Adam de sancto Edmundo, Willelmo de Stavenb' et multis aliis.

[a] *omitted* B.

William son of Fulk is not described as a canon of Lincoln; he received the prebend of Decem Librarum at some date between 25 September 1205 and 10 May 1206.

243. Godstow abbey

Notification of the settlement in the bishop's presence of a case between the prior and canons of Norton and the nuns of Godstow over the church of Easington, heard before G(eoffrey), abbot of Chester, O(sbert), abbot of Stanlow and B. dean of Chester, papal judges delegate. The canons had claimed that Easington was a chapel belonging to their church of Pyrton. By this composition the canons have remitted all right in the church of Easington and the nuns shall pay to the canons one bezant each year at Michaelmas for the sake of peace. Neither party shall claim any parochial rights over the other church and its parishioners. [24 August 1203 × 10 May 1206]

B = PRO E164/20 (Godstow cartulary) fo. 41r (xxviii r). s. xv in. C = Bodl. ms. Rawlinson B 408 (Godstow cartulary, English version) fo. 38v. s. xv ex.

Pd from C in *Godstow English Register* i no. 440.

Universis sancte matris ecclesie filiis ad quos presens scriptum pervenerit, Willelmus dei gratia Lincolniensis episcopus eternam in domino salutem. Noverit universitas vestra quod cum causa quedam verteretur inter priorem et canonicos de Northona ex una parte et sanctimoniales de Godestowe ex altera super ecclesia de Esendon', quam idem canonici petebant tanquam capellam ad ecclesiam suam de Piriton' de iure spectantem, coram G. de Cestria et O. de Stanlaue abbatibus et B. decano Cestrensi iudicibus a sede apostolica delegatis, partibus in presentia nostra ad componendum amicabiliter per assensum iudicum constitutis, controversia prefata hoc fine quievit, videlicet, quod prefati canonici totum ius quod ipsi vel ecclesia de Piriton' in ecclesia de Esendon' videbantur habere liberum et absolutum nobis presentibus iamdictis monialibus inperpetuum remiserunt et prefate moniales prefatis canonicis unun bizantium pro bono pacis annuatim ad festum sancti Michaelis inperpetuum persolvent; et quod parochianos ecclesie de Piriton' in prefata ecclesia de Esendon' ad divina iure parochiali non recipient nec ius aliquod parochiale ecclesie de Piriton' sibi vendicabunt nec canonici in ecclesia de Esendon'. Ne ergo contra hanc compositionem cuiquam venire liceat, eam presentis scripti testimonio et sigilli patrocinio roboravimus. Hiis testibus: magistro G. de Malbertorp'[a] et Thoma de Fiskerton', Lincolniensis ecclesie canonicis, Vacario[b] capellano, magistris W. filio Fulconis, A. de sancto Admundo, W. de Stavenbi et Hugone de Gloucestr', Rogero Bacun, P. de Cheuremunt, Carolo et Waleranno, clericis, et multis aliis.

[a] Masbertorp' B.   [b] vicario B.

Innocent III's commission to the judges delegate is pd *Letters of Pope Innocent III* no. 668 and dated ? 9 January 1198 × December 1205.

244. Greenfield priory

Inspeximus of bishop Hugh's general confirmation of possessions for the nuns of Greenfield [no. 70].   [24 August 1203 × 10 May 1206]

A = BL Harl. Ch. 43 H 25 (faded). Not endorsed; approx. 135 × 161 + 17 mm.; small fragment of seal (repaired), reddish-brown wax, no counterseal visible, on parchment tag, d.q.1. Scribe **IV**.

Universis Christi fidelibus ad quos presens scriptum pervenerit Will(elmu)s dei gratia Lincolniensis episcopus . salutem eternam in domino. Inspeximus cartam pii patris et predecessoris nostri bone

memorie Hugonis quondam Lincolniensis . episcopi . sub hac forma .
[*here follows no. 70*] Testibus . Hamone decano . Lincolniensis .
ecclesie . magistro Rogero de Rolveston' . et aliis. Nos igitur dicti
patris et predecessoris nostri vestigiis inherentes dicte domui de
Grenefeld' et monialibus in ea deo servientibus omnia prenotata sicut
eis racionabiliter collata sunt ipsis episcopali auctoritate confirmamus
et presenti scripto cum sigilli nostri patrocinio communimus . salvis
quantum ad ecclesias episcopalibus consuetudinibus et Lincolniensis
ecclesie dignitate. Testibus W. archidiacono Bukingham' . magistris .
G. de Malbertorp' . Ada de sancto Edmundo . T. de Fiskertun' .
canonicis Lincolniensibus . magistro W. filio . Fulconis . Petro .
Karolo . clericis . et multis aliis.

William son of Fulk became a canon of Lincoln at some date between 25 September
1205 and 10 May 1206 (see no. 259 below).

*245. Horsington church

*Institution of William de Milai to the church of Horsington on the
presentation of Rannulf de Milay.* [8 April 1206]

Mention of charter in a dispute over the advowson of Horsington church between
Geoffrey FitzPeter, earl of Essex and Rannulf de Milay, Trinity term, 1206.
Pd, *CRR* iv 185.

The previous incumbent was said to have died on Easter day [2 April 1206] and the
institution took place on the following Saturday.

246. Kirkham priory

*Grant to the canons of Kirkham of an annual pension of half a mark
from the church of Cold Overton, to be paid to them by whoever holds
the* personatus. [24 August 1203 × 10 May 1206]

B = Bodl. ms. Dodsworth 7 (copies of charters in St Mary's Tower, York) fo.
210r. s. xvii med. C = Bodl. ms. Fairfax 7 (Kirkham cartulary, abstract only)
fo. 34r. s. xv ex.

Universis Christi fidelibus ad quos presens scriptum pervenerit,
Willelmus dei gratia Lincolniensis episcopus salutem eternam in
domino. Noverit universitas vestra nos divine pietatis intuitu concessisse dilectis in Christo filiis canonicis de Kirkeham annuam
pensionem dimidie marce de ecclesia de Caldoverton' ipsis ab eo qui
dicte ecclesie personatum gesserit singulis annis inperpetuum per-
solvendam. Quod ut 'ratum et' firmum permaneat inperpetuum,
presenti scripto et sigilli nostri patrocinio communimus, episcopali
auctoritate qua fungimur confirmantes; salvis in omnibus episcopalibus consuetudinibus et Lincolniensis ecclesie dignitate. Testibus:

magistro Ada*a* de sancto Edmundo, T. de Fiskertun, canonicis Lincolniensibus, magistro W. filio Fulconis, W. persona de Cleipol, Waler(anno) de Lincoln, G. de Iwardebi, clericis, et multis aliis.

a Ada *omitted* B.

William son of Fulk is not described as a canon here; the prebend of Decem Librarum was collated to him by bp William 25 September 1205 × 10 May 1206 (see below, no. 259).

*247.   Knighton manor

Final concord between the bishop and R(obert) son of R(obert), earl of Leicester, concerning the manor of Knighton.

[24 August 1203 × 24 March 1204]

Mention of charter as no. 12 in a list of the Knighton section of the second book of the lost cartulary of Leicester abbey (Bodl. ms. Laud misc. 625, fo. 81r (lxxxv r)).

Pd, J. Nichols, *History of Leicestershire* iv 1. 235.

The entry in this Leicester abbey rental notes that the final concord was sealed for greater security with the seals of king John, archbp Hubert Walter, bp Herbert of Salisbury, bp Eustace of Ely and bp John of Norwich. King John confirmed the settlement on 24 March 1204 (*Reg. Ant.* i no. 212; *Rot. Chart.* 125).

*248.   Knighton manor

[?] Charter relating to the manor of Knighton.

[24 August 1203 × 24 March 1204]

Mention of charter as no. 16 in a list of the Knighton section of the second book of the lost cartulary of Leicester abbey (Bodl. ms. Laud misc. 625, fo. 80v (lxxxiiii v)).

Pd, J. Nichols, *History of Leicestershire* iv 1. 235

The list merely gives the bp's initial, so it could either be William of Blois or Walter of Coutances. As bp William had a dispute over the manor of Knighton (see *Reg. Ant.* iii nos. 871–2) it seems probable that he may be involved in this particular instance. For the possible date see above.

*249.   Kyme priory

? Confirmation to Kyme priory of a pension of two and a half marks from the church of All Saints, Wainfleet.

[24 August 1203 × 10 May 1206]

Mention of charter in the first institution roll of bp Hugh II.

Pd, *RHW* i 13.

For a similar charter of St Hugh, see no. 82.

*250. Leicester abbey

Appropriation of the church of Barrow-on-Soar to the abbey of Leicester. [24 August 1203 × 10 May 1206]

Mention of grant in the Leicester archdeaconry 'matricula' of bp Hugh II.

Pd, *RHW* i 253.

251. Lichfield cathedral

Confirmation for the common fund of the church of Lichfield of the church of Thornton [by Horncastle], given by Robert Marmiun and confirmed by bishop Hugh [no. 90]. The dean and canons of Lichfield are to possess the church in proprios usus *after the death of Peter the clerk, the present perpetual vicar.* [24 August 1203 × 10 May 1206]

B = Lichfield D. & C., Magnum Registrum Album fo. 221v. s. xiv in.

Pd (calendar) from B in *Lichfield M.R.A.* no. 515.

Universis sancte matris ecclesie filiis ad quos presens scriptum pervenerit, Willelmus dei gratia Lincolniensis episcopus eternam in domino salutem. Ad universitatis vestre notitiam volumus pervenire nos auctoritate episcopali confirmasse commune Lich' ecclesie ecclesiam de Thorniton' quam ex donatione Roberti Marmiun et confirmatione venerande recordationis Hugonis Lincolniensis episcopi predecessoris nostri canonice optinuerunt, ita quidem quod post decessum Petri clerici eiusdem ecclesie vicarii perpetui liceat eiusdem ecclesie de Lich' decano et canonicis predictam ecclesiam de Thorniton' cum omnibus ad eam pertinentibus in usus proprios commune sue convertere et perpetuo possidere; salvis episcopalibus consuetudinibus et Lincolniensis ecclesie dignitate. Quod ut ratum inconcussumque permaneat, id presenti scripto et sigilli nostri munimine roboravimus. Hiis testibus: Rogero Lincolniensis ecclesie decano, Roberto de Mamecestr' archidiacono Norh', magistro Alexandro de Alnestowe et Thoma de Fiskerton', canonicis Lincolniensis ecclesie, magistris Willelmo filio Fulconis, Ada de sancto Admundo et Gilberto de Schardeburgh, Vacario capellano, Hugone de Rollieston', Ricardo de Tingherst, Gilberto et Carolo, clericis, et multis aliis.

Marmiun's grant is ibid. no. 513. William son of Fulk is not described as a canon of Lincoln here; the prebend of Decem Librarum was collated to him by bp William 25 September 1205 × 10 May 1206 (no. 259).

252. Lincoln cathedral

Confirmation, having inspected bishop Robert [Chesney's] charter [EEA i no. 161], of his grant exempting the prebends of the church of

*Lincoln from all episcopal rights and demands, so that the archdeacons
shall have no power to demand anything from the prebends or from the
churches which belong to the common of Lincoln, or to implead their
parishioners. The same liberty is granted to the church of Searby which
is assigned to the lights of the church of Lincoln, the church of Leighton
[Bromswold] belonging to the subdeanery of Lincoln, and the church of
All Saints [in the Bail], Lincoln belonging to the chancellorship of
Lincoln.*   [24 August 1203 × 25 September 1205]

> B = Lincoln D. & C. A/1/5 (Registrum Antiquissimum) no. 906. s. xiii in.
> C = Lincoln diocesan records, misc. roll 6 (inspeximus of Walter de Gray,
>   archbp of York (1215-55), no. 3 (damaged).
> Pd from B in *Reg. Ant.* i no. 288; from C in *RRG* 516.

Hiis testibus: Rogero de Rolveston' decano Lincolniensis ecclesie,
magistro Willelmo de Montibus cancellario, magistro Willelmo de
Bramfeld' subdecano, magistro Girardo de Rowell', magistro Waltero
Blundo, Hugone de sancto Eadwardo*a* et multis aliis.

> *a* Edwardo C.

> Searby is not mentioned in bp Chesney's charter. William de Bramfeld, subdean of
> Lincoln, was murdered on 25 September 1205. For a similar charter of bp Hugh I
> see no. 102.

253. Lincoln cathedral

*Ordinance, made with the advice and good will of Roger of Rolleston,
the dean and the chapter of Lincoln, providing that everyone who is a
canon of Lincoln at the time of his death shall have the power of
disposing of the fruits of his prebend for one year from the day of his
death. The bishop also provides that each of the vicars of the
prebendaries shall receive every year half a mark beyond his accustomed stipend.*   [24 August 1203 × 25 September 1205]

> B = Lincoln D. & C. A/1/5 (Registrum Antiquissimum) no. 910. s. xiii in.
> Pd from B in *Reg. Ant.* i no. 293; *LCS* i 115-16.

Testibus: magistris W. de Bramfeld subdecano, G. archidiacono
Bedford', Alexandro de Bedefordia, Philippo de Malbertorp', Gerardo
de Rowell', T. de Fiskerton', Lincolniensis ecclesie canonicis, magistro W. filio Fulconis, Eudone preposito et aliis.

> Subdean Bramfeld was murdered on 25 September 1205.

254. Lincoln cathedral

*Confirmation for the common of the canons of Lincoln, at the request of
master Ralph of Swaton, of Ralph's grant of the church of Scredington.*

The bishop also confirms master Ralph's gift to the common of the two bovates of land in Scredington which Jungwine held, with a toft and croft and all appurtenances. [24 August 1203 × 25 September 1205]

B = Lincoln D. & C. A/1/5 (Registrum Antiquissimum) no. 940. s. xiii in.
Pd from B in *Reg. Ant.* iii no. 1003.

Hiis testibus: Rogero de Rolveston' decano Lincolniensis ecclesie, magistro Willelmo de Montibus cancellario, magistro Willelmo de Bramfeld' subdecano*a*, magistro Girardo de Rouuell', magistro Waltero Blundo, Hugone de sancto Edwardo et multis aliis.

a Lincolniensis ecclesie *follows here but is marked for deletion.*

For a similar confirmation by bp Hugh I see no. 104. Note that the witnesses are exactly the same as in no. 252. The murder of subdean Bramfeld on 25 September 1205 provides a *terminus ad quem* for this document.

255. Lincoln cathedral

Confirmation of the composition made between R(oger), the dean and the chapter of Lincoln, and the abbot and canons of Barlings in respect of a dispute over the church of Scothern.
[24 August 1203 × 10 May 1206]

B = Lincoln D. & C. A/1/5 (Registrum Antiquissimum) no. 167. s. xiii in.
Pd from B in *Reg. Ant.* i no. 218.

Testibus: magistris G. de Rowelle, A. de sancto Edmundo, T. de Fiskerton, canonicis Lincolniensibus, magistro W. filio Fulconis, R. de Calcwelle, R. de Stowe, R. de Rowell', clericis, et multis aliis.

Master William son of Fulk is not yet described as a canon of Lincoln; he received the prebend of Decem Librarum 25 September 1205 × 10 May 1206 (see no. 259). The actual composition is not recited in this confirmation. It is pd ibid. no. 217; the dispute concerned certain tithes in Scothern which had of old belonged to the prebend of All Saints, Hungate. The abbot of Barlings at the time was Robert; the prebendary of All Saints Richard of Linwood.

256. Lincoln cathedral

Mandate to all the archdeacons and officials of the diocese of Lincoln to cause the faithful of every household in the diocese to be moved to a more regular observance of the yearly pentecostal processions.
[24 August 1203 × 10 May 1206]

B = Lincoln D. & C. A/1/5 (Registrum Antiquissimum) no. 913 (no witnesses). s. xiii in.
Pd from B in *Reg. Ant.* i no. 297; *Eynsham Cartulary* ii no. 707.

For a similar mandate of bp Hugh I and for a note on pentecostal processions see no. 92.

257. Lincoln cathedral

Grant to the dean and chapter of Lincoln to compel all canons who do not make residence to appoint suitable vicars to fill their place. The bishop also grants them liberty to exercise canonical justice against those persons who do injury to the common, saving in all things the right and authority (potestas) *of the bishop. Archdeacons, deans and other officials of the bishopric of Lincoln are not permitted to absolve persons excommunicated or placed under interdict by the chapter except they act on an episcopal or capitular mandate, and they are commanded to carry into effect the sentence of the chapter.*

[24 August 1203 × 10 May 1206]

B = Lincoln D. & C. A/1/5 (Registrum Antiquissimum) no. 915 (no witnesses). s. xiii in.

Pd from B in *Reg. Ant.* i no. 299.

This grant closely follows a similar grant by bp Hugh I (no. 93).

*258. Lincoln cathedral

Indulgence of forty days for those contributing alms towards the building of the cathedral church of Lincoln. Thirty-three masses are to be celebrated in the cathedral each week for the brothers and sisters of the fraternity (of the cathedral), both living and dead.

[24 August 1203 × 10 May 1206]

Mention only, in list of indulgences to the cathedral fabric, in *Gir. Camb.* vii 217, app. F.

For the general fraternity of the cathedral established by Hugh I see above, no. 97. Walter is given as the name of the bp (i.e. Walter of Coutances, 1183–5), but like the editor of *Gir. Camb.* I incline to the view, taking into account the chronology and sense of the passage, that Walter is a scribal error for William (of Blois). This supposition seems to be partly confirmed by the reference later in the appendix to the indulgence (although this time of fifty (*sic*) days) and the thirty-three masses granted by bp *William* (ibid. 219). See also J. W. F. Hill, *Medieval Lincoln* (Cambridge 1948, repd 1965) 113, and K. Major, *Minster Yard* (Lincoln Minister pamph. 2nd ser., no. 7, 1974) 23.

259. Lincoln cathedral

Grant to the bishop's clerk, master William son of Fulk, of the prebend of Decem Librarum, on the resignation of Peter de Colonna, canon of Lincoln, which prebend the bishop had conferred upon Peter at the instance of pope Innocent III and which in the time of the bishop's predecessors had been held by master Simon de Trou and after him by master Alan of Buckden. William son of Fulk is to receive the ten

*pounds out of the farm of the archdeaconry of Lincoln, as his
predecessors had received them.* [25 September 1205 × 10 May 1206]

A = Lincoln D. & C. Dij/55/3/2. Endorsed: prebenda .x. li. (s. xiii); de prebenda
.x. librarum (s. xiii); approx. 142 × 125 + 20 mm.; seal missing, parchment tag,
d.q.1.

Pd from A in *Reg. Ant.* ii no. 350.

Omnibus Christi fidelibus ad quos presens scriptum pervenerit ʔ
Will(elmu)s dei gratia Lincolniensis episcopus salutem eternam in
domino. Noverit universitas vestra nos ad resignationem dilecti in
Christo filii Petri de Columpna Lincolniensis ecclesie canonici ʔ
dedisse et concessisse caritatis intuitu dilecto in Christo filio magistro
Willelmo filio Fulconis clerico nostro ʔ illam prebendam decem
librarum esterlingorum ʔ quam ad instantiam et petitionem domini
pape Innocentii tercii ʔ eidem Petro antea contuleramus . quam etiam
tempore predecessorum nostrorum magister Symon de Trou . et post
eum magister Alanus de Buggenden' habuerant ʔ perpetuo possidendam. Et ipsi magistro Willelmo dictas decem libras assignavimus
percipiendas ʔ ubi predicti canonici eas percipere consueverunt .
videlicet de firma archidiaconatus Lincolniensis ʔ per manum ipsius
archidiaconi . scilicet centum solidos ad Pascha . et centum solidos ad
festum sancti Michaelis. Ut autem hec nostra donatio et concessio
perpetuam obtineant firmitatem ʔ eas presenti scripto et sigilli nostri
patrocinio communivimus. Testibus . Rogero decano . Philippo
subdecano . magistris Girardo de Rowell' . Gilberto de Malbertorp' .
Adam de sancto Edmundo . et Thomas de Fiskerton' ʔ Lincolniensis
ecclesie canonicis . magistro Willelmo de Stavenb' . Alexandro de
Torkes' . Rogero . Petro . Waleranno et Karolo clericis ʔ et multis aliis.

Philip became subdean at some date after 25 September 1205.

260. Lincoln cathedral

*Appropriation to the church of Lincoln in augmentation of the common
of the canons residing there of the churches of Orston and Edwinstowe.*
[24 August 1203 × 10 May 1206]

B = Lincoln D. & C. A/1/5 (Registrum Antiquissimum) no. 931. s. xiii in.
C = ibid. A/1/6 (Registrum) no. 205. s. xiv med. (no witnesses).

Pd from B in *Reg. Ant.* iii no. 980.

The wording of this actum is identical with the appropriation deed of bp Hugh I
(no. 107), save for the change of the bp's name.

261.   Lincoln cathedral

Confirmation of the church of Wellingore for the common of the church of St Mary, Lincoln, saving the right of Alan of Wellingore, clerk, while he lives. This grant is for the maintenance of canons residing in the church of Lincoln.   [24 August 1203 × 10 May 1206]

> B = Lincoln D. & C. A/1/5 (Registrum Antiquissimum) no. 938. s. xiii in.
> D = ibid. A/1/6 (Registrum) no. 350. s. xiv med. There are no witnesses in either cartulary copy.
>
> Pd from B in *Reg. Ant.* iii no. 1000.

For a similar confirmation by bp Hugh I see no. 99. Shortly after this confirmation, the church of Wellingore was the subject of a dispute between the dean and chapter of Lincoln and the abbey of St Martin at Sées. A composition of July 1207 confirmed the church in perpetual possession of the common fund of Lincoln, on condition that the cathedral chapter paid twenty-four shillings a year to the abbey (*Reg. Ant.* iii no. 1001).

262.   Lincoln cathedral

Confirmation for the common of the cathedral church of St Mary of Lincoln of a mediety of the church of Glentham, granted by Gilbert of Glentham and Alfred his heir, and saving the right of Geoffrey of Glentham, clerk, while he lives.   [24 August 1203 × 10 May 1206]

> B = Lincoln D. & C. A/1/5 (Registrum Antiquissimum) no. 959a (no witnesses). s. xiii in.
>
> Pd from B in *Reg. Ant.* iii no. 1038.

For a similar confirmation by St Hugh and for details of the original grant see above, no. 100.

*263.   London, Haliwell priory

Confirmation to the nuns of Haliwell, Shoreditch, London, of an annual pension of five marks from the church of Welwyn.
                         [24 August 1203 × 10 May 1206]

> Mention of confirmation in the second institution roll of bp Hugh II, 1218-9.
> Pd, *RHW* i 136.

For a similar confirmation of St Hugh, see no. 112.

264.   Newnham priory

Confirmation for the canons of Newnham of certain churches and tithes, namely: the churches of Wootton and Wrestlingworth, the gift of Simon de Beauchamp [Bellocampo], the tithe of Nigel Malherbe in Houghton, two parts of the tithe of the demesne of Simon de Beauchamp

in Linslade, one mark from the mill [of Linslade] and the tithe of the
mill of Biddenham and of the mill of Risinghoe.

[24 August 1203 × 10 May 1206]

B = BL ms. Harl. 3656 (Newnham cartulary) fo. 56r. s. xv in. C = ibid. fo. 59r.
Pd from B in *Newnham Cartulary* no. 91; C noted ibid. no. 101.

Testibus: magistris A. Bed', G. de Rowell', A. de sancto Eadmundo
et aliis.

For the identification of the mill from which Newnham received one mark a year
see ibid. nos. 1, 3, 5–6, 87.

265. Newnhàm priory

General confirmation for the canons of Newnham of their possessions in
the diocese, namely: the churches of St Paul, Bedford, [Great]
Barford, Renhold, Stagsden and Salford, two parts of the church of
Southill, the churches of Cardington, Willington, and Goldington,
pensions of three and a half marks from the church of Ravensden, five
shillings from the church of Holcote, twenty six shillings from the
church of Gravenhurst, four marks from the church of All Saints,
Bedford, two parts of the garb tithes of the demesne of W[illiam] Druel
in Colworth, both assarts and cultivated lands, two parts of the tithes
of the demesnes of Keysoe, Aspley [Guise], Eversholt, Haynes, two
parts of the whole demesne of Simon de Beauchamp [Bellocampo] in
Stotfold, and of the demesne of Simon of Holwell, the tithes of the mill of
'Juel'', the tithes of three virgates of land in Biddenham of the fee of St
Paul, and two shillings from the land which was Hugh de Bokeland's
in the same village.   [24 August 1203 × 10 May 1206]

B = BL ms. Harl. 3656 (Newnham cartulary) fos. 57v–58r. s. xv in.
Pd from B in *Newnham Cartulary* no. 96.

Testibus: magistris W. archidiacono de Bukyngham, A. Bedeford' et
aliis.

William of Blois succeeded Roger as archdn of Buckingham in the course of bp
William's episcopate, but the precise date is not certain.

266. Newnham priory

Confirmation for the canons of Newnham of the church of Gravenhurst
on the presentation of William son of Brian and on the admission of
Nicholas, former archdeacon of Bedford, during the vacancy of the see of
Lincoln. The bishop has inspected the charters of William and the arch-
deacon. The perpetual vicarage of Simon de Bueles is safeguarded.

He shall hold the church with all appurtenances, paying to the canons an annual pension of twenty-six shillings.

[24 August 1203 × 10 May 1206]

B = BL ms. Harl. 3656 (Newnham cartulary) fo. 58r–v. s. xv in.
Pd from B in *Newnham Cartulary* no. 98.

Testibus: G. archidiacono Bed', R. archidiacono Buck' et aliis.

The date of this confirmation is probably early in bp William's episcopate, since William of Blois succeeded Roger as archdn of Buckingham during the pontificate. For Simon de Bueles and the Bueles family see Beds. Hist. Rec. Soc. 19 (1937) 161. Archdn Nicholas must have admitted the canons into the church during the vacancy between bp Robert Chesney and bp-elect Geoffrey Plantagenet (1166–1173), see also *Newnham Cartulary* no. 197.

*267.　Nocton priory

Letters patent to the king certifying that the prior and canons of Nocton are parsons of the churches of Nocton and Dunston, and that William de Aresci was admitted as vicar of the churches in his presence (when he was precentor of Lincoln), on the priory's presentation. The church of Nocton pays to the canons an annual pension of five marks, and the church of Dunston four shillings.　　　　[12 May × 4 June 1204]

Mention of letters patent sent in the course of a dispute between the prior of Nocton and the abbot of St Mary's, York over the advowson of the churches, Easter term 1204.

Pd, *CRR* iii 112.

William of Blois was precentor from *c.*1197 until his elevation to the bishopric in 1203 and these dates provide the limits for William de Aresci's admission as vicar of Nocton and Dunston.

268.　Nocton priory

Institution of Vacarius, priest, to the perpetual vicarage of Dunston, on the presentation of Alan, the prior and the canons of Nocton. Vacarius shall hold the church for as long as he lives, paying to the canons one silver mark a year for half of the garb tithes of the village, which the bishop has granted, with the consent of R(oger) the dean and the chapter of Lincoln, to the canons of Nocton in proprios usus after Vacarius' death.　　　　[25 September 1205 × 10 May 1206]

A = Lancashire Record Office, DDTO, K/1/10. Not endorsed; approx. 150 × 112 + 14 mm.; seal missing, parchment tag for seal, d.q.1. Scribe **III**.

Omnibus Christi fidelibus ad quos presens scriptum pervenerit ⋮ Will(elmu)s dei gratia Lincolniensis episcopus salutem eternam in domino. Noverit universitas vestra nos ad presentationem dilectorum

in Christo filiorum Alani prioris et canonicorum de Noketon' admisisse dilectum in Christo filium Vacarium capellanum ad perpetuam
vicariam ecclesie de Dunston' . ipsum que in eadem ecclesia canonice
perpetuum vicarium instituisse. ita quidem quod predictus Vacarius
eandem ecclesiam de Dunston' cum omnibus pertinentiis suis quoadvixerit tenebit . reddendo prefatis canonicis pro medietate decime
garbarum eiusdem ville quas de consensu .R. decani et capituli
Lincolniensis ecclesie eisdem canonicis de Noketon' post decessum
predicti Vacarii in proprios usus convertendas concessimus ꞉ unam
marcam argenti ad duos terminos solvendam . scilicet dimidiam
marcam ad Pascha et dimidiam marcam ad festum sancti Michaelis .
salvis episcopalibus consuetudinibus a sepedicto Vacario solvendis ꞉ et
Lincolniensis ecclesie dignitate. Quod ut futuris temporibus perpetuam obtineat firmitatem ꞉ presenti scripto et sigilli nostri patrocinio
communivimus. Testibus . Philippo subdecano . magistris . G. de
Rowell' . W. filio Fulconis . A. de sancto Edmundo . et Thoma . de
Fiskerton' ꞉ Lincolniensis ecclesie canonicis . magistro Willelmo de
Stavenb' . Roberto de Methringham' decano . Hugone capellano de
Noket' . Petro clerico . et aliis

Philip became subdean of Lincoln at some date after 25 September 1205.

*269.   Nocton priory

Ordination of the vicarage of Nocton
                                          [? 24 August 1203 × 10 May 1206]

Mention of charter of bp W. in the Lincoln archdeaconry institution roll of bp
   Hugh II in the record of Simon de Koleby's institution to the vicarage of Nocton
   and a fresh ordination of it during the twentieth pontifical year, beginning 20
   December 1228. 'Aliter ordinata est ut in carta W. quondam Lincolniensis
   episcopi quam habent canonici memorati.'
Pd, *RHW* iii 170.

Bp W. could of course be either William of Blois or Walter of Coutances.

*270.   Northampton, Holy Trinity hospital (Kingsthorpe)

*Confirmation for the master and brethren of the hospital of Holy
Trinity outside Northampton [Kingsthorpe] of an annual pension of
four silver marks from the church of Bletsoe in the name of a perpetual
benefice.*   [24 August 1203 × 10 May 1206]

Mention of confirmation in a charter of bp Hugh II, 1219 × 1223.
Pd, *Lib. Ant.* 104–5.

The hospital at Kingsthorpe was founded in 1200.

271. Nun Cotham priory

Admission of the nuns of Nun Cotham to that portion of the church of Croxton belonging to the gift of Robert son of Richard of Croxton, and on his presentation. [24 August 1203 × 10 May 1206]

B = Bodl. ms. Top. Lincs. d 1 (Nun Cotham cartulary) fo. 23br. s. xiii in.

[O]mnibus Christi fidelibus ad quos presens scriptum pervenerit, Willelmus dei gratia Lincolniensis episcopus salutem eternam in domino. Noverit universitas vestra nos ad presentationem dilecti in Christo filii Roberti filii Ricardi de Croxtun admisisse dilectas in Christo filias moniales de Cotun ad illam portionem ecclesie de Croxtun que ad donationem eiusdem R. pertinet ipsasque in eadem portione canonice instituisse, salvis in omnibus episcopalibus con-suetudinibus et Lincolniensis ecclesie dignitate. Quod ut futuris temporibus perpetuam obtineat firmitatem*a*, id presenti scripto sigilli nostri munimine roborato communivimus.*b* Hiis t(estibus).

a corrected from firmitatibus B.   *b one minim omitted* B.

Robert son of Richard of Croxton's grant and the confirmation by the cathedral chapter of Lincoln are both on fo. 23br of the cartulary.

272. Osney abbey

Confirmation, with the consent of R(oger) the dean and the chapter of Lincoln, for the canons of Osney of the church of Waterperry, to possess it in proprios usus *as they possessed it before he became bishop.*
[24 August 1203 × 10 May 1206]

B = Oxford, Ch. Ch. Lib., Osney cartulary fo. 120r (section 1) (witnesses omitted). s. xiii ex.

Pd from B in *Oseney Cartulary* iv no. 345.

For bp Hugh's admission of the abbey into possession of the *personatus* see no. 146.

273. Osney abbey

Confirmation, with the assent of the dean and chapter of Lincoln, for the canons of Osney of the churches of Hook Norton, Kidlington, Waterperry, Steeple Claydon and Stone, to possess them in proprios usus, *as they possessed them before he became bishop.*
[25 September 1205 × 10 May 1206]

B = BL ms. Cotton Vit. E xv (Osney cartulary) fo. 170r. s. xiii in.

Pd from B in *Oseney Cartulary* iv no. 32A.

Testibus: Rogero decano Lincolniensi, magistris Gerardo de Rowelle, Willelmo filio Fulconis, Adam de sancto Eadmundo et Thoma de Fiskint', Lincolniensis ecclesie canonicis, magistro Willelmo de Stavenb', Rogero Bacun, Petro de Cheuermund, Karolo et*a* Waleranno, clericis, et multis aliis.

a de B.

274. Oxford, St Frideswide's priory

General confirmation of possessions for the canons of St Frideswide, Oxford, namely: the church of St Frideswide in proprios usus, *with the chapels of Headington, Marston, Elsfield, and Binsey; in Oxford the chapels of Holy Trinity, St Michael at the South Gate and St Clement, and the churches of St Aldate's, St Peter ad Castrum (le Bailey), St Michael at the North Gate, St Edward, and St Mildred; the churches of Fritwell, Winchendon and Worminghall* in proprios usus; *sixteen pence from the church of Hampton Poyle (Philipeshamton') and two measures* (coddos) *of wheat, for tithes; two sheaves from the demesne of Churchill and the whole tithe of hay of the same, and of the newly-tilled land* (novalibus) *of the monks there; all the tithes of corn from the demesne of Adam de Thoni in Garsington; in Horspath from one demesne an acre of rye and an acre of oats, and from the other demesne in the same village an acre of rye, half a hide of the land of the church, two thraves of all corn, for tithe, and one thrave from each virgate of land in the same village; from the demesne of Cuddesdon one acre of wheat, another of rye, and a third of oats; from Chippinghurst twelve thraves of all corn; from Denton four thraves; and the tithes of one hide in Walton and half a hide in Cowley and half a hide in Thomley; the tithes of Langney; in Forest Hill one and a half acres of the demesne of the abbey of Osney, and one acre of the other demesne, and from each virgate of land in the village one thrave of all corn, for tithe, and the bodies of the dead of the same village with* prima divisa; *and from the demesne of Hamo Carbonel in Bainton two shillings, for tithes.* [24 August 1203 × 10 May 1206]

B = Bodl. C.C.C. ms. 160 (St Frideswide's cartulary) pp. 302–3, no. 459 (witnesses omitted). s. xiii ex. C = Oxford, Ch. Ch. Lib., St Frideswide's cartulary, p. 55a (witnesses omitted). s. xv med. D = ibid. p. 193a–b (witnesses omitted). E = ibid. pp. 357b–358a (witnesses omitted). F = ibid. p. 55b (charter mentioned in an inspeximus of Robert Marsh, the dean and the chapter of Lincoln, 2 Dec. 1259). G = ibid. pp. 59a–60a (in an inspeximus by the same, 18 Aug. 1261, with witnesses).

Pd from BG in *St Frideswide's Cartulary* i no. 43; other versions mentioned ibid. i nos. 63, 66, 253; ii no. 939.

Testibus: Willelmo archidiacono Bokyngham', magistris Alexandro de Elnestowe, Girardo de Gowell',*a* Ada de sancto Edmundo et

Thoma de Filkertona,*b* Lincolniensis ecclesie canonicis, magistris Willelmo filio Fulconis, Willelmo de Stavenesby, Gilberto de Ywardbie, Petro de Crevermont,*c* Karolo et Walerano, clericis, et multis aliis.

a recte Rowell'.   *b recte* Fiskertona.   *c recte* Chevermont.

William son of Fulk is not described as a canon of Lincoln; he received the prebend of Decem Librarum at some date between 25 September 1205 and 10 May 1206 (see above, no. 259). *VCH Oxfordshire* vi (1959) 158 identifies 'Philipeshamton'' as Hampton Gay, but I think that the church should be identified as Hampton Poyle (cf. *Place-names of Oxfordshire* i (EPNS xxiii, 1971) 213–14).

275. Oxford, St Frideswide's priory

Confirmation for the canons of St Frideswide, Oxford, of the church of All Saints, Oxford, and an annual pension of three marks from the church, saving the residue for the vicar who shall serve the church at their presentation.   [24 August 1203 × 10 May 1206]

B = Bodl. C. C. C. ms. 160 (St Frideswide's cartulary) pp. 298–9, no. 454. s. xiii ex.

Pd from B in *St Frideswide's Cartulary* i no. 369.

Testibus: W. Oxon', R. Noramton' et aliis.

Witnesses are presumably the archdns of Oxford and Northampton. The church of All Saints was part of the endowment of king Henry I (*Regesta* ii no. 1342).

276. Oxford, St Frideswide's priory

Confirmation for the canons of St Frideswide, Oxford, of the churches of All Saints, Oxford, and Churchill.
          [24 August 1203 × 10 May 1206]

B = Bodl. C. C. C. ms. 160 (St Frideswide's cartulary) p. 299, no. 455* (witnesses omitted). s. xiii ex.

Pd from B in *St Frideswide's Cartulary* i no. 370.

277. Oxford, St Frideswide's priory

Grant to the canons of St Frideswide, Oxford, of a pension of five marks from the church of St Michael, Northgate, Oxford, saving the possession of the vicar, who shall serve the church at their presentation. The vicar shall pay this pension to the canons each year.
          [24 August 1203 × 10 May 1206]

B = Bodl. C. C. C. ms. 160 (St Frideswide's cartulary) p. 299, no. 455 (witnesses omitted). s. xiii ex.

Pd from B in *St Frideswide's Cartulary* i no. 466.

This grant was confirmed by pope Innocent III in a bull of 17 February 1215 (ibid. no. 467; *Letters of Pope Innocent III* no. 990A) and by pope Honorius III on 21 November 1224 (*St Frideswide's Cartulary* no. 468).

278. Oxford, St Frideswide's priory

Confirmation for the house and canons of St Frideswide, Oxford, of the the church of Churchill, which Henry de Noers and Juliana his wife declared, in the bishop's presence, they had given to the canons. The bishop has seen their charter and also the confirmation by archbishop Richard [EEA ii no. 180]. [24 August 1203 × 10 May 1206]

B = Oxford, Ch. Ch. Lib., St Frideswide's cartulary pp. 228b–229a (no witnesses). s. xv med.

Pd from B in *St Frideswide's Cartulary* ii no. 1036.

The charter of Henry de Noers is ibid. no. 1025. For a probable confirmation by bp Hugh I see above, no. 149 and note. The Noers charter was also confirmed by archbp Hubert Walter of Canterbury (*EEA* iii no. 561).

279. Peterborough abbey

Inspeximus and confirmation of bishop Hugh's charter [no. 154] for Peterborough abbey concerning the grant of the church of Normanby by William de Roumare. [24 August 1203 × 10 May 1206]

B = Peterborough D. & C. ms. 1 (Swaffham's register) fo. 107v (xcii v). s. xiii med.

Universis Christi fidelibus ad quos presens scriptum pervenerit, Willelmus dei gratia Lincolniensis episcopus salutem in domino. Inspeximus cartam bone memorie H. predecessoris nostri sub hac forma: Omnibus Christi fidelibus ad quos presens scriptum pervenerit, H. dei gratia Lincolniensis episcopus salutem in domino. Noverit universitas vestra nos ad presentationem dilecti filii nostri Willelmi de 'Ru'mara*a* et cetera ut supra.*b* Nos autem predictam concessionem et confirmationem ratam et gratam habentes, eam presenti scripto et sigilli nostri patrocinio confirmamus. T(estibus): magistro A. de Alnestouue.

a Famara *originally written* B, *with the first two letters dotted for expunction and 'Ru' interlined.* *b* *a marginal note indicates bp Hugh's charter on fo. xci v (106v).*

This confirmation may date from early in bp William's episcopate since master Alexander of Elstow is not described as archdn of Bedford, an office he received during this episcopate.

280. Peterborough abbey

General confirmation of possessions for the almonry of Peterborough abbey, as in the confirmation by his predecessor, bishop Hugh [no. 155].   [24 August 1203 × 10 May 1206]

> B = Peterborough D. & C. ms. 1 (Swaffham's register) fo. 108r (xciii r). s. xiii med.

Universis sancte matris ecclesie filiis ad quos presens scriptum pervenerit, Willelmus dei gratia Lincolniensis episcopus eternam in domino salutem. Quotiens a Christi fidelibus in usus pauperum perpetuos beneficia conferuntur etc. ut supra.*a* Que omnia ut firma et inconvulsa omni tempore permaneant, presentis scripti serie et sigilli nostri confirmatione confirmamus. Hiis testibus: magistris A. de Almestouue, G. de Rouuell', G. de Malbertorp' et aliis multis.

a a marginal note indicates Hugh I's charter on fo. xci r (106r).

This document may have been issued early in bp William's episcopate since Alexander of Elstow is not described as archdn of Bedford.

281. Peterborough abbey

General confirmation of possessions for Peterborough abbey, as in the confirmation by his predecessor, bishop Hugh [no. 156].

[24 August 1203 × 10 May 1206]

> B = Peterborough D. & C. ms. 1 (Swaffham's register) fo. 108r (xciii r). s. xiii med.

Universis Christi fidelibus ad quos presens scriptum pervenerit, Willelmus dei gratia Lincolniensis episcopus salutem eternam in domino. Ne*a* ea que religiosorum congregationes etc. ut supra.*b* Hec omnia sicut eis rationabiliter concessa sunt auctoritate qua fungimur confirmamus et presenti scripto cum sigilli nostri patrocinio communimus; salvis in omnibus episcopalibus consuetudinibus et Lincolniensis ecclesie dignitate. T(estibus): magistris A. de Bedeford, G. de Malbertorp',*c* G. de Fouuell'*d* et aliis multis.

a added in the margin B.   *b a marginal note indicates Hugh I's charter on fo. xci v (106v).*
c corrected from Malbetorp' B.   *d presumably recte Rouuell'.*

282. Peterborough abbey

Inspeximus of a charter of Acharius, abbot of Peterborough, confirming to the abbey for the maintenance of hospitality all the tithes from every abbatial demesne, except Stanwick and Irthlingborough, since two sheaves of the demesne tithes of the last two places belong to the

sacristy of Peterborough and the third sheaf to the respective mother
churches of the manors. [24 August 1203 × 10 May 1206]

B = Peterborough D. & C. ms. 1 (Swaffham's register) fo. 108r–v (xciii r–v).
s. xiii med.

Universis Christi fidelibus ad quos presens scriptum pervenerit,
Willelmus dei gratia Lincolniensis episcopus eternam in domino
salutem. Noverit universitas vestra nos inspexisse cartam dilecti filii
nostri Acharii permissione divina abbatis Burgi sub hac forma con-
ceptam: Omnibus sancte matris ecclesie filiis ad quorum audientiam
presens carta pervenerit, Acharius permissione divina abbas ecclesie
sancti Petri de Burgo salutem ab eo qui dat salutem omnibus.
Universitati vestre notum esse volumus nos pio caritatis intuitu
petitione et concilio conventus eiusdem ecclesie Burgi concessisse et
dedisse et presenti carta confirmasse deo et sancto Petro et ecclesie
Burgi 'ad' sustentationem hospitalitatis eiusdem ecclesie omnes
decimas fructuum provenientium de omnibus dominiis nostris prefate
abbatie exceptis duobus dominiis, scilicet, de Staneuuige et de
Irtlingburch, unde due garbe totius decime predictorum duorum
dominiorum pertinent ad sacristiam prefate ecclesie de Burgo et tertia
garba totius decime predictorum dominiorum pertinet ad matrices
ecclesias predictorum maneriorum in Staneuuige et Irtlingburch.
Quare volumus ut prefata ecclesia de Burgo perpetuo prefatas decimas
ad prefate hospitalitatis sustentationem habeat et possideat bene et in
pace et sine omni diminutione. Quod ut stabile*a* et firmum perseveret,
presentem cartam sub sigillo nostro prefate ecclesie Burgi in futur-
orum memoriam dedimus et testibus hiis communivimus: magistro
Ivone de Lond', Roberto de Glemesford' et aliis pluribus. Nos itaque
dictam abbatis concessionem et donationem ratam et gratam habentes,
eam prout rite facta est episcopali auctoritate con[fo.108v]firmamus et
presenti scripto sigilli nostri appositione roborato communimus.
Testibus: magistro H. de sancto Edwardo, Willelmo de Marin',
Thoma de Fiskertona, canonicis Lincolniensibus et aliis.

a stabilem *originally written and 'm' deleted later* B.

Acharius was abbot of Peterborough 1200 × 1210.

283. Peterborough abbey

Mandate to all clergy and laity who owe any revenues to the sacristy
of Peterborough, enjoining them to pay what they owe as an annual
pension at the fixed times, and threatening penalties for the dis-
obedient. [24 August 1203 × 10 May 1206]

B = Peterborough D. & C. ms. 1 (Swaffham's register) fo. 108v (xciii v). s. xiii med.

VVillemus dei gratia Lincolniensis episcopus omnibus clericis et laicis qui sacristarie de Burgo redditum aliquem debent salutem et benedictionem. Vobis omnibus in virtute obedientie iniungimus quatinus terminis statutis quod sacristarie 'Burgi' in annuam*a* debetis pensionem*b* omni occasione postposita integre et sine molestia persolvatis. Sciatis itaque quod qui in hiis mandato nostro non obedierint tamquam inobedientes eos cohercere studebimus. Precipimus etiam archidiaconis et officialibus et decanis ad quos presentes littere pervenerint quatinus monachis de Burgo de hiis qui sacristarie redditum retinuerunt celerem exhibeant iustitiam. Valete.

a animam *written first* B, *then dotted for expunction and* annuam *interlined.*
b *altered from* portionem B.

For a similar actum of bp Robert Chesney (1148–66) see *EEA* i no. 220.

284. Ramsey abbey

Notification that on the first Sunday of Lent the following ordinance was made (ordinatum est et provisum) *at Ramsey, by authority of the archbishop of Canterbury and bishop William and with the advice of the abbots of Peterborough, Crowland, and Thorney, and the priors of Thetford and Dunstable, and the* maior et senior pars *of the convent of Ramsey, on the state of that monastery. The abbot shall have two monks of Ramsey as chaplains, to be witnesses, helpers, and advisers in all his affairs. One of them shall carry the abbot's seal and shall seal no letters patent without the advice of the* senior pars *of the convent. Two monks and the steward shall handle all outside business, if necessary after taking the abbot's advice. The same shall assign the income of the abbot's chamber to three treasurers of the monastery for safe keeping, to be expended as need arises. When the conventual revenue is insufficient, the deficit may be made up from the income of the abbot's chamber by the treasurer. Landed property which has been alienated is, so far as possible, to be recovered. Farmers of lands of the chamberlain and the almoner are to give security for their paying of rent and their management of the property. The allowance of food and drink and candles for the convent and guests is to be kept up to customary excellent standard, but should reductions become necessary they shall apply to the convent as well as to guests. The allowance for distribution as alms shall be kept at a sufficient level to merit the approval of God and man.*   [? 27 February 1205]

B = PRO E164/28 (Ramsey cartulary) fo. 192v (197v, clxviii v). s. xiv med.
Pd from B in *Ramsey Cartulary* ii no. cccxxviii; calendar in *EEA* iii no. 582.

The cartulary copy of this document is not cast in the form of an actum and has no title, address, or greeting. For the details of the visitation by archbp Hubert Walter and bp William and the dating of the document see *EEA* iii no. 582.

285. Royston priory

Inspeximus of bishop Hugh's appropriation of the church of Owersby to the prior and canons of Royston.   [24 August 1203 × 10 May 1206]

> B = PRO E41/237 no. 5 (transcript of Royston priory charters). s. xiii ex. C (incomplete) = BL Add. Ch. 46362 (leaf of Royston cartulary). s. xiv.

Omnibus Christi fidelibus ad quos presens scriptum*a* pervenerit, Willelmus dei gratia Lincolniensis episcopus salutem eternam*b* in domino. Universitati vestre notum fieri volumus nos venerabilis predecessoris nostri Hugonis Lincolniensis episcopi cartam inspecsisse hec verba continentem: Omnibus . . . [*no. 162*] . . . Bardolf. Nos itaque eiusdem H. pii predecessoris*c* nostri vestigiis inherentes dictam ecclesiam sancti Martini de Ouerisby dictis canonicis in usus proprios convertendam secundum subscriptam formam episcopali auctoritate confirmamus et presenti scripto sigilli nostri appositione roborato communimus. Testibus: G. Bedeford, R. Bukingeh' archidiaconis, magistris Alexandro de Halnerstowe, G. de Rowell', Thoma de Fyxkerton', canonicis Lincolniensibus, magistris etiam Hugone et Ada de sancto Eadmundo, W. de Staveneby, Carolo et Walerano clericis et multis aliis.

a omitted B.   *b* C *ends here at bottom of folio.*   *c* predecessores B.

Alexander of Elstow had succeeded Geoffrey as archdn of Bedford shortly before bp William's death, possibly 25 September 1205 × 10 May 1206.

286. Abbey of St-Évroul

Confirmation for the abbot and convent of St-Évroul of all their possessions in the diocese of Lincoln.

[25 September 1205 × 10 May 1206]

> B = PRO D.L. 41/3/25 (copies of charters for St-Évroul) mem. 1, no. 2 ss. xiii ex.–xiv in. C = BL ms. Cotton Otho B xiv (inventory of muniments of Sheen) fo. 112r (110, cviii). s. xv ex. Abstract only: 'Item confirmatio Willelmi episcopi Lincolniensis facta ei[s]dem abbati et conventui de sancto Ebrulfo de omnibus possessionibus suis in eodem episcopatu. Sigillum tamen eiusdem est perditum'.

Universis sancte matris ecclesie filiis ad quos presentes littere pervenerint, Willelmus miseracione divina Lincolniensis ecclesie minister humilis eternam in domino salutem. Quotiens a nobis petitur quod honestati et religioni convenire dinoscitur, animo nos decet libenti concedere et petentium desideriis congruum inpertiri suffragium. Eapropter iustis petitionibus virorum religiosorum abbatis videlicet et monachorum sancti Ebrulphi grato concurrentes assensu eis omnia que in parochia nostra in perpetuam liberam et quietam elemosinam habent et possedunt de donis et confirmacionibus comitis Leyc' et aliorum fidelium de quorum origine non est memoria, auctoritate nobis a deo concessa confirmamus et sub omnipotentis dei et beate Marie et nostra suscipimus protectione in quibus hec propriis duximus exprimenda vocabulis: apud Leyc' plenam decimam de omni dominio comitis de prepositura videlicet, de pontibus de Holegate de molendinis et piscationibus atque virgultis que modo in eadem villa sunt vel de novo[a] fient in tota foresta eiusdem ville, in defensis videlicet et in alta foresta, et alibi per totam forestam plenam decimam de omnibus pannagiis et herbagiis et venationibus et venditionibus et haraciis equorum et equarum et de omnibus fructubus et assartis et agriculturis et molendinis et furnis et piscationibus et censibus et ecclesiis et villis et capellis et obventionibus et porpresturis eius presentibus et futuris, et de omnibus rebus aliis que ex eadem foresta etiam si ad agriculturam redacta fuerit poterunt provenire et quitantiam herbagii et pannagii ad centum porcos conventus sancti Ebrulphi per annum, in defensis videlicet et in alta foresta et alibi per totam forestam Leyc'; infra muros civitatis Leyc' novem burgenses, extra vero quinque; decimam quoque dominicarum terrarum comitis eiusdem ville; in Belegrave etc. usque ibi; in Clenefeld' ecclesiam cum duabus virgatis terre et capell(as) de Branteston' et de Kereby cum decimis aliisque pertinentiis suis; in Merkesfeld' etc.; in Roteby duas partes decimarum totius dominii comitis de omnibus de quibus decima datur et accipitur et [b-]ita habet[-b] monasterium sancti Ebrulphi in omnibus dominiis de feudo Leyc' etc. usque illuc; in Bosseby decimas dominicarum terrarum de duabus aulis; in Humbyrston' decimam de duabus[c] aulis et unam virgatam terre; in Stokton' decimam de dominio et unam virgatam terre; in Evyngton' decimam de dominio etc.; in Torp Ernald' decimam de dominio; in Brantigby decimam[d] de dominio usque illuc; in Wykyngeston' decimam de dominio etc. Siquis autem hanc nostre donationis, concessionis et confirmacionis cartam aliquo modo contradicere vel contraire voluerit, omnipotentis dei et beate Marie virginis indignationem nostram et maledictionem se noverit incursurum. Ut igitur nostra donatio et concessio perpetua gaudeat firmitate eam presentis scripti pagina cum appositione sigilli nostri duximus reprobandam. Hiis testibus: Rogero

decano, Philippo subdecano, magistro Willelmo filio Fulconis, Thoma
de Fiskyrton', canonico Lincolniensis ecclesie, magistro Willelmo de
Staveneb', Petro de Cheuremont, Hugone de Walis, Karolo, Walerano
et multis aliis.

^a nova B.   ^{b–b} ita habet *provided from earl Robert's charter (see note below)*. B *has* in hunc.
^c auabus B.   ^d decimam *repeated* B.

> The wording of this confirmation from: apud Leyc ... to in Wykyngeston'
> decimam de dominio etc. follows almost word for word the grant of earl Robert of
> Leicester pd in J. Nichols, *History of Leicestershire* i 1 app. vii no. 2.
>   Philip succeeded G. as subdean of Lincoln cathedral shortly before bp William's
> death; G. had himself succeeded William de Bramfeld who was murdered on 25
> September 1205.

287. St Neot's priory

*Institution of John de Plesset, clerk, to the church of Knotting, on the
presentation of the prior and monks of St Neot's, saving to the monks
an annual pension of two aurei.*   [24 August 1203 × 10 May 1206]

> B = BL ms. Cotton Faust. A iv (St Neot's cartulary) fos. 39v–40r (38v–39r), no.
> xx. s. xiii med.

Universis Christi fidelibus ad quos presens scriptum pervenerit,
Willelmus dei gratia Lincolnienc' episcopus salutem [fo. 40r] eternam
in domino. Noveritis nos ad presentationem dilectorum in Christo
filiorum prioris et monachorum de sancto Neoto admisisse dilectum
filium Iohannem de Plesset' clericum ad ecclesiam de Cnotting'
ipsumque in ea personam instituisse, salva ipsis monachis annua
duorum aureorum pensione, salvis etiam in omnibus episcopalibus
consuetudinibus et Lincolniensis ecclesie dignitate. Quod ut in posterum perpetuam optineat firmitatem presenti scripto et sigilli nostri
patrocinio communimus. Testibus.

> Knotting was originally a chapel of Melchbourne. In 1176 the bp of Exeter
> arbitrated in a dispute between St Neot's and the Hospitallers over Knotting and
> adjudged that the chapel should remain to St Neot's and should be free of the
> mother church (fos. 112v–113r of B, cited in *VCH Bedford* iii 142).

288. Selby abbey

*Confirmation for the abbot and monks of Selby of the churches of
Stallingborough and Redbourne in proprios usus, saving suitable
vicarages to be ordained by the bishop with the consent of the abbot
and monks, namely, one of ten marks for Stallingborough and six
marks for Redbourne.*   [24 August 1203 × 10 May 1206]

> B = BL ms. Add. 37771 (Selby cartulary) fo. 206v. ss. xiii–xiv.
> Pd from B in *Selby Coucher Book* ii 299, no. mccxxiv.

Hiis testibus: Rogero decano etc.

> For descriptions of the vicarages in the time of bp Hugh II see *RHW* i 228
> (Redbourne — valued at five marks) and ibid. iii 204 (Stallingborough).

289. Spalding priory

*Notification that the prior and monks of Spalding have granted the
land in the bail of Lincoln in the parish of St Paul, which the bishop
held of them while he was precentor of Lincoln, to the bishop's nepos,
Henry de Marum, to hold for life, paying twelve pence a year at
Michaelmas for all service and exaction. All buildings that Henry shall
erect on this land shall come at his death with his land to the monks
without claim by Henry or his heirs.*

[25 September 1205 × 10 May 1206]

> B = BL ms. Harl. 742 (Spalding cartulary) fos. 281v–282r. s. xiv in.

Universis Christi fidelibus ad quos presens scriptum pervenerit,
Willelmus dei gratia Lincolniensis episcopus salutem in domino.
Noverit universitas vestra quod dilecti filii prior et monachi de Spald'
terram suam, quam de illis dum cantoris officio in ecclesia [fo. 282r]
Lincolniensi fungeremur in ballio Lincolniensi in parochia sancti
Pauli apostoli tenuimus, in presentia nostra concesserunt et carta sua
confirmaverunt dilecto nepoti nostro Henrico de Marum, tenendam
de ipsis in tota vita ipsius, reddendo ipsis annuatim pro omni servitio
et exactione xii denarios ad festum sancti Michaelis. Omnia autem
edificia que dictus Henricus in dicta terra construxerit post obitum
ipsius ad monachos de Spald' cum terra ipsa sine omni calumpnia eius
vel heredum suorum pervenient. In huius autem rei testimonium,
presenti scripto sigillum nostrum apposuimus. T(estibus): P. subdecano, magistro*ᵃ* W. filio Fulconis etc.

> *ᵃ* magistri B.

> Philip became subdean of Lincoln at some date after 25 September 1205. This
> charter was confirmed by the dean and chapter of Lincoln (fo. 282r of B); bp
> William's charter as precentor of Lincoln is on fo. 281v of B. Henry de Botiate
> (Butyate) quitclaimed this property to Spalding priory in 1224 (fo. 282r of B).

290. Spalding priory

*Institution of William (of Ely), the king's treasurer, to the church of
Surfleet, vacant by the resignation of Robert de Hardres, archdeacon
of Huntingdon, and on the presentation of the prior and monks of
Spalding; saving the vicarage of the archdeacon Robert. The latter
shall hold the church for life, paying to William an annual pension of*

one aureus. *In addition William shall pay to the prior and monks six silver marks a year, payable in three instalments.*

[25 September 1205 × 10 May 1206]

B = LAO Episcopal Reg. II (institution register of bp Dalderby) fo. 27v (in an inspeximus of bp Dalderby, 27 April 1309).

Omnibus Christi fidelibus ad quos presens scriptum pervenerit, Willelmus dei gratia Lincolniensis episcopus salutem in domino. Noverit universitas vestra nos, post resignationem ecclesie de Surflet' a dilecto filio Roberto Hardres archidiacono Huntedon' nobis factam, ad presentationem prioris et monachorum de Spalding' dicte ecclesie patronorum, admisisse dilectum filium Willelmum domini regis thesaurarium ad eandem ecclesiam ipsumque in ea personam canonice instituisse, salva vicaria prenominati Roberti in eadem ecclesia, qui ipsam ecclesiam cum omnibus pertinentiis suis quoadvixerit tenebit, reddendo inde prenotato Willelmo annuatim unius aurei pensionem et preterea sex marcas argenti dictis priori et monachis per manus prefati Willelmi annuatim solvendas ad tres terminos, scilicet, ad Pascha duas marcas et ad festum sancti Botulphi duas marcas et ad festum beati Nicholai duas marcas; salvis in omnibus episcopalibus consuetudinibus et Lincolniensis ecclesie dignitate. Quod ut perpetuam optineat firmitatem, presenti scripto sigilli nostri patrocinio roborato confirmamus. Hiis testibus: Philippo subdecano ecclesie Lincolniensis, magistris Gerardo de Rowell', Willelmo filio Fulconis, A. de sancto Edmundo*ᵃ*, et Thoma de Fiskerton', Lincolniensis ecclesie canonicis, magistro Willelmo de Staveneb', Rogero Bacun, Petro de Chieueremunt, Walerano et*ᵇ* Carolo, clericis et multis aliis.

ᵃ Admundo B.   *ᵇ* de B.

William de Bramfeld, subdean of Lincoln, was murdered on 25 September 1205 and was apparently succeeded by one Gilbert, who was himself succeeded by Philip before bp William's death. See H. G. Richardson on 'William of Ely, the King's Treasurer 1195–1215' in *TRHS* 4th ser., xv (1932) 45–90.

291.   Stainfield priory

Notification that the election of Petronilla, canonically elected as prioress of Stainfield, has been approved by Richard de Percy, the patron of the house. The bishop confirms that the assent of Richard and his heirs shall in future be required at an election of a prioress.

[24 August 1203 × 10 May 1206]

B = Syon House, Brentford, Mun. D.i.1a (Percy cartulary) fos. 160v–161r (no witnesses). s. xiv.

Pd from B in *Percy Chartulary* no. mviii.

For the election of Petronilla's successor, Constance, *ante* 1225 see *Mon. Angl.* iv 309–10, no. iv.

*292. Studley priory

Confirmation for the nuns of Studley of the church of Ilmer, given by Albritha daughter of David de Romenel and Thomas son of Bernard.
[24 August 1203 × 10 May 1206]

Mention of charter in Bodl. ms. Twyne 24 (extracts from a lost cartulary of Studley, s. xvii in) pp. 650–1, in connection with the appropriation of the church by bp Hugh II (ibid.). The bp is referred to as Peter (*sic*) not William. This confirmation is noted in J. Dunkin, *Oxfordshire: the history and antiquities of the Hundreds of Bullington and Ploughley* (2 vols., 1823) i 133.

*293. Sulby abbey

Confirmation for the abbey of Sulby of the church of Addington, given to them by Alnath Papillun.
[24 August 1203 × 10 May 1206]

Mention of charter produced in a dispute between Richard de Waterville and the abbot of Sulby over the advowson of the church, 1233.

Pd, *CRR* xv no. 831.

For a similar charter of Hugh I, see no. 193.

294. Swallow church

Institution of William, archdeacon of Buckingham, to the church of Swallow, on the presentation of Thomas de Lascelles, knight.
[25 September 1205 × 10 May 1206]

A = BL Harl. Ch. 84 D 2. No endorsement; approx. 122 × 69 + 15 mm.; fragment of seal (lower half of body) on parchment tag, reddish-brown wax, counterseal.

Universis Christi fidelibus ad quos presens scriptum pervenerit Willelmus dei gratia Lincolniensis . episcopus . salutem eternam in domino. Noverit universitas vestra nos ad presentacionem dilecti filii . Thome de Lascell' . militis . admisisse dilectum filium . Willelmum archidiaconum Bukingham' . ad ecclesiam de Sualue . ipsum que in ea canonice personam instituisse . salvis in omnibus episcopalibus consuetudinibus et Lincolniensis ecclesie dignitate. Quod ut inposterum perpetuam optineat firmitatem . presenti scripto et sigilli nostri patrocinio communimus. Testibus P. subdecano . Lincolniensi . magistris G. de Rowell' . G. de Malbertorp' . W. filio . Fulconis . T. de Fiskertun' . canonicis Lincolniensibus . magistris . W. de Staveneb' . W. de Tedeltorp' . R. de Bolehurst . et aliis.

Philip had become subdean some time after the murder of William de Bramfeld on 25 September 1205, although a subdean called Gilbert may have briefly held office before him. William of Blois, archdn of Buckingham, held the church of Swallow until his appointment as bp of Worcester in 1218 (*RHW* i 122–3).

*295. Thornton Curtis abbey

Confirmation for the abbey of Thornton [Curtis] of the church of Welton le Marsh, in the same form as bishop Hugh's confirmation [no. 197].
[24 August 1203 × 10 May 1206]

Mention of charter produced in a dispute between Walter de Hamby and the abbot of Thornton [Curtis] over the advowson of the church, 1222.

Pd, *CRR* x 42.

296. Tutbury priory

Institution of master Roger de Sumerford, canon of Lincoln, to the church of Stapleford, on the presentation of the prior and monks of Tutbury. Roger is to pay the priory an annual pension of three silver marks, twenty shillings at Christmas and twenty shillings at the Nativity of St John the Baptist.
[24 August 1203 × 10 May 1206]

B = College of Arms, ms. Arundel 59 (Tutbury cartulary) fo. 29r (witnesses omitted). s. xv med.

Pd from B in *Tutbury Cartulary* no. 26.

297. Wallingford priory

Confirmation of an agreement between the monks [? of Wallingford] and the parishioners of Stokenchurch over the cemetery at Stokenchurch.
[24 August 1203 × 10 May 1206]

A = Bodl. Berkshire Ch. 36 (badly damaged by damp; the whole of the right hand side of the document is missing. Some words are supplied conjecturally). No endorsement visible (the charter is mounted in a volume); approx. 104 (existing portion) × 55 + 15 mm.; seal and tag missing, slit for tag, d.q.1. Scribe **III**.

Universis Christi fidelibus ad quos presens scriptum pervenerit . Will(elmu)s dei gratia Lincolniensis [episcopus . . . Noverit] universitas vestra nos ratam et gratam habere conventionem factam inter mona[chos . . . ex una parte et] parrochianos de Stokenchirch' ex alia super cimiterio apud Stokenech[irch' . . .] super hoc inter ipsos confecto continetur eam que prout rite facta est auctorita[te nostra confirmamus et presenti scripto cum] sigilli nostri patrocinio communimus . salvis in omnibus episcopalibus consuetudinibus [et Lincolniensis ecclesie dignitate. Hiis testibus . . .] magistris A. de Bedef' . G. de [Mal]bertorp' . G. de Rowell' . T. de Fiskerton' [. . .

Willelmo filio] Fulcon[is] . W. de Stavenbi . Petro de Cheuermund' clerico et multis [aliis].

> Stokenchurch was a chapelry of Aston Rowant, a benefice in the patronage of Wallingford priory (*RHW* ii 3–4; *Lib. Ant.* 10); moreover the collection of charters of which this forms part all deal with the possessions of Wallingford priory, and this certainly seems to confirm the identity of the religious house involved.

298.   Walton chapel

Confirmation of a composition made between archdeacon William of Buckingham and William de Kaines, knight, before bishop Mauger of Worcester, chosen as judge by the parties, over the chapel of Walton and the tithes of William de Kaines's demesne belonging to the chapel. I. the chaplain of William de Kaines shall hold the chapel for as long as he lives, paying to the mother church of St Peter, [King's] Sutton a pension of two bezants or four shillings a year. When I. the chaplain dies or enters religion, the chapel shall revert in its entirety to [King's] Sutton church, at the disposition of the canon (of the prebend of Sutton-cum-Buckingham), either to hold himself or to assign to whomsoever he wishes. Divine service is to be celebrated once a week in the chapel, except Sundays. On the presentation of William de Kaines, archdeacon William has admitted I. the chaplain to the chapel in the presence of bishop Mauger, and afterwards William de Kaines gave the chapel to the mother church of [King's] Sutton and bishop Mauger assigned it to the archdeacon. Later Sir William gave his charter containing the composition, which bishop William has inspected, to the mother church.   [24 August 1203 × 10 May 1206]

> A = BL Harl. Ch. 84 D 3. Not endorsed; approx. 153 × 122 + 16 mm.; good specimen of seal (repaired), whitish-brown wax, counterseal, on parchment tag, d.q.i. Scribe **IV**.

Universis Christi fidelibus ad quos presens scriptum pervenerit Will(elmu)s dei gratia Lincolniensis episcopus . salutem in domino. Noveritis nos ratam et gratam habere composicionem factam in causa que vertebatur inter dilectos filios . Willelmum archidiaconum . Bukingham' . et Willelmum . de Kaines militem . coram venerabili fratre nostro Malgero dei gratia Wigorniensi . episcopo . iudice a partibus ita electo ut iusticia vel concordia mediante causam terminaret .· super capella de Waltun' et super decimis de dominico eiusdem militis tam de blado quam de aliis minutis decimis et aliis ad predictam capellam spectantibus videlicet quod .I. capellanus dicti W militis ad presentacionem ipsius militis et admissionem eiusdem .W. archidiaconi . et canonici matricis ecclesie tenebit dictam capellam cum omnibus predictis ad eam spectantibus toto tempore vite sue reddendo matrici ecclesie scilicet ecclesie sancti Petri de Sutun' ? duos bisancios vel quatuor solidos annuatim nomine pensionis ? ad duos terminos . scilicet medietatem ad festum sancti Martini . et medietatem ad Pentecosten. Si vero dictus .I. in fata concesserit vel vitam mutaverit ? predicta capella cum omni integritate sua ad predictam ecclesiam de Sutun' . in perpetuum revertetur . ita videlicet quod in disposicione canonici sit . eam vel in manu sua tenere . vel clerico cui voluerit assignare. Faciet autem canonicus prebende vel is cui capellam assignaverit semel in ebdomada excepto die dominico in quo non celebrabitur . in predicta capella divina celebrari. Ad presentacionem vero W. de Kaines predictus archidiaconus admisit predictum I. capellanum ad predictam capellam in presencia domini Wigorniensis. Predictus vero W. de Kaines post presentacionem et admissionem predicti .I. capellani ? predictam capellam cum omnibus predictis ad eam pertinentibus donavit predicte matrici ecclesie de Sutun' . quantum ad laici donacionem pertinet . et in manus dicti domini Wigorniensis . omne ius quod in eadem capella habuit per librum posuit . et ipsi dominus Wigorniensis per eundem librum predicto archidiacono predictam capellam cum omnibus predictis assignavit. Post omnia vero predicta dictus W. miles cartam suam dictam composicionem continentem quam inspeximus dicte matrici ecclesie contulit. Hanc igitur composicionem prout rite facta est episcopali auctoritate confirmamus et presenti scripto sigilli nostri patrocinio roborato communimus. Testibus A. archidiacono . Bedeford' . Vacario . T. de Fiskertun' . canonicis Lincolniensibus . magistro Symone . de Elnestow . T. de Olneia . W. de Cleipol . R. de Bukeb' . personis . et multis aliis.

William of Blois became archdn of Buckingham in the course of bp William's episcopate but no precise date is available.

299. Ware priory

Confirmation of the gift made by Robert, earl of Leicester, to prior Herbert of Ware of the house at Charley with lands and all other appurtenances and liberties, and one carucate of land in the assarts of Anstey. Both these gifts are contained in the earl's charter.

[24 August 1203 × 10 May 1206]

A = Archives dep. de l'Orne, H. 907. Endorsed: Confirmacio Willelmi . Linc' episcopi . de Charleia . et de terra de Anesty . et prato . (s. xiii); approx. 149 × 80 + 16 mm.; seal and tag missing, slits for tag, d.q.2.

Pd (calendar) from A in *CDF* no. 648.

Omnibus sancte matris ecclesie filiis ad quos presens scriptum pervenerit . Will(elmu)s dei gratia Lincolniensis ecclesie minister humilis
salutem in vero salutari. Ad universitatis vestre noticiam volumus
pervenire : nos episcopali auctoritate confirmasse donationem quam
dilectus filius nobilis vir . Robertus comes Leicestr' fecit Herberto
priori de Wares . scilicet domum de Charleie . cum terris et cum
omnibus aliis pertinentiis et libertatibus sicut carta eiusdem comitis
testatur . unam etiam carrucatam terre in essartis de Ainesti sicut in
eadem carta continetur : in puram et perpetuam elemosinam. Et ut
hec nostra confirmatio perpetuam optineat firmitatem : eam presenti
scripto et sigilli nostri patrocinio communimus. Hiis testibus . magistro Alexandro et Vacario capellano et Thoma de Fiskerton' Lincolniensis ecclesie canonicis . magistris Willelmo filio Fulconis Adam de
sancto Ædmundo . Willelmo de Stavenebi . Gileberto de Iwarebi
clerico . Gamaliele persona de Nouesle   Ricardo persona de
Belegr(av)a . Gilberto de Clenefeld' . Petro et Carolo clericis et multis
aliis

> It is not clear whether earl Robert of Leicester was alive or dead at the time the
> confirmation was issued; he died on 20 or 21 October 1204. William son of Fulk is
> not described as a canon of Lincoln; he received the prebend of Decem Librarum at
> some date between 25 September 1205 and 10 May 1206. Ware was a cell of the
> abbey of St-Évroul.

300. York minster

*Appropriation, made with the consent of the cathedral chapter, to the
chapter of York of the church of Lissington, saving a suitable vicarage.*
[24 August 1203 × 10 May 1206]

> B = BL ms. Cotton Claud. B iii (York Minster cartulary) fo. 27r–v (25r–v). s. xiii
> ex. C = York Minster Muniment Room, L2/1 (Magnum Registrum Album of
> York Minster) part ii, fo. 31r. s. xiv med.
>
> Pd from B in *York Minster Fasti* ii no. 76.

Testibus: R. decano, R. thesaurario, magistris R. de Lindwud'[a], R.
de Holm[b], G. de Rowell', W.[c] filio Fulconis, A. de sancto Edmundo,
T. de Fiskerton'[d], canonicis Lincolniensibus et aliis.

[a] Lindwd C.   [b] Holme C.   [c] Willelmo C.   [d] Fiskton' C.

> This appropriation had not taken effect by 1269 (*York Minster Fasti* ii 117–8; *Rot.
> Grav.* 35), presumably because of disputes between the chapter and the local
> family, the Rigsbys. In 1202 Gilbert of Rigsby was involved in litigation with York
> over the advowson (*Lincs. Assize Rolls 1202–9* 14); and in 1268 by a final concord
> John son of Thomas of Rigsby recognised the right of the York chapter to the
> advowson, for a payment of forty shillings (*York Minster Fasti* ii 117).

APPENDIX I

ADDITIONAL ACTA AND MENTIONS OF ACTA OF THE
BISHOPS OF LINCOLN 1123–1185

Since the publication of the first Lincoln volume in 1980 several additional acta or references to lost acta have come to light and are included in this appendix. I am also grateful to Dr Brian Kemp who has pointed out that 'Eston'' mentioned in actum no. 230 in volume I, should have been identified as Aston in Hertfordshire.

ALEXANDER

*I. Elstow abbey

Gift to the abbess and nuns of Elstow of ten shillings a year from his rent of Buckden.   [22 July 1123 × 20 February 1148]

> Mention of gift in a confirmation of king Henry II, enrolled on the confirmation roll 2 Henry VIII (roll 37, m.8).
>
> Pd, *Letters and Papers of Henry VIII* i 294–5 no. 485 (54); S. R. Wigram, *Chronicles of the Abbey of Elstow* (1885) 28, 39.

*II. Kenilworth priory

Confirmation for the priory of Kenilworth.
                                [*c.*1125 × 20 February 1148]

> Mention of charter in a general confirmation by archbp Richard of Canterbury, Oct. 1181 × 16 February 1184.
>
> Pd, *EEA* ii no. 142.
>
> Kenilworth priory was founded by Geoffrey de Clinton *c.*1125. There is no copy of bp Alexander's confirmation in the Kenilworth cartularies.

*III. Launde priory

? Confirmation for Launde priory of the churches of Loddington, Tilton, Frisby-on-the-Wreak, Weston by Welland, Welham and Ashby St Ledgers.   [22 July 1123 × 20 February 1148]

> Mention in an inspeximus by bp John Dalderby of Lincoln, dated 20 January 1314, of a charter of bp Richard Gravesend of Lincoln confirming these churches to

Launde 'ad instar bone memorie Alexandri, Hugonis, Roberti predecessorum nostrorum'. Gravesend's confirmation is dated 29 November 1266. The confirmations of Robert Chesney and St Hugh survive (*EEA* i no. 143; ibid. iv no. 84). Bp Dalderby's inspeximus is in LAO, Ep. Reg. III fo. 295r.

Launde priory was founded some time between 1119 and 1125.

IV. Louth Park abbey

Foundation of the abbey of Louth Park   [1139]

Mention pd *EEA* i no. 47.

Since the publication of the first Lincoln volume, I have located a transcript of the 'Alvingham Priory Book' referred to by Bayley in his *Notitiae Ludae* (Louth 1834) 118–19. In the last decade of the 19th century the volume was in the possession of F. J. Ingoldby of Louth and was the subject of correspondence in *Lincolnshire Notes and Queries* iii (1892–3) 183–6; iv (1894–5) 85–7. Canon T. Longley made a transcript of the volume at this time (*Lincolnshire Archives Committee: Archivists' Report 1954–5*, 25) and this transcript survives among his papers.

B = LAO, Longley ms. 5/29 (copy of English register of Alvingham priory, now lost) fo. 82a–b of original manuscript. s. xix ex.

Alexander by the grace of God bishop, to all his successors sendeth greetinge. It is very profitable and necessarie, consideringe the malice of these dayes and the troubles of temptation which dayly throughe infidelite are seene to growe, to provide some deede of justice and puritie in this moste miserable lyfe, which may be of force before the face of the almightie, to helpe or procure the remission of our synnes: wherfore by the counsaile of my clergie and assent of my whole chapter of the church of St Marie of Linkholne I am disposed to found an abby of moonkes of St Marie of the Fountaynes accordinge to the order of the blessed St Benedict and custoomes of *(blank in ms.)* in my woode, namely in my parke on the south side of my towne called Louth, which parke I have graunted wholie and free from all terrene service to almightie God and the blessed virgen Marie his moother, and to the use of the munkes which are appointed for the service of God in that place and further I have confirmed it to their possession by good securitie, except that part which is called Wlstanwde, in which part not withstandinge I have graunted them all the pasture for their swyne, as they have in their owne proper part. I have given and graunted unto them also all the land without the parke from Wlstanwde unto the brinke of the water of the river in breadth towards the north as it is devided by the ditch of the way to the south, which land doth retch in length to the south part even to the boundes betwixt Louth and Cockrington. In lyke manner I have given [fo. 82b] unto them one myll for ever to possess upon the same water. Therfore I am purposed to give unto them this gifte free and quit from all earthlie servitude, and whatsoever elce for the savation^a of my soule, the soule of my soveraigne lord king Henrie, and the soule of Roger bishop of Salsburie myne uncle, and the soules of all my parents and for the state of the Church of our foresaid abby, shall give in almes by these letters and seale of our chapter of the church of the blessed virgen St Marie of Linkholne and in the signe of the holie crosse + I doe confirme in the yere of our Lorde MCXXXIX. Therefore whosever will eyther encrease or defend this my almes in true charritie for his person and abilitie, peace be unto him, health and everlastinge blessinge of almightie God, but whosoever shall presume cruelie to deminish it or rashlie to violate it, as much as perteineth unto the episcopale authoritie of our sea^a (except he doth amend and correct that his malice), being admonished and forwarned by the eclesiasticale authoritie we pronownce unto him for the ostinacie^a of his presumpsion the daunger of everlastinge salvation^b and the losse of eternall lyfe in the iudgment of excomunication.

^a sic. ^b sic, presumably for damnation.

*V. Northampton, St James's abbey

Confirmation of possessions for the abbey of St James, Northampton.
[c.1145 × 20 February 1148]

Mention of confirmation in a general confirmation of St Hugh, 1186 × 1200.
Pd, *EEA* iv no. 133.

St James's abbey was founded c.1145 × 1150. No copy of Alexander's charter can now be located in the fire-damaged cartulary of the abbey (BL ms. Cotton Tiberius E v).

ROBERT CHESNEY

*VI. Alvingham priory

? Confirmation of an agreement made between Alvingham priory and Louth Park abbey over [? Wold] Newton, Swinethorpe, and Binbrook.
[19 December 1148 × 27 December 1166]

Mention of document at the end of an agreement made between abbot Ralph of Louth Park and prior Geoffrey of Alvingham, 1174, in Bodl. ms. Laud misc. 642 (Alvingham cartulary) fo. 130v. s. xiii ex.

. . . Preterea scriptum R. Lincolniensis episcopi inter nos de Neutona, Suinehop et Binebrock' inconcusse tenebitur.

*VII.   Bradenstoke priory

Confirmation for the canons of Bradenstoke of the gifts of William of Aston in North Aston.   [? *c*.1151 × 27 December 1166]

> Mention of confirmation in charters of William son of Robert of Aston and Robert son of Osbert of Aston, grandsons of the donor, 1197/8 × 1226.
>
> Pd, *Bradenstoke Cartulary* nos. 497, 664.

William had given the church of North Aston and certain land in the parish (cf. ibid. nos. 549, 566, 662). Mention is also made in the grandsons' charters of the assent and confirmation of archdn Robert of Oxford and Robert's notification is ibid. no. 661. Robert Foliot became archdn *c*.1151 and it is possible that the bp's confirmation dates from the same time.

VIII.   Bullington priory

Confirmation for the priory of Bullington of the churches of 'Wittena', Ingham, Spridlington and Langton [by Wragby], given to them by Simon son of Simon and Philip de Kyme.

[September 1152 × 27 December 1166]

> B = BL ms. Add. 6118 (abstract by Gervase Holles of the Bullington priory cartulary, now lost) fo. 439r. s. xvii med.

Robertus Lincolniensis episcopus confirmat donationem ecclesiarum*a* de Wittena et de Ingham et de Spridlington et de Langton quas Simon filius Simonis et Philippus de Kim' dederunt. Test(es) Walterus abbas de Bardeneia, Henricus abbas de Kim', Radulfus de Disci archidiaconus*b* Lund', Willelmus Clement capellanus episcopi.

a ecclesiae B.   *b* archidiacono B.

> 'Wittena' has not been identified among the churches given to Bullington by the Kyme family (see *Danelaw Charters* nos. 1–3; *Gilbertine Charters* 91–2 nos. 1–2; *EEA* i no. 286). It may possibly be a scribal error for Winthorpe. Abbot Walter of Bardney first occurs on 22 January 1155; abbot Henry of 'Kim'' is probably to be identified with the abbot of Combe who occurs 1157 × 1163 (*Danelaw Charters* no. 58; *HRH* 130). Ralph de Diceto became archdn of Middlesex at some date between September 1152 and *c*.June 1153. He and bp Robert and Simon son of Simon attest a confirmation of Philip de Kyme for Bullington of the churches of Bullington and Langton (*Danelaw Charters* no. 2).

IX.   Kirkstead abbey

Confirmation of the agreement made between the monks of Kirkstead and the Knights Templars of 'Aneheide' (Mere) over land at Dunston and Nocton. Richard of Hastings, the Master of the Templars in England has surrendered whatever claim the Templars had in the land. The monks have given forty marks to the Templars and they shall possess the land free and quit.   Lincoln, 22 January 1155

A = Lancashire Record Office, DDTo. K/19/5. Endorsed: Hanehate (s. xiii); Concordacio inter nos et milites templi de terra de Dunestun et Noctuna (s. xiii); xxiii; hanheth (? s. xiv); approx. 181 × 199 + 13 mm.; seal missing, slit for seal-tag; hec carta dupl(icata) written on turn-up.

Rob(ertus) . dei gratia episcopus Lincolniensis . omnibus sancte ecclesie fidelibus clericis et laicis ⸴ salutem et benedictionem. Nostre sollicitudinis est . commendare memorie causas que auctoritate nostri testimonii decise sunt . ne forte cuiusquam contrarie voluntatis obiectio rediviva contentione reducat in dubium quod provide diffinitum est . et gignat ex pace litigium. Eapropter karissimi omnium nostrum nosse volumus karitatem . quod dilectissimi filii nostri monachi de Kirkested' et milites de Templo . Aneheide qui aliquamdiu disceptaverant pro terra de Duneston' et Noketuna ⸴ perhenniter concordantur. Pro ipsorum pace perpetua placuit commendare memorie ⸴ formam reconciliationis eorum . per huius transactionis paginam . annum . tempus . diem et locum annotantes. Igitur anno ab incarnatione domini millesimo . centesimo . quinquagesimo quinto . tempore Henricus rex Anglorum . et dux Normann(orum) et Aquitan' et comes Andeg' quo venerat primum Lincol' . post coronationem suam . xi^{ma} . die kalendarum Februarii . foras murum civitatis Linc' ab aquilone . deposuit Ricardus de Hasting' magister omnium templariorum Anglie in manus nostras quicquid reclamationis et calumnie . quicquid etiam iuris . milites Templi vel fratres iuste vel iniuste in prefata terra se habuisse contenderant. Hoc plane fecit unanimi consensu pari que collaudatione commilitonum et fratrum suorum . scilicet Gualteri de Dorobernia . Roberti . de Bulonia . Roberti de Lunem . Roberti Rufi . Gualteri Rufi . et Gilleberti. Sciendum etiam quod hec controversia decisa est . mediantibus quadraginta marcis ⸴ quas monachi dederunt templariis terminis constitutis . eoque modo remansit terra prefata monachis libera et quieta. Et iccirco transactionem decisionem que inter monachos et milites prefatos habitam ⸴ per omnia confirmamus . nec in totum partem ve ⸴ aliqua ratione convelli decernimus ⸴ sed habere censemus perpetuam firmitatem. Si quis autem deinceps litem contra monachos inde innovare temptaverit ⸴ ille se et eum ante deum novit . quia nititur ea que sunt utiliter finita rescindere. Huius rei testes sunt . abbas Gualo de sancto Laurentio . abbas Radulfus de Luda . abbas Walterus de Bardeneia . abbas Eadwardus de Croiland' . Gillebertus de Sempingeh' . Umfridus subdecanus . Willelmus filius Osberti archidiaconus . Rogerus de Amari precentor . Rogerus Parvus . Baldricus de Sigillo . Simon cell(erarius) de Sart' . Michael .

cell(erarius) de Luda . Walterus capellanus de Bardeneia . Radulfus de Timberlund . Robertus de Bilingh' .

From the endorsement this document is clearly Kirkstead abbey's copy of the agreement.

From the mention of the king's visit to Lincoln it is clear that this confirmation is using the Christmas reckoning of the year of grace, not the Annunciation. For the identification of 'Anehcidc' see *Final Concords* II lvi; *Records of the Templars* 241 n. 10 and introd. clxxviii–ix. It was part of a large Lincolnshire heath lying in the parishes of Dunston, Nocton, Metheringham, Blankney, Harmston, Coleby and Boothby Graffoe. Despite my comments on *EEA* i no. 137 of the period 1148 × 1150, it is now probable that the reference in archbp Theobald's confirmation (*Theobald* no. 143) may relate to this document. In this instance compare the charter of Richard of Hastings, the Master of the Temple, dated 22 January 1155 (*Records of the Templars* 241–2, no. 1 '. . . in manus Teodbaldi venerabilis Cantuariensis archiepiscopi Anglorum primatis et apostolice sedis legati, et Roberti episcopi Lincolniensis apud Lincolniam in locis campestribus civitatis eiusdem . . .').

*X.   Lessay abbey

General confirmation of churches for the abbey of Lessay.
[19 December 1148 × 27 December 1166]

Mention of a charter produced in a dispute between the abbot of Lessay and the abbot of Peterborough and Humphrey son of William over the advowson of Sudbrooke church, 1202.

Pd, *Lincs. Assize Rolls 1202–9* no. 449.

For the original grant of Sudbrooke church see *CDF* no. 922; the assize roll entry also mentions the production as evidence of a confirmation of king Henry I (*Regesta* ii no. clxxvii) and a confirmation of archbp Hubert Walter (*EEA* iii no. 523A). This charter is presumably the one of bp Robert produced (along with king Henry's charter) in an assize of darrein presentment between Gerard de Canvill and Lessay abbey over the church of 'Brocebi' (? Brattleby), May 1200 (*Rot. Cur. Reg.* ii 251).

XI.   Lewes priory

Dr M. J. Franklin of Wolfson College, Cambridge, has kindly pointed out to me the existence of a 13th-century copy of a purported charter of bp Chesney confirming churches and possessions in the Lincoln diocese for Lewes priory (PRO E40/14946, catalogued in the name of bp Grosseteste, 1235–53). Dr Franklin has edited the document and discussed it in an article 'Another Lewes forgery?' to be published shortly in the *Journal of the Society of Archivists*.

XII.   Lincoln, St Katharine's priory

Grant to the canons of the hospital of Lincoln of the chapel of St Philip and St James in Newark castle, together with the tenth part of all tolls paid in Newark, except at fairs, houses surrounding Newark parish

church to the north and east, and two bovates of land in the fields of
Newark.   [19 December 1154 × 27 December 1166]

> B = LAO Ep. Reg. I (register of bp Oliver Sutton) fo. 124v (in an inspeximus of
>   bp Sutton, dated 12 February 1295).
> Pd from B in *Reg. Sutton* v 86–7.

Hiis testibus: domino Martino thesaurario, magistro Malgero, magistro Laurentio, magistro Radulfo, magistro Henrico de Norht', domino Waltero Dar', Thoma capellano, Waltero capellano de Neuwerk', Remigio priore Schal' et Radulfo canonico eius.

> This charter incorporates some gifts (but by no means all) made at the time of the
> bp's foundation of St Katharine's, and indeed the lost foundation charter (*EEA* i
> no. 163) could well have been several separate deeds of gift. The witness-list
> contains the earliest known reference to prior Remigius of Shelford. Shelford
> priory was founded *temp.* king Henry II, so this document must date from after the
> king's accession, 19 December 1154. Martin probably became treasurer of Lincoln in
> the early 1150s (*EEA* i no. 80n). St Katharine's priory was founded soon after 1148.

XIII.   Lincoln, St Katharine's priory

Confirmation of a charter of William Foliot(h) granting the church of
Saxby and two bovates of land to the canons of the church of St
Sepulchre, Lincoln, which the bishop has founded.
                                  [19 December 1148 × 27 December 1166]

> B = LAO, Ep. Reg. I (register of bp Oliver Sutton) fo. 124v (in an inspeximus of
>   bp Sutton, dated 12 February 1295).
> Pd from B in *Reg. Sutton* v 87–8.

... et bonorum virorum testimonio communimus, Roberti archidiaconi, Radulfi abbatis de Parco Luthie, Philippi abbatis de Revesby, Radulfi medici, Hervei de Rauceby canonici, Willelmi de Chesney.

> Both abbot Ralph and abbot Philip first occur in 1155 although they could have
> become abbots some years before. At first sight, the claim by bp Chesney that he
> was the founder of St Sepulchre's hospital seems at variance with the accepted
> foundation of this hospital by his predecessor, Robert Bloet (see *EEA* i app. i
> no. 2). However, the close association between St Katharine's priory, which
> Chesney did found (see ibid. no. 163), and St Sepulchre's led to some confusion in
> nomenclature and St Katharine's is sometimes referred to as St Sepulchre's (*AASR*
> xxvii (1904) 267; J. W. F. Hill, *Medieval Lincoln* (Cambridge 1948) 345). In 1236
> by a final concord William Foliot's nephew, Jordan Foliot, acknowledged the
> advowson of Saxby to belong to St Katharine's priory, the gift of his uncle (*AASR*
> xxvii 272).

XIV.   See of Lincoln

Return made to king Henry listing the knights of the fee of St Mary,
Lincoln, and the service they owe to the bishop, and indicating which

*knights were enfeoffed in the time of king Henry I and which have been
enfeoffed since that time. The bishop also records his* servitium
debitum *of sixty knights due to the king.*   [1166]

> B = PRO E164/12 (Black Book of the Exchequer) fos. 108–109. s. xiii in.
> C = ibid. E164/2 (Red Book of the Exchequer) fo. 112. s. xiii med.
>
> Pd from B in T. Hearne ed., *Liber Niger Scaccarii* (1774) i 260–3; from C in *Red
> Book of the Exchequer* i 374–6.

*XV.   Notley abbey

*? Confirmation for the canons of Notley of the church of Caversham, on
the presentation of earl Walter Giffard (of Buckingham), the abbey's
founder.*   [c.1162 × 1164]

> Mention of the document in a charter of archdn R(obert Foliot) of Oxford in
> Oxford, Christ Church, Notley charter roll mem. 3: '. . . auctoritate instru-
> mentorum Roberti Lincolniensis episcopi et presentatione Walteri Giffard
> comitis fundatoris abbatie de Nutel' . . .'

The 'instruments' mentioned may have have been the confirmation and a mandate
to the archdn to put the abbey into corporal possession of the church. The abbey
was founded in 1162 or earlier (cf. *Oxoniensia* vi 23) and earl Walter died in 1164.
The church of Caversham was among the original endowments of earl Walter and
his wife (*Mon. Angl.* vi 278, no. i).

XVI.   Abbey of St-Évroul

*Confirmation for abbot Bernard and the convent of St-Évroul of all
their possessions in the diocese of Lincoln.*   [c.1158 × 1159]

> B = PRO D.L. 41/3/25 (copies of charters for St-Évroul) mem. 1, no. 1 (edge
> slightly damaged). ss. xiii ex.–xiv in.

Robertus dei gratia Lincolniensis episcopus omnibus sancte matris
ecclesie fidelibus salutem. Suscep'ti' cura regiminis nos religiosorum postulationibus ammonet prebere assensum simul et con-
sensum, ut in hoc fidelium unica devotio gratiorem consequatur
affectum. Sunt enim eorum beneficia prelatorum auctoritate
munienda et in suis necessitatibus discretionis intuitu protegenda.
Eapropter dilecte fili in domino Bernarde abbas sancti Ebrulphi et
successoribus tuis abbatibus et monachis in eodem monasterio dei
servitio mancipatis tam presentibus quam futuris bona que in presen-
tiarum prefatum monasterium possidet in parochia nostra aud in
futurum deo iuvante rationabilibus modis fidelium largitione poterit
adipisci confirmamus et pendentis sigilli auctoritate eidem, salva in
omnibus Lincolniensis ecclesie dignitate, in perpetuam elemosinam
communimus et sub nostra protectione suscipimus, in quibus dignum
duximus hec propriis annotanda vocabulis: apud Leyc' plenam

decimam de omni dominio comitis, de prepositura videlicet, de
pontibus de Holegate de molendinis et piscationibus atque virgultis
que modo in eadem villa sunt vel de novo fient in tota foresta eiusdem
ville, in defensis videlicet et in alta foresta, et alibi per totam forestam
plenam decimam de omnibus pascuagiis et herbagiis et venationibus et
venditionibus et haraciis equorum et equarum et de omnibus fructibus
et assartis et agriculturis et molendinis et furnis et piscationibus et
censibus et ecclesiis et villis et capellis et obventionibus et porpresturis
eius presentibus et futuris, et de omnibus rebus aliis que ex eadem
foresta etiam si ad agriculturam redacta fuerit poterunt provenire et
quitantiam herbagii et pannagii ad centum porcos conventus sancti
Ebrulphi per annum, in defensis videlicet et in alta foresta et alibi per
totam forestam Leyc'; infra muros civitatis Leyc' novem burgenses,
extra vero quinque; decimam quoque dominicarum terrarum comitis
eiusdem ville; apud Belegrave etc. usque illum locum; in Clenefeld
ecclesiam cum duabus virgatas terre et capell(as) de Buceston' et de
Kereby cum decimis aliisque pertinentiis suis; in Merkenesfeld' etc.;
in Roteby duas partes decimarum totius dominii comitis de omnibus
de quibus decima datur et accipitur, et ita habet monasterium sancti
Ebrulphi in omnibus dominiis de feodo Leyc'; in Groby etc. usque
illum locum; in Bosceby decimas dominicarum terrarum de duabus
aulis; in Humbirston' decimas de duabus aulis et unam virgatam
terre; in Stocton' decimam de dominio et unam virgatam terre; in
Evinton' decimam de dominio etc.; in Thorpernald' decimam de
dominio; in Brantigby decimam de dominio etc.; in Wykygiston'
decimam de dominio etc. Siquis autem hanc nostre concessionis et
confirmationis cartulam sciens infringere attemptaverit, dei indignationem et nostram maledictionem se sciat incursurum et in huius rei
testimonium presenti scripto sigillum nostrum apposuimus. Valete.

a an extra minim inserted in this word B.

Bernard is said to have been abbot of St-Évroul for less than a year before he was
deposed in 1159. His successor, abbot Robert II succeeded in Septuagesima week
(February) 1159 (?1159/60) (*Gallia Christiana* xi col. 822. cf. *Delisle* i no. lxxxix).
Bp Chesney's charter is mentioned in *Gallia Christiana* xi col. 823. I am most
grateful to Dr Marjorie Chibnall and Professor Christopher Brooke for their help
with the dating of the abbots of St-Évroul at this period.

XVII.   Priory of St-Fromond

*Confirmation for the monks of St-Fromond of the churches in Stamford
given to them by Richard du Hommet, the king's constable, namely the
churches of All Saints [in the Market], St John, and St Michael
[Cornstall].*   [19 December 1154 × ? early 1165]

B = BL Add. Ch. 66079 (roll of charters of priory of St-Fromond, dioc. Coutances), m. 1d. s. xv.

Robertus dei gratia episcopus Lincolniensis omnibus sancte matris ecclesie filiis salutem. Universitati vestre sit notum nos concessisse et carta nostra confirmasse deo et sancto Fromundo[a] et monachis sancti Fromundi ecclesias in Stanford' quas eis dedit Ricardus de Humez constabularius regis, sicut carta ipsius testatur, scilicet, ecclesiam omnium sanctorum que fuit Azelini presbiteri et ecclesiam sancti Iohannis que[b] fuit Reginaldi presbiteri, sancti Michaelis que Goderici presbiteri[c]. T(estibus): Nicholao de Sigillo, Martino[d] thesaurario Lincolniensi, magistro Radulpho, Willelmo capellano, Gaufrido, Rein(ero), Petro decano, Alexandro[e], clericis Stanford'.

[a] Fromunddo *with the first 'd' erased.*   [b] *followed by* R, *dotted for expunction.*
[c] *presumably this last section should read:* ... ecclesiam sancti Michaelis que fuit Goderici presbiteri.   [d] Marco B.   [e] Alexander B.

Richard du Hommet was the constable of Normandy for Henry Plantagenet as duke of Normandy and as king of England (crowned 19 December 1154) (*Regesta* iii xxxvii). He died in 1180. Nicholas de Sigillo attests this confirmation without his archidiaconal title (Huntingdon). He was appointed archdn probably at some date between 1164 and early 1165, and certainly not later than 1166 (*Le Neve* 27; cf. W. J. Millor and C. N. L. Brooke eds., *The Letters of John of Salisbury* ii (Oxford 1979), no. 140).

XVIII. Thorney abbey

Confirmation of the settlement made by earl Gilbert de Clare [of Hertford] at Northampton, in the presence of the bishop, earl Simon (de St Liz) and others, promising to give one hundred shillings' worth of land to the abbot and brethren of Thorney when he recovered his inheritance, on account of his violent harassment of the abbey.

[19 December 1148 × 24 November 1152]

B = CUL ms. Add. 3021 (Thorney cartulary) fo. 207r, no. xii. s. xiv in.

Reverentissimo patri ac domino Teobaldo dei gratia Cantuariensi archiepiscopo et totius Anglie primati venerabilibusque fratribus suis coepiscopis, abbatibus, prioribus omnibusque sancte ecclesie fidelibus, clericis videlicet et laicis, Robertus humilis ecclesie Lincolniensis minister salutem et debitam venerationem. Cum multa pluribus ecclesiis intulisset dampna Gislebertus comes de Clara, pro quibus anathematis innodationem incurrerat, ecclesiam Thorniensem gravibus et immoderatis incommodis violenter afflixerat. Tandem prefate ecclesie satisfacere volens et abbati fratribusque eiusdem loci affuit Northampt' et in presentia nostra et multarum religiosarum personarum et comitis Simonis et aliorum plurium baronum fecit compositionem cum abbate et fratribus Thorneye, donans et concedens eis pro illatis dampnis et iniuriis centum solidatas terre de propria hereditate sua de qua plenariam facturus est eis investituram primo dimidio anno quo recuperabit hereditatem suam. Hanc siquidem dedit et concessit teneuram in elemosinam perpetuam et libere et quiete possidendam. Quod ut ei melius crederetur et ut firma esset compositio, iuravit in presentia nostra se finaliter tenere. Hoc idem perhibemus et nostri sigilli auctoritate confirmamus. Bene valeatis.

> Earl Gilbert died on 24 November 1152 (*Regesta* iii no. 170). The earl's successors did not in fact fulfil his promise to the abbey (S. Raban, *The estates of Thorney and Crowland* (Cambridge 1977) 36).

XIX.   Westminster abbey

Indulgence of twenty days to all those visiting the tomb of Edward the Confessor, who has been canonised by pope Alexander (III).   [? 1163]

B = Westminster Abbey Mun. bk. 11 ('Domesday') fo. 393r (417r). s. xiv in.

R. dei gratia episcopus Lincolniensis abbatibus, archidiaconis, decanis et omnibus fidelibus nostre sollicitudini obnoxiis salutem. Ex summi pastoris pia admonitione obstricti tenemur in celestibus thesauros recondere quia nec vetustatis incommoda sentient et effractorum declinabunt insidias. Inde est quod omnes nobis in Christo devotos pia exortatione et paterno monemus affectu quatinus piissimi regis Anglorum et gloriosissimi confessoris Edwardi corpus elemosinis et devoto visitent obsequio, quem summus pontifex Alexander consentiente matre nostra Romana ecclesia canonicavit et innumerabilibus exigentibus meritis in cathalogum confessorum sublimavit. Eapropter nos confisi de gratuita dei misericordia omnibus sanctissimum confessorem cum elemosinis suis in celebrationibus depositionis et translationis eius et a vigiliis earum in quindecim dies visitantibus de iniuncta sibi canonice penitentia xx relaxamus dies et omnium beneficiorum et orationum inperpetuum ecclesie nostre participes constituimus. Valete.

> Edward the Confessor was canonised by a bull of pope Alexander dated at Anagni on 7 February 1161 (fo. 387v of B; *JL* 10654). Fo. 393r of B also contains a similar indulgence (this time for forty days) issued by bp Richard Belmeis II of London (1152–1162). It is very probable that this indulgence was issued in 1163 or thereabouts on the occasion of the Confessor's translation on 13 October 1163 (F. Barlow, *Edward the Confessor* (1970), 279–84, 309–27; *Councils and Synods* I part ii 849–50).

XX. Westminster abbey

Confirmation to Elias the clerk of the perpetual vicarage of the church of Datchworth, at the petition of abbot Laurence of Westminster and archdeacon Richard of Poitiers, the parson of the church. Elias is to pay two aurei *a year to archdeacon Richard but if the latter should give up the church or die, then the pension shall be paid to the church of Westminster. While he lives Elias shall pay nothing more than these two* aurei. [*c*.1164 × 27 December 1166]

B = Westminster Abbey Mun. bk. 11 ('Domesday') fo. 227r (238r). s. xiv in.

Robertus dei gratia Lincolniensis episcopus Nicholao Huntend' archidiacono totique clero de Huntend' et Hertfordsir' salutem. Dilecto filio nostro Elie clerico utiliter providere cupientes, venerabilium*a* amicorum nostrorum Laurentii abbatis Westm' et domini Ricardi Pictav' archidiaconi petitione, perpetuam ecclesie de Dachewrd' vicariam auctoritate episcopali in perpetuam elemosinam ei concedimus, confirmamus et presentis scripti testimonio corroboramus, sicut tenor carte predicti abbatis et conventus Westm' exprimit, ita scilicet quod Elias ecclesiam illam possideat cum omnibus pertinentiis suis et cum omni fructuum integritate et reddet annuatim predicto Ricardo Pictav' archidiacono, qui eiusdem ecclesie persona constitutus est, duos aureos tantum. Si vero Ricardus Pict' archidiaconus eidem ecclesie cesserit vel decesserit prescripto tenore et conditione idem Elias ecclesie Westm' annuatim reddet illos duos aureos et ecclesiam illam habebit cum omnibus pertinentiis suis et cum omni fructuum integritate qua prius eam possidebat et ita quod ab eo quamdiu vixerit nichil preter hos duos aureos de iure exigi possit. T(estibus): magistro Ricardo precentore Lincolniensi, Martino thesaurario, magistro Radulfo, magistro Henrico, Ricardo Barr', Thoma capellano, magistro Rogero, magistro Petro, Ricardo clerico, Willelmo clerico, Laurentio.

a venenerabilium *sic* B.

Nicholas de Sigillo probably became archdn of Huntingdon in 1164 or early 1165. For Richard of Ilchester, archdn of Poitiers and later bp of Winchester see *TRHS* 5th ser., 16 (1966) 1–21.

GEOFFREY PLANTAGENET

XXI. Bullington priory

Admission of the convent of Bullington into possession of a mediety of the church of [South] Ferriby, and the church of St Peter, Burgh

[-le-Marsh] and the chapel of St Mary in Burgh ad proprios usus,
William the clerk of Appleby having resigned whatever right he had in
the church of [South] Ferriby into the hand of Robert Code.

[? 12 October 1175 × 23 January 1181]

B = BL ms. Add. 6118 (abstract by Gervase Holles of the Bullington priory
cartulary, now lost) fo. 439r–v. s. xvii med.

G. Lincolniensis electus voluit Willelmum clericum de Appelbi
quicquid iuris habuit in ecclesia de Feribi in manu Roberti Code
resignare, et conventum [fo. 439v] de Bulington in ipsius ecclesiae
medietatem et in ecclesiam sancti Petri de Burc et capellam sanctae
Mariae eiusdem ville ad proprios usus in perpetuo possidendas
instituisse: salva Lincolniensis ecclesiae dignitate in omnibus.

This charter probably dates from around the time *EEA* i no. 286 was issued. The
church and chapel at Burgh was the subject of a dispute with the abbot and convent
of Grimsby, settled in Bullington's favour in 1193 (*Danelaw Charters* no. 15). A
version of *EEA* i no. 286 precedes this document in the cartulary transcript
(fo. 439r).

XXII.   Nuneaton priory

Notification that David de Armenteres has granted to R(ichard),
bishop of Winchester, in the bishop-elect's presence, the right of
patronage of the church of Burley (on the Hill) to dispose of as he
wishes to a religious house. The bishop-elect has approved this grant,
confirming that the religious house which shall receive the church shall
enjoy all the fruits and income, provision being made for the priest
serving the church.   [? January 1177 × January 1181]

B = BL Add. Ch. 47543 (inspeximus by the Official of the Consistory Court of
Lincoln, 1453), no. 3.

G. dei gratia Lincolniensis electus universis sancte matris ecclesie filiis
ad quos presentes littere pervenerint salutem in domino. Univer-
sitatem nostram scire volumus quod dilectus filius noster David de
Armenteres in nostra presentia constitutus venerabili fratri nostro
Ricardo Wyntoniensi episcopo ius patronatus quod habebat in ecclesia
de Burgele concessit et dedit, ita ut predicto episcopo liceat libere et
absolute ecclesiam predictam loco religioso cui voluerit conferre
imperpetuum possidendam, et nos hanc concessionem approbavimus
que sigilli nostri impressione duximus roborandam; statuentes ut viri
religiosi seu femine quibus predictus episcopus memoratam ecclesiam
decreverit conferendam fructusque omnes obventiones de ipsa pro-
venientes plene et integre percipiant, deductis hiis que nec iam fuerint
ad usus sacerdotis qui in ecclesia illa debet deservire; salvo nobis in

omnibus iure pontificali et parochiali. Hiis testibus: Herberto Cantuariensi archidiacono, Hugone de Nunant' Luc'[a] archidiacono,
Radulfo de Dici Lund' archidiacono, Roberto de Burneh' archidiacono de Bukingeh', Guarino precentore Boroic'[b] ecclesie, Ricardo
capellano Lincolniensis electi, magistro Hugone de Gah', Stephano de
Norfolc', magistro Gregorio Lund', magistro Petro, David capellano,
Willelmo de Curenn', Petro de Malling', Ricardo filio Walkeini[c].

[a] sic, for Lexoviensi.   [b] sic, possibly for Ebroic'.   [c] sic, presumably for Walkelini.

Herbert Poer is said to have been appointed archdn of Canterbury in 1175 and
Ralph de Diceto became dean of St Paul's, London, at some date between January
1180 and January 1181. This document contains the earliest reference to Robert of
Burnham as archdn of Buckingham: his predecessor, David, last occurs in
September 1176 and is thought to have died in January 1177. St Hugh includes this
church in his general confirmation of the possessions of Nuneaton priory in the
diocese, 1186 × 1188 (see above, no. 139).

XXIII. Nuneaton priory

*Similar notification about the gift of the right of patronage of the church
of Burley (on the Hill). At the request of bishop Richard of Winchester,
the bishop-elect has granted the church to the nuns of (Nun)eaton.*

[? January 1177 × January 1181]

B = BL Add. Ch. 47543 (inspeximus by the Official of the Consistory Court of
Lincoln, 1453), no. 4.

G. dei gratia Lincolniensis electus universis sancte matris ecclesie filiis
salutem in domino. Noverit universitas vestra quod dilectus filius
noster David de Armenteres in presentia nostra constitutus venerabili
fratri nostro R. Wyntoniensi episcopo ius patronatus quod habebat in
ecclesia de Burgelea concessit et dedit, ita ut predicto episcopo liceat
libere et absolute ecclesiam predictam loco religioso cui vellet conferre
imperpetuum possidendam, sicut carta ipsius David et nostra testantur. Nos vero postmodum divine pietatis intuitu ad petitionem et
presentationem predicti venerabilis fratris nostri Ricardi Wyntoniensis episcopi concessimus et dedimus prescriptam ecclesiam cum
omnibus pertinentiis suis ecclesie de Eatton' et monialibus deo
servientibus in liberam et puram elemosinam perpetuo possidendam,
salvo nobis iure pontificali et parochiali. Et ut hec nostra concessio et
donatio rata et firma permaneat, eam presenti carta et sigilli nostri
appositione corroboramus et confirmamus. Hiis testibus: H. Cantuariensi, R. de Disci Londoniensi, Laurentio Bedeford' archidiaconis,
Ricardo capellano, magistro Roberto de Cantebr', magistro Iohanne
de Burneham, magistro Hugone de Gaherst, magistro Roberto de

Salos, magistro Petro de Stowa, Iohanne de hospitali, Braund' clerico, et multis aliis.

See above for the date. Laurence first occurs as archdn of Bedford October×December 1181 but his predecessor, Nicholas, last occurs April 1174×summer 1178, so he could have been appointed some considerable time earlier.

WALTER OF COUTANCES

*XXIV.   Simon de Arderne

Confirmation to Simon de Arderne for his service of all the land which Robert son of Fulk held in Langford.
[? December 1183×3 March 1185]

Mention of the confirmation (ascribed to bp William of Blois) in a confirmation by R. the dean and chapter of Lincoln.

Pd, *Reg. Ant.* iii no. 942.

For the correct identification of bp W. as Walter of Coutances and dean R. as Richard FitzNeal (probably appointed December 1183) and further details of this Langford land see *Reg. Ant.* viii xxi–xxiii and ibid. x xlix. For bp Chesney's grant to Robert son of Fulk see *EEA* i no. 140.

*XXV.   Merevale abbey

? Grant to the church of Shawell of an annual payment of one mark for the tithes of the grange which the monks of Merevale have in the parish.
[3 July 1183×3 March 1185]

Mention of the payment made by the monks 'auctoritate W. de Constantiis quondam Lincolniensis' in the so-called *matricula* of bp Hugh of Wells.

Pd, *RHW* i 250.

APPENDIX II

REFERENCES TO ACTS OF THE BISHOPS 1186–1206

Specific references to lost episcopal charters have been included in the main text, but sometimes the bishop's actions are recorded without any clear indication whether an evidentiary document was issued or not. Such instances have been collected together in this appendix.

HUGH I

1 Indulgence of thirteen days enjoined penance to those present at his enthronement, 29 September 1186 (*Gesta Henrici II* 353).

2 Order that the monks of St Albans should not be permitted to say or hear mass within the Lincoln diocese and that no one subject to the bishop's authority, under pain of excommunication, should receive the monks into their houses or should buy, sell, or exchange goods with them, 1186, shortly after his enthronement (*Gir. Camb.* iv 95).

3 Synodal decrees issued by the bishop, to be observed by all his subjects, clerical and lay. The eight precepts and prohibitions chiefly concern irregularities on the part of archdeacons, their officials and parochial clergy, 1186 (*Gesta Henrici II* 357, cf. *Magna Vita* ii 37). These decrees are repd in R. M. Woolley, *St Hugh of Lincoln* (1927), 62–3 and pd in translation in G. G. Perry, *The Life of St Hugh of Avalon, Bishop of Lincoln* (1879), 204–5; and H. Thurston, *The Life of St Hugh of Lincoln* (1898), 326–7.

4 Institution of master N. to the vicarage of Stallingborough (*Selby Coucher Book* ii p. 213, no. mlxxiv).

5 Institution of W. de Castell to the church of Packington, saving a pension of ten shillings to the prior of Coventry (*RHW* i 251).

6 Institution of W. the chaplain to the chapel of 'Angodeston' (ibid. 251).

7 Institution of William to the vicarage of Swinford (ibid. 242).

8 Institution of Hugh to the church of Withcote (ibid. 268).

9 Institution of William de Hinglesham to the church of Foston, saving a pension of ten shillings to the monks of Lenton (ibid. 239).

10 Institution of William to the church of Bruntingthorpe (ibid. 240).

11 Institution of Peter to the church of Claybrooke (ibid. 241).

12 Institution of William de Akervill to the church of South Kilworth and institution of master (*blank*) le Reveneys to the vicarage (ibid. 242).

13 Institution of Thomas to the church of Edmondthorpe (ibid. 242).

14 Institution of Thomas to the church of Sapcote (ibid. 244).

15 Institution of Peter to the church of Croft (ibid. 244).

16 Institution of Henry to the church of Thurlaston (ibid. 244).

17 Institution of Nicholas to the church of Nailstone (ibid. 247).

18 Institution of Henry son of Walkelin to a mediety of the church of Sheepy (ibid. 249).

19 Institution of Richard Midda to the church of Appleby (ibid. 249).

20 Institution of R. de Verdon to four portions of the church of Loughborough and institution of R. de Corlinstog' to the fifth portion of the church (ibid. 253).

21 Institution of Peter de Bakepuz to the church of Allexton (ibid. 258).

22 Institution of G. to the church of Cranoe (ibid. 261).

23 Institution of W. of Kibworth to the church of King's Norton, saving to the abbot of Owston 2 marks and half a stone (*petra*) of wax (ibid. 264).

24 Institution of W. to the vicarage of Kibworth Beauchamp, saving a pension of twenty shillings payable to the rector, H. de Mortimer (ibid. 265).

25 Institution of Reginald de Gaham to the church of Knipton (ibid. 266).

26 Institution of unnamed incumbent to the church of Norton by Twycross and grant of a pension of twenty shillings to the monks of Belvoir. (ibid. 249, cf. *HMC Rutland* iv 143. The unnamed incumbent was possibly William Furmentin).

27 Institution of Gerald of Wales to the church of Chesterton (*Gir. Camb.* i 263).

28 Consecration of the church of (Old) Clee in honour of the Holy Trinity and St Mary, 5 March 1193 (F. A. Greenhill, *Monumental incised slabs in the county of Lincoln* (Newport Pagnell 1986), 35; date mistranscribed in *Archaeologia* xliii 87; G. G. Perry, *The Life of St Hugh of Avalon* (1879), 364).

29 Dedication of the church of Little Cawthorpe mentioned in charters of Gilbert son of William of Legbourne and William son of Robert of Legbourne (Bodl. ms. Laud misc. 642 (Alvingham cartulary) fos. 137v, 138r).

30 Establishment of the prebend of Marston St Lawrence in Lincoln cathedral, mentioned in Lincoln D. & C. Dij/83/2/36 (document dated Wednesday before the Assumption [12 August] 1276): '. . . sanctus Hugo dictam portionem a duobus militibus comparavit et de ipsa canonicatum ordinavit in ecclesia Lincolniensi . . .'. For this prebend see *Reg. Ant.* iii nos. 894–7 and *Le Neve* 85.

31 The bishop appended his seal to an agreement between the monks of Louth Park and the convent of Alvingham. Alvingham gives to Louth Park three selions of land beside the gate of 'Calvecroft' grange [in Cockerington] and its part of one selion in Newland, in recompense for certain lands Louth Park abbey claimed against Alvingham. 'Hec autem compositio facta fuit coram domino Hugone Lincolniensi episcopo et sigillo suo corroborata in crastino sancti Gregorii anno ab incarnatione domini m°.c°.xc.v.' [13 March 1196] (Bodl. ms. Laud misc. 642 (Alvingham cartulary) fo. 61v).

32 Ordination of the vicarage of Henlow (C. R. Cheney, *From Becket to Langton: English Church Government 1170–1213* (Manchester 1956), 182, 192–3).

33 Modification in the rule of the lay brothers of the order of Sempringham with regard to dress and food, made before the bishop with the assent of the general chapter of the order, 1186 × early 1189. Mention of the modification made 'coram bone memorie Hugone Lincolniensi episcopo' in the *Vita* of St Gilbert, pd in *Un Procès de canonisation à l'aube du xiiie siècle (1201–1202): Le Livre de saint Gilbert de Sempringham*, ed. R. Foreville (Paris 1943) app. i, p. 82; *The Book of St Gilbert*, ed. R. Foreville and G. Keir (Oxford 1986), *Life* c. 25 and introd. For the lay brothers' revolt see *Procès* app. ii, pp. 83–9; M. D. Knowles, 'The Revolt of the Lay Brothers of Sempringham' in *EHR* l (1935) 465–87; R. Graham, *S. Gilbert of Sempringham and the Gilbertines* (1903) 19–23. Dr Graham ascribes the changes in the rule to 'about 1187' but there is no firm evidence for this date. The

Q

Vita account states that it happened shortly before St Gilbert's death, which occurred on 4 February 1189.

34 Excommunication of the persecutors of Geoffrey Plantagenet, Archbishop of York, 1191 (*Gir. Camb.* iv 393).

35 The bishop appended his seal to an agreement between Hamo, the dean of Lincoln cathedral, and the prior and canons of Thurgarton over the church of Sutton (in Ashfield). 'Ad plenam etiam securitatem cyrograffum istud confectum est et sigillorum tam domini H. Lincolniensis episcopi quam prefati H. decani et capituli Lincol' et capituli de Thurg' appositione confirmatum', *c.*September 1189 × March 1195 (Southwell Minster ms. 3 (Thurgarton cartulary) fo. 145r, cf. *Reg. Ant.* iii no. 922).

36 Excommunication (with other prelates) of count John, 10 February 1194 (*Chronica Rogeri de Hovedene* iii 237).

37 Excommunication of Geoffrey, the chief forester (*Magna Vita* i 114), and subsequent absolution (ibid. 118–19).

38 Excommunication of all who had tried to deprive William of Hartshill of his inheritance, 1194 (*Magna Vita* ii 22).

39 Constitutions forbidding the marriage of those who had not yet reached the years of discretion (ibid. 24).

40 Prohibition forbidding any priest or devout Christian to be present at the wedding of the young daughter of Thomas and Agnes de Saleby, and the subsequent suspension of the priest who had celebrated the marriage, the sequestration of the benefice and the excommunication of those who had flouted the prohibition (ibid. 24).

41 Excommunication of a forester (ibid. 27).

42 Prohibition forbidding Richard de Waure, deacon, to implead Reginald de Argentan in a secular court, and later excommunication (ibid. 28, 30).

43 Excommunication of the adulterous wife of Oxford (ibid. 31–2).

44 As a judge delegate, the bishop ordered that William, a clerk of the York diocese should be restored to his church (ibid. 32).

45 Prohibition forbidding archdeacons, their officials, and rural deans from imposing fines on offenders (ibid. 38).

46 General decree forbidding any parish priest on one of his manors to bury a deceased person, particularly an adult, if he himself were there (ibid. 77).

47 Excommunication of the bailiff of the earl of Leicester (ibid. 157).

48 Excommunication of Pons, the bishop's steward (ibid. 203).

49 Restoration, with Archbishop of Canterbury, in accordance with the mandate of Pope Celestine III, of the monks at Coventry cathedral and removal of the secular canons installed by Bishop Hugh de Nonant in 1190. (*Ann. mon.* iv 49; *Diceto* ii 159 gives the date of the restoration of the monks as 18 January 1198; *Gervase* i 550 gives 11 January 1198).

Postscript

Professor Cheney has discussed in detail two formularies (Baltimore, Walters Art Gallery ms. W. 15, ff. 79v–81v and Lambeth Palace ms. 105, f. 271v) which might even have been compiled by a clerk in Hugh's household.[1] The formularies contain references to H. bishop of Lincoln (or in the Baltimore ms. 'bishop of London'), one of which, about the schools of Northampton, is actum 135 in this present collection.

The others relate to forms of documents concerning the bishop in the capacity of a papal judge delegate, viz. Baltimore ms. f. 79v (*De iudice committente vices suas*) and f. 80v (*sic debet fieri citatio a iudice delegato*); the Lambeth ms. contains a version of the former sub-delegation and a letter addressed to the bishop by T. archdeacon of Wiltshire (*siquis clericus ab uno diocesi ad aliam transmigrare voluit a prelato suo huiusmodi litteras debet impetrare*).

[1] *EBC* 124–8. For further discussion of these and other formularies see J. E. Sayers, *Papal Judges Delegate in the Province of Canterbury 1198–1254* (Oxford 1971), 46–54; F. D. Logan, 'An early 13th-century papal judge-delegate formulary of English origin' in *Studia Gratiana* xv (1967) 73–88.

WILLIAM OF BLOIS

50 Ordination of a vicarage in the church of Pulloxhill in the patronage of the priory of Dunstable, 1204 (*Ann. mon.* iii 28).

51 Commission of delegates to hear a case brought by Ralph of Carlton against Thomas, the parson of Kirkby, on the grounds that he had tried to withdraw from a contract to sell Ralph corn after receiving part of the purchase price (mentioned in a mandate of Archbishop Hubert Walter of Canturbury, 1203 × 1205) (*HMCR Various Collections* i 237).

[*It is possible that some of the following references to bishop W. in Hugh of Wells' rolls could be to Walter of Coutances (1183–5), although it is likely that most are to William.*]

52 Institution of master Thomas to the church of Heather (*RHW* i 247).

53 Grant of a pension of twenty shillings payable to R. de Iwardeby by the parson of Asfordby (ibid. 256).

54 Institution of Richard to the church of Higham on the Hill (ibid. 248).

55 Institution by authority of the Lateran Council of G. to the church of Knossington (ibid. 263).

56 Institution of Walter de Meuton to a mediety of the church of Melton Mowbray, saving to the patrons, Lewes priory, a pension of twelve marks (ibid. 269).

57 Institution of Peter to the church of Scraptoft (ibid. 264).

APPENDIX III

Although the *Magna Vita* provides many details of Hugh's travels and encounters, few of these events can be dated with any precision. For instance, we are told by Adam that Hugh returned almost every year to the charterhouse at Witham, sometimes once and sometimes more often, but chiefly in the autumn months when he could send most of his household to their homes (*Magna Vita* ii 70–1). These visits, understandably, are only mentioned in the *Magna Vita* and no specific information is available which would aid the compilation of an itinerary. An asterisk by the place-date indicates an occurrence as a witness to a royal charter. These precise dates may be misleading unless it is recalled that at present we do not know at what stage the royal charter received the list of witnesses and the time- and place-dates (see *English Episcopal Acta* iii app. iii p. 308 for a more detailed discussion of this point). A specific study of Hugh's journey to France in 1199 has been made by Dom Paul Piolin, *Voyage de Saint Hugues, évêque de Lincoln, à travers l'Anjou et le Maine en l'année 1199* (Angers 1889).

HUGH OF AVALON

1186

May 25	elected bishop at Eynsham	*Diceto* ii 41–2
Sept. 14	as bishop-elect attends Council at Marlborough	*Gesta Henrici II* i 352
Sept. 21	consecrated bishop at Westminster	*Diceto* ii 42; *Gesta Henrici II* i 352–3
between 21 and 29 Sept.	St Albans	*Gir. Camb.* iv 94–5
Sept. 29	enthroned at Lincoln	*Gesta Henrici II* i 353
	shortly afterwards visits Stow	*Gir. Camb.* vii 109

1187

Feb. 11	Canterbury	*Gervase* i 353
late Feb.	travelled to France	*Eyton* 277

1188

Feb. 11	Geddington	*Magna Vita* i xlv; *Gervase* i 409–10

June 16	ambassador to Philip II of France — Winchelsea	*Gervase* i 432–3; *Gesta Henrici II* ii 40

1189

March × June	Le Mans*	*Delisle* ii no. dcclxviii
Whitsun week	La Ferté-Bernard	*Gesta Henrici II* ii 66
July 20	licence to go to England — between Chaumont-en-Vexin and Trie	*It. Ric.* 2
	At some point during this year the bishop was at Buckden	actum no. 157
Aug. 13	crosses to Normandy	*It. Ric.* 2
Sept. 3	attends king Richard's coronation at Westminster	ibid. 3
Sept. 12–18	Geddington*	ibid. 6–8
Sept. 15–16	Pipewell	*Gesta Henrici* II ii 85; *Chronica Rogeri de Hovedene* iii 15
Sept. 20	Warwick*	*It. Ric.* 9
Nov. 29	Canterbury	ibid. 18
Dec. 1	Canterbury*	ibid. 19
Dec. 5	Canterbury*	ibid. 21
Dec. 6–7	Dover*	ibid. 21–2

1191

In the course of this year Hugh travelled round a great part of the diocese visiting religious houses including Godstow abbey		*Gesta Henrici II* ii 231
Sept.	Oxford	*Magna Vita* i xlvi; *Gir. Camb.* iv 397–8
Oct.	Reading	ibid.
Oct. 9	London	*Chronica Rogeri de Hovedene* iii 144

1193

| March 5 | consecrated Clee church | F. A. Greenhill, *Monumental incised slabs in the county of Lincoln* (Newport Pagnell 1986), 35 |
| June | ? Canterbury | *It. Ric.* 76 |

1194

Feb. 10	Westminster	ibid. 84
March 28	Nottingham*	ibid. 86
March 30	Nottingham	*Chronica Rogeri de Hovedene* iii 240
April 16	Winchester*	*It. Ric.* 88
April 17	Winchester	ibid. 89
April 23	Bishop's Waltham	ibid. 91

In the course of this year the bishop was at Buckden (*Magna Vita* ii 85)

1195

| Jan. 15 | York | *Chronica Rogeri de Hovedene* iii 278, 281 |

1196

July 7	Rouen	*It. Ric.* 114

1197

Nov. 11	Lincoln (blesses abbot of Eynsham)	*Gervase* i 543–4
Dec. 7	Oxford	*Magna Vita* ii 98–9; *Gervase* i 549
	Hugh goes to Normandy and finds the king at Château Gaillard; Portjoie; and then returns to England	*Magna Vita* ii 101, 103

1198

? in 1198	Peterborough Buckden	ibid. 115–16
after 11 May	Bermondsey	ibid. 81–2
Aug. 25	Rouen	*It. Ric.* 133
Aug. 28	Château Gaillard	*Magna Vita* ii 101
? September	Rouen	ibid. 107, 109
April 1198 × April 1199 (last year of Richard I's reign)	Rochester Canterbury	ibid. ii, 7, 9
late 1198 or early 1199	London Cheshunt near St Albans	ibid. ii 124, 126, n. 1, 127

1199

*c.*Feb.	spent 3 weeks in Normandy	ibid. ii 130
early March	set out for Anjou and stayed for same time at a manor of St Nicholas, Angers	ibid. ii 130
late March/early April	He was probably at Angers when informed that the king had received a fatal wound	ibid. ii 134
? April 3	La-Haye-des-Bons-Hommes	ibid. ii 130; Piolin 7
after April 6	on his way to the king's funeral he visits Queen Berengaria at Beaufort-en-Vallée	*Magna Vita* ii 136
April 10	Saumur	ibid. ii 136
April 11	conducts Richard I's funeral service at Fontevrault abbey	ibid. ii 137; *It Ric.* 145
April 14	Chinon	ibid. ii 138 cf. 137
	In King John's company the bp visited Saumur and the tombs of Henry II and Richard I at Fontevrault	ibid. ii 138
April 18	celebrated Easter? at Fontevrault/Beaufort-en-Vallée	ibid. ii 142
April 19	Hugh set out for England La Flêche, and St Peter's abbey in the suburbs of Le Mans	ibid. ii 146–7
April 20	left Le Mans and reached Sées — shortly afterwards he visited the abbey of Persigny, and returned through Normandy to England	ibid. ii 147–8

May 27	attends king John's coronation at Westminster	*Chronica Rogeri de Hovedene* iv 90

1200

Easter	Stow	*Magna Vita* i 109
May 12	Les Andelys	*Rot. Chart.* 66b
May 22	present at the treaty of Le Goulet	*Magna Vita* ii 149
May 31	he began his travels to Burgundy	
	(*the following places are given in the order they were visited. The precise dates of visits are of course impossible to determine.*)	*ibid* ii 92, 153–184
	Les Andelys	
	Meulan	
	abbey of St Denys	
	Paris	
	Joi	
	Troyes	
	hospital of St Anthony (St Didier de la Mothe)	
	Grenoble	
	La Grande Chartreuse	
	St Domninus	
	Avalon	
	Villarbenoît	
	St Maximin	
	Avalon	
	Bellay	
	La Grande Chartreuse	
	Arvières	
	Lugny	
	Val St Pierre	
	Cluny	
	Cîteaux	
	Clairvaux	
	Reims	
	St Omer	
	Clairmarais	
	Dover	
	Canterbury	
	London	
*c.*Sept. 18– Nov. 16	last illness at the Old Temple, London	*ibid.* ii 184–5
Nov. 16	died in London	*ibid.* ii 184, 197, 208; *Ann. Mon.* i 202
Nov. 17	The body disembowelled and the bowels buried near the altar steps in the Temple church, London	*Magna Vita* ii 218
	The body brought from London to Lincoln	
Nov. 18	Hertford	
Nov. 19	Biggleswade	
Nov. 20	Buckden	
Nov. 21	Stamford	
Nov. 22	Ancaster	

Nov. 23	Lincoln	ibid. ii 225
Nov. 24	buried beside the altar of St John the Baptist in Lincoln cathedral	ibid. ii 232; *Ann. mon.* i 202

WILLIAM OF BLOIS

1203

Aug. 24	consecrated at Canterbury	*Canterbury Professions* no. 143

1204

March 15	Bridgnorth*	*Rot. Chart.* 122b
March 22	Westminster*	ibid. 123
Aug. 3	Oxford*	ibid. 135b, 136b

1205

? Lent	Ramsey	actum no. 284

1206

May 10	died	*Chronica Majora* ii 495; *Ann. mon.* iv 394

INDEX OF PERSONS AND PLACES

Arabic numerals (occasionally with extra items distinguished as A, B, and C) indicate the continuous series of acta and small roman numerals refer to the pages of the introduction. In the third appendix the entries are indexed by page number; in appendices I and II by the entry number. The letter W following a number indicates a witness. When a name occurs often as witness, the series of such entries is preceded by 'witness'. With English and Welsh place-names the pre-1974 counties are noted, and followed, where now changed, by the present administrative divisions. Two additional abbreviations: ch. for church, and ment. for mentioned, have been used in this index.

A

A., mr 135

Ab Kettleby, Ketleby (Leics), ch. of St Helen 84

Abbefelde, Abefeld', Geoffrey de 3

Abbend', see Abingdon

Abi, see Aby

Abingdon, Abbend' (Berks/Oxon), Ben. abbey of 2, 3; abbot of, see Hugh; kitchen of 3; monks and chaplains of, see Nicholas; Richard; sick brethren of 2

Abinton (in Lavendon, Bucks) 72

Aburn', see Aubourn

Abwaldebi, see Aswardby

Aby, Abi (Lincs), ch. of 70

Acharius, abbot of Peterborough 282

Acra, see Castle Acre

Adam son of Reginald, vicar of Towthorpe 69

Addington, Little (Northants), ch. of 193, 293

Addlethorpe, Hardelistorp (Lincs), ch. of 183; rector of, see Gene, Roger de

Adlingfleet (Yorks W. R./Humb), William of, knight 200

Æisseby, see Ashby St Ledgers

Aggleptort, see Authorpe

Agnes daughter of Jocelin 174

– daughter of Pain son of John 67, 242

Aia, Wigar de 155, and see Eye

Aignesford, see Eynsford

Ailby, Alebi (Lincs), Gunter of 70

– Herbert of 70

– Walter of 70

– William of 70

Ailwin son of Godegose 67, 242

Aimeric, archdn of Durham 232W

Ainesti, see Anstey

Ainho, see Aynho

Aissebi, see Ashby Magna

Aisterlund (near Ailby and Saxby, Lincs) 70

Akele, see Oakley

Akervill, William de, rector of South Kilworth, app. II(12)

Alan, prior of Nocton 268

– rector of Wrangle 206

– son of count Henry of Goëllo 223

Albeniac', Albini, see Aubigny

Aldermaston (Berks), mr Absolom of 42

Alebi, see Ailby

Alexander III, pope 24, 167n., 207n., app. I(XIX)

– archdn of the West Riding alias Stow 13W, 15W, 43W, 71W, 201n., 203; official of the ch. of Lincoln sede vacante 203; vicar of Doddington and Thorpe on the Hill 210

– bp of Lincoln xxx, xxxi, xxxiv, xxxvi, 67, 78n., 84n., 133, 189n., 242, app. I(I–V)

– mr, 209W; canon of Lincoln 299W

– chaplain 188AW

– clerk, of Aubourn 20

– clerk of Stamford app. I(XVII)

– prior of Canons Ashby 31n.

Alice 40B

Alkborough, Hautebarg(e) (Lincs/Humb) 181

– ch. of 181

– William of, vicar of Spalding 180n.

Allexton (Leics), ch. of app. II(21); rector of, see Bakepuz, Peter de

Almaria, Amari, Richard de, archdn of the West Riding alias Stow 203n.; precentor of Lincoln app. I(XX)

– Roger de, archdn of the West Riding alias Stow and precentor of Lincoln 117n., app. I(IXW)

Alnest', Alnestouu(e), Alnestow(e), see Elstow

Alneto, see Aunay

Alricheseia, see Arlesey

Alsavia, see Halse

Alstan, chaplain 188AW

Alvingham (Lincs), ch. of St Ethelwold 4

– Gilb. priory of 4, 5, app. I(IVn., VI); app.
  II(31); prior of, see Geoffrey
Alwin son of Godegos, see Ailwin
Amari, see Almaria
Anagni (Italy) app. I(XIXn.)
Ancaster (Lincs) p. 211
– ch. of 117
Andelys, Les (Château Gaillard, Eure) p.
  211
Andrew, chaplain, canon of Lincoln 74W,
  212W
– monk 188AW
Aneheide (Mere, Lincs), Templars of app.
  I(IX)
Angers (Maine-et-Loire), Ben. abbey of St
  Nicholas 181n., p. 210; abbot of, see
  William
Angod, clerk 115W, and see also Blackolvest'
'Angodeston' (unidentified, Leics), chapel of
  app. II(6); rector of, see W.
Anjou (France) p. 210
Ansketil, Anketil, Asch', prior of Nostell 25
  & n., 136
Anstey, Ainesti (Herts) 299
Apostolorum, see Philip
Appleby (Leics), ch. of app. II(19); rector
  of, see Midda, Richard
Appleby, Appelbi, clerk of, see William
Apulia, Simon de, dean of York 214Cn.
Arcels, Seer de 16
Arderne, Simon de app. I(XXIV)
Ardr', see Hardres
Aresci, Thomas de 129
– William de, vicar of Nocton and Dunston
  267
Argentan, Reginald de app. II(42)
Aristotle, mr, vicar of Hemingford 159
Arlesey, Alricheseia (Beds), ch. of 205;
  vicarage of 205
Armenteres, Armenters, David de 139, app.
  I(XXII, XXIII)
– Henry de 130
Arvières (France) p. 211
Asfordby (Leics), rector of app. II(53)
  see also Esford'
Arthingworth, Erningworde (Northants), ch.
  of St Andrew 84
Asch', see Ansketil
Ashby Foleville, Esseby (Leics), ch. of St
  Mary 84
Ashby Magna, Aissebi (Leics), ch. of 40
Ashby St Ledgers, Æisseby (Northants), ch.
  of 84, app. I(III)
Ashby, West, Askebi (Lincs), ch. of 74;
  rector of, see William
Aspley Guise (Beds) 265
Aston, Robert son of Osbert app. I(VIIn.)
– William of app. I(VII)
– William son of Robert of app. I(VIIn.)
Aston, North (Oxon), ch. of app. I(VII)
Aston Rowant (Oxon) 297

Astwick (Beds), chapel of 41
Astwick, Estvic, Estwic (near Brackley,
  Northants) 24
Astwood, Estwerde (Bucks), chapel of 127
Aswardby, Abwaldebi (Lincs) 16
– ch. of 223
Attington (Oxon), knight's fee in 231
Aubigny, Albeniac', Albini, Aubeni, Cecily
  d' 19n., 173
– Ralph d' 20n.
– Robert d' 19n.
– William d' 173
– William III d' 225
Aubourn, Aburn' (Lincs), ch. of xxxviii, 20;
  clerk of, see Alexander
'Auco' (? Ayot St Peters, Herts), ch. of 168
Aunay, Alneto (Calvados), Cist. abbey of 6;
  abbot of, see Christian; John I; Vivian
Aunest', see Elstow
Authorpe, Aggleport (Lincs), chapel of 171
Avalon, Avalun', Avaluns (Yonne) p. 211
– Hugh of, bp of Lincoln xxi–xlii passim;
  enthronement of app. II(1); household of
  xxiv–vii; kinsmen of xxv–vi; seal of xl–xlii;
  acta 1–215; ment. 228, 238, 241, 244,
  249n., 251, 252n., 254n., 256n., 257n.,
  258n., 260n., 261n., 262n., 263n., 278n.,
  279–181, 285, 293n., 295, app. I(IIIn.,
  Vn., XXIIn.)
– Peter of, brother of the bp 7, 52W, 85W
– mr William of 141W; canon of Lincoln
  xxvi, 73W
Aylesbury, Eilesberi (Bucks), mr Richard of,
  vice-archdn of Oxford 147W
Aynho, Ainho (Northants) 8
– ch. of 204; rectors of, see Diceto, Ralph de;
  Vireneto, Ralph de; vicar of, see Turbert
  son of Turbert; vicarage of 204
– hospital of St James 8
Ayot St Peters (?), Auco (Herts), ch. of 168
Azelin, priest, rector of All Saints, Stamford
  app. I(XVII)

B

B., dean of Chester 243
– prior of Witham 62W, 241Wn.
Bacon, Bac', Baccun, Bact', Bacun, Roger
  xxv, xxvii, witness: 2, 56, 105, 122, 179,
  187, 204, 223, 243, 273, 290
Badintona, see Bainton
Baggeherste, William de 67W
Bain, river (Lincs) 16n.
Bainton, Badintona (Oxon) 156, 274
– Robert of 156
Bakepuz, Peter de, rector of Allexton app.
  II(21)
Baldwin, archbp of Canterbury xxiv, xxxix,
  1, 36n.
Banbury, Bannebir' (Oxon) xxxviiin.
– bp's fee outside 160

– clerk of, *see* W.
– tolls of market 67, 242
Bard', *see* Bardolf
Bardney, Bard', Bardeneia (Lincs) 16
– Ben. abbey of 9–17, 217–19; abbot of 17,
   and see also Matthew; Robert; Walter;
   abbot's clerk, *see* Geoffrey
– chaplain of, *see* Walter
– dean of, *see* Bardney, Richard of
– Richard of 11W; dean 13W–15W
Bardolf, Bard', Bardulf, Hugh 118, 195n.
– Robert witness: 120, 121, 162, 178, 209,
   285; canon of Lincoln 195n.; rector of
   Hambleden 195
Bareswrd(e), mr Simon de 211W
Barford, Great (Beds), ch. of 265
Barkwith, Robert of, lord of Poolham 10n.
Barlings (Lincs), Prem. abbey of 220, 255;
   abbot of 220n., *and see also* Robert
Barnack, Bernake (Northants/Cambs), ch. of
   151
Barnoldby-le-Beck, Bernelobi (Lincs/Humb),
   ch. of 223
Barnwell (Cambs), prior of 234n.
Barnwell All Saints, Bernewella (Northants),
   ch. of 170
Barr', Richard app. I(XXW)
Barrow-on-Soar (Leics), ch. of 250
Barrowby, Berehebr', Bereheby, Bergebi
   (Lincs), mr Samson of 48W, 130W
– William, dean of 48W
Bartholomew, bp of Exeter 169, 287n.
Barton (in the Clay) (Beds), ch. of 157
Barton-on-Humber (Lincs/Humb), chapel of
   All Saints 16; ch. of St Peter 16
Barton Seagrave, Barton', Berton'
   (Northants), ch. of 75–7; rector of, *see*
   Piun, Stephen de
Barton (Westcott) (Oxon), ch. of 60, 63
– Alexander of 60
Basset, Gilbert 23
– Richard 84
Bassingthorpe, Torp (Lincs) 189
Bath and Glastonbury, bp of, *see* Savaric;
   Wells, Jocelin of
Baumber (Lincs) 16
Beyeux (Calvados), bp of, *see* Henry
Beachampton, Bechhamton' (Bucks),
   mediety of ch. of St Mary 114
Beauchamp, Bello Campo, Hugh I de 11,
   (?) 29
– Hugh de (nephew of above) 11
– Simon de, rector of Edlesborough 11
– Simon de (another) 41n., 125, 126n., 264
– William de 41n.
Beauchief (Yorks W. R./S. Yorks), Prem.
   abbey of 18
Beaufoe, mr Robert de 176
Beaufort-en-Vallée (Maine et Loire) p. 210
Beaulieu (Beds), Ben. priory of 19
Beauport, de Bello Portu (Côtes-du-Nord),

Prem. abbey of St Mary 223
Beauver, *see* Belvoir
Bechhamton', *see* Beachampton
Becket, Thomas, chancellor 48n.
Bedford, Bed', Bedef', Bedeford(e),
   Bedefordia, archdn of, *see* Deeping,
   Geoffrey of (?); Elstow, Alexander of;
   Laurence; Nicholas
– ch. of All Saints 265
– ch. of St Paul 265; prebendaries of St Paul
   126
Bedford, mr Alexander of xxv, witness: (no
   description) 62, 90, 125, 126, 134, 209,
   210, 264, 265, 281; canon of Lincoln 74,
   79, 132, 140, 204, 206, 212, 229, 253
– I. of, reeve of Northampton 135
– mr John of 72W; parson of Milton Ernest
   19
– mr Robert of xxv, 72W, 75W, 139W,
   162W, 209W; canon of Lincoln 101;
   precentor of Lincoln 72n., 75., 120W,
   121n., 139n., 162., 209n.
– mr Warin of 130W
Beelsby, Belesbi (Lincs/Humb), ch. of 223
Beesby, Besebi (Lincs/Humb), ch. of 223
Begbroke (Oxon), ch. of 224; rectors of 224;
   vicar of, *see* Thomas; vicarage of 224
Bek, Thomas, bp of Lincoln 218n.
Belchford, Beltisford' (Lincs), mediety of ch.
   of 182, 184; rector of, *see* Malebisse,
   Alexander; Paris, Peter son of William of;
   St Edward, John of
Belgrave, Belegrave (Leics) 286, app.
   I(XVI); rector of, *see* Richard
Belesbi, *see* Beelsby
Bellay (Seine et Oise) p. 211
Bellinge, Bellinga (Northants), dean of, *see*
   Ralph
Bello Campo, *see* Beauchamp
Belmeis, Richard II, bp of London app.
   I(XIXn.)
Beltisford', *see* Belchford
Belton, Beltun' (Rutl/Leics), chapel of 84
Belvoir, Beauver, Belver (Leics), castle of
   225
– Ben. priory of 20, 225, app. II(26)
Benedict, abbot of Peterborough 152, 181n.,
   188AW, 214
– abbot of St Mary, Stratford Langthorne
   211
Benedicta, lady 118
Benjamin, vicar of Hallaton 85
Bennington, Long, Benigton' (Lincs), ch. of
   172; vicarage of 172
Berehebr', Bereheby, Bergebi, *see* Barrowby
Berengaria, queen of England p. 210
Bermondsey (London) p. 210
– Clun. priory of 21, 22, 22A, 226; prior of
   226n.
Bernake, *see* Barnack
Bernard, abbot of St-Évroul app. I(XVI)

– cook 150
Bernecestr', *see* Bicester
Bernelobi, *see* Barnoldby-le-Beck
Bernewella, *see* Barnwell All Saints
Bernewude, Bernwd', William de, preceptor
   of the Temple, London 206W
Berton(a), *see* Barton Seagrave; Steeple
   Barton
Bertram, prior of Durham 237
Besebi, *see* Beesby
Bicester, Bernecestr' (Oxon), ch. of 23
– Aug. priory of 23
Biddenham (Beds) 264, 265
Bidun, Halina(l)d de 144
Bigesworde (? Biggleswade, Beds), tithes of
   118
Biggleswade (Beds) p. 211
Bigot, William 16
Bilingh' (? Billinghay, Lincs), Robert de app.
   I(IXW)
Billing, Little (Northants), ch. of 130
   see also Bellinge
Billingborough (Lincs), ch. of 177
Billinghay, *see* Bilingh'
Binbrook, Binebrock' (Lincs) app. I(VI)
Binsey (Oxon), chapel of 274
Birthorpe (in Stow by Threckingham,
   Lincs), chapel of 174, 175
– Walter of 175n.
Bishop's Waltham (Hants) p. 209
Bisshoppesdun', Osbert de, rector of
   Horncastle 74
Blackbourton, Burtona (Oxon), chapel of
   142, 144, 148
– Hugh of 142
Blackolvest', Blaculuest', Angod de 79W,
   80W
   see also Angod
Blankney (Lincs) app. I(IXn.)
Blatherwycke, Blarwic (Northants), ch. of St
   Mary Magdalen 84
Bledlington, *see* Bridlington
Bletsoe (Beds), ch. of 270
Blockesham, *see* Bloxham
Bloet, Robert, bp of Lincoln xxx, 106n.
Blois, Bleis, Blesensis, Bleys (Loir et Cher),
   mr William of 25n., 205W; bp of Lincoln
   xxi–xlii *passim*; household of xxvii–viii;
   seal of xl–xlii; acta 216–300; ment. 90n.,
   92n., 93n., 97n., 99n., 100n., 102n., 104n.,
   106n., 107n., 112n., 149n., 154n., 155n.,
   app. I(XXIVn.); precentor of Lincoln 267,
   289; rector of St Nicholas, Durham xxiiin.;
   subdean of Lincoln 13W–17W, 20W, 25n.,
   47W, 106W, 171W, 175W, 176W, 205n.
– – *nepos* of, *see* Marum, Henry de
– William of (another), archdn of
   Buckingham 219W, 225W, 229W, 244W,
   265W, 274W, 298; bp of Worcester xxvii,
   294n.; prebendary of Sutton cum
   Buckingham (Lincoln) 298; rector of

Swallow 294
Bloxham, Blockesham, Blokesham (Oxon),
   ch. of 67, 211, 242
Blund, mr W. 225W
– mr Walter 171W, 252W, 254W
Boby, Bobi, Hugh de 26W; steward of the bp
   xxvi, 179W, 212W; *see also* Bony
Bocland, Bokeland, Geoffrey de, rector of
   Walkern 230
– Hugh de 265
Bohun, Roger de 141W
Bokeland, *see* Bocland
Boland' (? in Aby, Lincs) 70
Bolandewang (? in Aby, Lincs) 70
Bolebec, Herbert de, knight 81
Bolehirst, Bolehurst' (? Bolnhurst, Beds),
   Roger de 73W, 219W, 294W; *see also*
   Rolehyrst'
Boloigne, Godfrey de 130
Bonby in Lindsey (Lincs/Humb), ch. of 167
Boniface, archbp of Canterbury xxiiin., 199n.
Bony, (? Boby), Hugh de 26W
Boothby Graffoe (Lincs) app. I(IXn.)
Bos', *see* Bosell'
Bosceby, *see* Bushby
Bosco, Arnold de 139
– Geoffrey de 7
– William de 6W
Bosegat', Bosegayt', *see* Bozeat
Bosell', Bos', Busello, Bussello, mr Theobald
   de xxv, 117W; canon of Lincoln 3W, 73W,
   206W
   see also Buzas
Bosseby, *see* Bushby
Botiate, *see* Butteyate
Boultham (Lincs), ch. of 16
Bourne (Lincs), abbot of 46n.
Bowden, Little, Bugged' (Leics), ch. of St
   Nicholas 84
Bozeat, Bosegat', Bosegayt' (Northants), ch.
   of 133, 134; vicarage of 134
Bracchel(e), Braccheleia, *see* Brackley
Bracebridge (Lincs) 16
Braci, Gilbert de 144
– William de 144
Brackley, Braccel(e), Braccheleia
   (Northants), hospital of St John the
   Evangelist xxxivn., 24; master of, *see*
   Salomon
Bradel', Bradell', R. de 205W
Bradenstoke (in Lynham, Wilts), Aug. priory
   of app. I(VII)
'Bradewad' (unidentified), mill of 16
Bradwell, Bradwelle (Bucks), chapel of 127
Brafield on the Green (Northants), ch. of 130
Braimuster, Odo de 231
Bramfeld, William de, subdean of Lincoln
   223n., 252W–254W, 286n., 290n., 294n.
Brampton Ash, Bramthona (Northants), ch.
   of 170
Branteston', *see* Braunston

Brantigby, *see* Brentingby
Braose, Giles de, bp of Hereford 216n.
Bratoft (Lincs), demesne tithes of 16
– Geoffrey of 16
Brattleby (?) (Lincs), ch. of app. I(X)
Braund, clerk app. I(XXIIIW)
Braunston, Branteston', Buceston' (Leics), chapel of 286, app. I(XVI)
Braybrooke (Northants), tithes of 130
– Andrew of 130
Breithebuskewang' (in Swaby, Lincs) 70
Breitt(on), Alice le 52n.
– Hugh le 52n.
  see also Bret
Brellingt', *see* Bridlington
Brentingby, Brantigby (Leics) 286, app. I(XVI)
Bret, Simon le 206, 207 (*iuvenis*)
  see also Breitt(on)
Brewer, William, bp of Exeter 221n., 222n.
Bridgnorth (Salop) p. 212.
Bridlington, Bledlington, Brellingt', Brid', Bridel' (Yorks E. R./Humb), Aug. priory of 25–7; canons of, *see* Elias; William; prior of, *see* H.; Hugh
Bridport (Dorset), mr John of, rector of St Mary, Oxford 68
Brigehesl', *see* Brigsley
Briggemilne (in pa. Sutton, Northants/Cambs) 155
Brigsley, Brighesl' (Lincs/Humb), ch. of 223
Brizenorton (Oxon), ch. of 60, 63
'Brocebi' (unidentified, ? Brattleby, Lincs), ch. of app. I(Xn.)
Brocklesby, Broclosbi (Lincs/Humb), mediety of ch. of All Saints 124; sixth part of ch. 123
Broughton, Brocton' (Beds), ch. of 127
Broughton (Hunts/Cambs), ch. of 157
Bruntingthorpe (Leics), ch. of app. II(10); rector of, *see* William
Bubbenhill, Bubenhill' (? Bubnell, Derbys), William de, vicar of Saddington 54, 55, 238
Buceston', *see* Braunston
Buckden, Buggeden', Buggenden', Bukedene (Hunts/Cambs) 157, app. I(I), pp. 209–11
– mr Alan of, canon of Lincoln and prebendary of Decem Librarum 259
– mr Simon of, bailiff on the bp xxvin.
Bucketorp, mr Robert de 68
Buckingham, archdn of, *see* Blois, William of; Burnham, Robert of; David; Roger; Swafeld, Stephen de
– earl of, *see* Giffard, Walter
Budeford', Richard de, rector of Chipping Norton 66
Bueles, Simon de, vicar of Gravenhurst 266
– family 266n.
Bugged', *see* Bowden, Little
Buggeden', Buggenden', *see* Buckden
Bukeb', (? Long Buckby, Northants), R.,

rector of 298W
Bukedene, *see* Buckden
Bullington, Bulington (Lincs), ch. of St James 28, app. I(VIIIn.)
– Gilb. priory of St Mary xxxivn., 28, app. I(VIII, XXI)
Bulonia, Robert de, Templar app. I(IX)
Burc, *see* Burgh-le-Marsh
Burch, *see* Peterborough
Burgefurn', Thomas 70
– William 70
Burgele(a), Burgeleya, *see* Burley on the Hill
Burgh-le-Marsh, Burc (Lincs), ch. of St Mary 28, app. I(XXI)
– ch. of St Peter 28, app. I(XXI)
Burgo, *see* Peterborough
Burguell', *see* Burwell
Burgundy (France) p. 211
Burley on the Hill, Burgele(a), Burgeleya (Rutl/Leics), ch. of 139, app. I(XXII, XXIII)
Burneham, *see* Burnham
Burnel, Roger 177
Burnham, Burneham, Alard of, archdn of London 122n.
– mr John of app. I(XXIIIW)
– mr Robert of, archdn of Buckingham, app. I(XXIIW)
Burton (by Lincoln) 16
Burton, Hugh de 144
Burtona, *see* Blackbourton
Burwell, Burguell' (Lincs), chaplain of, *see* Herbert
– ch. of 171
– Ben. priory of 171
Bury St Edmunds (Suff), abbot of, *see* Samson
Busello, *see* Bosell'
Bushby, Bosceby, Bosseby (Leics), 286, app. I(XVI)
Bushmead (Beds), Aug. priory of 29, 228
Bussello, *see* Bosell'
Butteyate, Botiate, Butyate (in Bardney, Lincs) 16
– Henry of 289n.
Buzas (? Bosell'), Theobald de 141W

C

Cadeby, South (Lincs), ch. of St Peter 178.
Caen, Kaanes (Calvados) 155n.
– ch. in 167
Caignes, *see* Kaynes
Caisneto, *see* Chesney
Calcwelle, R. de 255W
Caldoverton', *see* Cold Overton
Caldwell (Beds), Aug. priory of 30
Calvecroft Grange (in Cockerington, Lincs) app. II(31)
Camera, Simon de, archdn of Wells and rector of Monkton 33n., 34; bp of Chichester 221, 222

Campania, Gilbert de 70
Camvill, Thomas de 57
Canons Ashby, Esseby (Northants), Aug.
  priory of 19, 31; prior of, see Alexander
Cant', see Kent
Cantebr', Mr Robert de app. I(XXIIIW)
Cantelu, Emecina de 44n.
– Walter de 44n.
Canterbury, Cant' (Kent) xxxii, pp. 208–212
– archbp of, see Baldwin; Boniface; Dover,
  Richard of; Theobald; Walter, Hubert
– archdn of, see Poer, Herbert
– ch. (metropolitan) of Christ Church or
  Holy Trinity 1, 32–8
– vacant see of 221
– John of, former archbp of Lyon, rector of
  Eynsford 33
Cantia, see Kent
Canvill, Gerard de app. I(X)
Canwick (Lincs), prebend of 110
Capella, Robert de, xxvi, witness: (no
  description) 2, 8, 10, 11, 39, 52, 56, 68, 70,
  71, 78, 81, 85, 89, 102, 103, 105, 106, 114,
  115, 117, 123, 124, 143, 145, 146, 152,
  160, 171, 207, 208, 210; canon of Lincoln
  61, 90, 132, 140, 148, 177, 179, 187,
  188A, 206
Carbonel, Hamo 274
Cardington (Beds), ch. of 265
Carlton, Ralph of app. II(51)
Carlton Kyme, prebend of (in Lincoln
  cathedral) 96
Carn', John de 128n.
Carun, Gervase de, rector of Sherington 128
Cassington (Oxon), chapel of 61, 62; vicarage
  of 62
Castell, W. de, rector of Packington app.
  II(5)
Castle Acre, Acra (Norf), Clun. priory of St
  Mary 39
Castor, Castre (Northants/Cambs), ch. of
  156
Catesby, Cattesbi, Chastebi (Northants), ch.
  of 40
– Cist. priory of St Mary 40
Catesden', see Gaddesden, Little
Cattecroft (? in Aby, Lincs) 70
Caversfield (Oxon), ch. of 120, 121
Caversham (Oxon/Berks), ch. of app. I(XV)
Cawthorpe, Little (Lincs), ch. of St Helen 4,
  app. II(29)
Celestine III, pope 40A, 40B, 42n., 152n.,
  154n., 166, 198n., 211, 214, 214A, 214B,
  214Cn., app. II(49)
Cella, John de, abbot of St Albans 211
Cestresham, see Chesham
Cestreton, see Chastleton
Chalfont St Peter (Bucks), ch. of 121
Charlbury (Oxon), ch. of 60, 62, 63
Charleie, see Charley
Charles, clerk (of bp William) xxvii, witness:

219, 228, 243, 244, 251, 259, 273, 274, 285,
  286, 290, 299
Charley, Charleie (Leics) 299
Chartreuse, La Grande (Isère) p. 211
Charwelton, Cherweltona (Northants), ch. of
  136, 137; rector of, see Ulian
Chastebi, see Catesby
Chastleton, Cestreton (Oxon), ch. of 144
Château Gaillard (Les Andelys, Eure) p. 210
Chaumont-en-Vexin (Loir-et-Cher) p. 209
Checkendon (Oxon), ch. of 43; rector of, see
  Rolleston, Hugh of; Rolleston, Roger of;
  vicar of, see Pentir, William de
Cheddington, Chetend' (Bucks), ch. of 137
Cherweltona, see Charwelton
Chesham, Cestresham (Bucks), mediety of
  ch. of 53, 88
Cheshunt (Herts) p. 210
Chesney, Caisneto, Adeliza 137n.
– Hugh de 60
– Matilda de 23
– – son of, see FitzGerald, Warin
– Robert, bp of Lincoln (1148–66)
  xxx,xxxvi, xli, xlii, 11, 13n., 26, 39, 44n.,
  50n., 56, 61, 78n., 83., 84n., 87, 88n., 102
  103, 109, 110, 116n., 117n., 127n., 131n.,
  133n., 137, 169, 174, 199n., 204, 229n.,
  252, 266n., 283n., app. I(IIIn., VI–XX,
  XXIVn.)
– Simon 137n.
– William de app. I(XIIIW)
Chester, abbot of, see Geoffrey
– bp of, see Muschamp, Geoffrey
– constable of, see John
– countess of, see Lucy
– dean of, see B.
– earl of, see Rannulf
Chesterton (Oxon), ch. of, app. II(27);
  rector of, see Wales, Gerald of
Chetend', see Cheddington
Chethun, Gilbert 160
Cheueremund', Cheuremunt, Chevermont,
  Chevermund, see Kirmond
Chicheley, Chicheeleia (Bucks), ch. of 127
Chichester, bp of, see Camera, Simon de
Chicksands (Beds), ch. of 41
– Gilb. priory of 41
Chieueremunt, see Kirmond
Child, Ralph 176
Chinon (Indre-et-Loire) p. 210
Chipping Norton (Oxon), ch. of 66; rector
  of, see Budeford, Richard de
Chippinghurst (Oxon) 274
Christian, abbot of Aunay 6n.
Church Langton (Leics), ch. of 87
Churchill (Oxon), ch. of 149, 276, 278
– tithes of 274
Cirencester (Glos), Aug. abbey of 42
Cîteaux (Côte-d'Or) p. 211
Claindon', see Steeple Claydon
Clairmarais (Pas-de-Calais) p. 211

Clairvaux (Aube) p. 211
Clapham, Clopham (Beds), chapel of 30
Clare, Clara, Gilbert de, earl of Hertford
    app. I(XVIII)
Claybrooke, Claybroke (Northants), ch. of
    139, app. II(11); rector of, see Peter
Claydon, see Steeple Claydon
Claypole, Claipol', Cleipol (Lincs), mediety
    of ch. of 17; rector of, see W.
Clee, Old (Lincs/Humb), ch. of Holy Trinity
    & St Mary app. II(28), p. 209
Clement V, pope 234n.
Clement, William, bp's chaplain app.
    I(VIIIW)
Clenefeld', see Glenfield Frith
Clere, Robert de 211W
Clinton, Geoffrey de 61, 75n., app. I(II)
Clopham, see Clapham
Clopton, Cloptona (Northants), ch. of 170
– William of 155
Cluny (Sâone et Loire) p. 211
Cnotting', see Knotting
Cockayne Hatley, see Hatley
Cockerington (Lincs) app. I(IV)
    see also Calvecroft grange
– , North (Lincs), ch. of St Mary 4
– , South (Lincs), ch. of St Leonard 4
Code, Robert app. I(XXI)
Codesdone, see Cuddesdon
Cogenhoe (Northants), Henry of 130
Coggeshall, Ralph 97n.
Colchester, Col', Colecestr' (Essex), Ben.
    abbey of 229, 230
Cold Ashby, Coldesseby (Northants), chapel
    of 50; vicar of 50
Cold Overton, Caldoverton' (Leics), ch. of
    246
– tithes of 130
Coleby, Koleby (Lincs), app. I(IXn.)
– Simon of, vicar of Nocton 269n.
Colecestr', see Colchester
Coleville, Colevill, family 6n.
– Henry de 231
– Philip de 6n.
Colewrda, Colewrthe, see Culworth
Colmworth (Beds) 29
– chaplain of, see William
Colonna, Columpna, Peter de, canon of
    Lincoln and prebendary of Decem
    Librarum 259
Combe, Kim' (Warw), abbot of, see Henry
Conan son of count Henry of Goëllo 223n.
Constable, Alice la 86
Constance, prioress of Stainfield 291n.
Cople (Beds), ch. of 41
Corby, Corbi (Northants), third part of ch.
    of 187, 188
Corlinstog', (?Costock, Notts), R. de, rector
    of fifth portion of the ch. of Loughborough
    app. II(20)
Cornwall, John of xxiv

Cornwell (Oxon), ch. of 60, 63
Cotes-by-Stow (Lincs), ch. of 208
Coteshmore, see Cottesmore
Cothingham, see Cottingham
Cottesmore, Coteshmore, Cotteshmor'
    (Leics) 179
Cottingham, Cothingham (Northants), ch. of
    156
Cotun(a), see Nun Cotham
Couleia, see Cowley
Coutances (Manche), John of, archdn of
    Oxford, later bp of Worcester 59, 69, 80n.,
    142n; dean of Rouen and prebendary of
    Grantham (in Salisbury cathedral) 69
– Walter of, bp of Lincoln, later archbp of
    Rouen xxiii, xxx, xxxi, xl, 20n., 39, 44n.,
    96n., 199n., 203n.,217n., 224n., 248n.,
    258n., 269n., app. I(XXIV, XXV)
Couture, La, Cultura (Le Mans, Sarthe),
    Ben. abbey of 232, p. 210
Coventry, bp of, see Muschamp, Geoffrey
– prior of app. II(5)
– priory of 43, app. II(49)
Cowley, Couleia (Oxon), ch. of 144
– tithes of 274
Crakethweit (? in Aby, Lincs) 70
Cran', see Cranwell
Cranel', Alexander de, rector of Great
    Harrowden 192
Cranewell', see Cranwell
Cranfield (Beds), ch. of 157
Cranford, Craneford' (Northants), ch. of 133
Cranoe (Leics), ch. of app. II(22); rector of,
    see G.
Cranwell, Cran', Cranewell' (Lincs), mediety
    of ch. of 12; rector of, see Neville, Walter
    de; vicar of, see Stainby, William of;
    vicarage of 12
Crawley, Little, Parva Crawleia (Bucks),
    mediety of chapel of 127
Crawley, North, Magna Crawleia (Bucks) 4th
    part of ch. of 127
Creis (in Brackley, Northants) 24
Crevequer, Daniel de 85
Croft (Leics), ch. of app. II(15); rector of,
    see Peter
Croft (Lincs) 16
Crowland, Croiland' (Lincs), Ben. abbey of
    St Guthlac 44–47, 233, 234; abbot of 284,
    and see Edward; Henry
Croxden (Staffs), abbot of 179n.
Croxhag' (?in Aby, Lincs) 70
Croxton, Croxtun (Lincs/Humb), ch. of 271
– Robert son of Richard of 271
Cruce Roys, see Royston
Cuchewald, see Cuxwold
Cuddesdon, Codesdone (Oxon) 3, 274
Cuddington (Bucks), chapel of 161
Cultura, see Couture, La
Culworth, Colewrda, Colewrthe (Northants),
    ch. of 31

– Robert son of William of 31
– Thomas son of William of 31n.
Cumberworth, Cumbrewrd' (Lincs), ch. of
70
Cumin, John, archbp of Dublin 179n.
Curenn', William de app. I(XXIIW)
Cuxwold, Cuchewald (Lincs), ch. of 138;
vicarage of 138
Cyrencestr', I. 8

D

Dachewrd', see Datchworth
Dalderby, John, bp of Lincoln 84n., 121n.,
app. I(IIIn.)
Damian, mr 188AW
Dar', Walter app. I(XIIW)
Datchworth, Dachewrd' (Herts), ch. of app.
I(XX); rector of, see Ilchester, Richard of;
vicar of, see Elias; vicarage of app. I(XX)
Daventry, Daventre, Davintr' (Northants),
Clun, priory of xxxiii, 48–50
David, mr 139W
– archdn of Buckingham 78n., app.
I(XXIIn.)
– chaplain app. I(XXIIW)
– earl of Huntingdon 72, 130, 131n.
– I, king of Scotland 60, 131
Davintr', see Daventry
Decem Librarum, prebend of (in Lincoln
Cathedral) 242n., 246n., 251n., 255n., 259,
274n., 299n.; prebendary of, see Buckden,
Alan of; Colonna, Peter de; Trou, Simon
de; William son of Fulk
Deene, Dene (Northants), ch. of 209; rector
of, see Edmund; vicar of see Simon;
vicarage of 209
Deeping, Dep', Depighe, Deping(e),
Depingis, Depyng', Dyeping', Geoffrey of
xxv, xxvii, witness: (no description) 2, 11,
13, 15, 17, 56, 61, 62, 71, 105, 134, 207,
208, 210; ?archdn of Bedford 10n., 232,
239, 253, 266, 285; canon of Lincoln 3, 14,
73, 132, 159, 177, 179, 187, 204; precentor
of Lincoln 10n., 223
Dene, Godfrey de la 211W
Dene, see Deene˙
Denton (Oxon) 274
Depighe, Deping(e), Depingis, Depyng', see
Deeping
Derby, Dereby, Roger of, canon of Lincoln
95, 101
'Derfletescroft' (?Lincs) 16
Derleig', Derl', mr Nicholas de 77W, 173W
Derwennehill' (?in Aby, Lincs) 70
Diceto, Dici, Disci, Ralph de, rector of
Aynho, later dean of St Paul's, London
204, app. I(XXIIn.); archdn of Middlesex
app. I(VIIIW, XXIIW, XXIIIW)
Dinton, Dunington' (Bucks), ch. of 67, 242

Disci, see Diceto
Dive, Diva, Guy de 179
– Hugh de 187
– Matilda de 187, 188
Doddeford', see Dodford
Doddington, Dudington' (Lincs), ch. of 210;
rector of, see Westminster, Nicholas of;
vicar of, see Alexander, archdn of the West
Riding alias Stow; vicarage of 210
Doddington, Great (Northants), tithes of 130
Dodeford', see Dodford
Dodestorp, see Dogsthorpe
Dodford, Dudeford', Dodeford, Doddeford'
(Northants), ch. of St Mary 114
– mr Richard of 49W, 115W, 130W
Dogsthorpe, Dodestorp (Northants/Cambs)
155, 156
Dorchester (Oxon), abbot of, see Eustace
Dorobernia, Walter de, Templar app. I(IX)
Doudeauville (Pas-de-Calais), abbot of 122,
and see Peter
Dover (Kent) pp. 209, 211
– Richard of, archbp of Canterbury xxxvi,
40A, 44n., 133n., 163n., 278, app. I(II)
Drax (Yorks W.R./N. Yorks), Aug. priory of
51, 235, 236
Druel, William 265
Dryburgh, Adam of 213A
Dublin, archbp of, see Cumin, John
Dudeford', see Dodford
Dudington', see Doddington
Duneston', see Dunston
Dunigtune, Dunington', see Dinton
Dunstable, Dunestapl(e), Dunnestapel',
Dunst', Dunstapull' (Beds), Aug. priory of
52, 53, app. II(50); prior of 284
– Robert of witness: 71, 105, 132, 187, 207
Dunston, Duneston' (Lincs), ch. of 129,
267, 268; vicar of 129, and see Aresci,
Wiliam de; Vacarius
– land in app. I(IX)
Durford (W. Sussex), abbot of 179n.
Durham, archdn of, see Aimeric
– bp of, see Puiset, Hugh du
– ch. of St Nicholas xxiiin.; rector of, see
Blois, William de
– priory of 237; prior of, see Bertram; monk
of, see Radinge, John de
Duston (Northants), ch. of 133
Dyeping', see Deeping

E

Eafeld, see Eastfield
Earls Barton (Northants), tithes of 130
Easby, sancta Agatha de Richem', Rich'
(Yorks N.R./N. Yorks), Prem. abbey of 54,
55, 238; abbot of, see Ralph
Easington, Esendon' (Oxon), ch. of 243
Eastfield, Eafeld (in Peterborough,
Northants/Cambs) 156

East Halton, *see* Halton, East

East Kirkby, *see* Kirkby

East Rasen, *see* Market Rasen

East Wykeham, *see* Wykeham, East

Easton-on-the-Hill (?), Estona (Northants), ch. of 156

Eastry (Kent), ch. of 32; rector of, *see* St Martin, Ralph of

Eatun, Etun' (unidentified), tithes of 229

Eatune, Henry de 67W

Eboraco, *see* York

Ecton (Northants), Stephen of, rector of Shillington 158

Edelberg', *see* Edlesborough

Edenestow(a), *see* Edwinstowe

Edenham (Lincs), ch. of 27

Edinburgh, Aug. abbey of Holyrood 56

Edith, widow 150

Edlesborough, Edelberg' (Bucks), ch. of 11, 16, 219; rector of, *see* Beauchamp, Simon de; vicarage of 219

Edlington (Lincs) 16

– ch. of 16; vicar of, *see* Steeping, Geoffrey of; vicarage of 10

Edmondthorpe (Leics), ch. of app. II(13); rector of, *see* Thomas

Edmund, bp's clerk, rector of Deene 209

Edward, abbot of Crowland app. I(IXW)

– the Confessor, King of England app. I(XIX)

Edwinstowe, Edenestow(a) (Notts), ch. of xxxv, xxxviin., 95n., 101, 106, 107, 260

Eia, *see* Kingsey

Eilesberi, *see* Aylesbury

Einesford, *see* Eynsford

Eisseby, *see* Ashby Folville

Elias, canon of Bridlington 26W

– vicar of Datchworth app. I(XX)
   see also Helias

Eliden', *see* Hellidon

Elkington, South (Lincs), ch. of All Saints 141

Elnestow(e), *see* Elstow

Elsfield (Oxon), chapel of 274

Elstow, Alnest' Alnestouu(e), Alnestow(e), Aunest', Elnestow(e), Halnerstowe, Halnestowe, Haunestou' (Beds), Ben. abbey of 57, app. I(I); abbess of, *see* Mabilia

– mr Alexander of xxv, xxvii, witness: (no description), 17, 61, 122, 166, 239; canon of Lincoln 14, 80, 177, 242, 251, 274, 279, 285; archdn of Bedford 279n., 285n., 298

– mr Simon of 298W

Elton (Hunts/Cambs), ch. of 157

Ely (Cambs), bp of, *see* Eustace; Longchamp, William de

– prior of 234n.

– William of, king's treasurer, rector of Surfleet 290

Emma, wife of William son of Helias 144,

146n.
   see also Waterperry, Emma of

Enderbi, *see* Wood Enderby

Engaine, Robert 72

Enganet, Roger 212W

Erareker (? in Aby, Lincs) 70

Ernald, abbot of Rievaulx 25

Erningworde, *see* Arthingworth

Ernulph, bp of Rochester 161

Esendon', *see* Easington

Esford' (? Asfordby, Leics), dean of, *see* Peter

Esseby, *see* Canons Ashby

Essex, earl of, *see* FitzPeter, Geoffrey

Estona, *see* Easton-on-the-Hill

Estona, Richard de 237n.

Estun' (unidentified), tithes of 229

Estvic, *see* Astwick

Estwerde, *see* Astwood

Estwic, *see* Astwick

Eton', *see* Nuneaton

Ettoneston', Hugh de 3W

Etun', *see* Eatun

Eudo the provost (?of Lincoln) 253W

Eugenius III, pope 16n.

Eustace, abbot of Dorchester 143n., 241W

– bp of Ely 32–8, 221, 222, 247n.

– clerk (? of Wilton) 80W, 174W

– priest of Godstow 67W

Evermue, Jollan de 71

– Reyner de 71

– Walter de xxxix, 71

Eversholt (Beds) 265

Everton (Beds), ch. of St Mary 168

Evington, Evinton', Evyngton' (Leics) 286, app. I(XVI)

Évreux(?), (Eure), precentor of, *see* Warin

Ewerby, Iwardebi, Iwardeby, Iwareb', Ywardbi (Lincs), Gilbert of 228W, 229W, 246W, 274W, 299W

– R. of app. II(53)

Exchequer, barons of the xxxiv, 192
   see also Scaccario

Exeter, bp of, *see* Bartholomew; Brewer, William; Marshal, Henry

Exton (Rutl/Leics), ch. of 130

Eye, Eie (in Peterborough, Northants/Cambs) 156
   see also Aia

Eynesbury (Hunts/Cambs), ch. of 239

Eynsford, Aignesford, Einesford (Kent), ch. of 32n., 33; rector of, *see* Canterbury, John of

– William of 72

Eynsham (Oxon) 59, p. 208

– Ben. abbey of xxxiv, 59–64, 240, 241; abbot of p. 210, *and see* Robert

– ch. of 60

– parish of 59, 62

– Adam of xxi, xxvi, xxvii, xxviii, xl, 111n., 120n., 206n., p. 208

F

Falueslei, *see* Fawsley
Farforth, Farford' (Lincs) 70
Fawsley, Falueslei (Northants), ch. of 48
Fenne, Ralph de 185, 186; daughter of, *see* Rochford, Albreda of
Ferham (? in Brackley, Northants) 24
Ferihi, *see* Ferriby, South
Feringes, Theobald de 212W
Ferriby, South, Feribi, Suthferiby (Lincs/ Humb), mediety of ch. of 27, app. I(XXI)
Ferté-Bernard, La (Sarthe) p. 209
Filey, Fiuel(e) (Yorks E.R./N. Yorks) 25
Fingest, Tingherst, Tinghirst' (Bucks), Richard of 3W, 73W, 251W
Firsby (Lincs), ch. of 16
– land in 16
Fiskerton, Fiskert', Fiskertona, Fiskertun', Fiskint', Fiskton', Fiskyrton', Fyxkerton' (Lincs), ch. of 156
– Thomas of xxvii, xxviiin., witness: (no description) 297, canon of Lincoln 219, 223, 225, 228–30, 242–4, 246, 251, 253, 255, 259, 268, 273, 274, 282, 285, 286, 290, 294, 298 300
FitzGerald, Warin 23
FitzHamon, Robert 194
FitzNeal, Richard, bp of London 214; dean of Lincoln app. I(XXIVn.)
FitzPeter, Geoffrey, earl of Essex 245
FitzRalph, Robert, archdn of Nottingham, later bp of Worcester 142n.
Fiuel(e), *see* Filey
Flamang, Robert 156
Flèche, La (Sarthe) p. 210
Fleet, Flet (Lincs), ch. of 39
Flore, Flora (Northants), ch. of 119
– tithes of 130
Folevil(l)e, Ralph de 84
Foliot(h), Jordan app. I(XIIn.)
– Robert, archdn of Oxford app. I(VIIn., XVn.)
– William app. I(XIII)
Folkingham (Lincs), ch. of 16
– land and tithes in 16
Fontevrault (Maine-et-Loire), Ben. abbey of p. 210
Ford, mr Ralph de 115W
Fordington, Fordingt' (Lincs), parson of, *see* Ralph
– Ralph of 14W
Forest Hill, Forstella (Oxon), chapel of 144
– land in 274
Fosse (Lincs), Cist. priory of 201n.
Foston (Leics), ch. of app. II(9); rector of, *see* Hinglesham, William de
Fotherby (Lincs), ch. of St Mary 141
Fotheringhay (Northants), tithes of 130
Fountains (Yorks W.R./N. Yorks), Cist. abbey of app. I(IV)

Foxley, Foxle (Northants), tithes of 130
– Richard 130
France p. 208
– king of, *see* Philip II
Freemantle (Hants) 215n.
Freiston, (Lincs), Ben. priory of 65
– William of 4n.
Frethegestahac, *see* Kirkby Underwood
Frisby-on-the-Wreak, Friseby (Leics), ch. of St Guthlac 84, app. I(III)
Friskney (Lincs), mediety of ch. of All Saints 28
Fritwell (Oxon), ch. of 274
Frivill', Drogo de 6W
Fryseby, mr William de 207W
Fulk, rector of Whaplode 44
Fulletby (Lincs), third part of ch. of St Andrew 28
Furmentin, William, rector of Norton by Twycross app. II(26)
Fyxkerton', *see* Fiskerton

G

G., rector of Cranoe app. II(22)
– rector of Knossington app. II(55)
Gaddesden, Little, Catesden', Gatesden' (Herts), ch. of 133
Gah', *see* Gaherst
Gaham, Reginald de, rector of Knipton app. II(25)
Gaherst, Gah', mr Hugh de app. I(XXIIW, XXIIIW)
Gait, le Gay, Gay(t), Robert 144, 145
Gamaliel, rector of Noseley 299W
Gant, Gaunt family 14n.
– Alice de, countess (of Lincoln) 174
– Gilbert I de, earl (of Lincoln) 11, 13–6, 219n.
– Gilbert de (another) 13n.
– Robert de 13n., 16
– Walter de 16, 27
Gargat(e), Robert 155
– Roger 120
Garsington (Oxon) 274
Garthorpe, Garthorp' (Leics), ch. of 235, 236; rector of, *see* Kirmond, Peter of
Gaunt, *see* Gant
Gay(t), *see* Gait
Geddington (Northants) pp. 208, 209
Gedney, Gedeneye (Lincs), ch. of 44n., 45, 46; vicar of 45
– tithes of 45
Gene, Genn', Roger de, rector of Addlethorpe 183
Geoffrey app. I(XVIIW)
– abbot of Chester 243
– archdn (?of Bedford) 232W
– brewer 155
– chief forester app. II(37)

– clerk of the abbot (of Bardney) 11W, 13W–15W
– dean (?of Stamford) 188AW
– dean of Stamford 187W
– king's chaplain, rector of mediety of ch. of Ulceby 207
– notary 120W, 121W
– prior of Alvingham app. I(VI)
– rector of Whaplode 44
– son of Geoffrey 155
Gernon, Gernun, family 168n.
– Richard 3
Giffard, Walter, earl of Buckingham 120, app. I(XV)
Gilbert, clerk 251W
– subdean of Lincoln 286n., 290n., 294n.
– Templar app. I(IX)
Gildeburg', see Guilsborough
Gilevill', Gilewill', mr Henry de, canon of Lincoln 79W, 80W, 228W, 239Wn.
Gippolf 16
Glaest', see Glaston
Glamford', mr Robert de 188AW
Glanvill, Gilbert, bp of Rochester 216n., 221, 222
Glaston, Glaest' (Rutl/Leics), ch. of St Andrew 84
Glatton (Hunts/Cambs), ch. of 122
Glemesford, Robert de 282W
Glenfield Frith, Clenefeld' (Leics), ch. of 286, app. I(XVI)
– Gilbert of 299W
Glentham, Glenham (Lincs), mediety of ch. of 100, 262
– Alfred of 100, 262
– Geoffrey of 100, 262
– Gilbert of 100, 262
Glentworth, Glentewrd', Glenworhe (Lincs), ch. of St Michael 123, 124
Glintona, John de 156
Gloucester, Glocestria, Gloucestr', Ben. abbey of 66; abbot of, see Thomas
– earl of 194, and see also William
– Mr Hugh of 232; rector of Little Woolstone and Toddington 243W
Goddington (Oxon), ch. of 57
Godfrey, bp of Winchester, see Lucy, Godfrey de
Godric, priest, rector of St Michael, Cornstall, Stamford app. I(XVII)
Godstow, Godestow(e) (Oxon), Ben. abbey of St Mary and St John the Baptist xxxviii, 67, 68, 211, 242, 243, p. 209
– priests of, see Eustace; Pain; Thomas; Waleran
Goëllo (Côtes-du-Nord), see Alan son of count Henry; Conan son of count Henry
Goldewelle (in Brackley, Northants) 24
Goldington (Beds), ch. of 265
Goslenus, prior of Spalding, see Jollanus
Goulet, Le (Seine-Maritime) p. 211

Goxhill, Gousl(a) (Lincs), ch. of 26; perpetual farmer of, see Hardres, Robert de
Grainsby, Grenesbi (Lincs), Eudo of 70
– Ralph of 70
Grande Chartreuse, La (Isère) p. 211
Grantham (Lincs)
– Borealis prebend (in Salisbury cathedral) 69; prebendary of, see Coutances, John of; Ingoldesby, William of
Grava, Grave, see Grove
Gravenhurst (Beds), chapel/ch. of 158, 265, 266; vicar of, see Bueles, Simon de
Gravesend, Richard, bp of Lincoln xlin., xlii, 19n., 44n., 84n., app. I(IIIn.); seal of 70n.
Gray, John de, bp of Norwich 221, 222, 247n.
– Walter de, archbp of York 252n.
Great Barford, see Barford, Great
Great Barton, see Barton, Great
Great Doddington, see Doddington, Great
Great Hale, see Hale, Great
Great Harrowden, see Harrowden, Great
Great Limber, see Limber, Great
Great Marlow, see Marlow, Great
Great Paxton, see Paxton, Great
Great Steeping, see Steeping, Great
Great Sturton, see Sturton, Great
Greenfield, Grenefeld' (Lincs), Cist. priory of xlii, 70, 244
Grenesbi, see Grainsby
Grenoble (Isère) p. 211
Grikke, Godwin 218n.
Grim, mr Richard, canon of Lincoln 61W, 90W, 148W, 204W
Grimoldby (Lincs), ch. of St Edith 141
Grimsby, Grimesbi, Grimesby (Lincs/Humb), Aug. abbey of 25, app. I(XXIn.); abbot of, see Richard
– Little, ch. of St Saviour 141
Grip, Robert, knight 155, 156
Groby (Leics) app. I(XVI)
Grosseteste, Grosteste, Mr Robert 130W; bp of Lincoln xxxi, 130n., app. I(Xn.)
Grove, Grava (in Evenley, Northants) 24
Grove, Grave (Oxon), tithes of 3
Gualo, abbot of Revesby (St Laurence) app. I(IXW)
Guilsborough, Gildeburg' (Northants) 179
Guisborough, Giseburn (Yorks, N.R./Cleveland), Aug. priory of xxxiii, 198
Guneben 70
Gunthorpe, Gunetorp (Northants/Cambs) 156
– Ivo of, knight 155
Gunnes 16

H

H., dean of Lincoln, see Hamo
– prior of Bridlington 198, 205W

Habrough, Haburg', Haburc (Lincs/Humb),
ch. of St Margaret 123, 124
Hackthorn (Lincs), mediety of ch. of St
Michael 28
Haddenham (Bucks), ch. of 81n., 161
Hag', see Haugh
Haggehurste, Hauggehurst, William de 211W
Hagworthingham (Lincs) 16
– ch. of 16
Haket, Beatrice 202n.
– Roland 202n.
Hale, Great, Hale (Lincs), ch. of 13, 16;
rector of, see Lacy, Gilbert de; vicarage of
218
– chaplain of, see Ralph
Halebode (?Halbotfen, Northants) 155
Halhton', see Hallaton
Haliwell, see London
Halnerstowe, Halnestowe, see Elstow
Hallaton, Halhton' (Leics), ch. of 85; vicar
of, see Benjamin
Halse, Alsavia, Halsow (Northants) 24
Halton, Halt', Gilbert de 13W, 15W
Halton, East, Halt', Hauton (Lincs/Humb),
ch. of St Peter 123, 124
Halton (Holgate) (Lincs) 16
Hambleden (Bucks), ch. of 194, 195; rector
of, see Bardolf, Robert
Hambleton, Hameldon', Hameledune
(Rutl/Leics), ch. of 212
Hamby, Walter de 197n., 295n.
Hameldon', Hameledune, see Hambleton
Hamelin the dean 4n., 141W, 171W
Hamerton, Hamertun' (Hunts/Cambs) 72,
229
– Clementia of 72
Hamo, archdn of Leicester xxv, 43W, 131W;
dean of Lincoln 12n., 25n., 43n., 47n.,
131n., 181n., app. II(35); witness: 2, 4, 8,
10–16, 20, 40, 41, 53, 60, 68, 70, 71, 77,
78, 84, 85, 102–5, 110, 117, 123, 141, 145,
146, 150, 154–8, 160, 165, 172–7, 188A,
191, 196, 205, 207, 244
– – clerk of, see William
– precentor of York 25
– son of Meinfelin 114
Hampton Gay, Hamton' Gaitorum (Oxon),
ch. of 144, 145, 274n.
Hampton Poyle, Philipeshamton' (Oxon), ch.
of 274
Hanging Houghton (by Lamport)
(Northants), tithes of 130
Hardelistorp, see Addlethorpe
Hardingstone (Northants), ch. of 130
Hardres, Ardr', Hard', Hardra, Hardre,
Hardrie (Kent), Richard de 26W, 212W
– Robert de xxvi, (no description) witness:
28, 130, 145, 146, 165, 178, 209; archdn of
Huntingdon xxvi, 5n., 44n., 130n., 145n.,
165n., witness 8, 10, 11, 13, 15, 26, 27, 39,
47, 50, 56, 78, 90, 102, 104, 117, 118,

122–4, 166, 174, 176, 188A, 196, 208, 212,
228; canon of Lincoln 44n., 199n.; farmer
of ch. of Goxhill 26; parson of Stainton le
Vale 5; vicar of Surfleet 290; vice-archdn of
Lincoln xxvi, 5n., 44n., 199n.
– – clerk of, see Luke
see also Hayden
Hardwick (Bucks), ch. of 21, 22, 22A, 226;
rector of, see Novo Mercato, James de;
Peverel, Hugh; vicar of, see Richard
Hareng, Walchelin 60
Harlestone (Northants), tithes of 130
Harmston (Lincs) app. I(IXn.)
Harpin, prior of Royston 162
Harringworth (Northants), tithes of 130
Harrold (Beds), Aug. priory of 72n.
Harrowden, Great, Harwedon' (Northants),
ch. of 192; rector of, see Cranel', Alexander
de; vicar of, see Helias
– tithes of 130
Hartshill, William of app. II(38)
Hartsholme (Lincs) 16
Harwedon', see Harrowden, Great
Hastings, Richard of, master of the Templars
in England app. I(IX)
Hatcliffe, Haudclive (Lincs/Humb), ch. of
223
Hathern, Hathurn (Leics), ch. of 88A; vicar
of, see T.
Hatley (Cockayne) (Beds), ch. of 126; vicar
of, see Tawell, Alan de
Haudclive, see Hatcliffe
Hauggehurst, see Haggehurste
Haugh, Hag' (Lincs) 70
– Amfred of 70
Haume, La (in Maxey, Northants/Cambs),
tithes of 153
Haunestou', see Elstow
Hautebarg(e), see Alkborough
Hauton, see Halton, East
Havedic (in Mumby, Lincs) 70
Hawerby, Hawaudebi (Lincs/Humb) ch. of
223
Hayden (?Hardres), Richard de, vicar of
Timberland 199
– Robert de, official of the bishopric of
Lincoln sede vacante 199
Haye-des-Bons-Hommes, La (France) p. 210
Haynes (Beds), ch. of 41
– tithes of 265
Hayrun, Alban 116
Headington (Oxon), chapel of 274
Heather (Leics), ch. of app. II(52); rector
of, see Thomas
Heckington, Hekington' (Lincs), ch. of 13n.,
14–6; rector of, see Rolleston, Roger of
Hehham, Simon dean of 10W
Heiford, see Heyford, Upper
Heigham, Nicholas, dean of Lincoln 105n.
Helias, mr. rector of Melton Mowbray 89
– son of William son of Acard 237

- vicar of Great Harrowden 192
  see also Elias
Hellidon, Eliden' (Northants), chapel of 40
Helpston, Helpestona (Northants/Cambs),
  Roger of 156
- Waleran of 156
Hemingford Abbots (Hunts/Cambs), ch. of
  St Margaret 159; vicar of, see Aristotle
Hemington, Hemmingtona (Northants), ch.
  of 170
Henry I, king of England 170n., 275n., app.
  I(IV, Xn., XIV)
- II, king of England 6n., 8n., 41n., 48n.,
  52n., 67, 144, 163, 188An., 207n., 242,
  app. I(In., IX, XIIn., XIV), p. 210
- - chaplain of, see Geoffrey
- - constable of, see Humet, Richard de
- III, king of England xxx, 71n.
- VIII, king of England app. I(I)
Henry, mr. app. I(XXW)
- abbot of Combe app. I(VIIIW)
- abbot of Crowland 44n., 46
- archdn of Stafford, rector of Hughenden 78
- bp of Bayeux 167n.
- clerk of Paston 155
- cook 155
- rector of Thurlaston app. II(16)
- son of Peter 130W, 131W; rector of St
  Peter, Northampton 132
- son of Walkelin, rector of a mediety of
  Sheepy app. II(18)
Herbert, archdn of Canterbury, see Poer,
  Herbert
- bp of Salisbury, see Poer, Herbert
- clerk, of Burwell 171W
- prior of St Neot's 60W
- prior of Ware 299
- son of Alard 16
- son of Matthew 197
Hereford, bp of, see Braose, Giles de
Heregereshag' (?in Rigsby, Lincs) 70
Herleham (in Withern, Lincs) 70
Herlesham (?in Brackley, Northants) 24
Hermeric, see Aimeric
Hertford p. 211
- earl of, see Clare, Gilbert de
Hethe, Hethre, Hethra (Oxon), ch. of 80
Heyford, Richard of 130
Heyford, Heiford (?Northants or Oxon), mill
  of 133
Heyford, Lower (Oxon), ch. of 60, 63
Heyford, Upper, Heiford, Heyford Warren
  (Oxon), manor of 23; lord of, see Insula,
  Robert de
Heyford Warren, see Heyford, Upper
Heynings, Heyninges (Lincs), Cist. priory of
  71
Hibaldstow (Lincs/Humb), mr Warin of,
  official of archdn of Bedford 72
High Toynton, see Toynton, High
Higham on the Hill (Leics), ch. of app.

II(54); rector of, see Richard
Hillegha, Simon de, rector of Stanground
  196
Hinchingbrooke (Hunts/Cambs), Ben. priory
  of St James 72, 73
Hinglesham, William de, rector of Foston
  app. II(9)
Hinton, Helias de 24
Histon (Cambs), knights' fees in 7
Hoby, Hugh de 27W
Hoiland', mr Gerard de 89W
Holcote (Beds), ch. of 265
Holegate (? in Leicester) 286, app. I(XVI)
Holewell', see Hollowell
Holles, Gervase app. I(VIIIn., XXIn.)
Hollowell, Holewel' (in Guilsborough,
  Northants) 179
Holm(e), Robert de, canon of Lincoln 300W
  see also Hulmo
Holwell (Leics), Simon of 265
Holyrood, see Edinburgh
Hommet, see Humet
Honington (Lincs) 189n.
Honorius III, pope xxxi, 46n., 277n.
Hontindon', see Huntingdon
Hook Norton, Okenarton' (Oxon), ch. of
  144, 273
Horncastle, Hornecastr' (Lincs), chapelry of
  74; rector of, see Bisshoppesdun, Osbert de
Horsington (Lincs), ch. of 245; rector of, see
  Milai, William de
Horspath (Oxon) 274
Horton, Hortona (Northants), ch. of 133
Hospitali, John de app. I(XXIIIW)
Hospitallers in England, prior and brethren
  of 169, 287n.
Houghton (unidentified), tithes in 264
Houghton (Hunts/Cambs), ch. of 157
Houghton by Lamport, see Hanging
  Houghton
Houghton, Little (Northants), ch. of 130
Houghton Regis (Beds), ch. of 163
Houton', Picot de 70
- Richard de 70
Howell, Huwell' (Lincs), ch. of 16
- Gerard of 17, 69n.
Hugh, mr (? of St Edward) 285W
- abbot of Abingdon 211 and W
- chaplain, canon of Lincoln 3W, 29W, 74W,
  140W, 179W, 212W
- chaplain of Nocton 268W
- prior of Bridlington 25
- prior of Pontefract 214A-C
- rector of Whaplode 44
- rector of Withcote app. II(8)
- son of Gilbert 16
- - brother of, see Ralph son of Gilbert
Hughenden, Uchenden' (Bucks), ch. of 78;
  rector of, see Henry, archdn of Stafford
- Nicholas of 78n.
Hulmo, Robert de 73W

see also Holm(e)

Humberstone, Humbirston', Humbyrston' (Leics) 286, app. I(XVI)

Humet, Hommet, Humez, Agnes de 6n.

– Richard de, constable of Normandy 6n., app. I(XVII)

– William de 179

Humphrey son of William app. I(X)

– subdean of Lincoln app. I(IXW)

Hungary, Hungr', Peter de, canon of Lincoln 159W

Huntingdon, Hontindon', Huntedon', Huntendona 72, 73

– archdn of, *see* Hardres, Robert de; Sigillo, Nicholas de

– archdeaconry of 118

– ch. of St Andrew 157

– earl of, *see* David

– priory of St James outside, *see* Hinchingbrooke

– *procurator vinee regis* of, *see* Robert

Huttoft (Lincs) 16

I

I., chaplain of William de Kaines 298

– prior of Warter 198

– scholar of Northampton 135

Iarum, *see* Yarm

Ibstone (Bucks), ch. of 143; rector of, *see* Richard

Iffley, Iftel', Ivetele, Yifteley (Oxon), ch. of 79, 144

Ilchester (Som), Richard of, archdn of Poitiers and rector of Datchworth app. I(XX); bp of Winchester 139, app. I(XXn., XXII, XXIII)

Ilmer (Bucks), ch. of 292

Ingelram, chaplain 8W, 77W, 148W

– chaplain of the dean of Lincoln xxvi, 122W, 166W

– priest 68W

Ingham (Lincs), ch. of All Saints 28, app. I(VIII)

Ingoldmells (Lincs) 16

Innocent III, pope 2n., 3n., 29n., 32, 36, 206n., 221, 243n., 259, 277n.

Insula, Robert de 174W

– Robert de, lord of Heyford Warren 23n.

Irnham (Lincs) 16

– ch. of 16

Irthlingburgh, Irtlingburch (Northants), ch. of 156

– tithes of 282

Isham (Northants), tithes of 130

Ivetele, *see* Iffley

Ivo son of Schaidman 16

Iwardebi, Iwardeby, Iwareb', *see* Ewerby

J

J., dean of Warwick 42

Jocelin, treasurer of Lincoln 43W

John, king of England xxxviii, 7, 73, 96n., 155n., 167n., 215n., 221, 223, 231n., 247, 267, pp. 210, 211; count of Mortain app. II(36)

– – treasurer of, *see* Ely, William of

John 40B

– I, abbot of Aunay 6

– bp of Norwich, *see* Gray, John de

– canon of Lincoln 172W

– cardinal deacon of St Maria in Via Lata 222

– clerk xxix, 67W

– clerk of Mareham on the Hill 74

– constable of Chester 117

– *de hospitali* app. I(XXIIIW)

– dean of Preston 114W

– sacrist (?of Lincoln cathedral) 102W

– scribe 89W

– son of Simon, rector of High Toynton 74

Joi (France) p. 211

Jollanus, Goslenus, prior of Spalding 183, 184n.

Jordan, son-in-law of Henry de Noers 149

– son of Godric 155

– vicar of Woking 191

'Juel' (unidentified), mill of 265

Jungwine 104, 254

K

Kaanes, *see* Caen

Kaynes, Caignes, Kaines, Hugh de 114n.

– Ralph de 114

– William de, knight 298

– – chaplain of, *see* I.

Keddington (Lincs), ch. of St Margaret 4

Kedelinton', *see* Kidlington

Kelstern, Kellesterne (Lincs), ch. of 198; rector of, *see* T.

Kenilworth, Kenell', Kenill' (Warw), Aug. priory of 75–80, app. I(II); prior of, *see* Robert; Silvester

Kensinton', Henry de 211W

– John de 211W

Kent, Cant', Cantia, Richard of xxv; archdn of Northampton 125n.; subdean of Lincoln 17n., 47n., witness: 3, 29, 50, 62, 73, 79, 80, 125, 126, 140, 179, 206, 212,241

– Theobald of 140W

Kereby, *see* Kirby Frith

Keten(a), *see* Ketton

Keteringe, *see* Kettering

Ketleby, *see* Ab Kettleby

Kettering, Keteringe (Northants), ch. of 156

Ketton, Keten(a) (Rutl/Leics) 179

Keysoe (Beds), ch. of 41

– tithes of 265

Kibworth, W. of, rector of King's Norton app. II(23)

Kibworth Beauchamp (Leics), rector of, *see* Mortimer, H. de; vicar of, *see* W.; vicarage of app. II(24)

Kidlington, Kedelinton' (Oxon), ch. of 144, 273

Killingholme, Kilvingeholm', Kilwingholm (Lincs/Humb), ch. of St Denis 123, 124

Kilworth, South (Leics), ch. of app. II(12); rector of, see Akervill, William de; vicar of, see Reveneys, (blank) le

Kim', see Combe

Kimble (Bucks), ch. of 120, 121

Kime, see Kyme

Kimpton, Kymmiton' (Herts), ch. of 118; vicarage of 118

Kinestorp', see Kingsthorpe

Kingesham (near Brackley, Northants) 24

King's Langley, Langel' (Herts), ch. of 137

King's Norton (Leics), ch. of app. II(23); rector of, see Kibworth, W. of

King's Sutton, Sutun' (Northants), ch. of St Peter 298

King's Walden (Herts), ch. of 116

Kingsey, Kingeseia, Eia (Bucks), ch. or chapel of 81, 161n.; rector of, see Whitefeld, Simon de; vicar of, see William

Kingsthorpe, Kinestorp' (Northants), ch. of 130
– hospital of Holy Trinity 270
– tithes of 156

Kinigt', see Kirmington

Kirby Frith, Kereby (Leics), chapel of 286, app. I(XVI)

Kirkby (? East Kirkby or Kirkby on Bain, Lincs), rector of, see Thomas

Kirkby Laythorpe, Kirkby by Sleaford, Kirkeby (Lincs), ch. of St Peter 9, 174

Kirkby on Bain, see Kirkby

Kirkby Underwood, Kirkeby (Lincs), mediety of ch. of 173
– wood of Frethegestahac 173n.

Kirkham, Kirkeham (Yorks E.R./N. Yorks), Aug. priory of 246

Kirklevington, Levington (Yorks N.R./Cleveland), ch. of 198

Kirkstead, Kirkested', Kyrk' (Lincs), Cist. abbey of St Mary 201n., app. I(IX)

Kirmington, Kinigt', Kirninton' (Lincs/Humb), ch. of St Helen 123, 124

Kirmond, Cheueremund', Cheuremund, Chevermont, Chevermund', Chieueremunt (Lincs), Peter of xxvii, xxviiin.; witness: 219, 223, 228, 230, 243, 273, 274, 286, 290, 297; rector of Garthorpe 235

Kirninton', see Kirmington

Kislingbury (Northants), tithes of 130

Knighton (Leics), manor of 247, 248

Knipton (Leics), ch. of app. II(25); rector of, see Gaham, Reginald de

Knossington (Leics), ch. of app. II(55); rector of, see G.

Knotting, Cnotting' (Beds), ch. of 169, 287; rector of, see Plesset, John de

Koleby, see Coleby

Kyme, Kime, Aug. priory of 82, 249
– Philip of, canon of Lincoln 96
– Philip of (another) app. I(VIII)
– Richard of, canon of Lincoln 175W; treasurer of Lincoln 300W
– Simon of 96
– Simon son of Simon of app. I(VIII)

Kyrk', see Kirkstead

L

La Couture, see Couture, La

La Haume, see Haume, La

La Sauve-Majeure, see Sauve-Majeure, La

Lacy, Laci, Gilbert de, rector of Great Hale 13

Lambeth, Lameh' (London), chapel dispute xli, 36

Landa, see Launde

Langford (Oxon) app. I(XXIV)

Langel', see King's Langley

Langley (Leics), Ben. priory of 83

Langney (in Binsey, Oxon) 274

Langtoft (Lincs), ch. of 233, 234; vicar of, see Maneton, Robert de; Robert; vicarage of 233, 234

Langton, see Church Langton

Langton by Wragby (Lincs), ch. of app. I(VIII)

Lanval, William de, and William his son 230

Lascelles, Lascell', Thomas de, knight 294

Lateran Council, Third (1179) app. II(55); Fourth (1215) 180n.

Laughton by Folkingham (Lincs), ch. of 176

Launde, Landa (Leics), Aug. priory of St John the Baptist 84, app. I(III); prior of, see Walkelin

Laurence app. I(XXW)
– mr app. I(XIIW)
– abbot of Westminster app. I(XX)
– archdn of Bedford 13W, 26W, 27W, 72W, 187W, 205W, app. I(XXIIIW)
– – official of, see Warin

Lavington, Lavingtun' (Lincs), ch. of 190

Lechlade, Lecchelad', Lechelad(e), Lectelad', Lich', Lichel', Lichelad(e), Lychel' (Glos), witness of xxv, witness: (no description) 6, 11, 39–41, 43, 68, 70, 75, 77, 81, 89, 102, 104, 106, 114, 123, 131, 134, 143–7, 160, 171, 174, 205, 208, 209; canon of Lincoln 67, 90, 132, 159, 172, 175, 187, 188A

Ledwell (Oxon), chapel of 144

Lee (Bucks) 120
– ch. of 121

Leeds, Liedes (Kent), Aug. priory of 85

Legbourne (Lincs), Cist. priory of 86
– Amfred of 4n.
– Gilbert son of William of app. II(29)
– William son of Robert of app. II(29)

Legr', *see* Leicester
Lehton', *see* Leighton Bromswold
Leicester, Legr', Leucestr', Leyc' 286, app. I(XVI)
- Aug. abbey of St Mary de Pratis 87, 88, 88A, 247n., 248n., 250; abbot of 88, *and see* Paul; R.
- archdn of, *see* Hamo; Raymond; Rolleston, Roger of
- earl of 286, *and see* Robert (junior and senior)
- - bailiff of app. II(47)
- forest of 286
- Hugh of, sheriff of Northampton 49n.
Leighton Bromswold, Lehton' (Hunts/Cambs), ch. of 102, 252
Lenton (Notts), monks of app. II(9)
Lessay (Manche), Ben. abbey of app. I(X); abbot of app. I(X)
Leucestr', *see* Leicester
Leukenore, *see* Lewknor
Levington, *see* Kirklevington
Lewes (E. Sussex), Clun. priory of xxix, 89, app. I(XI), app. II(56)
Lewknor, Leukenore (Oxon), ch. of 3
- mr Nicholas of 61, 62
Lexington, Henry, bp of Lincoln xxxi
- William, dean of Lincoln 124n., 208n.
Leyc', *see* Leicester
Lich', Lichel', Lichelad(e), *see* Lechlade
Lichfield, Lich' (Staffs), bp of, *see* Muschamp, Geoffrey; Nonant, Hugh de
- cathedral ch., dean and chapter of 90, 251; common fund of 251; treasurer of, *see* Sywell, Simon of
Liedes, *see* Leeds
Limber, Great, Magna Limberga (Lincs), ch. of 6; vicar of, *see* St Edward, Geoffrey of; vicarage of 6
Linchel', mr Richard de 157W
Lincoln app. I(IX), pp. 208, 210–2
- archdn of, *see* Peter
- - vice-archdn of, *see* Hardres, Robert de
- archdeaconry of 259
- bp of, *see* Alexander; Avalon, Hugh of; Bek, Thomas; Bloet, Robert; Blois, William of; Chesney, Robert; Coutances, Walter of; Dalderby, John; Gravesend, Richard; Grosseteste, Robert; Lexington, Henry; Plantagenet, Geoffrey; Sutton, Oliver; Wells, Hugh of
- - household of xxiv-viii
- - Official of the consistory court of app. I(XXII–XXIIIn.)
- bishopric of 111, app. I(XIV); fees of 160, app. I(XIV); manors of 113; vacancy administration of 266, *and see* Alexander; Hayden, Robert de
- cathedral ch. of, dean and chapter of xxiiin., xxxiii, xxxv, xxxviii, 12W, 91–110, 124n., 152W, 154n., 185, 252–62, 268,

271–4, 300, app. I(XXIVn.)
- - canons of 93, 99, 253, 257, *and see* Alexander; Andrew; Avalon, William of; Bardolf, Robert; Bedford, Alexander of; Bedford, Robert of; Bosell', Theobald de; Buckden, Alan of; Capella, Robert de; Colonna, Peter de; Deeping, Geoffrey of; Derby, Roger of; Elstow, Alexander of; Fiskerton, Thomas of; Gilevill, Henry de; Grim, Richard; Holme, Robert de; Hugh; Hungary, Peter of; Kyme, Philip of; Kyme, Richard of; Lechlade, Geoffrey of; Linwood, Richard of; Malberthorp, Gilbert de; Malberthorp, Philip de; Malebisse, Alexander; Mancetter, Robert of; Marin', William de; Ping', Walter de; Ralph *medicus*; Rauceby, Hervey of; Raymond; Rolleston, Roger of; Rowell, Gerard de; St Edmund, Adam of; St Edward, Geoffrey of; St Edward, Hugh of; Sampson; Swalcliffe, Richard de; Sywell, Simon of; Theobald; Trou, Simon de; Vacarius; William son of Fulk
- - chancellor of, *see* Montibus, William de; Swafeld, Stephen de
- - chancellorship of 102, 252
- - common fund of xxxv, 91, 93, 99, 100, 104, 106, 107, 252, 254, 260–2
- - dean of, *see* FitzNeal, Richard; Hamo; Heigham, Nicholas; Lexington, William; Marsh, Robert; Meopham, Richard de; Rolleston, Roger of
- - - chaplain of, *see* Ingelram
- - deanery of 95
- - general fraternity of 97, 258
- - lights of 102, 252
- - prebendal churches of 103
- - prebends of 95, 101, 102, 252; All Saints, Hungate (Lincoln) 255n., *and see* Canwick; Carlton Kyme; Decem Librarum; Marston St Lawrence; Melton Ross; Sutton cum Buckingham
- - precentor of, *see* Almaria, Richard de; Almaria, Roger de; Bedford, Robert of; Blois, William of; Deeping, Geoffrey of
- - precentorship of 103
- - residentiary canons of 106, 107
- - sacrist of, *see* John
- - subdean of, *see* Blois, William of; Bramfeld, William de; Gilbert; Humphrey; Kent, Richard of; Philip; Winemer
- - subdeanery of 102, 252
- - treasurer of, *see* Jocelin; Kyme, Richard of; Martin
- - vicars of 93, 257
- city:
- - bail of 289
- - ch. of All Saints in the Bail 102, 252
- - ch. of Holy Trinity, Wigford 155
- - hospital of St Sepulchre app. I(XIII)
- - parish of St Paul 289

-- Gilb. priory of St Katharine's outside 109, 110, app. I(XII, XIII)
- earl of, see Gant, Gilbert de; Roumare, William de; countess of, see Gant, Alice de
- mr Adam of 165W
- Waleran of 246W
- William of, dean 11W
  see also William son of Fulk of Lincoln
Lindwd', Lindwud, see Linwood
Linford, Little (Bucks), chapel of 127
Linslade (Bucks) 264
- ch. of 41
Linwood, Lindwd', Lindwud' (Lincs), Richard of, canon of Lincoln and prebendary of All Saints, Hungate xxviiin., 255n., 300W
Lissington (Lincs), ch. of 300; vicarage of 300
Litigt' (?), W., dean of 47W
Little Billing, see Billing, Little
Little Bowden, see Bowden, Little
Little Cawthorpe, see Cawthorpe, Little
Little Crawley, see Crawley, Little
Little Gaddesden, see Gaddesden, Little
Little Grimsby, see Grimsby, Little
Little Houghton, see Houghton, Little
Little Linford, see Linford, Little
Little Woolstone, see Woolstone, Little
Loddington, Lodinton' (Northants), ch. of 84, app. I(III)
London, Lond' 135, pp. 209–211
- archdn of, see Burnham, Alard of, and also Middlesex
- bp of, see Belmeis, Richard II; FitzNeal, Richard; Sainte-Mère-Église, William de
- canon of, see Sampson
- Haliwell Aug. priory, Shoreditch 112, 263
- Temple, preceptor of, see Bernewude, William de
- Temple, New 232
- Temple, Old p. 211
- mr Ivo of 282W
- William, clerk, of 206W
  see also Lund'
Long Bennington, see Bennington, Long
Long Buckby, see Bukeb'
Long Sutton, see Sutton, Long
Longchamp, William de, bp of Ely 58
Longthorpe, Thorp (Northants/Cambs) 155
Loughborough (Leics), ch. of app. II(20); rectors of portions of, see Corlinstog', R. de; Verdon, R. de
Louth, Luda (Lincs) 25, app. I(IV)
- Park, Cist. abbey of 113, app. I(IV), app II(31); abbot of, see Ralph; cellarer of, see Michael
Low Toynton, see Toynton, Low
Lower Heyford, see Heyford, Lower
Lucius III, pope 44n., 167n.
Lucy, countess of Chester 189
Lucy, Godfrey de, bp of Winchester 191,

216n.
Luda, see Louth
Ludford Magna (Lincs), ch. of 178
Luffield, Luffeld' (Bucks), Ben. priory of St Mary 114, 115
Lugny (Sâone et Loire) p. 211
Luke 208W
- mr 162W, 172W
- clerk of the archdn of Huntingdon xxvi, 123W, 124W
- ianitor 67W
Lund', mr Gregory app. I(XXIIW)
Lunem, Robert de, Templar app. I(IX)
Lusby (Lincs) 16
- ch. of 16
Luton, Luyton (Beds), ch. of 163
Lutton (Lincs), chapel of 39
Luvel, Walter 130
Luyton, see Luton
Lychel', see Lechlade
Lyme stream (? in Lusby, Lincs) 16
Lyon (Rhône), archbp of, see Canterbury, John of

M

Mabilia, abbess of Elstow 57n.
Mablethorpe, see Malberthorp
Makeseia, see Maxey
Malberthorp, Malbertorp (? Mablethorpe, Lincs), mr Gilbert de xxvii, xxviiin., witness: (no description) 280, 281, 297; canon of Lincoln 223, 225, 228, 230, 242–4, 259, 294
- Philip de, canon of Lincoln 253W
Malcolm IV, king of Scotland 56
Malebisse, Maleb', Alexander, rector of mediety of Belchford and canon of Lincoln 182
Malherbe, Nigel 264
Malling', Peter de app. I(XXIIW)
Malmecestr', see Mancetter
Malton (Yorks N.R./N. Yorks), Gilb. priory of 116, 117
Mancetter, Malmecestr', Mamecestr', Manecestr' (Warw), mr Robert of 166W; archdn of Northampton 232W, 242W, 251W, 275W; canon of Lincoln 74W
Maneton, Robert de, vicar of Langtoft, 234n.
Mans, Le (Sarthe) pp. 209, 210
- abbey of St Peter, see Couture, La
Mansfield (Notts), manor of 106n.
Map, Walter, archdn of Oxford 275W
Mapeham, see Meopham
Mar', see Marum
Mara, Peter de 60
Mareham on the Hill, Maringes (Lincs), ch. of 74; clergy of, see John; Reginald
Marin', William de, canon of Lincoln xxiiin., 282W
Maringes, see Mareham on the Hill

Marinus, clerk of the queen 211W
Market Rasen (Lincs), ch. of St Thomas 178
Market Stainton (Lincs) 16
Markfield, Merkesfeld', Merkenesfeld'
    (Leics) 286, app. I(XVI)
Marlborough (Wilts), Council of (1186) p.
    208
Marlow, Great (Bucks), ch. of 194
Marmiun, Robert 16, 90, 251
Marmoutier (Indre et Loire), Ben. abbey of
    127n.
Marsh, Robert, dean of Lincoln 274n.
Marshal, Henry bp of Exeter 221, 222
Marston (Oxon), chapel of 274
Marston St Lawrence (Northants), prebend
    of (in Lincoln cathedral) app. II(30)
Martin, treasurer of Lincoln app. I(XIIW,
    XVIIW, XXW)
Marton (Lincs), ch. of 109
Marum, Mar', Henry de, nepos of bp William
    289
– mr William de xxiiin., 13W–15W
Matilda, empress 67, 144, 242
Matteker (unidentified) 70
Matthew 3
– abbot of Bardney 10n.
– chaplain 188AW
Mauduyt, Robert 212W
Mauger, mr (? of Newark) app. I(XIIW)
– bp of Worcester 221, 222, 298
Mautune, see Melton Mowbray
Maxey, Makeseia (Northants/Cambs) 156
– ch. of 152; vicarage of 152, 153
Maxilla 40B
Mealton', see Melton Mowbray; Melton Ross
Meaux, Melsa (Yorks E.R./Humb), abbot of,
    see Thomas
Melchbourne (Beds), ch. of 287n.
Melehun, Melhun, see Melun
Meletona, Roger de 156
Melsa, see Meaux
Melton Mowbray, Mautune, Mealton'
    (Leics), mediety of ch. of xxix, 89, app.
    II(56); rector of, see Helias; Meuton,
    Walter de; Nuers, Robert de
Melton Ross, Mealton' (Lincs/Humb), ch.
    and prebend of 105
Melun (Seine et Marne) Melehun, Melhun,
    mr Robert de 130W
Meopham, Mapeham, Mepham (Kent), ch.
    of 32n., 35; rector of, see Virgil
– Richard de, dean of Lincoln 205n., 206n.
Merevale (Warw), Cist. abbey of app.
    I(XXV)
Merk, Eustace de 162
Merkesfeld', Merkenesfeld', see Markfield
Merton (Oxon), ch. of 60
Merton (Surrey), Aug. priory of 118, 119,
    167
Metheringham, Methringham (Lincs) app.
    I(IXn.)

– Robert of, dean 268W
Meulan (Seine et Oise) p. 211
Meuton, Walter de, rector of mediety of
    Melton Mowbray app. II(56)
Michael, cellarer of Louth app. I(IXW)
Midda, Richard, rector of Appleby app.
    II(19)
Middelton, (Milton), Robert de 19n.
Milai, Milay, Rannulf de 245
– William de 245
Milton, see Middelton
Milton Ernest (Beds), ch. of 19; parson of,
    see Bedford, John of; vicarage of 19n.
Missenden (Bucks), Aug. abbey of St Mary
    120–2
– ch. of 120, 121
– William of 120
Moneta, Geoffrey de 232W
Monkton, Muneketune (Kent), ch. of 32n.
Monte, Gilbert de 24
Montibus, Monte, mr William de
    xxv, witness: (no description) 39, 40, 130,
    131, 174, 208; chancellor of Lincoln 13–15,
    17, 20, 27, 41, 47, 156, 159, 175–7, 208n.,
    252, 254
Moppleshauue (unidentified) 156
Mora, Robert de 43W, 209W
Moreton (in Thame, Oxon), knight's fee in
    231
Morin, br., the almoner of the bp xxvii,
    206W
Mortimer, H. de, rector of Kibworth
    Beauchamp app. II(24)
– R. de 64n., 241n.
Moulton (Northants), ch. of 130
Muketon', mr William de 171W
Multifernan (Multyfarnham, Westmeath,
    Ireland), annals of 97n.
Mumby, Munbi (Lincs) 70
– Alan of 70
– Eudo of 70
Muneketune, see Monkton
Munfichet, Gilbert de 168
– Richard de 168
– William de 168n.
Murdac, Ralph 142, 144, 148
– Reginald 192
Mursley, Muresley (Bucks), ch. of 139
Muschamps, Muschamp, Geoffrey, bp of
    Chester (Coventry and Lichfield) 216n.,
    221, 222
– Mary de 192
– Robert de 192
Musteil, Roger 174

N

N., mr, vicar of Stallingborough app. II(4)
Nailstone (Leics), ch. of app. II(17); rector
    of, see Nicholas
Nehus, see Newhouse

Neuport, *see* Newport Pagnell
Neutona, *see* Wold Newton
Neuuert, *see* Newark
Neville, Neovill', Novilla, Hugh de 174
– Robert de 78W, 188AW
– Walter de 12, 116
Newark, Neuuert (in Peterborough,
    Northants/Cambs) 156
Newark on Trent, Newerc' (Notts), bailiff of
    (?) xxvin.
– castle app.I(XII)
– – chapel of St Philip and St James in app.
    I(XII)
– chaplain of, *see* Walter
– ch. of app. I(XII)
– tolls of app. I(XII)
– Sampson of 11W
    see also Mauger
Newburgh (Yorks N.R./N. Yorks), Aug.
    priory of 146n.
    see also Novo Burgo
Newehus, *see* Newhouse
Newerc', *see* Newark on Trent
Neweton (? Newton le Wold, Lincs) 70
Newhouse, Nehus, Newehus (Lincs/Humb),
    Prem. abbey of St Martial 123, 124
Newington, South (Oxon), ch. of 60,63
Newland (? Lincs/Humb) app. II(31)
Newnham (Beds), Aug. priory of St Paul
    125,126, 239,264–6
Newnham Murren, Niweham (Oxon), ch.
    and tithes of 3
Newport Pagnell, Neuport (Bucks), ch. of
    127
– Ben. priory of St Mary 127, 128; prior
    of 128n.
Newton in Aveland (Lincs), ch. of 130
Newton le Wold, *see* Neweton'
Newton on Trent (Lincs), ch. of 109
Nicholas, archdn of Bedford 52, 131n., 266,
    app. I(XXIIIn.)
– monk and chaplain of Abingdon 211W
– (I), prior of Spalding 154n., 181n., 183n.,
    184n.
– rector of Nailstone app. II(17)
Nigel, dean of Oxford 144W, 147W
Niger, mr Ralph 131W
Niweham, *see* Newnham Murren
Nocton, Noctuna, Noket', Noketon',
    Noketuna (Lincs) app. I(IX)
– chaplain of, *see* Hugh
– ch. of 129, 267; vicar of 129, *and see*
    Aresci, William de; Koleby, Simon de;
    vicarage of 269
– Park, Aug. priory of St Mary 129, 267–9;
    prior of 129n., 266n., *and see* Alan
Noers, Henry de 149, 278
– – nephew of, *see* Jordan
– Juliana de 149, 278
    see also Nuers
Noket', Noketon', Noketuna, *see* Nocton

Nonant, Hugh de, bp of Coventry and
    Lichfield app. II(49)
Norfolc', Stephen de app. I(XXIIW)
Norh'pt', Norh't, *see* Northampton
Norman 70
Normanby, Normannesbi (Lincs), ch. of
    154, 279
Normandy (France) 207n, pp. 209, 210
Normanton on Soar, Normant' super Sor
    (Notts), ch. of 237
North Aston, *see* Aston, North
North Cockerington, *see* Cockerington,
    North
North Crawley, *see* Crawley, North
North Ormsby, *see* Ormsby, North
North Willingham, *see* Willingham, North
Northampton, Norh'pt', Norh't, North'
    213n., 214, app. I(XVIII)
– Aug. abbey of St James xxxv, xxxvi, xlii,
    133, 134, app. I(V); abbot of, *see* Walkelin
– archdn of, *see* Kent, Richard of;
    Mancetter, Robert of; Savaric; Winemer
– chapel of St Thomas 130
– ch. of All Saints 130
– ch. of Holy Sepulchre 130
– ch. of St Bartholomew 130
– ch. of St Edmund 130
– ch. of St Giles 130
– ch. of St Gregory 130
– ch. of St Mary 130
– ch. of St Michael 130
– ch. of St Peter 130, 132; rector of, *see*
    Henry son of Peter; vicarage of 132
– earl of, *see* St Liz, Simon de
– hospital of Holy Trinity outside, *see*
    Kingsthorpe
– Clun. priory of St Andrew 130–2; prior of,
    see Trianel, Robert
– reeve of, *see* Bedford, I. of
– schools of 135; scholars, *see* I. and W.
– sheriff of, *see* Leicester, Hugh of
– synod at 42
– mr Alexander of 132W
Northon (unidentified) 70
Norton, Northona (in Runcorn, Ches), Aug.
    priory of 243
Norton, *see* Chipping Norton
Norton by Twycross (Leics), ch. of app.
    II(26); rector of, *see* Furmentin, William
Norton Disney (Lincs), ch. of 109
Norwich, bp of, *see* Gray, John de; Raleigh,
    William
Noseley, Nouesle (Leics), rector of, *see*
    Gamaliel
Nostell, Nostela, Nostle (Yorks W.R./W.
    Yorks), Aug. priory of St Oswald 136, 137;
    prior of, *see* Ansketil
Notley, Notle, Nutel', Nuttele(ga), Parco
    Nuthel' (Bucks), Aug. abbey of app.
    I(XV); abbot of, *see* R.; Robert
Nottingham p. 209

– archdn of, *see* FitzRalph, Robert
Nouesle, *see* Noseley
Novilla, *see* Neville
Novo Burgo, Robert de 179
 see also Newburgh
Novo Mercato, Henry de 21, 22
– James de 21n., 22, 22A, 226n.; rector of
 Hardwick 22A
– William de 22A
Nuers, mr Robert, de, rector of Melton
 Mowbray 89
 see also Noers
Nun Cotham, Cotun(a) (Lincs/Humb), Cist.
 priory of St Mary 138, 271
Nuneaton, Eton' (Warw), priory of the Order
 of Fontevrault 139, 140, app. I(XXII,
 XXIII)
Nutel', Nuttele(ga), *see* Notley

O

Oadby, Oudebi (Leics), ch. of St Peter 84
Oakham, Ocham, Okham (Rutl/Leics), ch. of
 212
Oakley, Akele (Beds), ch. of 30
Ocham, *see* Oakham
Odell, *see* Wahill(e)
Odo, rector of St Peter, Torksey 201n.
Oilli, Henry I de 144
– Henry de (son of above) 144
– Robert de 144
– Robert de (another) 144
Okenarton', *see* Hook Norton
Okham, *see* Oakham
Old Clee, *see* Clee, Old
Olney, Olneia (Bucks), T., rector of 298W
Ormsby, North (Lincs), ch. of St Helen 141
– Gilb. priory of xxxv, 141
Orston, Oskenton', Oskin(g)ton(a) (Notts),
 ch. of xxxv, xxxviin., 95n., 101, 106, 107,
 260
Osbert, abbot of Stanlow 243
– rector of Horncastle, *see* Bisshoppesdun,
 Osbert de
– rector of Skidbrook 202
Osen', Oseneia, *see* Osney
Osgodby (Lincs) 17
Oskenton', Oskin(g)ton(a), *see* Orston
Osney, Osen', Oseneia (Oxon), Ben. abbey of
 St Mary xxxvii, 79, 142–8, 272, 273; abbot
 of 274; annals of 145n., 146n.; chapel in
 front of abbey gate (St Thomas) 147
Oudebi, *see* Oadby
Oundle, Undele (Northants), ch. of 156
Ouerisby, Ouresbi, *see* Owersby
Overton, *see* Cold Overton
Owersby, Ouerisby, Ouresbi (Lincs), ch. of
 St Martin 162, 285; vicar of 162
Owston (Leics), abbot of app. II(23)
Oxendon (Northants), ch. of 42
– Philip son of Richard of 42

Oxford, Oxeneford', Oxinefordia, Oxonf', 67,
 68, app. II(43), pp. 209, 210, 212
– archdn of, *see* Coutances, John of; Foliot,
 Robert; Map, Walter
– archdeaconry of 3
– castle 144
– chapel of Holy Trinity 274
– chapel of St Clement 274
– ch. of All Saints 275, 276; vicar of 275
– ch. of St Aldate's 274
– ch. of St Ebbe 60
– ch. of St Edward 274
– ch. of St George 144
– ch. of St Giles 67, 242
– ch. of St Martin 3
– ch. of St Mary 68; rector of, *see* Bridport,
 John of
– ch. of St Mary Magdalen 144
– ch. of St Michael at the North Gate 274,
 277; vicar of 277
– ch./chapel of St Michael at the South Gate
 150, 274; vicar of, *see* Rolleston, Hugh of;
 vicarage of 150
– ch. of St Mildred 274
– ch. of St Peter ad Castrum (le Bailey) 274
– Council of (1197) 111n.
– dean of, *see* Nigel
– Aug. priory of St Frideswide's 144, 149,
 150, 274–8
– vice-archdn of, *see* Aylesbury, Richard of;
 Richard, mr
Oyry, Oyri family 44n.
– Emecina d' 44n.
– Fulk d' 44n., 45n., 46, 47
– Fulk d' (son of above) 44n.
– Geoffrey d' 44n.
– Geoffrey d' (another) 44n.
– Waleran d' 44n.

P

Packington (Leics), ch. of app. II(5); rector
 of, *see* Castell, W. de
Pain 6W
– priest of Godstow 67W
Painellus, *see* Paynel
Palefridus, Giffard 120
Pant', Jordan de 84
– Philip de 84
Papley, Pappele (Northants), tithes of 156
Papillun, Alnath 193, 293
Pappele, *see* Papley
Parco, Beatrice de 202n.
– Richard de 202
– William de 202n.
Parco Nuthel', *see* Notley
Paris (France) p. 211
– abbey of St Denis p. 211
– schools of xxiiin.
Paris, Parisiis, Peter of 230W
– Peter son of William of, rector of a mediety

of Belchford 182, 184n.
Partney, Parthenay (Lincs) 16
– chapel of St Mary 16
– ch. of St Nicholas 16
– clerk of, see Robert
Parvus, Roger app. I(IXW)
Paston, Pastona (Northants/Cambs), ch. of
  156
– clerk of, see Henry
– tithes of 155
– Ascelin of, knight 155
Pattishall, Pateshill(e), Pateshull', Pateshyll'
  (Northants), dean of, see Roger
– mediety of ch. of 67, 242
– Hugh of 73W
Paul, abbot of Leicester 40W, 88A
Paxton (? Great or Little, Hunts/Cambs) 130
Paxton, Great (Hunts/Cambs), ch. of 56
Paynel, Painellus, Gervase 127n., 139
– Sara 144
– William 144, 236n.
Peakirk, Peichirche (Northants/Cambs), ch.
  of 156
Pentir, William de, vicar of Checkendon 43
Percy, Richard de 291
Persigny (Sarthe), abbey of p. 210
Pery, see Waterperry
Peter 3
– mr app. I(XXW, XXIIW)
– abbot of Doudeauville, and later abbot of
  St John, Valenciennes 122n.
– archdn of Lincoln 13W, 15W
– chaplain of the queen 6W
– clerk 225W, 244W, 259W, 268W, 299W
– dean (of Stamford) app. I(XVII)
– dean of Esford' 89W
– – his brother, see Richard, mr
– rector of Claybrooke app. II(11)
– rector of Croft app. II(15)
– rector of Scraptoft app. II(57)
– vicar of Thornton by Horncastle 90, 251
Peterborough, Burch, Burgo (Northants/
  Cambs) 155, 156, p. 210
– Ben. abbey of 151–6, 170n., 181, 279–83;
  abbot of 284, app. I(Xn.), and see
  Acharius; Benedict; almonry of 154, 155,
  280; sacristy of xxxiv, 282, 283
Petronilla, prioress of Stainfield 291
Peverel, Hawisia 155
– Hugh, rector of Hardwick 21, 22, 226n.
– Robert, knight 155, 156
Philip II, king of France p. 209
Philip, abbot of Revesby app. I(XIIIW)
– Apostolorum 171W
– the priest (of Torksey) 200
– subdean of Lincoln, witness: 223, 259, 268,
  286, 289, 290, 294
Philipeshamton', see Hampton Poyle
Pict', Pictav', see Poitiers
Pikenot, William 174, 175
Pilat, Ralph 218n.

Pilsgate, Pillesgate (Northants), Geoffrey of
  156
Ping', Walter de, canon of Lincoln 29W
Pinsold, Alice de 60
– Stephen de 60
Pipewell (Northants) p. 209
Piriton', see Pyrton
Piun, Stephen de, bp's clerk, rector of Barton
  Seagrave xxvi, 76, 77
Plantagenet, Geoffrey, archbp of York xxiii,
  106n., 214, 214A–C, app. II(34); bp-elect
  of Lincoln 28n., 266n., app. I(XXI–
  XXIII)
Plesset, John de, rector of Knotting 287
Poer, Herbert, archdn of Canterbury app.
  I(XXIIn.); bp of Salisbury 11n., 216n.,
  221, 222, 247n.
– Hugh 50n.
Pointon (in Sempringham, Lincs), chapel of
  174
Poitiers, Pict', Pictav' (Vienne), archdn of,
  see Ilchester, Richard of
Polebrook, Pokebroc (Northants) 156
Pons, steward of the bp of Lincoln xxvi, app.
  II(48)
Pontefract (Yorks W.R./W. Yorks), prior of,
  see Hugh
Poolham (in Woodhall, Lincs), chapel of
  10n.
– lord of, see Barkwith, Robert of
Portjoie (France) p. 210
Postard, mr Ernulf 211W
– William, abbot of Westminster 211
Potton, Pottona (Beds), chapel of St Swithin
  131n.
– ch. of 131
Prestehag' (? in Rigsby, Lincs) 70
Preston (unidentified), dean of, see John
Preston Capes, Preston' (Northants), ch. of
  49; vicarage of 49n.
Preston Deanery (Northants), ch. of 130
Puiset, Hugh du, bp of Durham xxiii, xxv,
  214
Pulloxhill (Beds), vicarage of app. II(50)
Pyrton, Piriton' (Oxon), ch. of 243

Q

Quadring (Lincs), mediety of ch. of 185, 186
Quappelad', see Whaplode
Quincy, Saher de 239
Quinton (Northants), ch. of 130

R

R. abbot of Notley 24W, 53W
– abbot of St Mary de Pratis, Leicester 24
– archdn of Buckingham, see Roger
– archdn of Northampton, see Mancetter,
  Robert of
– rector of Bukeb' (? Long Buckby) 298W

Radinge, John de, monk of Durham 237
Radingiis, mr Nicholas de 73W
Raines, Rennes, William de 173n.
Raleigh, William, bp of Norwich 221n.
Ralph, mr app. I(XIIW, XVIIW, XXW)
– abbot of Easby 55n.
– abbot of Louth Park app. I(VI, IXW, XIIIW)
– canon of Shelford app. I(XIIW)
– chaplain of bp Hugh xxvi, xxvii, 205W
– chaplain of (Great) Hale 13W, 15W
– dean of Bellinge 49W
– *medicus*, canon of Lincoln app. I(XIIIW)
– parson of Fordington 13W–15W
– son of Gilbert 16
– – brother of, *see* Hugh son of Gilbert
– son of Restwald 156
– uncle of Gerard de Rowell 13W, 15W
– weaver 160
Ramburc', Henry de 230W
Ramsey, Rames' (Hunts/Cambs), Ben. abbey of xxxix, 157–9, 284, p. 212; abbot of 284, *and see* Robert; seal of 284; almoner of 284; cellarer of 158; chamberlain of 284; monks of 284; sacristy of 159; steward of 284; treasurer of 284
– mr Herbert of 157
Rannulf, earl of Chester 16, 189
Ratby, Roteby (Leics) 286, app. I(XVI)
– ch. of 140
Rauceby (Lincs), Hervey of, canon of Lincoln app. I(XIIIW)
Ravendale, Ravendal (Lincs/Humb), ch. of 223
– manor of 223
Ravensden (Beds), ch. of 265
Raymond xxv, witness: (no description) 104, 105, 115, 117, 123, 124, 207, 210; archdn of Leicester 17, 47n., 56(?), 62, 118, 122, 134, 148, 166, 187(?), 206; canon of Lincoln 14, 132, 159, 204
Reading (Berks) p. 209
Redbourne (Lincs/Humb), ch. of 288; vicarage of 288
Reginald, chaplain, rector of Mareham on the Hill 74
– priest, rector of St John, Stamford app. I(XVII)
Reims (Marne) p. 211
Reiner app. I(XVII)
– deacon 188AW
Remigius, prior of Shelford ap. I(XIIW)
Renhold (Beds), ch. of 265
Rennes, *see* Raines
Revell, Richard 73
Reveneys, (*blank*) le, vicar of South Kilworth app. II(12)
Revesby, Revisbi (Lincs), abbot of 182, *and see* Gualo; Philip
Rewin, Adam de 3
– Robert de 3

Rich', Richem', *see* Easby
Richard I, king of England 74, 111n., 125n., p. 209, 210
Richard, mr 4W, 178W
– abbot of Grimsby 25, 205W
– archbp of Canterbury, *see* Dover, Richard of
– bp of Winchester, *see* Ilchester, Richard of
– brother of Peter, dean of Esford' 89W
– chaplain app. I(XXIIIW)
– chaplain of the bp app. I(XXIIW)
– clerk app. I(XXW)
– dean of Bardney, *see* Bardney
– monk and chaplain of Abingdon 211W
– precentor of Lincoln, *see* Almaria, Richard de
– priest 118
– rector of Belgrave 299W
– rector of Higham on the Hill app. II(54)
– rector of Ibstone 143
– rector of Low Toynton 203
– son of Hernisius, rector of Skidbrook 202
– son of Nigel 114, 139
– son of Robert 84
– son of Walkelin app. I(XXIIW)
– subdean of Lincoln, *see* Kent, Richard of
– usher 160
– vicar of Hardwick 21, 22
– mr. vice-archdn of Oxford 144, *and see also* Aylesbury, Richard of
Richmond, *see* Easby
Rievaulx, Rievall' (Yorks N.R./N. Yorks), abbot of, *see* Ernald
Rigsby, Riggesbi (Lincs) 70
– Gilbert of 70, 300n.
– Herbert of 70
– Jodlan of 70
– John son of Thomas of 300n.
– Rocelin of 70
Risinghoe (in Goldington, Beds) 264
Roade, Roda (Northants), ch. of 133
Robert, abbot of Bardney 17n., 171W
– abbot of Barlings 255n.
– abbot of Eynsham 62–4
– – *nepos* of, *see* Wares, William de
– abbot of Notley 52W, 85W, 114W, 130W, 143n., 157W
– abbot of Ramsey 157, 159
– II, abbot of St-Évroul app. I(XVIn.)
– archdn of Huntingdon, *see* Hardres, Robert de
– archdn of Northampton, *see* Mancetter, Robert of
– archdn of Nottingham, *see* FitzRalph, Robert
– chaplain 62W
chaplain of Walmesgate 171
– clerk of Partney 13W–15W
– dean of Metheringham 268W
– earl of Leicester 140, 286n.; (senior) 24, 88An.; (junior) 24, 247, 299

– precentor of Lincoln, *see* Bedford, Robert of
– prior of Kenilworth 76
– prior of St-Fromond 188A
– *procurator vinee regis* of Huntingdon 72
– son of Ernis 26
– son of Fulk app. I(XXIV)
– son of Gilbert 86
– son of Hugh 84
– son of Philip 40
– son of Randolph (*or* Rannulph) 18
– son of Roger 8
– (? de Maneton), vicar of Langtoft 234
– vicar of Woking 191
Rocelin the priest (of Torksey) 200
Rocester, *see* Rouecestre
Roches, de Rupibus, Peter des 232; bp of Winchester 221, 222, 232n.
Rochester (Kent) p. 210
– bp of, *see* Ernulph; Glanvill, Gilbert
– cathedral priory of St Andrew 161; monks of 81n.
Rochford, Albreda de 185, 186n.
– Waleran de 185, 186n.
Roda, *see* Roade
Rodhewel', Roell', *see* Rowell
Roger, mr 41W, app. I(XXW)
– br., the almoner 206W
– archdn of Buckingham 265n., 266W, 285W
– bp of Salisbury app. I(IV)
– chaplain 139W, 162W, 209W
– chaplain of the king 6W
– clerk 225Wn., 259W
– dean of Lincoln, *see* Rolleston, Roger of
– dean of Pattishall 130W
– master of the Order of Sempringham 109, 110
– son of Aza 130
– son of Jocelin 174
– son of Richard 8
– – his son, *see* Robert son of Roger
Rolehyrst', Rolehust', Roger de 3W, 230W
see also Bolehirst
Rolleston, Rollestan', Rollieston', Rolv',
    Rolvest', Rolveston', Rolvestun',
    Rolweston', Rotholveston', Rothulveston',
    Rulveston', Hugh of xxv, 8W, 14W,
    78W–80W, 187W, 204W, 210W, 212W,
    251W; rector of Checkendon 43; vicar of St
    Michael at the South Gate, Oxford 150
– mr Roger of xxiv, xxvi, witness: (no
    description) 10, 11, 25n., 40, 43, 48, 49, 52,
    60, 75, 81, 85, 89, 102, 103, 114, 115, 120,
    121, 130, 131, 141, 143n., 144–7, 157, 160,
    162, 165, 173, 174, 178, 182, 191, 205, 209,
    244; archdn of Leicester 2, 4, 8, 14, 15,
    25n., 39, 47, 48n., 49n., 52n., 56(?), 60n.,
    61, 67n., 68, 70, 71, 78, 81n., 85n., 90,
    102n., 104–6, 114n., 115n., 118n., 120n.,
    123, 130n., 132, 143n., 145n., 147n., 150,
    158, 160n., 162n., 165n., 171, 173n.,
174n., 175, 176, 182n., 187(?), 188A,
    191n., 204, 205n., 210; canon of Lincoln
    67W, 172W; dean of Lincoln 4, 17W, 28n.,
    36n., 41n., 47n., 50W, 74W, 79W, 80W,
    106n., 108, 117n., 118n., 122W, 124W,
    134W, 141n., 148W, 166, 171n., 172n.,
    174n., 175n., 176n., 177n., 178n., 212W,
    215n., 229W, 232W, 251W, 252W, 253,
    254W, 255, 259W, 268, 272, 273W, 286W,
    288W, 300W; rector of Checkendon 43;
    rector of Heckington 14, 15
Rollos, Richard (II) de 54, 238
Rollright (Oxon) 62
– ch. of 63
Romar', *see* Roumare
Rome 214A, 214B
– St Peter's 214A
Romenel, Albrotha de 292
– David de 292
Rosie, *see* Royston
Roteby, *see* Ratby
Rothersthorpe, Thorop', Throp'
    (Northants), ch. of 133
Rouecestre (? Rocester, Staffs), Ralph de
    162n.
Rouell', *see* Rowell
Rouen (Seine-Maritime) p. 210
– archbp of, *see* Coutances, Walter
– dean of, *see* Coutances, John of
Roumare, Romar' Rumar(a), Alice de 40A
– William de 6, 154, 189, 279; earl of Lincoln
    40A
Rowell, Rodhewel', Roell', Rouell',
    Rouuelle, Rouwell(e), Rowelle, Rowll', mr
    Gerard de xxv, xxvii, witness: (no
    description) 13, 15, 17, 24, 40, 41, 62, 84,
    102, 124, 126, 134, 152, 165, 166, 171, 174,
    207, 252, 254, 264, 280, 281, 297; canon of
    Lincoln 29, 73, 74, 79, 80, 140, 175, 177,
    212, 223, 229, 230, 253, 255, 259, 268, 273,
    274, 285, 290, 294, 300; uncle of, *see* Ralph
– Hugh de 74W
– R. de 255W
– Ralph de 13W–15W
– Richard de 230W
– Samson de 171W
Royston, de Cruce Roys, Rosie (Herts), Aug.
    priory of 162, 285; prior of, *see* Harpin
Rufus, Robert, Templar app. I(IX)
– Walter, Templar app. I(IX)
Rumar(a), *see* Roumare
Rumeli, Alice de 24
Rupibus, *see* Roches
Rye, Hubert de 176
Ryhall (Rutl/Leics), ch. of 130

S

Saddington, Sadyngt', Sadyngton (Leics),
    ch. of 54, 55, 238; vicar of, *see* Bubbenhill,
    William de

Sai, Jordan de 60
St Agatha, *see* Easby
St Albans (Herts) pp. 208, 210
– Ben. abbey of 163, 164; abbot of 164n.,
   and see Cella, John de; monks of 118, app.
   II(2)
St Didier de la Mothe (France) p. 211
St Domninus (France) p. 211
St Edmund, de sancto Admundo,
   Eadmundo, Edmundo, mr Adam of xxvii,
   xxviiin., witness: (no description) 228, 242,
   243, 251, 264, 285, 299; canon of Lincoln
   223, 229, 244, 246, 255, 259, 268, 273, 274,
   290, 300
St Edmund's, *see* Bury
St Edward, de sancto Edwardo, Geoffrey of
   xxv, 6, 75W, 120W, 121W, 139W, 209W;
   vicar of Great Limber and canon of Lincoln
   6
– Hugh of xxv, xxviiin., witness: (no
   description) 2, 6, 8, 10, 39–41, 52, 56, 68,
   71, 75, 78, 81, 84, 85, 102–5, 117, 122–4,
   132, 134, 143, 160, 165, 171, 172, 205, 206,
   210, 252, 254; canon of Lincoln 282
– John of, rector of Belchford 184
St-Évroul, de sancto Ebrulpho (Orne), Ben.
   abbey of xxx, xxxvi, 286, 299n., app.
   I(XVI); abbot of, *see* Bernard; Robert II
St-Fromond, S. Fromundus (Manche), Ben.
   priory of xxxix, 165–7, 188A, app.
   I(XVII); prior of, *see* Robert
St Ives (Hunts/Cambs), Ben. priory of 159
St John, de sancto Iohanne, John of 60, 144
– Roger of 142, 144
– William of 144
St Laurence, *see* Revesby
St Liz, Simon I de, earl of Northampton
   132n.
– Simon III de, earl of Northampton 131,
   app. I(XVIII)
St Martin, mr Ralph of, rector of Eastry 32
St Maximin (Isère) p. 211
St Neot's, de sancto Neoto (Hunts/Cambs),
   ch. of St Mary 168
– Ben. priory of 168–70, 239, 287; prior of,
   see Herbert
St Omer (Pas-de-Calais) p. 211
St Prix, Sanctus Preiectus de Vermendes
   (Aisne), monks of 130
St Remigius, de sancto Remigio, Robert of
   144
St Valéry, de sancto Walerico, Bernard of 144
– Bernard of (son of above) 144
Sta Maria in Via Lata, cardinal deacon of, *see*
   John
Sainte-Mère-Église, William of, bp of
   London 221, 222
Saleby (Lincs), ch. of St Margaret 178
– Agnes of app. II(40)
– Thomas of app. II(40)
Salford (Beds), ch. of 265

Salisbury (Wilts), bp of, *see* Poer, Herbert;
   Roger
– canons of, *see* Coutances, John of;
   Ingoldesby, William de
– prebend of, *see* Grantham (Borealis)
Salomon, master of Brackley hospital 24
– – father of, *see* Swetman
Salos, mr Robert de app. I(XXIIIW)
Saltby (Leics), ch. of 51
Saltfleet (?) (Lincs) 16
Saltfleetby (Lincs), ch. of St Peter 86
Sampson, Samson, mr 188AW
– abbot of Bury St Edmunds 32–38
– canon of Lincoln 28W, 178W
– canon of London 178W
Sancta Cruce, William de 206W
Sancto Edmundo, *see* St Edmund
Sancto Edwardo, *see* St Edward
Sancto Iohanne, *see* St John
Sancto Walerico, *see* St Valéry
Sandford St Martin, Sandford, Sanford
   (Oxon), chapel of 144
Sandy, Sandeya (Beds), tithes of 229
Sanford, *see* Sandford St Martin
Sapcote (Leics), ch. of app. II(14); rector of,
   see Thomas
Sarsden (Oxon), chapel of 240
Sart' (?), Simon, cellarer of app. I(IXW)
Saumur (Maine et Loire) p. 210
Sausthorpe (Lincs), Robert of 203
Sauve-Majeure, La, Sancta Maria Silve
   Maioris (Gironde), Ben. abbey of 171
Savaric, archdn of Northampton, later bp of
   Bath 192, 193n., 216n., 221
Savigny, Savign' (Manche), Cist. abbey of
   xli, 172
Saxby (Lincs/Humb), ch. of 167, app.
   I(XIII)
Saxilby, Saxelbi, Saxolebi (Lincs), ch. of St
   Botolph 123, 124
Scaccario, Andrew de 212W
'Scalflet' (? Saltfleet) 16
Scampton (Lincs), ch. of 16
– land and tithes in 16
Scardeburg, Schardeburgh, Gilbert de 251W
Scelton, *see* Skelton in Cleveland
Schalby, John de xxiiin.
Schitebroc, *see* Skidbrook
Scot, Scottus, Roger 81W
Scoteny, Scotenay, Hugh de 4n.
– Lambert de 5
– Thomas de 5n.
Scotere, *see* Scotter
Scothern (Lincs), ch. of 255
Scotland, king of, *see* David I; Malcolm IV;
   William I
Scotter, Scotere (Lincs), ch. of 156
Scraptoft (Leics), ch. of app. II(57); rector
   of, *see* Peter
Scredington (Lincs) 104, 254
– ch. of 104, 254

Searby, Seuerbi (Lincs), ch. of 102, 252
Sées (Orne) p. 210
– Aug. abbey of St Martin 261n.
Sempringham, Sempingeh', Sempingh',
  Simpingeham (Lincs), ch. of St Andrew
  174
– Gilb. priory of St Mary xl, 173–7;
  fraternity of 110; nuns of 9, 12n.
– lay brothers of the Order of app. II(33)
– master of the Order of, see Roger
– Order of xxxiii
– Gilbert of app. I(IXW); app. II(33)
Septem Fontibus, Henry de 211W
– Ralph de 211W
Seuerbi, see Searby
Shawell (Leics), ch. of app. I(XXV)
Sheen (London), Carthusian priory of 286n.
Sheepy (Leics), mediety of ch. of app.
  II(18); rector of, see Henry son of Walkelin
Shelford (Notts), canon of, see Ralph
– prior of, see Remigius
Shepshed (Leics), soke of 88An.
Sherington, Srinton (Bucks), ch. of 127, 128;
  rector of, see Carun, Gervase de; vicarage
  of 128
Shifford (Oxon) 62
Shillington (Beds), ch. of 158; rector of, see
  Ecton, Stephen of; vicarage of 158
Shiplake (Oxon), ch. of 120, 121
Shwalucliva, see Swalcliffe
Sifrewast, Robert de 88
Sigillo, Baldric de app. I(IXW)
– Nicholas de app. I(XVIIW); archdn of
  Huntingdon app. I(XXn.)
Silvester, prior of Kenilworth 79n.
Simon, archdn of Wells, see Camera, Simon
  de
– cellarer of Sart' app. I(IXW)
– dean of Hehham 10W
– dean of Whittlebury 130W
– earl of Northampton, see St Liz, Simon de
– son of Nigel 155
– son of William 16
– vicar of Deene 209
Simpingeham, see Sempringham
Sinesuuald (in Warmington, Northants) 155
Siwell(e), see Sywell
Sixhills (Lincs), ch. of All Saints 178
– Gilb. priory of St Mary 178
Skelton in Cleveland, Scelton (Yorks
  N.R./Cleveland), ch. of 198
Skendleby (Lincs) 16
– chapel of St James 16
– ch. of St Peter 16
Skidbrook, Schitebroc, Skidebrok (Lincs),
  ch. of 202; rectors of, see Osbert; Richard
  son of Hernisius; Walter; William
Snelland (Lincs), ch. of 220
– Helto of 220
– Robert of 220n.
Snouthecròf, Snothecroft (? in Rigsby,

Lincs) 70
Soloman, see Salomon
Sorel, Simon 24
– Thomas 24
Sotby (Lincs) 16
– ch. of 16
Souldern (Oxon), ch. of 60, 63, 64, 241n.;
  vicar of, see Wares, William de; vicarage of
  64
South Cadeby, see Cadeby, South
South Cockerington, see Cockerington,
  South
South Elkington, see Elkington, South
South Ferriby, see Ferriby, South
South Kilworth, see Kilworth, South
South Newington, see Newington, South
South Stoke, see Stoke, South
South Thoresby, see Thoresby
Southcote, Suthcote (in Stone, Bucks),
  chapel of 144
Southill (Beds), two parts of ch. of 125, 265;
  vicar of 125
Southorpe, Sutorp, Suttorp (in
  Peterborough, Northants/Cambs) 155, 156
Southrey (Lincs) 16
Southwick, Suwic' (Hants), Aug. priory of St
  Mary 179
Spalding, Spald' (Lincs), Ben. priory of
  154n., 180–4, 289, 290; prior of, see
  Jollanus; Nicholas
– vicar of, see Alkborough, William of;
  William; vicarage of 180
Spratton, see Sproxton
Spridlington (Lincs), ch. of St Aubin 28,
  app. I(VIII)
– ch. of St Hilary 16
– tithes of 16
Sproxton (? Spratton) (Leics), tithes of 130
– Achard of 130
Srinton, see Sherington
Stafford, archdn of, see Henry
Stagsden (Beds), ch. of 265
Stainby, Stigh', Stighenbi (Lincs), William
  of, vicar of a mediety of Cranwell 12; canon
  of York 12n.
Stainfield (Lincs), Ben. priory of 185, 186,
  291; prior of 185n., 186n.; prioress of, see
  Constance; Petronilla
Stainton, see Market Stainton
Stainton le Vale, Staynton (Lincs), ch. of St
  Andrew 5; parson of, see Hardres, Robert
  de
Stallingborough (Lincs/Humb), ch. of 288,
  app. II(4); vicar of, see N.; vicarage of 288
Stamford, Stanf', Stanford' (Lincs) p. 211
– castle 167
– ch. of All Saints in the Market 166, 167,
  188, 188A, app. I(XVII); rector of, see
  Azelin
– ch. of St Andrew 188
– ch. of St Clement 188

- ch. of St George 167
- ch. of St John 165–167, app.I(XVII);
  rector of, *see* Reginald; vicar of, *see*
  Stamford, Samson of; vicarage of 165
- ch. of St Martin 156, 188
- ch. of St Mary at the Bridge 237
- ch. of St Mary Bynwerk 237; rector of, *see*
  Stamford, Henry of
- ch. of St Michael Cornstall 167, app.
  I(XVII); rector of, *see* Godric
- ch. of St Paul 167
- clerk of, *see* Alexander
- dean of, *see* Peter
- prior of St Leonard's 237n.
- Ben. priory of St Michael's xxxix, 166, 187,
  188, 188A
- Achard of 188An.
- Geoffrey of, dean 187W
- mr Henry of, rector of St Mary Bynwerk,
  Stamford 237
- mr Samson of, vicar of St John, Stamford
  165, 166
Stanes, *see* Stone
Staneuuige, *see* Stanwick
Stanf', Stanford', *see* Stamford
Stanground, Stangrund' (Hunts/Cambs), ch.
  of 196; rector of, *see* Hillegha, Simon de
Stanlow, Stanlaue (Ches), abbot of, *see*
  Osbert
Stanton St John (Oxon), ch. of 60, 63
Stanwick, Staneuige, Staneuuige
  (Northants) 282
- ch. of 156
Stapelford, dean of, *see* Symeon
Stapleford (Leics), ch. of 296; rector of, *see*
  Sumerford, Roger de
Stapleford, Stapelford', mr R. of 166
Staughton, Stoctun' (Great, Hunts/Cambs *or*
  Little, Beds) 72
Stavenebi, Stasnebi, Stavenb(i),
  Staveneb(y), Stavenesby, mr William de
  xxvii, witness: 219, 223, 225n., 228, 242,
  243, 259, 268, 273, 274, 285, 286, 290, 294,
  297, 299
Staynton, *see* Stainton le Vale
Steeping, Great (Lincs) 16
- ch. of 16
Steeping, Geoffrey of, bp's clerk and vicar of
  Edlington 10; *see also* Deeping, Geoffrey
  of
Steeple Barton, Bertona (Oxon), ch. of 142,
  144
Steeple Claydon, Claindon' (Bucks), ch. of
  144, 273
Stephen, mr 16W
- archdn of Buckingham, *see* Swafeld,
  Stephen de
- chancellor of Lincoln, *see* Swafeld, Stephen
  de
Stigh', Stighenbi *see* Stainby
Stivecle, *see* Stukeley

Stixwould, Styk', Stykeswald' (Lincs) 189
- Cist. priory of xxxv, xxxvi, xxxviin., 189,
  190
Stochingha (in Brackley, Northants) 24
Stoctun', *see* Staughton
Stoke by Clare (Suff), Ben. priory of 191
Stoke, South (Oxon), ch. of 60, 62, 63
Stokenchurch, Stokenchirch', Stokenechirch'
  (Bucks), cemetery of 297
- parishioners of 297
Stokes (unidentified), tithes of 156
Stokton', Stocton' (? Stoughton, Leics) 286,
  app. I(XVI)
Stone, Stanes (Bucks), ch. of 144, 273
Stoneleigh (Warw), abbot, of, *see* William
Stonesby (Leics), ch. of 65
Stotfold (Beds), ch. of 41
- tithes of 265
Stoughton, *see* Stokton
Stow (Lincs) pp. 208, 211
Stow *alias* West Riding (of Lindsey),
  Westreing', Westreng', Westrid' (Lincs),
  archdn of, *see* Alexander; Almaria, Richard
  de; Almaria, Roger de; Thornaco, William
  de; William son of Osbert
Stow by Threckingham (Lincs), ch. of St
  Aethelthryth 174, 175
Stowa, mr Peter de app. I(XXIIIW)
Stowe, Stowa (Bucks), ch. of 144
Stowe, R. de 255W
Stowe Nine Churches (Northants), tithes of
  130
Stratford Langthorne (Essex), abbot of, *see*
  Benedict
'Strattona' (?Great Sturton, Lincs) 16
Stretton (? Rutl/Leics), tithes of 130
Strubby, Strubi (Lincs) 16
- Henry of 70
- Ivo of 70
- Stuchbury (Northants), ch. of 130
Studham, Stodham (Beds), ch. of 52
- Alexander of 52
- Robert of 52n.
- family 52n.
Studley (Oxon), Ben. priory of 292
Stukeley, Stivecle (Hunts/Cambs) 72
- tithes of 130
Sturton, Great (?) Lincs 16
Stuteville, William de 13n.
Styk', Stykeswald', *see* Stixwould
Sualeclif *etc.*, *see* Swalcliffe
Sudbrooke (Lincs), ch. of app. I(X)
Sudwell(e), *see* Sywell
Suinehop, *see* Swinethorpe
Sulby, Suleby (Northants), Prem. abbey of
  192, 193, 293; abbot of 193n., 293
Sulgrave (Northants), ch. of 130
Sumerford, mr Roger de xxv, 48W, 89W,
  115W, 166W; canon of Lincoln 172W, 296;
  rector of Stapleford 296
Surfleet, Surflet' (Lincs), ch. of 290; rector

of, *see* Ely, William of; vicar of, *see*
Hardres, Robert de; vicarage of 290
Suthcote, *see* Southcote
Suthferiby, *see* Ferriby, South
Sutorp', *see* Southorpe
Sutton (unidentified) 70
Sutton, Suttona (in Peterborough,
Northants/Cambs) 155
– Thorold of 155
see also Briggemilne
Sutton, Oliver, bp of Lincoln xxii, 30n.,
51n., 113n., 120n., 192n., 218n., app.
I(XIIn., XIIIn.)
Sutton Bassett, Sutton' (Northants), chapel
of 84
Sutton cum Buckingham, prebend of (in
Lincoln cathedral) 298; prebendary of, *see*
Blois, William of, archdn of Buckingham
Sutton in Ashfield (Notts), ch. of app. II(35)
Sutton-le-Marsh (Lincs) 16
Sutton, Long, Suttun' (Lincs), ch. of 39
Sutton, *see also* King's Sutton
Suttorp, *see* Southorpe
Suualeclive, *see* Swalcliffe
Suwella, *see* Sywell
Suwic', *see* Southwick
Swaby, Swabi (Lincs) 70
Swafeld, mr Stephen de xxv, witness: archdn
of Buckingham 13, 15, 27, 47, 79, 80, 88n.,
106, 161, 166, 175, 176; chancellor of
Lincoln 24, 52, 60, 67, 77, 81, 103, 117,
143n., 144–7, 157, 174, 196
Swalcliffe, Shwalucliva, Sualeclif,
Sualeclive(e), Sualevecl', Suualeclive,
Swalecliv(e), Swaleclyve, Swalew',
Swaleweclif(-a, -e), Swaluecliva,
Waleweclliva, Mr Richard de, witness: (no
description) 2, 8, 10, 11, 14, 24, 39–41, 50,
52, 56, 60, 68, 70, 71, 78, 81, 84, 85, 89,
102–6, 114, 115, 117, 123, 124, 134, 143n.,
155, 160, 161, 165, 171–4, 176, 205, 207,
208, 210; canon of Lincoln 29, 61, 74, 77,
79, 80, 90, 132, 140, 148, 159, 175, 177,
187, 188A, 204, 206, 212
Swallow, Sualue (Lincs), ch. of 294; rector of,
see Blois, William of, archdn of Buckingham
Swaton (Lincs), mr Ralph of 104, 254
Swavesey (Cambs), prior of 234n.
Swein 8
Swetman father of mr Salomon 24
Swinethorpe, Suinehop (Lincs) app. I(VI)
Swinford (Leics), vicar of, *see* William;
vicarage of app. II(7)
Snewit wood (? in Aby, Lincs) 70
Symeon, dean of Stapelford' 89W
Syresham (Northants) 24
Sywell, Siwell(e), Sudwell(e), Suwella
(Northants) mr Simon of xxv, witness: (no
description) 60, 104, 115, 130, 131, 144,
147, 172, 201n.; canon of Lincoln 67, 175,
223; treasurer of Lichfield 201n.

T

T., rector of Kelstern 198
– rector of Olney 298W
– mr, vicar of Hathern 88A
Tadmarton, Thademerton' (Oxon), ch. of 2
Tamiseford, *see* Tempsford
Taplow (Beds), ch. of 120, 121
Tawell (? Tathwell, Lincs), mr Alan de,
vicar of Hatley 126
Tealby (Lincs), ch. of All Saints 178
Tedeltorp', *see* Theddlethorpe
Templars, knights app. I(IX)
see also Aneheide (Mere)
– master of, in England, *see* Hastings,
Richard of
see also Bulonia, Robert de; Dorobernia,
Walter de; Gilbert; Lunem, Robert de;
Rufus, Robert; Rufus, Walter
Tempsford, Tamiseford (Beds), ch. of 169
Testard, Gilbert 70
Tewkesbury (Glos), Ben. abbey of 194, 195
Thademerton', *see* Tadmarton
Thame (Oxon) 143n., 231n.
– Cist. abbey of 231n.
Theddlethorpe, Tedeltorp' (Lincs), W. de
294W
Theobald, archbp of Canterbury xxxvi, 44n.,
133, app. I(IXn., XVIII)
– (? de Bosell'), canon of Lincoln 61W
– steward of Westminster 211W
Theodoric, vicar of Woking 191
Therfield (Herts), ch. of 157
Thetford (Norf), prior of 284
Tholi 16
Thomas, abbot of Gloucester 66
– abbot of Meaux 198
– chaplain app. I(XIIW, XXW)
– priest of Godstow 67W
– rector of Edmondthorpe app. II(13)
– mr, rector of Heather ap.II(52)
– rector of Kirkby app. II(51)
– rector of Sapcote app. II(14)
– rector of Thornborough 115
– son of Bernard 292
– steward 67W
– vicar of Begbroke 224
Thomley (Oxon) 274
Thoni, Adam de 274
Thorre, *see* Torre
Thoresby, Toresbi (? South Thoresby,
Lincs) 70
Thorkesey, *see* Torksey
Thorn' *see* Thorney
Thornaco, mr William de, archdn of Stow
xxxviiin.
Thornborough, Torneberge(e) (Bucks), ch.
of 114, 115; rector of, *see* Thomas;
vicarage of 115
Thorneton', *see* Thornton by Horncastle
Thorney, Thorn' (Cambs), Ben. abbey of

196, app. I(XVIII); abbot of 284

Thornhaugh, Turnauue (Northants/Cambs) 156

Thornton by Horncastle, Thorneton', Thorniton' (Lincs), ch. of 90, 251; vicar of, see Peter

Thornton Curtis, Torenton (Lincs/Humb), Aug. abbey of xxxiii, 197, 198, 295; abbot of 197n., 295n.

Thorop', Thorp', see Longthorpe; Rothersthorpe

Thorp Arnold, Torp Ernald', Thorpernald' (Leics) 286, app. I(XVI)

Thorpe on the Hill, Thorp (Lincs), ch. of 210; rector of, see Westminster, Nicholas of; vicar of, see Alexander, archdn of the West Riding alias Stow; vicarage of 210

Thuatt 16

Thurgarton, Thurg' (Notts), Aug. priory of 199, app. II(35)

Thurlaston (Leics), ch. of app. II(16); rector of, see Henry

Thurlby (by Bourne), Turlebi (Lincs), ch. of St Firmin 188

Tiedolf Barnewde (? in Aby, Lincs) 70

Tilton on the Hill, 'Tilt' (Leics), ch. of St Peter 84, app. I(III)

– Everard of 84

Timberland, Timberlund (Lincs), ch. of 199; vicar of, see Hayden, Richard de; vicarage of 199

– Ralph of app. I(IXW)

Tingherst, see Fingest

Tiningonam, see Tyringham

Tinton' maior, see Toynton, High

Tinwell, Tineuuelle (Leics), ch. of 156

Tiwe, Hugh de 144

Toddington, Todingedona (Beds), ch. of 232; rector of, see Gloucester, Hugh of

Torenton, see Thornton Curtis

Torksey, Thorkesey, Torkes', Torkesey (Lincs), ch. of All Saints 200

– ch. of St Mary 200

– ch. of St Peter 200, 201; rector of, see Odo

– nuns of St Peter (Fosse) 201

– Aug. priory of 200; prior of 200

– Alexander of 259W

Torneberge(e), see Thornborough

Torp, see Bassingthorpe

Torp, Thurstan de 155

Torp Ernald', see Thorp Arnold

Torpel (Northants) 156

– Roger of 156

Torre, Thorre (Devon), Prem. abbey of 202

Torrington, West (Lincs), ch. of St Mary 174

Tot, Robert de 156

Tounecroft (? in Lusby, Lincs) 16

Towthorpe (in Londonthorpe, Lincs), chapel of 69; vicar of, see Adam son of Reginald; vicarage of 69

Toynton, High, Tinton' maior (Lincs), ch.

of 74; rector of, see John son of Simon

Toynton, Low (Lincs), ch. of 203; rector of, see Richard

Trentesic 70

Trentham (Staffs), Aug. priory of 182

Trianel, Robert, prior of St Andrew's, Northampton 6n.

Trie (Oise) p. 209

Trou, mr Simon de, canon of Lincoln and prebendary of Decem Librarum 259

Troyes (Aube) p. 211

Trubleville, Drogo de 131W

Trussebut, Geoffrey 207

Turbern 8

Turbert son of Turbert, vicar of Aynho 204

Turnauue, see Thornhaugh

Turre, Simon de 72

Turville, Richard de 121

– William de 120, 121

Tutbury (Staffs), Ben. priory of 296

Twafletes (unidentified) 70

Tynghirst', see Fingest

Tyringham (?), Tiningonam (Bucks), ch. of 127

U

Uchenden', see Hughenden

Ulceby (Lincs/Humb), mediety of ch. of 207

Ulian, rector of Charwelton 136

Undele, see Oundle

Upton, Uptona (Northants), chapel of 130

– mill of 133

Urban III, pope 44n.

Utterby (Lincs), ch. of St Andrew 141

V

Vacarius, mr xxvii, 117W

– canon of Lincoln 298W, 299W

– chaplain xxvii, 230W, 243W, 251W

– priest, vicar of Dunston 268

Val St Pierre (France) p. 211

Valenciennes (Nord), abbot of, see Peter

Valognes family 112

Vaudey (Lincs), abbot of 46n., 234n.; prior of 46n.

Verdun, Verdon, Bertram de 6n., 80

– R. de, rector of four portions of the ch. of Loughborough app. II(20)

Vesci, William de 116

Villarbenoit (France) p. 211

Vireneto, Viren', Virin', Ralph de 123W, 124W; canon of Lincoln 175W; rector of Aynho 204

Virgil 188AW

– rector of Meopham 33n., 35

Vis de Lu, John 72

Vivian, abbot of Aunay 6n.

W

W., abbot of Waltham 25
– clerk of Banbury 166W
 dean of 'Litigt' 47W
– rector of 'Angodeston' app. II(6)
– rector of Claypole 229W, 246W, 298W
– scholar of Northampton 135
– vicar of Kibworth Beauchamp app. II(24)
Wacelin, mr William 72W, 75W, 120W,
 121W
Waddon, Ralph de 164n.
Wahill(e), Odell, Simon de 67, 242
Wainfleet (Lincs) 16
– ch. of All Saints 82, 249
Walcot, Walecot(e) (Lincs) 181
– chapel of 181
Walcot, Walecote (in Southorpe,
 Northants/Cambs) 156
Walden (Essex), Ben. priory of 204; prior of,
 see William
Waleran, chaplain 211W
– clerk xxvii, witness: 219, 225, 230, 243,
 259, 273, 274, 285, 286, 290
– priest of Godstow 67W
Wales, Gerald of, rector of Chesterton, app.
 II(27)
Walewecliva, see Swalcliffe
Walis, Hugh de 286W
 see also Wells
Walkelin, abbot of St James, Northampton
 130W
– chaplain, witness: 43, 72, 77, 146, 173
– chaplain of bp xxvi, 144W, 147W
– prior of Launde 49W, 130W, 154W,
 188AW
Walkern, Walcra, Walcre (Herts), ch. of 230;
 rector of, see Bocland, Geoffrey de;
– tithes of 229
Wallingford (Berks/Oxon), Ben. priory of 297
Walmsgate, Walmesgar' (Lincs), chaplain of,
 see Robert
– ch. of 171
Walter, 6W
– abbot of Bardney app. I(VIIIW, IXW)
– abbot of Waltham 205
– chaplain of Bardney app. I(IXW)
– chaplain of Newark app. I(XIIW)
– constable 160W
– deacon 67W
– rector of Skidbrook 202
– son of Winemer 130
– Hubert, archbp of Canterbury xxv, xxxiin.,
 24n., 29n., 32n., 36–38, 46, 60n., 72n.,
 83n., 86n., 102n., 119n., 151n., 155n.,
 190n., 206n., 211, 216, 223, 237, 247,
 278n., 284, app. II(49, 51)
– – clerk of, see St Martin, Ralph of
Waltham, Walth' (Essex), Aug. abbey of 205,
 206; abbot of, see W.; Walter

Waltham, (Lincs/Humb), ch. of 223; soke of
 223
Waltham on the Wolds (Leics), ch. of 139
Walton, Waltun' (Northants), chapel of xl,
 298
Walton (Oxon) 274
Wardley, Warle (Rutl/Leics), ch. of St Mary
 84
Ware, Wares (Herts), Ben. priory of xxx,
 299; prior of, see Herbert
Wares, William de, vicar of Souldern 64
Waresley, Weresle (Hunts/Cambs) 72
Wargarthweit (? in Aby, Lincs) 70
Warin, mr, official of (archdn of) Bedford 72
– precentor of Évreux (?) app. I(XXIIW)
Warle, see Wardley
Warmington, Wermentona (Northants) 155
– ch. of 156
Warter, Wartre (Yorks E.R./Humb), Aug.
 priory of 105, 207; prior of, see I.
Warwick p. 209
– dean of, see J.
Wateleia, Wateleya, see Wheatley
Waterperry, Waterperi, Pery (Oxon), ch. of
 144, 146, 272, 273
– Emma of 146
– William of 146
Waterville, Richard de 193n., 293n.
Watford (Northants), ch. of 133
Watford, Eustace of 213n.
Watlington, Watlinton' (Oxon), ch. of 144
Waure, Richard de app. II(42)
Wdecroft, William de 156
Wdetorp', Alan de 70
– William de 70
Weekley, Wickeleia (Northants), ch. of 133
Welbeck, Well' (Notts), Prem. abbey of St
 James 208
Weldon, Weled' (Northants), ch. of St Mary
 84
Welham, Welleham (Leics), ch. of St
 Andrew 84, app. I(III)
Well', see Welbeck
Well', Robert de 70
– William de 70
Welleham, see Welham
Wellingore (Lincs), ch. of 99, 261
– Alan of 99, 261
Wellow, see Grimsby
Wells (Som), archdn of, see Camera, Simon
 de
– canon of, see Wells, Jocelin of
Wells, Hugh of, bp of Lincoln xxi, xxiin.,
 xxvi, xxviii–xxxii, xxxivn., xxxviii,
 xlin., xlii, 18n., 29n., 30n., 51n., 54n.,
 65n., 81n., 82n., 85n., 97n., 108n., 109n.,
 112n., 137n., 138n., 149n., 153n., 180n.,
 181n., 194n., 195n., 202n., 215n., 221n.,
 228n., 241n., 249n., 250n., 263n., 269n.,
 270n., 288n., 292n., app. I(XXV)
– Jocelin of, canon of Wells, later bp of Bath

and Glastonbury 221, 222
Welton le Marsh (Lincs), ch. of 197, 295
Welwyn (Herts), ch. of 112, 263
Weresle, *see* Waresley
Wermentona, *see* Warmington
Werrington, Widerintona (Northants/
Cambs), Alfric of 155
– Odo of 155, 156
– Ralph of 156
Werveldich (in Brackley, Northants) 24
West Ashby, *see* Ashby, West
West Riding (of Lindsey), Westreing';
Westreng', Westrid', archdn of, *see* Stow
West Torrington, *see* Torrington, West
West Wykeham, *see* Wykeham, West
Westcott Barton, *see* Barton (Westcott)
Westenges (unidentified) 70
Westminster, Westm', Westmonasterium
(London) 37, 73n., pp. 208, 209, 211, 212
– Ben. abbey of St Peter xxxviii, 209–12,
app. I(XIX, XX); abbot of, *see* Laurence;
Postard, William
– chapel of St Katharine 1, 32, 36, 38
– council of (1199) 215n.
– steward of, *see* Theobald
– mr Nicholas of, rector of Thorpe on the
Hill and Doddington 210
Weston by Welland, Weston' (Northants),
ch. of St Mary 84, app. I(III)
Weston on the Green, Westona (Oxon), ch.
of 144
Weston Turville (Bucks), ch. of 121
Westreing', Westreng', *see* Stow
Whaplode, Quappelad' (Lincs), ch. of 44;
rectors of, *see* Fulk; Geoffrey; Hugh;
vicarage of 44n.
Wheatley, Wateleia, Wateleya (Oxon), tithes
of 3
Whitefeld, Simon de, rector of Kingsey 81
Whittlebury, Witlingb', Witlyngbere
(Northants), dean of, *see* Simon
Whitton, Whiten' (Lincs/Humb), ch. of 208
Wickeleia, *see* Weekley
Wicumb', *see* Wycombe, High
Widerintona, *see* Werrington
Wiern', *see* Withern
Wigston, Wykygiston', Wykyngeston' (Leics)
286, app. I(XVI)
Willen, Wilingis (Bucks), ch. of 127
William I, King of England 212
– II, King of England 106n., 161
William I, King of Scotland 72
William, 85W
– abbot of St Nicholas, Angers 181n.
– abbot of Stoneleigh 42
– canon of Bridlington 26W
– chancellor of Lincoln, *see* Montibus,
William de
– chaplain app. I(XVIIW)
– chaplain of the bp xxvi, 205W
– chaplain of Colmworth 29, 228

– clerk app. I(XXW)
– clerk of Appleby app. I(XXI)
– clerk of 'Eia', vicar of Kingsey 81
– clerk of the dean 8W
– clerk of London 206W
– clerk of the York diocese app. II(44)
– dean of Barrowby 48W
– earl of Gloucester 194n.
– monk of 188AW
– prior of Walden 204
– rector of Bruntingthorpe app. II(10)
– rector of Skidbrook 202
– rector of West Ashby 74
– son of Acard 237n.
– – son of, *see* Helias
– son of Adam 213
– son of Brian 266
– son of Burchard 130
– son of Fulk, mr, xxvii, xxviiin., witness:
(no description) 74, 207, 228–30, 242–4,
246, 251, 253, 255, 274, 289, 297,
299; canon of Lincoln and prebendary of
Decem Librarum 219, 225n., 229n., 230n.,
242n., 244n., 246n., 251n., 255n., 259,
268, 273, 274n., 286, 290, 294, 299n., 300
– son of Fulk of Lincoln 17W
– son of Godric 155
– son of Hacon 16
– son of Helias 144, 146n.; son of, *see below*
William; wife of, *see* Emma
– son of Henry 143
– son of Hervey 213n.
– son of Osbert, archdn (of Stow) app.
I(IXW)
– son of Otuer 70
– son of Peter, rector of Wingrave 164
– son of Toke 8
– son of Ulf 13W, 15W
– son of William son of Helias 144, *see also*
Waterperry, William of
– subdean of Lincoln, *see* Blois, William of;
Bramfeld, William de
– vicar of Kingsey 81
– vicar of Spalding 180
– vicar of Swinford app. II(7)
Willingham, North (Lincs), ch. of St
Thomas 178
Willington (Beds), ch. of 265
Willoughby by Skendleby (Lincs) 16
Wilton, Wiltona, Wiltun', Wylton', Eustace
de, xxv, witness: 8, 10, 11, 29, 39–41, 52,
61, 68, 70, 74, 78, 79, 81, 84, 85, 102–4,
106, 114, 115, 117, 123, 124, 140, 143, 152,
160, 165, 171, 172, 179, 188A, 212
Wimar, *see* Winemer
Winceby (Lincs) 16
Winchelsea (Sussex) p. 209
Winchendon (Bucks), ch. of 274
Winchester (Hants) p. 209
– bp of, *see* Ilchester, Richard of; Lucy,
Godfrey de; Roches, Peter des

Winemer, Wimar, mr 24W; archdn of
Northampton 24n., 25n., 47W, 90W,
106W, 155W, 156W, 166W, 175W, 176W,
188AW, 205n., 214A-C; subdean of
Lincoln xxiv, xxvi, 24n., 25n., 28W, 104W,
110W, 178W
Wingrave (Bucks), ch. of 164; rector of, see
William son of Peter
Winterhard, William son of Walter 16
Winterton (Lincs/Humb), ch. of 117
Winthorpe (Lincs), ch. of St Mary 28, (?)
app. I(VIIIn.)
Winton', mr Hamo de 158W
Wisiton, see Woolstone, Little
Witeringe, see Wittering
Witham (Som), charterhouse of xxiii, 213A;
p. 208; prior of, see B.
Witham-on-the-Hill, Witham (Lincs), ch. of
27
Withcote (Leics), ch. of app. II(8); rector of,
see Hugh
Withern, Wiern' (Lincs) 16, 70
Witlingb', Witlyngbere,see Whittlebury
Wittena' (unidentified, ? for Winthorpe), ch.
of app. I(VIII)
Wittering, Witeringe (Northants/Cambs) 156
Witton, see Wyton
Wivelingh', Durand de 71W
Wlstanwde (in Louth, Lincs), app. I(IV)
Wlurikehag' (in Rigsby, Lincs) 70
Woburn, Woburne (Beds), Cist, abbey of 53
Wodeford, see Woodford
Wodint', Ascelin de 156
Woking (Surrey), ch. of 191; vicars of, see
Jordan; Robert; Theodoric
Wold Newton (?), Newtona (Lincs/Humb)
app. I(VI)
Wollaston (Northants), tithes of 130
Wood Enderby, Enderbi (Lincs), ch. of 74
Woodford, Wodeford (Northants), tithes of
156
Woodthorpe (Lincs) 16
Woolsthorpe, Wullestorp, Wulstorp (Lincs),
ch. of 225

– tithes of 225
Woolstone, Little, Wisiton (Bucks) ch. of
232; rector of, see Gloucester, Hugh of
– manor of 232
Wootton (Beds), ch. of 264
Wootton (Northants), tithes of 130
Wootton (Oxon), clergy chapter at 59, 62
Worcester, bp of, see Blois, William of;
Coutances, John of; Mauger
Worminghall (Bucks), ch. of 274
Wrangle, Wrengl(e) (Lincs), ch. of 206;
rector of, see Alan; vicarage of 206
Wrestlingworth (Beds), ch. of 264
Wullestorp, Wulstorp, see Woolsthorpe
Wycombe, High, Wicumb' (Bucks) 23
– ch. of 67, 242
Wykeham, East (Lincs), ch. of St Mary 178
Wykeham, West (Lincs), mediety of ch. of St
Edward 178
Wykygiston', Wykyngeston', see Wigston
Wylton', see Wilton
Wymeswold (Leics), ch. of 18
Wythyn' (unidentified), tithes of 130
Wyton, Witton (Hunts/Cambs), ch. of 157

                              Y

Yardley Hastings (Northants), tithes of 130
Yarm, Iarum (Yorks N.R./Cleveland),
chapel of 198
Yarnton (Oxon) 59, 62
Yifteley, see Iffley
York 214An., p. 209
– abbot of St Mary's 129n., 267n.
– archbp of, see Gray, Walter de;
Plantagenet, Geoffrey
– cathedral chapter of 300; canons of 214A,
and see Stainby, William of; dean of, see
Apulia, Simon de; precentor of, see Hamo
– clergy of the province 214Cn.
– Official of the court of 105n., 207n.
– Henry of 67W
Ywardbi, see Ewerby

INDEX OF SUBJECTS

Arabic numerals (occasionally with extra items distinguished as A, B, and C) indicate the continuous series of acta and small roman numerals refer to the pages of the introduction. In the third appendix the entries are indexed by page number; in appendices I and II by the entry number.

A

abbey, foundation of app. I(IV)
– repair of, endowment for 45, 157
– violent harassment of app. I(XVIII)
  see also almonry; chamberlain; infirmary;
  monks, sick; priory; treasurers *and under*
  names of individual houses
abbot, benediction of 64n., p. 210
absolution 257
address xxx, xxxi
admission, *see* institution
adultery 40B, app. II(43)
advocatus 39, 52, 81, 125, 131, 206
advowson, *see* church
agreement, composition xxxvi, xxxix, xl
– over cemetery 297
– over chapel 10n., 298
– over church 46, 79n., 109, 122, 144, 188A,
  198, 239, 243, 255, app. I(VI) (?), app.
  II(35)
– over land app. I(IX), app. II(31)
– over tithes 46, 298
almoner of abbey 284
– of bishop xxvii, 206 & n.
almonry of abbey 152, 154, 155, 280
alms, distribution of 215n., 284
ambassador p. 209
amen, *see apprecatio*
anathema xxxvii
appeal 36, 58, 214A
apprecatio xxxviiin.
appropriation of churches, grants *in proprios*
  usus xxii, xxiii, xxxiii–v, 5, 18, 19, 26, 30,
  39, 41, 44, 48–50, 59, 65, 67, 106, 107,
  109, 115, 118, 119, 123–5, 128, 132, 134,
  138, 141, 148, 162, 175–7, 187, 190, 193,
  206–8, 219, 242, 250, 251, 260, 272–4, 285,
  288, 292n., 300, app. I(XXI)
arbitration, award of 36n.
archbishops, *see names under* Canterbury;
  Dublin; Lyon; Rouen; York
archdeacons xxiii
– powers of 102, 252
  see names under Bedford; Buckingham;
  Canterbury; Durham; Huntingdon;
  Leicester; Lincoln; London; Middlesex;
  Northampton; Nottingham; Oxford;

Poitiers; Stafford; Stow; Wells
  see also official; vice-archdeacon
archdeaconry, farm of 259
archives, ecclesiastical xxi–ii
arenga xxxii–iii, xxxvii
assarts 16, 70, 156, 188, 265, 286, 299, app.
  I(XVI)
  see also breach
assault 135
assize of darrein presentment app. I(X)
aureus 11, 198, 204, 210, 224, 287, 290, app.
  I(XX)

B

bailiff of bishop xxviin.
– of earl app. II(47)
barn 130
barons of the Exchequer xxxiv, 192
benefice, perpetual 270 *and see* church;
  institution
bezant 243, 298
bishop(s):
– fee of 160, app. I(XIV)
– household of xxiii–viii, pp. 206, 208
– seizure of possessions of 111
  see also names under Bath; Bayeux;
  Chester; Durham; Ely; Exeter; Hereford;
  Lichfield; Lincoln; London; Norwich;
  Rochester; Salisbury; Winchester;
  Worcester
blessings (used in acta) xxxv
books (for parish church) 158
boonwork 160
boundaries, recited 29
bovates 16, 70, 104, 181, 198, app. I(XII,
  XIII)
breach (*brechia*) 3
  see also assart
bread, hastybere 181
bread and ale, monastic allowance 180
burial of bishop pp. 211–2
– of King Richard I p. 210
– rights and ceremonies xxi, 24, 61, app.
  II(46)

C

candles, allowance of 284
canonisation app. I(XIX)
canons (of cathedrals), see names under
    Lincoln; London; Salisbury; York
cardinal, see names under John
carucate 16, 23, 181, 299
castles, see names under Belvoir; Château
    Gaillard; Newark; Oxford; Stamford
cathedral church
– building of 97n., 98, 108n., 258
– services, division of the psalter 108
    see also canons; dean; fraternity; treasurer;
    vicars choral
cemetery, see churchyard
certification, letters of 267
chamberlain of abbey 284
chancellor of bishop xxvi
chancery, royal xxxix
chapels 10n., 16, 24, 36, 38–41, 50, 60–2, 74,
    81n., 84, 121, 127, 130, 131n., 142, 144,
    155, 158, 161, 171, 174, 175, 181, 190, 191,
    198, 240, 243, 274, 286, 287, 298, app.
    I(XII, XVI, XXI), app. II(6)
– mediety of 148
– permission to build 147
chaplain(s), bishop's xxvi, and see names
    Capella, Robert de; Clement, William;
    Eynsham, Adam of; Ralph; Richard;
    Walkelin; William
chapter, ruridecanal 59, 62
    see also cathedral church
charter(s), inspected but not recited by
    bishop 11, 24, 31, 39, 52, 56, 57, 61, 71,
    73, 83n., 102, 120, 121, 137, 149, 161, 163,
    168, 169, 173, 179, 194, 206, 220, 223, 225,
    238, 252, 266, 278, 298
charters, royal xxxiv
cheese 180
chirograph 239, app. II(35)
church(es), confirmations/grants of 4, 5, 6n.,
    11, 13–16, 26–8, 31, 39, 40, 52, 56, 57, 60,
    63, 67, 70, 72, 74, 75, 80, 84, 86–8, 90, 99,
    100, 104, 112n., 114–21, 123, 124, 126,
    127, 129–34, 137–9, 142, 144, 149, 151,
    152, 154, 156, 159, 161, 163, 168–74, 178,
    186–8, 188A, 190, 194, 197, 200, 206, 210,
    212, 220, 223, 233, 236, 238, 240–2, 244,
    251, 254, 261, 262, 264–6, 272–6, 278, 279,
    281, 286, 288, 292, 293, 295, app. I(III,
    VIIn., VIII, X, XI, XIII, XV–XVII, XX,
    XXII, XXIII)
– consecration of xxi, app. II(28), p. 209
– exchange of 167
– portions of: medieties 12, 17, 27, 28, 53,
    60, 67, 85, 88, 89, 100, 114, 124, 127, 141,
    173, 178, 182, 184–6, 207, 242, 262, app.
    I(XXI), app. II(18, 56); two parts of 5,
    125; third part of 187, 188; four portions of
    app. II(20); fourth part of 127; fifth

portion of app. II(20); sixth part of 123,
    124
– repair of 158
– restoration of, to priory 191, 192
    see also chapels; disputes; settlements
churchyard, cemetery, agreement over 297
– confirmation of priory site in 201
– consecration of xxi
citations xxi, 36, 38, 214A
clerk(s), bishop's xxiii–v
clothing (for religious) 223, 232, app. II(33)
commissions xxi, 243n.
common fund, see names under Lichfield;
    Lincoln
common pasture 29, 70
composition, see agreement
concord, (final) 57n., 105, 170n., 247,
    300n.
confessions 24, 215n.
confirmation of children xxi
confirmations (of possessions) xxi, xxii, xxxii–
    vii, xxxix, xl and passim
    see also agreements; chapels; churches;
    land; pensions; settlements; tithes
consanguinity, ties of 40A
consecration of bishop 221n., pp. 208, 212
– of churches and churchyards xxi, app.
    II(28), p. 209
constitutions, marriage app. II(39)
contract, withdrawal from app. II(51)
corn 118, 130, 196, 229, 274, 298, app.
    II(51)
coronation of Richard I p. 209
– of John p. 211
corroboration clause, corroboratio xxxv–vii
Councils, see names under Lateran;
    Marlborough; Oxford; Westminster
court, king's 44n., 105, 125n.
– secular app. II(42)
croft 104, 119, 254
cursus curie romane xxix
customs, episcopal xxv

D

dataries, episcopal xxvi, xxx, xxxviii
dates and dating elements xxx, xxxviii–ix, 20,
    157, 211, app. I(IX)
deans (of cathedrals), see names under
    Lincoln; London; Rouen; York
– rural, see names under Bardney;
    Barrowby; Bellinge; Chester; Esford;
    Geoffrey; Hehham; Lincoln, William of;
    Metheringham; Oxford; Pattishall;
    Preston; Stamford; Stapelford;
    Whittlebury
    see also chapter, ruridecanal
dedication of church app. II(29)
    see also consecration
dignity of the church of Lincoln xxxv

dispositive clauses xxxii, xxxiii, xxxv, xxxvi, xl

disputes:
– between archbishop Geoffrey Plantagenet and the bishop of Durham 214
– between archbishop Geoffrey Plantagenet and the chapter of York 214A–C
between archbishop Hubert Walter and Christ Church, Canterbury 36–38
– over archidiaconal procurations 234n.
– over churches, advowsons 5n., 12, 19n., 21n., 22n., 22An., 26n., 32–38, 44n., 53, 57n., 64n., 69n., 79, 86n., 105, 109, 125n., 128n., 129n., 164n., 166, 175n., 182, 185n., 188A, 191, 192, 193n., 198, 203, 211, 220, 226, 232, 239, 241n., 243, 245n., 255, 267n., 287, 293n., 295n., 298, 300n., app. I(X, XXIn.)
– over manor 232, 248n.
– over status of chapel 243
– over tithes 25, 298
– see also agreements; settlements
dress, see clothing
drink, allowance of 284
dues, see offerings

E

earthquake 97n.
'ego' used in acta xxxvi, 25 and n., 189, 201
election of bishop 221, 222, p. 208
– of prioress xxxiv, 291
empress, see names under Matilda
enthronement of bishop app. I(I), p. 208
eschaetors, royal 111
Exchequer, barons of the xxxiv, 192
exchange 167
excommunication, excommunicates 91, 93, 111, 215n., 227, 257, app. II(2, 34, 36–8, 40–3, 47, 48)
excuse, letters of 216n.
exemption, grant of xxxvii, 102, 103, 242, 252

F

fabric of the cathedral 97, 98
familia of bishop xxii, xxiv–ix, xxxviii
farm of archdeaconry 259
– of benefice 26
– of lands 284
– of tithes 130
fee of the abbey 159
final concord, see concord
fines, imposition of app. II(45)
fishing, fisheries 25, 158, 286, app. I(XVI)
food, allowance of (for religious) 232, 284, app. II(33)
forester app. II(37, 41)
forgery app. I(XI)
formularies xxix, 135n., pp. 206–7

fraternity of the church of Lincoln 97, 258
– of the order of Sempringham 110

G

glebe land 118, 119, 150, 172, 239
goods, detention of 135
granges 53, 158, app. I(XXV), app. II(31)
grants xxxix, and see churches; land; pensions; tithes
grants in proprios usus, see appropriation of churches
greeting, see salutation
guests, see hospitality

H

hay 274
hens 180
herbage 286, app. I(XVI)
hide 8, 274
horse-stud 286, app. I(XVI)
hospitals, see names under Aynho; Brackley; Kingsthorpe; Lincoln, St Sepulchre's
hospitality for guests, endowment for 147, 158, 159, 212, 282
hunting 286, app. I(XVI)

I

iconomus 24
immunities 135, 147
see also exemption
induction mandates xxi
indulgences of xxxiin., 97n., 98, 258, app. I(XIX), app. II(1)
infirmary of abbey 155
see also monks, sick
injunctio xxiv–v
inscriptio xxx–xxxi
inspeximus xxxix, 29n., 36, 188A, 228, 241, 244, 279, 282, 285
see also charter(s), inspected but not recited
institution in benefice xxii, xxxviii, xlii, 6, 10–15, 21, 22, 22A, 43, 44n., 54, 55, 64, 66, 69, 74, 76–8, 81, 85, 88A, 89, 90, 136, 140, 145, 146, 150, 164, 165, 180, 182–5, 188A, 192, 193n., 195, 196, 199, 202–5, 209, 224, 230, 234, 235, 238, 245, 266–8, 269n., 271, 287, 290, 293, 296, 298, app. I(XXI); app. II(4–27, 52, 54–7)
interdict 91, 93, 257
intitulatio xxx–xxxi
invocation xxxv
itineraries of bishops pp. 208–12
ius parochiale app. I(XXII, XXIII)
ius pontificale app. I(XXII, XXIII)

J

judicial duties xxii
jurisdiction, capitular xxxiii
– spiritual, of archbishop of York 214C
justice, ecclesiastical 91, 93, 94, 257
justices, royal xxxiv, 105, 192, 213, 227n.

K

kings, *see names under* Henry I, II, III,
VIII; Edward the Confessor: John;
Richard I; William I, II
see also France; Scotland
knights' fees, grant/confirmation of 7, 16, 231
– return of, of St Mary's, Lincoln app. I(XIV)
– tithes of 4, 155

L

land, agreement over app. I(IX), app. II(31)
– arable 233n.
– grants/confirmations of 8, 16, 23, 24, 29,
68, 70–3, 84, 104, 130, 150, 155, 156, 160,
179, 181, 189, 228, 244, 254, 265, 274, 280,
281, 286, 289, 299, app. I(VII, XII, XIII,
XVI, XVIII, XXIV)
– dispute over app. I(IX)
– newly-tiled 274
– plea of 213n.
lay brothers (of Sempringham) app. II(33)
legata 118, 180
legation 58
legitimacy, proof of 213
licences xxi
life-interest of clergy in benefice etc.
safeguarded 5, 13, 19, 44, 61, 62, 132, 158,
197, 202, 206, 230, 261, 262
lights, endowments for 102, 157, 161, 211,
252

M

mandates xxx, xxxvii, xlii, 32–6, 38, 91, 93,
94, 111, 135, 257, 283, app. I(XVn.), app.
II(51); papal 32n., 36, 37, 166, 214A, app.
II(49)
manor 23, 106n., 161, 223, 282, p. 210
– dispute over 232, 247, 248
manse 153
market 242
marriage, forbidden app. II(40)
– cases 40A, 40B
– constitutions app. II(39)
marsh 70, 218n.
mass(es), 258, app. II(2)
– purchase of wine for 130
mass-pennies 180
'*matricula*' 18n., 51n., 54n., 65n., 250n.
matrimonial cases 40A–B
see also marriage

meadow 16, 53, 70, 72, 73, 155, 158, 172,
233n.
measurements, *see* bovate; carucate; hide;
virgate
merchants 180
messuage 8, 16, 24, 53, 155
mills 16, 29, 84, 130, 133, 155, 179, 229,
264, 265, 286, app. I(IV, XVI)
missives xxx, xxxvii, xlii
monks, sick, endowment for use of 2, 157
see also infirmary
murder (of subdean) 223n., 252n., 253n.,
254n., 286n., 290n., 294n.

N

narrative clauses xxxiii
non-appearance of cited party 38
non-residence 93, 94, 257
notary 121W
notification xxxiii–iv
nullity decree 40A

O

oath 17, 20, 53, 143, 239
oats 274
obedience, *see* profession
offerings 10, 22, 45, 59, 62, 81, 118, 119,
153, 156, 158, 161, 172, 180, 205, 218n.,
233, 234, 239, 286, app. I(XVI)
officials,
– archdeacon's 72n., *and see also*
vice-archdeacon
– episcopal 91–4, 257
– *sede vacante* 199, 203
orders, letters of xxi
ordinations (of clergy) xxi, xxii
– of vicarages xxii, *and see under vicarages*
ornaments (for parish church) 158

P

palfrey 180
pannage 24, 229, 286, app. I(XVI)
papal judge delegate xxii, xxxiv, xxxvii,
xxxviii, 25, 32–8, 42, 166, 182(?), 191, 198,
211, 214, 214A–C, 234n., 243, app. II(44),
p. 207
– formulary p. 207
park 218n., app. I(IV)
pascuage app. I(XVI)
patron of priory 291
patronage, right of 143
see also church; presentation
pedage 113
penance 40An.
pensions (from churches and clergy) xxxix, 2,
3, 9–15, 17, 21, 22, 44, 51, 54, 55, 63, 64,
66, 68, 69, 74–9, 81, 82, 85, 88A, 89, 90,
101, 105, 112, 120–2, 126, 130, 143, 150,

152, 155–7, 159, 165, 167, 172, 179, 181,
182, 184, 188A, 195, 196, 198, 204, 210–2,
220, 223, 224, 230, 232–6, 238–41, 243,
246, 249, 263, 265–8, 270, 274, 275, 277,
280, 281, 283, 287, 290, 296, 298, app.
I(XX, XXV), app. II(5, 9, 23, 24, 26, 53,
56)
pentecostal processions xxxiii, 92, 256
pepper, payable as pension 63
personatus 85, 145, 146, 185, 192, 246, 272n.
and see also church
Peter's Pence 62
pigs 286, app. I(XVI)
plea of land 213
– of service 227n.
see also prohibition
ploughing 160
popes, *see* Alexander III; Celestine III;
Clement V; Eugenius III; Honorius III;
Innocent III; Lucius III; Urban III
preamble xxxii–iii, xxxvii
prebend(s), assignment/establishment of 95,
app. II(30)
– confirmation/grant of 96, 105 (*in
prebendam*), 110, 259
– disposal of fruits of, of deceased canon 253
– exemption of 102, 252
presentation, letter of xlii, 183n., 184n., 237
– right of 17, 239
see also church; patronage
prima divisa 274
priory, confirmation of site 201
see also abbey
proctor 192, 232
procurations, archidiaconal 234n.
profession of obedience 1, 214n., 216
prohibition about burial app. II(46)
– from imposing fines app. II(45)
– to attend and conduct wedding app. II(40)
– to implead app. II(42)
prohibition clauses xxxvii
protection, letters of 217
psalter, division of the 108
purpresture 286, app. I(XVI)

Q

quitclaim, *see* renunciation
quo warranto proceedings 200n.

R

reaping 160
recommendation, letter of 213A
register, episcopal xxii
regulations for lay brothers of Sempringham
app. II(33)
religious house, *see* abbey; priory
religious life, future entry to, 149
removal of secular canons app. II(49)

rents 16, 72, 150, 155, 179, 223, 265, 286,
289, app. I(I, XVI)
renunciation of claims, rights etc. xxxviii, xli,
20, 25, 42, 109, 154n., 166, 170n., 176,
181, 198, 211, 232, 237, app. I(IX, XXI)
repair of monastery, *see* abbey
residence of cathedral canons xxxiii, 93, 94,
99, 100, 106, 107, 257, 260, 261
residence requirement of vicar 50, 123, 138,
152, 154
resignation 43, 191, 204, 237, 259, 290
restitution, to be made 214A; promised app.
I(XVIII)
restoration of church to clerk app. II(44)
– of church to religious 32–5, 191
– of monks of Coventry app. II(49)
revolt, of lay brothers of Sempringham app.
II(33)
roofs (of abbey), repair of, *see* abbey
rye 274

S

sacristy of abbey 159, 282, 283
salt and salterns 16, 70
salutation xxxi–ii
sanctio xxxv–vii
schools, scholars xxiii, 135, p. 206
scribes xxix
– 'casual' xxix
seal of abbot 284
– of bishop, and sealing xxviii, xl–xlii; seal
examples 24, 73, 84, 114, 115, 123, 124,
144, 160, 173, 209; appended to agreement
app. II(31, 35); seal of bishop Gravesend
attached to actum of bishop Hugh 70
seal bags, use of 114, 144
selions app. II(31)
sequestration app. II(40)
servants, household, of abbey 147
service, divine:
– performance of 298
– division of the psalter for 108
service, feudal, secular: 16, 160, 289, app.
I(XIV, XXIV); quit of 8, 189
– plea of 227n.
servitium debitum app. I(XIV)
settlements of disputes xxxiii, xxxvi, xxxviii,
17, 25, 36, 37, 45n., 46, 47, 53, 79, 105,
122, 166, 169, 182, 188A, 198, 211, 232,
234n., 239, 243, app. I(XVIII)
see also agreements; disputes
sheep 70
sick monks, endowment for use of 2, 157
see also infirmary
soke 88An., 223
steward of abbey 284
– of bishop xxvi, *and see names* Boby, Hugh
de; Pons
stole, episcopal 215n.
suspension, papal 214C

– of priest app. II(40)

synod(s), diocesan xxi, 42; at Northampton 192

– decrees of app. II(3)

synodals 81, 147

T

tallage 53

testament of bishop 215

thraves 274

tithes 3, 10, 16, 22, 24, 25, 45–7, 53, 70–2, 81, 118, 119, 130, 144, 153, 155, 156, 158, 167, 180, 188, 196, 205, 218n., 219, 225, 229, 233, 234, 239, 244, 255n., 264, 265, 268, 274, 280–2, 286, 298, app. I(XVI) (XXV)

titles xxx–xxxi

toft 70, 104, 155, 218n., 233n., 254

tolls xxxvii, 67, 113, 242, app. I(XII)

transactio 17, 20

treasures (of abbey) 284

– of cathedral, *see names under* Lichfield; Lincoln

treaty (of Le Goulet) p. 211

V

vacancy administration xxiiin., xxvi

– of archbishopric of Canterbury 221, 222

– of see of Lincoln, institution during 44n., 199, 203, 266

– of parish church 226

see also official

valediction xx, xxxvii-viii

vicarages 30, 39, 46, 47, 48n., 49n., 50, 62, 90, 115, 123, 125, 128, 129, 132, 134, 138, 158, 192, 199, 205–8, 218, 219, 224, 267, 269, 275, 277, 288, 290, 300, app. II(4, 7, 12, 32, 50)

– perpetual 6, 10, 12, 22, 26, 43–5, 54, 55, 64, 69, 81, 85, 88, 88A, 118, 119, 126, 150, 153, 154, 159, 162, 165, 172, 180, 182, 191, 204, 209, 210, 233, 234, 238, 251, 266, 268, app. I(XX)

vicars, personal residence obligations of 50, 123, 138, 152, 154

vicars choral, to be appointed 93, 94, 257

– stipend of 253

vice-archdeacon, *see names under* Lincoln; Oxford

virgate 24, 72, 155, 160, 265, 274, 286, app. I(XVI)

visitations xxi, 284, p. 209

W

wax, payable as a pension 63, 88A, 157, app. II(23)

wedding, *see* marriage

wheat 23, 274

will, bequest by 68

see also testament

wine, purchase of, for mass 130

witness-lists xxx, xxxv, xxxvii, xxxviii

ENGLISH EPISCOPAL ACTA

I. LINCOLN 1067–1185. Edited by David M. Smith. 1980.

II. CANTERBURY 1162–1190. Edited by C. R. Cheney and Bridgett E. A. Jones. 1986.

III. CANTERBURY 1193–1205. Edited by C. R. Cheney and E. John. 1986.

IV. LINCOLN 1186–1206. Edited by David M. Smith. 1986.